DONALD ROSS
AND THE
HIGHLAND
CLEARANCES

Dedicated to my parents Malcolm and Sandra, my darling wife Emma, and my wonderful daughters, Katie and Ann – the first Scottish bairns born in my family since 1906.

Katie and Ann Ross.

DONALD ROSS
AND THE
HIGHLAND CLEARANCES

'Yet Still the Blood is Strong'

ANDREW ROSS

AMBERLEY

From the lone shieling of the misty island
Mountains divide us, and the waste of seas –
Yet still the blood is strong, the heart is Highland,
And we in dreams behold the Hebrides.

Canadian Boat Song

Jacket illustrations: Front: Ruined blackhouse at Samadalan, Knoydart. *Back:* Skye crofter, from *ILN*, 3 March 1888. *Back flap:* Ross clansman, from McIan's *Clans of the Scottish Highlands*.

First published 2023

Amberley Publishing
The Hill, Stroud
Gloucestershire, GL5 4EP

www.amberley-books.com

Copyright © Andrew J. Ross, 2023

The right of Andrew J. Ross to be identified as the Author of this work has been asserted in accordance with the Copyright, Designs and Patents Act 1988.

All rights reserved. No part of this book may be reprinted or reproduced or utilised in any form or by any electronic, mechanical or other means, now known or hereafter invented, including photocopying and recording, or in any information storage or retrieval system, without the permission in writing from the Publishers.

British Library Cataloguing in Publication Data.
A catalogue record for this book is available from the British Library.

ISBN 978 1 3981 0426 6 (hardback)
ISBN 978 1 3981 0427 3 (ebook)

1 2 3 4 5 6 7 8 9 10

Typesetting by SJmagic DESIGN SERVICES, India.
Printed in the UK.

Contents

Text Illustrations		8
Preface		10
Acknowledgements		13
Abbreviations		15
1	The Miller of Skibo	16
2	John Ross, Millwright	33
3	Donald Ross, the New Miller of Skibo	42
4	Eviction	47
5	House Breakers	53
6	Money Trials and Tribulations	57
7	Charles Edward Gordon	65
8	Glencalvie Clearance	74
9	A New Life in Glasgow	81
10	Agent for the Poor	97
11	Glasgow Court Cases	108
12	Strathaird Evictions	119
13	Barra Exodus	131
14	Highland Destitution	140
15	The Hebridean Benevolent and Industrial Society	150
16	HMS *Hercules*	157

17	Weeping in the Isles	166
18	Knoydart Evictions	184
19	Boreraig and Suishnish Clearance	207
20	The Massacre of the Rosses	220
21	The Crimean War	246
22	Harriet Beecher Stowe	251
23	Famine Relief	256
24	The Glasgow Celtic Society	269
25	Miscellaneous Letters	274
26	Fraud	280
27	A New Life in Nova Scotia	285
28	The Legacy of Donald Ross	296

Notes	302
Illustration sources and credits	324
Appendix 1: The addresses of Donald Ross from the Glasgow Post Office directories	326
Appendix 2: The published pamphlets of Donald Ross	328
Appendix 3: The addresses of Donald Ross from the Nova Scotia directories	330
Bibliography	332
Index	342

Map of Sutherland, with a vignette of Inveraray Castle, Argyll.

Text Illustrations

Dedication: Katie and Ann Ross.
Frontispiece: Map of Sutherland.
p. 16. George Dempster.
p. 17. Skibo Castle.
p. 18. Clashmore Inn.
p. 23. George [Soper] Dempster.
p. 24, left. The Marquis of Stafford.
p. 24, right. The Countess of Sutherland.
p. 29, top. Borthwick Castle and church.
p. 29, bottom. The grave of George [Soper] Dempster.
p. 31. The family tree of the Miller of Skibo.
p. 40. Church of the Holy Rood, Stirling.
p. 41. Asylum for Indigent Old Men, Glasgow.
p. 43. Bill for meal written by Donald Ross.
p. 48. Bundle of Dornoch Sheriff Court documents.
p. 50. Parliament House, Edinburgh.
p. 54. Letter from John Gordon to John Ross.
p. 58. Inverness Court and bridge.
p. 66. The reading of the Protest in St Andrew's Church, Edinburgh.
p. 75. Map of Easter Ross.
p. 76. Rev. Gustavus Aird.
p. 81. River Clyde, Glasgow.
p. 86. Fiddler's Close, Glasgow.
p. 89. Glasgow Green.
p. 90. Buchanan Street, Glasgow.
p. 91, top. Buchan Street, Gorbals.
p. 91, bottom. Map of Glasgow.
p. 93, top. Trongate Street, Glasgow.
p. 93, bottom. Queen Victoria and Prince Albert's visit to Glasgow.
p. 94. Govan.
p. 95. RMS *Persia*.
p. 96. Cathcart.
p. 98. William Campbell of Tullichewan.
p. 109, left. Henry Glassford Bell.
p. 109, right. Sir Archibald Alison.
p. 110. Appeal written by Donald Ross.
p. 122. Prof. John Shank More.
p. 123. Broadford Hotel, Skye.

Text Illustrations

p. 125, top. A Skye blackhouse.
p. 125, bottom. Inside a Skye blackhouse.
p. 127, top. Cill Criosd Church, Skye.
p. 127, bottom. Ford at the head of Loch Slapin, Skye.
p. 159. HMS *Hercules*.
p. 167. The gravestone of Rev. John Forbes, Skye.
p. 189, top. Map of Loch Hourn.
p. 189, bottom. Airor jetty, Knoydart.
p. 194. Ruined blackhouse at Doune, Knoydart.
p. 196. St Anthony's Chapel, Knoydart.
p. 200. The eviction of Catharine Mackinnon, Inverie.
p. 207. Map of Suishnish, Skye.
p. 208. Map of Boreraig, Skye.
p. 214. The eviction of Duncan and Flora Macrae, Suishnish.
p. 227. Map of the site of the Massacre of the Rosses.
p. 239. Grace Ross of Ca-dearg.
p. 251. Harriet Beecher Stowe.
p. 273. The 2nd Grand Gathering of The Glasgow Celtic Society.
p. 275. The Earl of Elgin.
p. 289. Dartmouth, Nova Scotia.
p. 290. The Red Mill, Dartmouth.
p. 292. The Marquis of Lorne and Princess Louise.

Preface

Donald Ross was baptised on 7 March 1813 in the font of Dornoch Cathedral. As he had his head wetted his proud parents could not have imagined that their son would be the subject of a book, written by one of their great-great-great-great-grandsons, 200 years later.

In the year 2000 my future father-in-law gave me a copy of John Prebble's *The Highland Clearances*. Being English I knew little about Scottish history and had the typical romantic view of tartan, bagpipes, haggis, whisky and mountains. My Glasgow-born grandfather, Andrew Morrison Ross, died in 1952, when my London-born father was very young, so any Scottish stories were not passed on. When reading Prebble's book, I was particularly horrified by a chapter entitled *The Massacre of the Rosses*, an event that was reported by Donald Ross.

In 2004 I started investigating my own family history, and on our honeymoon, armed with a copy of my grandfather's birth certificate, my wife and I visited the General Records Office for Scotland, now called the National Records of Scotland, in Edinburgh. We were pleased to find the 1866 marriage record of my great-great-grandfather John Sutherland Ross who was a Printer Compositor Foreman for the *Paisley Herald*. In 2008 an employment opportunity enabled us to move from London to Edinburgh and I continued my family research. I soon got back to the 1833 parish marriage record of my great-x3-grandfather, John Ross, Millwright in Golspie, Sutherland – I had come from a line of Highlanders!

The following year my wife and I attended the Ross Clan Gathering in Tain, Ross & Cromarty. We visited the Historylinks Museum in Dornoch, Sutherland and found John Ross listed in the 1822 statute labour list for Dornoch, below the name of his father Donald Ross, Miller. A bit more searching resulted in us excitedly running across the road to St Barr's churchyard, next to Dornoch Cathedral where we found the Miller's grave, marked by a magnificent tablestone. With time, and more trips to the NRS I steadily populated the family tree with the Miller's ten children and their descendants.

Preface

The Miller's seventh child, my great-x4-uncle, also named Donald Ross, married the significantly older May Bayne, though they seemed to disappear after the 1841 census. Thanks to a hint on the Ancestry website I found them in the 1851 census in Glasgow where he was working as a 'Writer,' but I didn't know that this actually meant lawyer, until a casual conversation with one of my colleagues enlightened me. Later I found Donald in the Glasgow Post Office directories, on-line at the National Library of Scotland website, though initially I thought there were two of them until I realised he was using both work and home addresses. By chance, in January 2014, I picked up Prebble's book again, looked in the index and there was Donald Ross listed as 'lawyer and journalist of Glasgow,' the author of *The Massacre of the Rosses*! Given that this was a common name I couldn't begin to believe it was the same person until I found a Dornoch Council Minute on the Am Baile website, where he put a stop to the 2nd Duke of Sutherland running a road through St Barr's graveyard, and the on-line British Newspaper Archive where he was listed in an 1845 appeal to help the victims of the Glencalvie Clearance. Both these records and the 1841 census gave his address as 'Rosebank, Dornoch.' Any remaining doubts vanished when I found a legal document at the NRS where Donald and his siblings were listed as the executors of their mother's will and he was referred to as 'Writer in Glasgow.'

Prebble was the first person to write substantially about Donald's pamphlets and newspaper articles. What was known about Donald was nicely summed up in the anonymous preface to the 1977 Journeyman Press's re-print of *The Russians of Ross-shire, or Massacre of the Rosses*. It commenced, 'Accurate information about Donald Ross has unfortunately been difficult to come by. *The Russians of Ross-shire* is itself quite rare, and his other pamphlets are only accessible in public collections. But it is known that he was a lawyer in Glasgow, and spent much energy in publicising the brutality of the clearances, and helping to alleviate the distress caused to the evicted.' It ended 'had it not been for those few years of intense activity by this one man, little or nothing would have reached us of the cruelty and sufferings imposed on the evicted families of Knoydart and Strathcarron.' Thanks to the internet, and numerous trips to libraries and archives, I have found so much more about this man. What follows is a detailed account of his fascinating life, from humble miller to hero, then rapid downfall and emigration, amidst the backdrop of one of the darkest and most shameful chapters in Scottish history. This book is not meant to be a critique of the Highland Clearances, more an account of the efforts of one man to publicise atrocious events and his unceasing efforts to help the poor. His rare pamphlets, newspaper articles and letters reveal a fascinating insight into life and suffering in Scotland in the 1840s and 50s. Like any good journalist Donald was prone to exaggeration, so wherever possible I have sought other sources to corroborate what he wrote. In many cases I have succeeded, in others not, which leaves open to question whether he was recording the truth or embellishing it.

Donald Ross and the Highland Clearances

Although I have looked at as many articles and records as possible, I don't pretend for one minute to have seen everything, and this has been hindered by the Coronavirus pandemic, which prevented a trip to Nova Scotia. I'm sure that with time, as more and more records and documents become available on-line, other lost gems will come to light. I have endeavoured to examine and check all primary references for accuracy though sadly I have been unable to find an image of Donald Ross.

While writing this book a couple of coincidental events happened which truly surprised me. The first was unexpectedly stumbling across John Ross's grave in a large graveyard in Stirling in June 2015, while trying to find a way to bypass some steps with an occupied double buggy. At the time I thought he had been buried in Glasgow! After my wife and I moved to the Scottish Borders our neighbours recommended we attend Borthwick Church in North Middleton and our daughters were baptised there. In July 2015 I spotted the grave of George Dempster of Skibo near the entrance to the churchyard, the same George Dempster who had evicted my ancestors from the Skibo Estate in the 1840s. I had been reading newspaper articles about him the evening before but had no idea where he was buried!

I very much hope that this book will be of interest to anyone inquiring into Scottish history, of use to social historians and students of the Highland Clearances, and is a worthy complement to other books on the subject.

Andrew J. Ross

Acknowledgements

I would like to thank my parents Malcolm and Sandra Ross, and wife Emma Ross for their continuous support and patience; my father-in-law, John De Boise, for giving me a copy of Prebble's *The Highland Clearances*; David Forsyth (formerly National Museums Scotland) and Morag Bremner (formerly Tain & District Museum and Clan Ross Centre) for their encouragement and enthusiasm; Hugh Cheape (University of the Highlands and Islands) and Donald Cameron for discussion; Mike Taylor (formerly National Museums Scotland) for suggesting additional leads; John and Adelaide Borthwick for suggesting my wife and I visit Borthwick Church; Dugald Ross (Staffin Dinosaur Museum) for the translation of *Am Ministear*; the Duke of Buccleuch and Queensberry KT for permission to quote correspondence by Sir John McNeill (NRS GD371/288); Golspie Mill, Dunrobin Castle and the Friends of the Church of the Holy Rude (Stirling) for information; Ann Hearle for information about Hollins Mill; Krisztina Fenyő for copies of newspaper articles; Rachel Russell for giving me the print of Edinburgh and map of Inverness-shire; Alastair McIntyre for the photo of Grace Ross and information about her family and the massacre site; Jason Ubych (Tain & District Museum) for information about the massacre; Pam Keown for the photo of Ann Ross and information about her family; the manager of Dornoch Castle Hotel for showing me one of the old prison cells; Roland Haechler and Bettina Fischer for permission to photograph Sandaig Chapel; Joyce Wylie for the photo of Donald's grave; the librarians of the National Library of Scotland (Edinburgh), Central Library (Edinburgh), Mitchell Library (Glasgow), National Museum of Scotland (Edinburgh), British Library (London), SSC Library (Edinburgh), Inverness Reference Library, Fort William Library, V&A National Art Library (London) and the following university libraries: Edinburgh, Aberdeen, Glasgow, Sabhal Mòr Ostaig (Highlands and Islands), St Andrews, Imperial College (London), Oxford and Cambridge for access to books, pamphlets and letters or supplying information about items in their collections; the archivists and curators at the National Records of Scotland (Edinburgh), Historylinks Museum (Dornoch),

Stirling Council Archives, Highland Archive Centre (Inverness), Edinburgh City Archives, Skibo Castle, Blair Atholl Castle and Estate Archives, National Archives (Kew), Halifax Municipal Archives (Nova Scotia), Nova Scotia Archives (Halifax) and Nova Scotia Museum for access to their documents and records or supplying information about items in their collections; Lynne Mahoney of Historylinks Museum (Dornoch), National Library of Scotland, National Records of Scotland and the Carson Clark Gallery (Edinburgh) for supplying copies and/or permission to reproduce images from their collections, and my friends and colleagues for putting up with me talking about Donald Ross *ad nauseum*.

Abbreviations

AUL	Aberdeen University Library
BL	British Library
CUL	Cambridge University Library
DNHHL	Historylinks Museum, Dornoch
EUL	Edinburgh University Library
GUL	Glasgow University Library
FWL	Fort William Library
HCA	Highland Archive, Inverness
HIES	Highland and Island Emigration Society
ILN	*Illustrated London News*
IRL	Inverness Reference Library
JOGJ	*John O' Groat Journal*
MLG	Mitchell Library, Glasgow
NAK	National Archives, Kew
NBDM	*North British Daily Mail*
NLS	National Library of Scotland, Edinburgh
NRS	National Records of Scotland, Edinburgh (including the National Archives of Scotland)
NSA	New Statistical Account of Scotland
OS	Ordnance Survey
OSA	Old Statistical Account of Scotland
OUL	Oxford University Library
SAUL	St Andrews University Library
SCA	Stirling Council Archives
SMO	Sabhal Mòr Ostaig (University of the Highlands and Islands)
TANDM	Tain & District Museum
V&AL	Victoria & Albert Museum, National Art Library

1

The Miller of Skibo

Donald Ross was named after his father, who was the Miller of Skibo born in about 1764 in the Parish and Royal Burgh of Dornoch, Sutherland, Scotland. The Miller and 'his father, who bore the same name, had, for nearly a century together, been tenants and Millers of the Mill of Skibo' and was buried near 'his predecessors for the last five generations' in 1838[1] The earliest dated record, quoted in a court document, was written by the laird of the Skibo Estate, George Dempster:

George Dempster in 1793, the Laird of Skibo.

The Miller of Skibo

Donald. Whatever meliorations [improvements] you make either on your mill, or by stone houses covered with straw or heather, or stone fences round your garden or fields, I will allow by appraisement, in case of your removal.

At Skibo, 3rd Nov. 1792 George Dempster

Your present value of the mill is £2.3.6. Two pounds, 3/6. G D

Subsequently the Miller made 'extensive meliorations and erections at and upon the said mill of Skibo and Kiln thereof.'[2] He also had a small farm named Ryre. He was a tenant-at-will, *i.e.*, he did not have a lease, and as such could be evicted at short-notice, but at least he had the re-assurance that he would receive compensation. The mill was situated in the village of Clashmore, one mile E.N.E. of Skibo Castle.

Clashmore was described as 'a modern and thriving village, about three miles west of Dornoch, situate[d] partly on the estate of Sutherland and partly on that of Skibo, being divided only by a small burn which separates these properties, and by the parliamentary road to Caithness, which passes through the village. A neat and commodious inn graces this rising place,' built in 1819.[3]

The Miller was listed in the statute labour lists, which were set up to maintain roads, from 1822 to 1838, living at Clashmugach, and he was paying four shillings rent per year.[4] Today Clashmugach is an area situated immediately N.W. of Clashmore though in the Miller's day it included the N.W. quadrant of Clashmore.

Skibo Castle in 1890, before it was purchased and extended by Andrew Carnegie.

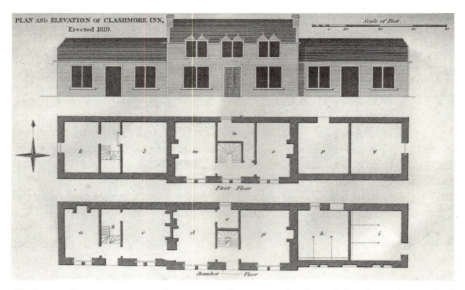

Clashmore Inn. a tap room, b pantry and stores, c kitchen, d family parlour, e bed closet, f lobby and stairs, g dining room, h stable, i mailcoach stable, k men servants' bedroom, l maid servants' bedroom, m bedroom, n bed closet, o bedroom, p hayloft, q hayloft.

Millers were the first harvesters of water-power and most places of inhabitancy near a running water source had a mill.[5] In Sutherland, at the beginning of the 19th century, the mills were described as 'contrivances of the most wretched and feeble nature, erected in hovels little better than the ordinary huts of the country.'[6] At Clashmore in 1790 'the Mill and houses at that time had been made of turf' and 'the Mill, Mill-dams and Mill-leads all were swept away by a flood.'[7] The Miller re-built the mill and built a cottage, kiln, barn, byre (cattle shed), stable and cart-shed, all of stone and thatched, and he enclosed his fields and garden with stone walls. Locals recalled that in 1809 the house 'was then a feal or turf one and it was pulled down and built of stone, clay and lime and there were two vents in the house – there was a byre also of stone and turf, which was thrown down and a steading of stone lime and clay built ... after the death of Mrs Dempster,' who died in 1810. Another account recorded that the house was thatched sometime after 1811 and 'there was a byre in front and stable and barn behind the house – the byre was built with stone and clay and the roof of divots and ... the same was on the stable and barn.' In 1810 the mill was thatched with broom or heather and 'old Mill dams and leads constructed of natural hollows in the moor to the north of the Mill and a few turf and stones had been erected at the lowest part of them to contain the water.'[8] The Miller constructed four small dams on the Sutherland Estate, however in 1830 the Marquis of Stafford (later 1st Duke of Sutherland) drained these dams and paid about £70 for the construction

The Miller of Skibo

of a new dam 'to contain a great quantity of water.' In 1835-6 the Miller rebuilt the cottage and steading, and in his will left half of the cottage to his eldest son, John.[9] The mill and other properties were valued at £32 in 1810, £163 in 1830 and £170 at the Miller's death in 1838.[10] A later lease described the 'Miller's Croft' and indicated where his cottage was, which is still there today but with a slate roof.[11]

The watermill is not marked on the first detailed map of the area as it had been demolished before then, however the mill dam is marked and the pond is still there today. It was recorded that 680 yards of 'catch-water drain' led to the dam to fill the pond when it rained.[12] The mill would have been situated on the south-west Skibo Estate side of the burn and probably had a vertical external under-shot water wheel, though may originally have been a horizontal 'click' mill.[13] The sluice on the map would have been used to regulate the water flow to the mill. There were 74 yards of 'water lead, from parliamentary road to mill excavation' so this places the mill immediately north of the row of buildings that form the upside-down T-shape on the map, which may have been the steading.

A typical thatched cottage in the Highlands had an open fire in the centre and food was cooked in a large iron pot hanging on a chain. In the early 19th century potatoes became a substantial part of the Highland diet and three varieties: 'kidney, pink-eyed and round red' were extensively cultivated in Sutherland. Tenants that lived near the sea boiled them in 50:50 sea and freshwater. Some were mashed and left to cool and the next morning the mash was sliced and toasted. Another mainstay of the Highland diet was a mixture of bear (or bere, an indigenous barley), peas and beans which were ground up by the mills to make 'meal.' The 'Sutherland pea' was a 'small dwarfish grey pea' grown by the south-east coast, sometimes with beans sown among them.[14] Meal was measured in bolls, which comprised four firlots. The standard Linlithgow firlot was fixed at 21¼ pints.[15] In Sutherland 110 bolls and two firlots of barley were equivalent to 100 Linlithgow bolls.[16] The 'Blainsley white oat' was grown along the south-east coast and 'a small grey or black oat' by crofters. Once harvested and milled, oatmeal was used to make 'pottage' (porridge) with milk for breakfast, and oatcakes for dinner; and bear-meal was baked into thin bear-bread.[17] Wheat had been experimentally grown on the landowner's farms at Skibo and Dunrobin and a small amount of rye was sown with oats by crofters. Ovens and the home-baking of bread only took off in the late 19th century, although many towns would have had a baker before then.

Estate farmers were 'thirled' to the mill, *i.e.* they had to take their crop to the landowner's mill and a percentage, 'multures,' went to the miller. The Thirlage Act of 1799 encouraged landlords to cease this feudal practise and Dempster abolished thirlage on the Skibo Estate.[18] This allowed millers to become more independent and competition increased, so some mills fell into rack and ruin while others prospered. Some built kilns to provide the extra service of drying the crops before milling. Rents were set based on fiars prices and these were based on the average prices of various crops from the previous year.

Locally quarried stone was often used for millstones, though good quality stone was quarried elsewhere and transported by sea.[19] Initially the miller did all the mechanical repairs but as the machinery became more sophisticated skilled millwrights were required to keep everything in good working order. The miller was one of the more important persons in the village; he and his family never went hungry and often grew their own crops and kept livestock. The miller was also one of the few to own a horse and cart, necessary for transporting the sacks of grain to the mill, or meal to customers or market.[20]

The Miller of Skibo married Ann Gordon on 28 January 1797. Ann, who was born sometime from 1778 to 1781, would have been 16-19 years of age when she married the Miller, who was 14-17 years older.[21] Ann's father was William Gordon and his will included the details of his two wives and fifteen surviving children, however he fathered seven children by his first wife and ten by his second. Ann was born to his first wife, Marian McKenzie. William married his second wife, Ann 'Nanny' Forsyth on 5 March 1790 and he died on 8 December 1824 at about 74 years of age.[22] His gravestone is in St Barr's Churchyard, next to Dornoch Cathedral, though the inscription is no longer readable. Cowper & Ross recorded 'Wm Gordon, Skibo 3.12.1821[6? -] and An...' though had misread the date.[23]

The Miller married Ann in the only church in the parish, Dornoch Cathedral, although not strictly a cathedral as it no longer had a bishop. The ceremony was administered by Rev. John Bethune, who was the minister from 1778 to 1816. He wrote the Dornoch Parish entry for *The* [old] *statistical account of Scotland* and a memorial to him is inside the cathedral. Rev. Donald Sage described Bethune as 'an elegant classical scholar, a sound preacher, and one of the most finished gentlemen I ever remember to have seen.'[24] At the time nearly everyone went to church so the Miller and his wife would have listened to Bethune's sermons, who preached two hours in Gaelic and two hours in English.[25] Dornoch Cathedral was dilapidated at that time with its west aisle (nave) in ruins. In 1786 Bethune complained to the Countess of Sutherland about the 'nauseous and unhealthful' environment due to the practice of the dead being buried in the church. This resulted in the floor being raised seven feet, a new pulpit and pews installed, and the roof ceiled. In 1788 the church heritors agreed that lofts could be built in the aisles to allow more people to attend services, and in 1816 a gallery was built in the chancel, with an outside staircase.[26] William Daniell produced a wonderful view of Dornoch from when he travelled down the east coast of Scotland in 1818.[27] However, a plan of the cathedral from 1815 shows that he painted the ruined west aisle in the wrong place.[28]

Five fairs a year took place in St Barr's Churchyard and Sage provided a detailed description from when he was a schoolboy.[29] Goods traded included livestock, meat, butter, cheese, tallow, wool, flax, stockings, shoes, timber, oil, beer, whisky, vegetables and fruit, including gooseberries, pears and currants.[30] The Miller probably sold meal at the fairs. Later a north-south track through the churchyard was converted to a foot-path, the fairs were moved to North Street and the churchyard was surrounded by a wall to stop pigs from entering and digging into the graves.[31] On market days fights often broke out at the 'miserable little inn thatched with heather' and a new inn, a 'large white house in High Street' was built by the Marquis.[32] As a child, Sage roamed through the woods of Skibo, so he probably knew the Miller and his wife, though did not mention them in his posthumous memoir.

There were only rough tracks in the 18th century and transport was generally by foot or horseback. Road building in Sutherland started in 1807 and the parliamentary road through Clashmore was built in 1810.[33] 1819 saw the first mail coach travel from Tain in Ross & Cromarty, through Sutherland, to Thurso in Caithness. The road running from Clashmore south to the Meikle Ferry was built in about 1820.[34] Trade diminished during the early 19th century due to new fairs opening elsewhere and a survey of 1832 described Dornoch as 'a place of no importance, having no Trade or Manufacture, and no Harbour.'[35] In 1831 there was an outbreak of Cholera which affected Golspie and Helmsdale up the coast, but Dornoch escaped thanks to a drive to clean up the town and keep outsiders out.[36]

The Laird of Skibo's seat was Skibo Castle, which has a long history and changed hands many times.[37] In 1756 the estate was purchased by William Gray who wished to restore the castle and make the estate prosperous, and the 'mills were put back into production.'[38] In 1787 the estate, comprising 3,946 acres, was purchased by George Dempster, a former Member of Parliament, for £11,500.[39] About forty families lived there and paid a total of £170 in rent. Dempster considered it to be 'the only habitable spot in Scotland I ever was possessed of.'[40] He purchased adjacent lands in the Parish of Creich and wrote:

> There may be about 200 families living on these estates, with the exception of the *mains*, or house-farm, of each place. The farms are of small extent in regard to arable ground. They produce some corn and potatoes, hardly sufficient to maintain the families of the tenants. The tenants pay their rents by the sale of cattle, which are fed in their houses, on straw, through the winter, and pick up a miserable subsistence on the waste and common ground of the estate, during the summer... The estates furnish some wood, with which, and the swarded surface of the ground, cut into the form of large bricks, they make houses and offices for themselves, covering them with the same swarded turfs, cut thinner, and resembling slates in their form. Once in three years, all the earthy part of these houses is thrown on the dunghill, and new houses built again of the same materials. The cattle commonly occupy one end of the house, during the winter season. Some holes in the walls and roofs serve for windows and chimneys. An iron pot, for boiling their food, constitutes their principal furniture.

Nothing can exceed the wretched appearance of these habitations. As to the occupation of the people, the women begin to earn a little money by spinning. The young men go early in the spring to the south country, and hire themselves for all kinds of country labour; towards harvest, many of the women also go the same way, to assist in cutting down and getting in the crop. They all return before winter, and are said to pass their time round good fires of peat, which the country every where furnishes, and do very little work. In the south country, however, to which they go, they are remarked for their assiduity, and are said to be indefatigable in executing all manner of task work. Those, who remain at home, attend to the concerns of their corn, potatoes, and cattle, and to the providing of their fuel from the neighbouring peat mosses... It need hardly be mentioned, that the inhabitants are in general poor;– that is, possess little money or goods, except a stock of very indifferent cattle.[41]

Surplus cattle were periodically driven south to sell, known as the 'Skibo Drove.'[42] In 1793 Dempster received 'a little bull and cow from Bengal exactly the size of a good English sheep.'[43] Four decades later diminutive 'Skibos' were bred by the tenants to pay the rent and sold for 'fanciful' prices.[44]

Dempster, known as 'Honest George,' saw the value of his tenants and encouraged them to make improvements, including agricultural experimentation, which resulted in his farms becoming more efficient. In 1792 he informed Sir Adam Fergusson that his Skibo tenants were 'building so many stone houses, garden walls and stone enclosures, that stone itself grows scarce and valuable.'[45] In November he wrote to all the tenants of Clashmugach promising 'that when they are removed from their possessions, they shall be allowed by appraisement full meliorations for improving their houses' and was good to his word during the time he was laird.[46] In 1796 he passed on the estate to his half-brother Captain John Hamilton Dempster, who was lost at sea on a voyage from Bombay to China in 1801. The estate was inherited by the captain's son, also named George Dempster, who died that same year and thus it passed on to the captain's daughter Harriet Dempster. She married William John Soper who adopted the surname of Dempster. On 24 November 1806 William Soper Dempster agreed to adhere to George Dempster's letter to the Miller and amended it accordingly. Harriet died on 17 October 1810 and the estate was inherited by her 6-year-old son George Soper Dempster as 'heir of entail,' even though her husband was still alive.[47] Joseph Wall stated 'the Soper-Dempsters seem to have left little record,' which was true for William, but not for his son George, who never used the Soper part of his name.[48]

George [Soper] Dempster was educated at the United College at St Andrews and studied law at Trinity College, Cambridge.[49] He was called to the bar in Edinburgh in 1826 and was mentioned as part of the counsel in an assault

The Miller of Skibo

George [Soper] Dempster c.1855, the Laird of Skibo, who evicted Donald Ross and his family.

case, along with William Pitt Dundas.[50] On 8 May 1827 Dempster married William's sister, Joanna Hamilton Dundas in Borthwick Church, now in North Middleton, Midlothian. She was the youngest daughter of Robert Dundas of Arniston, who was Lord Chief Baron of the Court of Exchequer.[51] William became the first Registrar General at 'The General Registry Office of Births, Deaths and Marriages,' now the National Records of Scotland. George and Joanna did not have any children.[52]

Dempster contributed to the legal courts in Dornoch and in 1844 fined two young men £30 each for running an illicit distillery, but they didn't pay so were imprisoned in Dornoch Jail for three months.[53] In 1851 he presided over a Justice of the Peace Court in Dornoch over offences against the Excise laws and fined John Murdoch £12 10s for selling a bottle of home-brewed beer for 2½d.[54] Dempster embraced the life of a highland laird and 'kept harriers, rode and fished, and became an admirable shot.'[55] He was a member of the Royal and Ancient Golf Club of St Andrews, the Caledonian Hunt and the Royal Body Guard of Archers.[56] He was also a member of the Highland Society of Scotland, was regularly a Steward for the Northern Meeting, and in 1846 was appointed an Extraordinary Director of the Highland and Agricultural Society of Scotland.[57] In 1835 he received a gold medal for his experimentation of plantations and planted nearly three million trees on over 1,100 acres.[58]

The neighbouring Sutherland Estate was owned by George Granville Leveson-Gower and Elizabeth Gordon. Elizabeth inherited the estate and Dunrobin Castle near Golspie, at only one year of age, when her parents died in 1766.[59] A petition to the House of Lords by her trustees resulted in her being given the title Countess of Sutherland in 1771 and she married Leveson-Gower (Viscount Trentham) in 1785.[60] In 1803, on the death of his father, Leveson-Gower inherited the title Marquis of Stafford and several large English estates making him the wealthiest man in Britain.[61] In 1833 he became the Duke of Sutherland, thus Elizabeth became the Marchioness of Stafford in 1803 and the Duchess of Sutherland in 1833.[62]

The Miller and his family probably lived a charmed existence when the estate was owned by the benevolent elder George Dempster. Elsewhere landlords were evicting their tenantry to make way for sheep farming, which they considered 'improvements.' The Highland Clearances were neatly summed up by the Rev. John Kennedy of Dingwall:

> ... the body of the people in the Highlands became distinguished as the most peaceable and virtuous peasantry in Britain. It was then that they began to be driven off by ungodly oppressors, to clear their native soil for strangers, red deer and sheep ... in the very recklessness of cruelty, families by hundreds were driven across the sea, or were gathered, as the sweepings of the hill-sides, into wretched hamlets on the shore.[63]

Above left: George Granville Leveson-Gower in 1811, the Marquis of Stafford, who later became the 1st Duke of Sutherland. The Marquis had the mill pond built to power Clashmore Mill.

Above right: Elizabeth Gordon in 1806, Countess of Sutherland and Marchioness of Stafford, who later became the 1st Duchess of Sutherland.

However, it was more complicated than that.[64] Contemporary reports are polarised either describing the horrific treatment of the poor crofters and cottars (land-less labourers) or defending the actions of the improving landlords. James Loch, Commissioner to the Marquis and Marchioness of Stafford, was typical of the latter and considered that the men on the Sutherland Estate, 'when not in the pursuit of game, or of illegal distillation' spent their time 'in indolence and sloth.'[65]

Much has been written on the subject and it is worth pointing out that emigration had become commonplace in the second half of the 18th century and clearances on a small scale had taken place, though were barely recorded. Native sheep and goats lived in Sutherland, and small flocks were kept by the locals, but both were almost completely wiped out by disease in the winter of 1806/7.[66] Large scale sheep farming started to take off in the Highlands in the last quarter of the 18th century, due mainly to the efforts of Sir John Sinclair in Caithness, compiler of the OSA and President of the Board of Agriculture, and Sir John Lockhart Ross of Balnagown, Ross & Cromarty.[67] Many clearance victims emigrated abroad, particularly to the North American colonies, but some lost their lives through disease or being shipwrecked. Others ended up in the larger Scottish towns and cities or settled on other estates, only to be evicted again later.[68]

A useful source is the *Farmers' Magazine* which commenced in 1800 and by 1804 had a circulation of over 4,000 copies, though ceased production in 1825.[69] It was printed in Edinburgh and many of its articles were about Scotland, however they were often anonymous or authored with initials or pseudonyms. It reveals the agricultural knowledge and thinking of the time, such as the best ways of cultivating different crops, arguments over different breeds of livestock and descriptions of new labour-saving mechanical contraptions. There are seasonal county reports containing varying levels of details on the weather and how the crops were doing, which demonstrate how fragile Highland subsistence farming was; some years good, in other years desperate. There are many articles on sheep and the merits of the different breeds, though the Cheviot was the favourite for the Highlands. Some articles deplore traditional shared run-rig farming practices, however many small tenants were converting to crofting, where the crofter was the tenant of their own plot of land, which was then often subdivided and sub-let to cottars.[70] Surprisingly there are also articles about the poor law, labour costs, thirlage, leases, depopulation and emigration. Anonymity allowed some writers to get away with writing extreme views which were unfortunately taken seriously and evolved with time. Some of these articles are shocking to read and with a strong air of foreboding expose how the Highland Clearances were inevitable. E.g. 'A Constant Reader' wrote 'The farmers from the South Country, if they do migrate to the Highlands, will carry with them a most abundant supply of that capital and knowledge, without which the aboriginal inhabitants never could have moved one inch out of their primitive barbarism... Who, then, in his senses, would employ rude and ignorant natives in the grand and arduous task of improvement, where enlightened agriculturists can be procured for the same laudable purpose?'[71] There were a few voices defending the Highlanders' virtues such as the elder George Dempster, who wrote under his own name and 'Domesticus,' but the tide of opinion was against them and the writing was on the wall for the poor Highlanders' old way of life.

In the early 19th century, a major program of evictions took place on the Sutherland Estate, known as the Sutherland Clearances. Although they were done in the Marquis and Marchioness's names, local stonemason Donald MacLeod considered they 'were generally absentees, and while they gave-in to the general clearing scheme, I have no doubt they wished it to be carried into effect with as little hardship as possible. But their prompters and underlings pursued a more reckless course, and, intent only on their selfish ends, deceived these high personages.'[72] The most notorious clearance happened along Strathnaver in the north of the county. Some recent publications regard 1807 as the year the Cheviot sheep were first introduced there, based on Loch's *Account*, however Cheviots were mentioned as being there in 1801.[73] In 1809 William Young and Patrick Sellar arrived in Sutherland and were responsible for a clearance in 1814, after Sellar had acquired the leases. Sellar was arrested and charged with culpable homicide, due to cases of death caused by exposure after the people were forcibly evicted. However, Sellar was acquitted and this gave the green light to further major evictions, overseen by Loch.[74] The largest took place in 1819 when 3,331 people (704 families) were evicted, of which 2,304 were re-settled on the margins of the estate.[75] MacLeod wrote graphic descriptions of the people being forcibly evicted and their houses set on fire.[76] He sent copies of the 1841 1st edition of his pamphlet to the 2nd Duke of Sutherland, Loch and others, and the fact that the Duke, who could have employed the best lawyers in the land, did not to take him to court over the allegations speaks volumes.[77] Another detailed account was written by Sage who gave his last service in Strathnaver in May 1819 and on returning shortly afterwards saw the smouldering ruins.[78] Today tourists can see the remains of house foundations along the Strathnaver Trail.[79]

A clearance happened close to Clashmore in 1813, at Sidera/Cyderhall. The tenants were moved to Birichen Muir and were evicted again in 1841.[80] Many emigrated to Nova Scotia. The Miller and his family must have known about this and other clearances on the Sutherland Estate as large meetings to discuss emigration took place nearby at the Meikle Ferry Inn in 1819, until they were declared illegal by Loch under the Seditious Meetings Act.[81]

The introduction of sheep changed the landscape as they are selective feeders preferring young grass, thus allowing coarser plants to take over, whereas cows keep coarse plants in check.[82] In the 1840s changes were beginning to be noticed and in 1845 Prof. James F. W. Johnston gave a talk in Golspie, chaired by George [Soper] Dempster. Johnston said that the valleys of Sutherland were 'becoming a waste as formerly, and will soon become useless, even for pasture for flocks... What was to be done? Just apply the hand of man. Plough, subsoil, lime, drain, and manure the land, and it will raise crops.'[83] Johnston's advice was contrary to the sheep farm 'improvement' ethos of Sutherland and fell on deaf ears. Later, as sheep farming became less profitable and the large tenant farmers moved away, much of the Highlands were converted into deer parks and became the hunting grounds for the rich.

George [Soper] Dempster was closely acquainted with the Marquis, Marchioness, Loch, Young and Sellar, who probably greatly influenced how he and his factor managed the Skibo Estate. In 1827 Dempster, the Marquis, Earl Gower (later the 2nd Duke of Sutherland), Sellar and others, were judges of sheep for the Highland Society.[84] In 1828, as Chair of a meeting of the Freeholders of Sutherland, Dempster proposed, seconded by Young, that Lord Francis Leveson-Gower (Earl Gower's brother) should be MP for Sutherland, who was unanimously re-elected.[85] Dempster was often the Chancellor of the committee that set the annual fiars prices and Sellar was on the committee.[86]

In 1833 Dempster advertised the farms of Maikle, Balblair, Ardahlie, Rheemore and Acharry to be let, and three years later advertised lands at Langwell and Achievaich for sale, including the Right of the Meikle Ferry.[87] The sale was to pay off debts of £5,150. Prior to this he had to get an Act of Parliament to overturn the Law of Entail on these lands, which showed that he had spent £14,074 on estate improvements.[88] This law ensured that land had to be inherited by the next of kin, however it was a ball and chain for landowners who were saddled with debt as they were unable to sell their lands without going through the expensive legal process first. In 1840 Dempster attended a meeting in Edinburgh for arranging petitions to parliament 'to promote an extensive system of emigration from the highlands and islands.'[89] At another meeting to discuss a motion 'for obtaining an *official* inquiry into the Pauperism of Scotland,' Dempster considered that 'the means of inquiry already existing in Scotland are sufficient.'[90] In 1841 he stood against Loch as parliamentary candidate for the Northern Burghs in the General Election, though Loch won.[91] In 1844, at a dinner after a Cheviot Sheep Show in Sutherland:

> Mr Loch then gave [a toast to] the health of his friend Mr Dempster of Skibo – the greatest resident proprietor in the county, and who did everything to promote the comfort and prosperity of those around him. In these acts of kindness, hospitality, and beneficence, Mr Dempster was cordially seconded by his excellent and respected lady. As a country gentleman he was indefatigable and public-spirited. He had set a good example as an improver, and followed up the best methods of drainage, planting. &c., thereby adding greatly to the value of his

estate, to the beauty of the country, and the employment of the people. Mr Dempster's health was drank with great applause.[92]

The Duke of Sutherland died in 1833 and was buried in Dornoch Cathedral.[93] Shortly afterwards a 105 foot high memorial statue was erected on Ben Bhraggie overlooking Golspie.[94] The Duchess paid for a major renovation of the cathedral, including the removal of the raised floor and galleries, and re-building the west aisle, though unfortunately many original features were destroyed in the process.[95] Sage and MacLeod described the 'revolting spectacle' of the dead being exhumed and 'thrown into large trenches,' which led to the saying 'The Sutherlands clear you even after you're dead.'[96] The Duke's coffin was moved to the new vault and the Duchess was buried there when she died in 1839.[97]

The Miller of Skibo died of jaundice in April 1838, either on the 15th as per his death record or 16th as on his gravestone. His grave is marked by a large tablestone, behind the Plaiden Ell which was used to measure cloth on market days.[98] The tablestone is made of quartzite or hard sandstone and is probably what was used for millstone. The inscription reads:

> Erected
> IN
> Memory of Donald Ross
> Late Miller of Skibo
> who Departed
> this Life April 16th 1838
> Aged 74 years

Given the hardness of the stone it has survived the ravages of time and the lettering, although overgrown by lichens, has remained readable, unlike many of the other contemporary gravestones.

After a case in the House of Lords in 1857, it was reported that Dempster had been 'freed from entail.' The decision was appealed by his sister, Eleanor [Soper] Dempster as heir substitute, however The Lords dismissed her appeal.[99] The estate was heavily burdened with debt so in 1861 Dempster sold the lands of Balblair for £13,500 and three years later advertised the farm of Pulrossie Mains to be let.[100] In 1866 he sold the remaining Skibo Estate and resigned as Convener of the County of Sutherland, and adverts appeared in the *Inverness Courier* for the sale of livestock and other items.[101] Dempster spent the rest of his life at Ormiston Hall, East Lothian.[102] His last notable deed was to donate a painting of his great-uncle to the Scottish National Portrait Gallery.[103] Dempster died in 1889 in Edinburgh and was buried in the graveyard of the re-built Borthwick Church, which re-opened in 1864.[104] An inventory of Dempster's estate was valued at £34,278.[105] Joanna died on 25 March 1890 in Edinburgh and was buried with her

The Miller of Skibo

Old postcard of Borthwick Castle and church, North Middleton; where George [Soper] Dempster and Joanna Dundas were married and buried. The white marble crosses near the entrance to the graveyard mark Dundas family graves.

The pink granite gravestone of George [Soper] Dempster and Joanna. The white marble cross on the right marks the grave of Joanna's brother, William Pitt Dundas.

husband, near to the graves of other members of the Dundas family. The leaded inscription on the gravestone reads:

> GEORGE DEMPSTER
> OF SKIBO
> BORN 26TH FEBRUARY 1804
> DIED 6TH FEBRUARY 1889
> JOANNA HAMILTON
> DUNDAS
> WIFE OF GEORGE DEMPSTER
> BORN 1806, DIED 1890

In 1898 the Skibo Estate was purchased by philanthropist Andrew Carnegie who greatly extended the castle and today the estate is a prestigious golf resort.

The Miller and his wife had ten children, born from 1798 to 1821. Their first eight children would have been baptised at Dornoch Cathedral by Bethune, and the last two by Rev. Angus Kennedy after he took over in 1817.[106] The baptisms would have happened quickly after birth as Highlanders were very superstitious and believed that an unbaptised child could be 'carried off by the fairies.'[107] Jean was born in 1810 and given the absence of further records then it is likely that she died young. For there to be two Ann Rosses born very close to each other suggests that the first one died in infancy, though exactly when is uncertain as deaths were not recorded in the parish until 1821.[108]

It is not known how many of the Miller's children went to school, though it is likely that they received some schooling. Calder mentioned a school at Clashmore known as Skibo School, built by George Dempster, and Mrs Dempster 'set apart a room in the Castle, where she gave sewing and needlework lessons to the young girls,' however it is uncertain which George and Mrs Dempster Calder was referring to.[109] There was also a school in Dornoch and Sage described it from when he attended it in 1801-3.[110] By 1816 along 'the whole line of coast betwixt the Meickle Ferry and the Ord, there are very few old people who do not understand the English language, and ... very few young ones who cannot speak it fluently.'[111] In the 1820s there was a drive to build schools to educate the poor in the Highlands, so by 1834 there were seven in the Parish of Dornoch.[112] 500 children attended school in the winter of 1833/4, but there were still 250 children in the parish, between six and fifteen years of age, who were unable to read. Sage described the various games and amusements that the pupils participated in including 'club and shinty ... pancake-cooking on Pasch Sunday, and in February, the cock-fight' on Shrove Tuesday.[113] They probably knew many of the rhymes and games that children in Golspie were reciting/playing, described by Nicholson.[114]

The Miller of Skibo

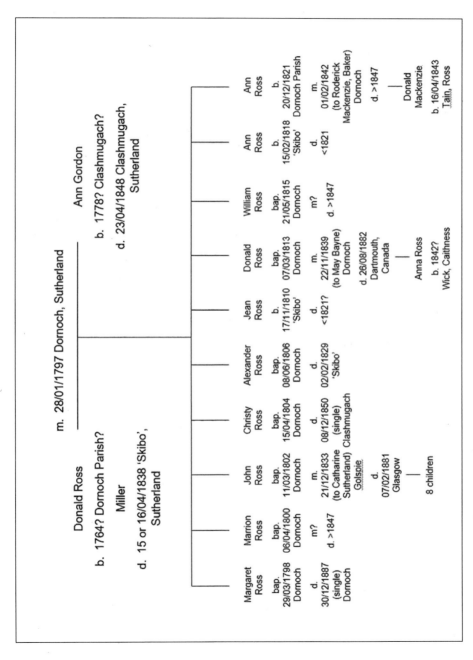

Part of the family tree of the Miller of Skibo.

The story of the Miller's first son, John, is in the next chapter. His second son, Alexander, was listed as the Miller's son in the statute labour lists for 1822 and 1823, so presumably he worked at the mill.[115] From 1826 to 1828 he was in the 'List of exemptions' so was not fit for work. He died in 1829, only twenty-two years of age. The Miller's third son, Donald, the main subject of this book, mentioned that the grave of his brother was near to that of his father.[116] Little is known about the Miller's fourth son, William, who was listed in the statute labour lists in 1832 and 1839.[117] In 1841 it was mentioned that he was a 'Wright at Glasgow.'[118]

The Miller's four surviving daughters, Margaret, Marrion, Christy and Ann were, in 1841, living with their widowed mother, presumably in the house built by their father. Christy was working as a dressmaker. Also living with them was lodger and baker Roderick Mackenzie, and James Ross, aged twelve, however it is not known how he was related. Ann married Mackenzie in 1842 at Dornoch Cathedral and the following year gave birth to a son. The following year Mackenzie emigrated to North America and presumably took his family with him.[119] In 1845 Marrion was added to the Poor Roll and received nine pence per week, which increased to 1s 6d in 1847.[120] In 1848 Donald, William, Margaret, 'Merran', Christy, and Ann Ross were listed as executors of their mother's will, however this is the last known record for William, Marrion and Ann.[121] Christy died in 1850. In 1848 Margaret was also added to the Poor Roll and was initially given 1 shilling a week, which was increased to 1s 6d in 1855.[122] By 1865 she was living in Dornoch, in 1867 her allowance was increased to two shillings per week and in 1870 she was paying 20s 5d rent per year.[123] Occasionally she was given items such as flannel, a petticoat and a blanket. In 1872 her relief was increased to 2s 6d and remained until she died in 1887, aged eighty-nine, having outlived most, if not all of her siblings.

2

John Ross, Millwright

John Ross was baptised in Dornoch Cathedral on 11 March 1802. He was listed in the statute labour lists in 1822 and 1823, so presumably worked at Clashmore Mill with his father.[1] On 21 December 1833 he married Catharine Sutherland in St Andrew's Church, Golspie, situated up the coast from Dornoch.[2]

Catharine was born in Dornoch sometime from 1815-9 and was 13-17 years younger than John. John was working as a millwright, probably at Golspie Mill on the Sutherland Estate. There are two mills marked on the first detailed OS map surveyed in 1873, and there was also a flax mill on Golspie Burn, but it's not marked on the map, so presumably was no longer in operation.[3] The older 'Flour Mill,' where John probably worked, is now a ruin. The 'Meal Mill' wasn't built until 1863 and is still being used as a flour mill today. In March 1835, when their first child was born, John was a carpenter. Over the next twenty-one years they had eight children and five of these went on to have large families.

By May 1836 they had moved back to Clashmore and John was working as a millwright at his father's mill, which continued until 1843.[4] They initially lived at Rosebank and in 1837 John was listed as a joiner and meal dealer, so probably also delivered the meal to customers.[5] In the 1841 census John's occupation is given as 'Sp. Deal.' as then he was also a spirit dealer selling whisky.

In August 1839 a 'Feu Contract' (lease) was drawn up between George [Soper] Dempster and William Christie, Accountant in Golspie, for a piece of ground. On this ground John, 'with the consent of the said George Dempster built a Dwelling House and Shop' bounded on 'the South by the Parliamentary Road measuring Ninety feet westward from the abutment of the Bridge which crosses said Road; On the west by a line drawn due North from the West end or Gable of said Dwelling House to the Burn of Clashmugach measuring one Hundred and six feet and on the East and North by the said burn.'[6] The plot and house are clearly marked on the first OS map, immediately west of the bridge on the north side of the road, but the house occupying the site today was probably built later. The feu duty was ten shillings per year, due at Whitsunday, and if two years went by with it unpaid then the contract was null and void. In October 1839 John was licenced for selling spirits in his own house at Clashmore and proceeded to sell whisky on commission for Messrs Christie.[7] The illicit distillation of whisky, or uisge beatha in Gaelic, was on the wane as the 1823 Act to Eliminate Illicit Distilling made it easier to obtain a licence and gave Customs and Excise Officers more powers while curbing corruption.[8] Whisky back then was different to what is drunk today as it was usually consumed soon after production.[9] John subsequently sold his house to William Christie though continued to live there and paid him rent.[10] In 1843 John's 'spirit cellar' was reported by Rev. Angus Kennedy as being the only licensed spirit shop in Dornoch Parish.[11]

John made several appearances at the Dornoch Small Debt Court, either pursuing money owed to him, or others pursuing him for money, however most of the cases were unsuccessful.[12] Cases heard at Dornoch Sheriff Court provided a lot more details. In February 1839 John took Hugh Ross, Tacksman of Farm 1821, Dornoch to court over an unpaid account.[13] In 1837 John had supplied Hugh with seventeen quantities of oat meal and one of salt, for a total of £13 17s 9d. Hugh denied he owed John money and stated 'he received eight Bolls two firlots and two pecks of oat meal from the pursuer as Agent for Mr. James Davidson General Agent Golspie, and paid Mr Davidson for the same by delivering over to him six quarters of oats.' John replied that Davidson credited the oats to Hugh on another account. Four witnesses were summoned, who all worked for Hugh. On 14 June Sheriff-substitute Alexander Gordon decided in favour of John. Hugh appealed, however John questioned why Hugh had not requested Davidson as a witness, 'a person above all suspicion and one who would in a moment have settled the question.' The verdict remained and John was also awarded expenses of £5 10s 1d after tax.

Another protracted case provided fascinating details of his whisky dealing. In July 1840 Donald Sutherland, Distiller at Dalmore Distillery, Alness, Ross & Cromarty submitted adverts to the *Inverness Courier* looking for customers for his whisky 'distilled colder than water; and he flatters himself a single trial will prove it equal, if not superior in quality to any Spirits made in the North.'[14] John wrote to Sutherland on 31 July:

> I have been Keeping a cellar in my House here, for the Messrs Christies of the Helmsdale Distillery on the following conditions Vizt, they were at the Expense of paying the Licence £3.5.6 for me themselves, and sent their own Horse and Cart to the cellar with Such quantities of Spirits as I required, from time to time, first at 7/9 [7s 9d] pr Gallon & afterwards at 8/ pr Gallon after the additional duty, and allowed me at the rate of Sixpence pr Gallon for my trouble on the Sales I effected, the proceeds of which I was regularly to remit them every month. To give you an idea

of the extent of the Sales I made for them I beg to State, that I remitted them £178.11.8 Sterling within the last 8 months, altho [sic] it was merely a commencement, but from the unfortunate Situation of Messrs Christies's affairs now, it is likely that they cannot Supply me with any more Spirits, and the reason of my writing you at present is to ascertain if you would be inclined to furnish me with Spirits from your Distillery on the same terms, or if you would be at the expenses of Sending the Spirits to the South Side of the meikle Ferry from where I could get it here at my own expense. ... I could put up a Sign Board with Dalmore Distillery upon it, and I would punctually remit you the proceeds every month. I could also be of Service to you in procuring orders, and effecting Sales for you, in other parts of this County.[15]

Sutherland replied 'my price per Gallon is 8/- 10up, but as you state you would put Dalmore Distillery Cellar on your board, and remit the Cash for what Whisky you get regularly every month, I have no objections to make a trial with you, and allow you off that price 6d. per Gallon.' John agreed and wrote 'I hope you will forward from 60 to 100 gallons for the first, by your earliest Convenience in Charge of a Carefull [sic] person to the South side of the Meikle Ferry, Giving me 24 hours previous notice.' Sutherland replied on 13 August to say he would send his own cart with a hogshead (large barrel) of whisky to the south side of the ferry the following morning. He produced an invoice for '70 Gallons Aqua. 10up @ 8/' totalling £28. 'Aqua' is short for *aqua vitae* meaning the 'water of life;' 'up' refers to the alcohol content and means under proof, whereas 'op' is over proof and has a higher alcohol content.

This was the start of an amicable arrangement between the two men with regular correspondence, and John received a consignment every couple of months. To make sure he was paid regularly, Sutherland drew up bills with the Caledonian Bank, Dornoch. A bill could be drawn up by someone who was owed money, to receive a loan from a bank. The bill would be signed by both parties and the bank would then agree (or not) to pay the money minus a small fee ('discount'). The person that owed the money then had from one to four months to repay the money ('retire the bill') to the bank, otherwise a Protest was lodged with the court and both parties were liable for interest and expenses. A bill could be paid off using another bill, which again would be discounted, with another period to pay it back. John had to retire Sutherland's bills within a month or two, or if it was a large delivery then the payment was often divided over two or three months. The quantities demonstrate the demand for whisky in that part of Sutherland at that time.

On 26 December John received 128 gallons of 10up for the usual price of 8s per gallon and 13 gallons of 11op at 10s per gallon. Sutherland also furnished John with an account which showed that over 4 months John had received 342¼ gallons for £138 11s, which is equivalent to £12,600 today.[16] On 14 January 1841 John wrote to Sutherland requesting another delivery, 'I hope you can reduce the price a Sixpence per Gallon, as I can get it Cheaper elsewhere.' On 27 January an invoice was written out for 140¼ gallons of 10up at 7s 3d per gallon and 25 gallons of 11op at 9s 3d per gallon, totalling £62 8s 1d.

On 26 July John wrote to Sutherland requesting another delivery though clearly cracks were beginning to appear in their arrangement: 'I hope you will be more Punctual in what day you mean to forward the aqua to the ferry as I was disappointed two or three times after going with the Carts to the Ferry ... I hope you will be sure for to see the Casks full before sending them away from you as there was one of the Casks Short of the quantity two gallons and a half ... you will give me credit for the intake in the Casks and Licence which amounts to £6-7-6.' Sutherland replied 'I will cause my man to Wait with the Whiskey two or three hours if you are not waiting it at this side of the ferry, but if you dont get the Casks full it is not my fault for no Cask leaves here but which is full to the Bung & I cannot be accountable for any intake ... if you allow the Whisky to lie at the ferry all night, when no doubt liberties are taken with it the fault is your own.' John replied on 31 July 'Cask No 95 had been pierced and 2 & ½ Gallons abstracted from it ... pieces of Broom put into the holes made in the casks ... it occurs to me that we should just split the loss betwixt us.' Sutherland relented and although John was invoiced for a delivery of 146 gallons priced at £52 15s 9d Sutherland agreed a deduction for 'half of the intake' and the cost of the licence and wrote out a bill for exactly £50. John then had money troubles and struggled to retire this and the next bill. In October he asked Sutherland to renew a bill for £25 however Sutherland replied 'You have at present Value for £75 worth of Whiskey & yet you ask me to renew a £25. You must be well aware, that even if I could do so, the Bank would at once see it was a renewal, which might have the effect of their losing Confidence in you.'

On 5 January 1842 John requested another consignment and 143 gallons were delivered nine days later with a bill for £55 10s payable within two months. John wrote to Sutherland on 7 March requesting a bill 'for £35 and remit the proceeds to Mr. Fraser Banker Dornoch and I will be prepared to pay him £20 on or before the Draft falls due ... money is very scarce at present here.' It appears Sutherland declined as on 15 March John sent him 'a Bill for £24 which I hope you will return in course of Post to retire the other which will be due.' So John had taken out a loan of £24 to finish paying off the bill for £55.

On 2 May John was invoiced for 139¾ gallons plus 16 gallons for Miss Joan Ross, Innkeeper at Spinningdale, for a total of £60 16s 6d, payable in two instalments within two and three months. John must have realised he was in trouble financially as he wrote 'with my acceptance to you per £24 odds now in the Bank, would make me obligant to you to the extent of £85, which is considerably more than I am due you, as you will see from the enclosed Accompt Current ... the difference betwixt us arises from you having omited [sic] to give me credit for the allowance of 6d per gallon for selling your whiskey, and what I paid for the Licence, in terms of our original agreement.' Mr Mackenzie of Dalmore Distillery immediately replied that Sutherland was away however 'if I rightly understand the terms, upon which, you have all along been supplied, with Whisky from this Distillery, I consider your claims ... nothing short of a complete assumption, and as far as I know, warranted neither by any writ, or agreement of Mr Sutherland.' John then wrote a long letter to Sutherland on 16 May outlining their original agreement. Sutherland replied 'unless the bill is accepted in due course for the Amount, I will take it up & place it in the hands of a man of business to prosecute for non acceptance ... you will find that tricks will not do with me.' Sutherland followed it up with a letter on 10 June 'I have now looked over the a/c you sent here in my absence in the South, and feel astonished how you dared present such to me.' He then went on to detail their transactions and considered from January 1841 he had charged the nett price, and at times charged less than the full price of the whisky. 'I have acted all along with a different feeling towards you & consider myself ill requited now, by an attempt being made to take the advantage.' John replied that 'upon the 27 January 1841 you reduced the price to 7/3d and yet you have now the modesty to desire me to credit you with 8/ on that occasion, thereby overcharging myself 3d on that transaction, but you will find that I am not Such a Simpleton as you take me to be ... the only difference betwixt us is the charge of 6d per gallon made by me in terms of our original agreement upon which I all along acted in good faith towards you, and I defy you to show that you ever intimated to me, that you was to discontinue that allowance.'

Sutherland visited John on 23 June to settle their differences. John gave him £7 9s cash and a bill was drawn up for £27 signed by both of them, to be paid within two months. However, on 4 July Sutherland wrote 'I observe the first proportion of your unaccepted Dft. to me per £60.16.6 Stg for the last supply of Aqua you got, is due tomorrow the 5th inst. and I now beg to intimate to you, that unless the said proportion of said bill be paid, the matter must instantly be put in the hands of a man of business to recover.' John replied that he was surprised because as far has he was concerned the £7 9s cash and £27 bill had settled the account. 'If you attempt to give me any trouble after this, I am perfectly able to defend myself in any action you may think proper to raise against me.' Sutherland sent him a copy of the account and considered that John still owed him £29. The account included the full prices without deductions, even though at times Sutherland had charged John less. 'I have now to intimate for the last time that unless this sum be immediately settled with me, steps will require to be taken for its recovery.' John wrote a long reply on 29 July and considered the account 'to be quite erroneous' because it omitted the 6d commission, 'But if you are determined to annoy me for any alleged Balance on our past transactions, while I deny that I owe you one shilling on that score I shall cut any future transactions with you, and Defend myself.' That same day Sutherland had a court Summons drawn up for the £29 he considered he was owed, however held off having it served.

On 28 March 1843 the Summons was delivered to Catharine, as John was out. This started a court battle which dragged on, resulting in a huge bundle of seventy-seven documents, some of which were drawn up by John's lawyer uncle, John Gordon. The bundle included most of the correspondence, including eighteen letters written by John. John's Defences outlined the series of events and their agreement as he saw it, which maintained that he was owed 6d per gallon commission on the sales he made since January 1841 and thus did not owe Sutherland anything. On 9 August Sutherland's Replies argued that they had settled their original agreement at the end of 1840. 'On 27th January 1841 the Pursuer forwarded to the Defender the whole whisky ordered by his letter of the 14th, and at the same time sent him an Invoice stating the price of 8/- per gallon in Correspondence with the former practice. The amount of the whisky at this sale was of £67:19:6d. But on 12th February 1841 the Pursuer drew on the defender for the price of the whisky, not at the invoiced price of 8/- less 6d of discount or allowance, but at the net rate of 7/3 mentioned in the Pursuer's letter of 16th January. The exact amount was thus £62.8.1d.' However, this was incorrect as the original invoice clearly stated a price of 7s 3d and neither the invoice nor Sutherland's letter mentioned that the price was nett. John's letters were submitted as evidence, although this did not include a potentially crucial one that John wrote on 21 January 1841; was this deliberate because it jeopardised Sutherland's case? John's Answers denied that he 'was ever informed, or given to understand that the agreed on Commission of six pence per Gallon on his sales was to be discontinued' and 'that the prices Invoiced were the net prices.' The Dalmore Distillery Cellar sign 'remained up in front of his House, until about the latter end of the month of October 1842, when the cargo of spirits he received from the Pursuer in the month of May previously was exhausted.' In just over two years John had sold 1,427¾ gallons of Dalmore whisky and had paid Sutherland £548 13s 1d, equivalent to about £50,000 today.

Sheriff-substitute Gordon gave his verdict on 26 January 1844 in favour of Sutherland but reduced the amount owed by £1 14s 9d for the 'intake.' He reasoned that 'On 14 January 1841 the Defender asks for a reduction of the price to 7/6 per Gallon (=7/ nett). The Pursuer hesitates to make so large a reduction, but ultimately agrees to reduce the price to 7/3. This obviously means 7/3 nett, for any other construction involves, without the smallest external evidence to support it, the strong improbability that the seller volunteered to reduce his price 3d pr Gallon below what the Pursuer ever asked him to do.'[17] Sutherland's expenses of £6 4s 10s were signed off by Sheriff Hugh Lumsden on 12 April. The verdict would have been a massive blow to John as he then owed Sutherland about £26, plus over £6 expenses.

It appears John had been sampling too much of his stock as his lodger and lawyer uncle, John Gordon, drew up a Petition on 9 May which he lodged with Dornoch Sheriff Court under oath:

John Ross, Millwright

That for a considerable time back, John Ross Millwright at Clashmore aforesaid, and residing in the House there belonging to the Heirs of the now deceased Mr. William Christie, sometime of Golspie, and Catherine Sutherland or Ross his wife, also residing there, without any just cause whatever, have both and each of them conceived the most deadly malice and ill will towards the Petitioner, and have each of them on divers occasions within the last three years in particular assaulted, maltreated and abused the Petitioner, and made various attempts to deprive him of his life, but as this was generally, when the said John Ross was in a state of inebriation, the Petitioner was induced from time to time to overlook their improper and reprehensible conduct...

1844 May 3} ... That upon the Petitioner's return home from Court the same evening, about four o Clock P.m., he was repeatedly assaulted and insulted by the said Catherine Sutherland or Ross, who violently and in the most outrageous manner obstructed and prevented him from going up to his writing office in the said House ... who used the most indecent and opprobrious epithets towards the Petitioner and with oathes and imprecations avowed and declared she would sooner cut his Throat and set fire at once to all his Processes, Papers, and effect...

...That about ten o Clock again on the same evening the Petitioner accompanied by two respectable Neighbours proceeded to his Room in order to go to his Bed there, when he was once more most grossly assaulted and Knocked down by the said John Ross, by a violent blow in the breast, by which he was Knocked down, and nearly deprived of life and were it not that he was able with great difficulty to make his escape, he would undoubtedly be Killed on the spot.[18]

The Sheriff-substitute ordered John and Catharine 'to keep the Petitioner John Gordon harmless and skaithless in his person property and goods for the period of twelve Calendar months each under the penalty of Eight Pounds six shillings & eight pence sterling'; and failing that, to be imprisoned.

Just when you think it couldn't get any worse Gordon lodged a Summons with the Court on 5 July claiming that John owed him £67 9d![19] Gordon must have done this to spite John knowing there was no way he could afford to pay it. Gordon provided copies of six accounts along with a summary from May 1837 to February 1844. John in his Defences denied 'owing the Pursuer one farthing of the amount for which he is here prosecuted,' submitted three letters from 1841 in which Gordon admitted he owed John money and an account in which John claimed Gordon owed him £27 2d, including the rent. John considered 'The only account twixt the pursuer and defender is that for defending him at the instance of Mr. Donald Sutherland Dalmore, and which is stated by the pursuer at Seventeen Pounds Sterling.' Gordon lodged Replies but on 23 August the Sheriff considered the Defences and Replies were not prepared correctly and ordered them to be withdrawn. John was

The Church of the Holy Rood (Greyfriars), Stirling, from the Ladies' Rock. Photo by James Valentine c.1868. The cupola over the Martyrs Monument on the left was placed in 1867; the row of old hogsback stones to the right of the path were removed and replaced by vertical stones, of which the first was erected in 1869.

permitted to lodge new Defences but on 4 October 1844 the Sheriff-substitute considered 'in respect of no Defences being lodged for the Defender holds him as confessed and Decerns against him in absence.' Gordon was permitted expenses of £2 14s 3d, on top of the £67 9d owed, the total being equivalent to £7,000 today!

In 1846 John and his family were evicted and by the birth of their fifth child on 31 December 1847, had moved to Stirling. Stirling is dominated by its castle and in 1841 the local ministers mentioned the 'Many excellent dwelling-houses and splendid shops, and elegant suburban villas.'[20] However, a subsequent report described filthy open sewers with 'no public necessaries; and the common stairs and closes, and even the public streets, are used, habitually, as such, by certain classes of the community.' In 1851 John and his family were living in St John Street, however lodging houses there harboured 'the lowest description of mendicants and vagrants.'[21] At the top of the street is the Church of the Holy Rood (=Greyfriars or High Church), divided into East and West.[22] John and his family probably attended the services and the four youngest children may have been baptised there. In 1841 Stirling had nineteen schools and very few children and adults could not read or write, so presumably their children were educated.[23] By 1856 they had moved to The Craigs, and from

John Ross, Millwright

at least 1860 up to his wife's death on 21 December 1867 were living at 74 High Craigs. In 1870-1 John was living at 75 Upper Craigs.[24]

The various records referred to John as a millwright, carpenter, joiner, coach wright or cartwright. On 22 April 1850 he became a Burgess of the Mechanics after presenting a Bill of Entry and paying two pounds, which gave him trade benefits.[25] In about 1848, John had become one of the four Town Officers, thus he had a responsible role with a regular salary of twelve shillings per week. Their uniform, supplied by the council, was a 'gaudy livery of scarlet, their heads adorned with cocked hats, and bearing halberts, the brightness of which, however, intimated that they had very little duty to perform except that of show' and the officers 'went about their duties in an easy, sleepy fashion.'[26] The officers, along with the Town Drummer, led processions on gala days, public parades and the funerals of eminent men. They also acted as police before there were proper policemen in Stirling. John may have been amongst the party that waited on the railway platform when Queen Victoria and her entourage passed slowly through on 14 August 1849, on her way to Perth from Glasgow.[27] John was probably one of the officers who, in March 1850, were asked to 'perambulate the Streets on the Sabbath and to report the Licensed Houses in the practice of giving drink to persons on that day.' On 19 December 1853 it was reported 'that the Magistrates had dismissed John Ross' but no reason was given.[28]

In the 1870s John moved to Glasgow and died of senility on 7 February 1881 in the 'Old Man's Asylum.' The Asylum for Indigent Old Men was more of an old people's home than an asylum for the mentally ill, situated at 81-83 Rottenrow. His children returned his body to Stirling and buried him in the old cemetery of the Church of the Holy Rood, with his deceased wife and two children who had died young. Their grave is situated very close to the west side of the tower, which may indicate John was well respected in the town.[29]

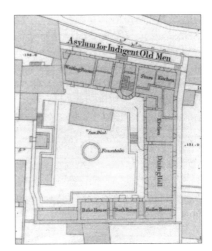

Plan of the Asylum for Indigent Old Men, Rottenrow, Glasgow, surveyed 1857. John Ross died there in 1881.

3

Donald Ross, the New Miller of Skibo

Donald Ross was baptised on 7 March 1813 in Dornoch Cathedral by Rev. John Bethune. As a boy he had kept pet rabbits, didn't learn English until he was fourteen and only went to school for three months.[1]

Donald first appeared in the statute labour list for Dornoch in 1837 however he would have been twenty-four by then, so where had he been?[2] On 22 November 1839 he married Marjory Bayne in the newly renovated Dornoch Cathedral by Rev. Angus Kennedy. His wife was born in the small village of Huntingtower, three miles W.N.W. of Perth. She was baptised on 16 October 1796 at Tibbermore Church, so she was sixteen years older than Donald. In the baptism record her name had been crossed out and replaced with May.

They only had one child, Anna, listed in the 1851 census as nine years old, born in Wick, Caithness, however, there does not appear to be a birth record nor any connection of the family with Caithness. Given that May was forty-six at the time of Anna's birth, then she was probably adopted. Each year, during the herring season, Wick's population increased dramatically due to the influx of fishermen and female fish gutters, which led to increased promiscuity.[3] Perhaps Anna was the result of such a liaison.

Donald took over as the Miller of Skibo after his father's death in 1838 and worked closely with his brother John. The earliest evidence of Donald's handwriting is a bill dated 1840, for ½ boll of oatmeal and ½ boll of barley meal for £1.[4] Miss Jess Davidson sublet 'the farm of Rosebank in the parish of Dornoch, held by her under Tack from George Dempster Esquire of Skibo to Donald Ross, then a Miller residing at Clashmore, for the space of nine years from the term of Whitsunday, 1839.'[5] Donald was listed as living at Rosebank in the 1841 census, the statute labour lists for 1840-1843 and the Dornoch Sheriff Court Jury Rolls for 1842-1844.[6] Donald's mother stated 'her son, who had grown up to manhood, was attending to the mill as Miller, to the entire satisfaction of the tenants.'[7]

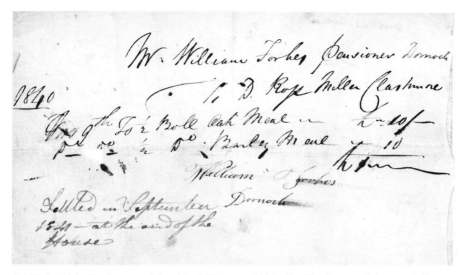

A bill for ½ boll of oatmeal for 10 shillings and ½ boll of barley meal for 10 shillings; the earliest known example of Donald's handwriting.

On 12 April 1845 Donald had an Interdict drawn up by Charles Spence SSC against the 2nd Duke of Sutherland, the Heritors of the Parish of Dornoch and the Magistrates of the Royal Burgh of Dornoch. This was to prevent them from putting a road through St Barr's Churchyard, near to where Donald's father and brother were buried.[8] Donald 'had erected a monumental stone over his father's grave' which was to be 'cleared away to make room for the foundation of a dyke [wall], to enclose that portion of the churchyard.' As part of the preliminary works, a post had been 'dug and planted' into his brother Alexander's grave. On 21 April Donald stated he had 'ascertained that the Magistrates of Dornoch are the only and real Respondents, and that the Duke of Sutherland and the other Heritors of Dornoch, are not the parties who have carried on the operations complained of.' However, the town council minutes of the same date recorded 'the Clerk ... had written to Mr George Sutherland Taylor, agent for the principal Heritor and for the Provost ... stating the fact that the Magistrates had not interfered or sanctioned any interference with the Churchyard.'[9] Their Answers to the Interdict stated 'the paling complained of was put up without any authority or interference on the part of the Magistrates of Dornoch.'[10] At their next meeting on 9 May the Magistrates added they had 'no funds for the execution of improvements at their disposal.'[11] So if the Duke, Heritors and Magistrates were not responsible, who had instigated the work? Either way, the Interdict was not contested, so the Miller of Skibo's tablestone and the Plaiden Ell were saved. That same year Donald was mentioned as a miller at Clashmore, with his brother John, in a subscription list of a Gaelic book, however they had been evicted from the mill before then.[12]

The 2nd Duke of Sutherland was named George Granville Leveson-Gower after his father. In 1823, as Earl Gower, he married his cousin Lady Harriet Elizabeth Georgiana Howard and became the 2nd Duke when his father died in 1833.[13] The Sheriff of Lanarkshire, Archibald Alison, described the Duke as 'a pleasing, intelligent man, reserved in his manners, and unfortunately afflicted with deafness, which precluded him from taking part in general conversation.'[14] He was often referred to as the 'Good Duke' however Donald MacLeod described him as 'a simple, if not a silly, narrow minded gentleman, who concerns himself very little, about even his own pecuniary affairs; he entrusts his whole affairs to this set of vile, cunning knaves, called factors, and the people are enslaved so much that it is now considered the most foolish thing a man can do [is] to petition his Grace.'[15] Earl Gower played a part in the earlier 'improvements' on the Sutherland Estate and when he became Duke they continued, but on a lesser scale.[16] In 1840 his factors advised him to issue a proclamation that he would, in 'an act of high-sounding generosity' cancel all rent arrears due by the small tenantry, with the condition that 'no future arrears would be allowed, and that all future defaulters should be instantly removed, and their holdings (not let to tenants, but) handed over to their next neighbour', which had the effect of reducing the number of small tenants and increasing the size of the large farms.[17] In the winter of 1840-1 'shoals of vagrants were apprehended in various parts of this county, and brought to Dornoch. After a close investigation, the entire party ... were marched to the Meikle Ferry, from thence to be transmitted to the celebrated Black Isle in Ross-shire, "time out of mind, the beggars' domicile."'[18] By 1850 the Duke was the largest landowner in western Europe and the Sutherland Estate covered about 1.1 million acres. He died in 1861 and with time the fortunes of the successive Dukes of Sutherland diminished.[19] The 2nd Duchess was Queen Victoria's Mistress of the Robes and Alison described her as 'Possessed early in life of great natural beauty and a fine figure... That she possesses in a very high degree the favour of her sovereign is well known, and has been publicly evinced on many occasions. Six Cabinet Ministers are at this moment her connections by blood or marriage, and she enjoys greater political influence than ever has been possessed by any lady since the days of Sarah, Duchess of Marlborough.'[20]

Charles Spence was instrumental in the direction that Donald took in his life. He was born in 1795 in Kirkwall, the capital of the Orkney Isles, and was probably baptised in St Magnus Cathedral. By about 1819 he had moved to Edinburgh working as a lawyer and became a Solicitor before the Supreme Court in 1831. Spence also became an estate agent, an agent for a life assurance company and was involved with a lot of charities, often holding executive roles.[21] He lived and worked in Edinburgh for over forty years and would have seen many changes, such as the building of the Scott Monument.[22]

Spence discovered an old legal document 'lying under dust, unmolested, in the Advocates' Library, Edinburgh' which stated 'the land was bound to maintain the disabled poor in so much of the necessaries of life as was considered sufficient to sustain life.'[23] He used this 'ancient Poor-law of Scotland' in a case brought before the Supreme Court in 1843, supporting widow Elspeth Duncan, who had eight children. She received a shilling to eighteen pence a week for winding bobbins and 3s 6d a week from the church. The judges had a debate about what was 'needful sustentation' and the Lord President considered 'A mere pittance sufficient to keep them from starvation would not do; for it must be enough to prevent their health being injured by its scantiness.' The majority of the judges ruled that 'the allowance therein awarded was not sufficient as needful sustentation for the family,' so the Heritors of the Parish of Ceres in Fife were instructed to increase the widow's relief payments.[24] Over a year later the widow had not received a penny more, so Spence took the Heritors to court and they immediately paid the widow £15 12s in arrears.[25] MacLeod then supplied Spence with seventy-two cases from Sutherland, plus some from other counties.[26] Many other cases followed and Spence wrote 'The revival of the ancient poor law is now producing throughout the country the happiest effects. Numbers of poor persons are obtaining, by force of law, that reluctant justice from the heritors of which they have been by far too long deprived.'[27]

A Royal Commission was set up in 1844 to investigate the condition of the poor in Scotland, resulting in the *Poor Law Inquiry (Scotland)* report. Duncan McNeill, Lord Advocate, then prepared the *Poor Law Amendment (Scotland) Bill*, which was read in the House of Commons on 2 April 1845.[28] Dempster, in a long letter to the Lord Advocate, considered the bill would be 'ruinous to the landholders.'[29] The second reading of the bill took place on 12 June.[30] Mr S. Crawford said that in Sutherland 'there was no protection for the poor; they were without hope, and the country was in a state of desolation.' This was refuted by Loch who said 'I can say that there is no set of tenantry in the world that form so anxious a care to their landlord' and gave a selected account of the improvements. Edward Ellice retorted 'the condition of the people now showed that the [improvement] system had not led to good, for the state of the population was wretched in the extreme.' Mr P. M. Stewart considered the bill 'gave power to the powerful, and threw additional burdens on the oppressed poor of Scotland.' The bill was amended and was passed by the House of Lords on 29 July.[31] In a nutshell, provision of relief for the poor was to be overseen by a Board of Supervision and administered by parish Parochial Boards to distribute relief payments to people on the Poor Roll, and to provide medical help for the sick. Sir John McNeill, Duncan's brother, was appointed the Chair of the Board. Landowners and landlords were expected to pay for the relief and applications for relief were assessed by an Inspector of the Poor.

On 20 May 1845 a meeting was held in Edinburgh to set up 'an association for protecting the interests of the poor.'[32] At a public meeting on 31 May it was agreed that it would be called the *Scottish Association for Protection of the Poor*. Rev. James Begg gave a rousing speech 'They would send a voice across the hills – a voice which would be understood by every Highlander – a voice which would declare that the people of this country would never allow their fellow-countrymen to be treated as slaves, or their rights and privileges to be trodden under foot.'[33] Initially Spence and Robert Somers were Joint Secretaries though later Spence became the sole Secretary.[34] Somers was another outspoken critic of the Highland Clearances; in 1844 he wrote a pamphlet on the *Scottish Poor Laws* and for a while was an assistant to Hugh Miller, who was editor of *The Witness*.[35] In October 1847 Somers travelled to the Highlands to report on the effects of the potato famine and wrote a series of letters to the *North British Daily Mail*, which he later published as a book entitled *Letters from the Highlands*. In 1849 he became the editor of the *NBDM*.

At the association's next meeting on 5 June, chaired by Spence, it was considered the 'Poor-Law Bill at present before Parliament ... instead of conferring a boon on the unfortunate pauper, only increased the facilities of the heritor to defeat his claim to needful sustentation.'[36] In August Spence reported nine cases where he had helped people get increased poor relief payments, and he mentioned seventy-two other cases that had been taken up by the association.[37] The following year Spence wrote to *The Scotsman* complaining that 'the Board of Supervision has *denied the poor the privilege of stating their complaints against parishes by means either of counsel or of agents*.'[38] At the first annual meeting in June 1846, Spence reported that 'the association had been the means of getting additional support to many poor persons.'[39]

In 1850 Spence became the Treasurer of the Royal Patriotic Society of Scotland, set up in 1846 to 'improve physically the condition of the humbler classes, chiefly through the medium of their own instrumentality, by aiding them to economize and to develop their resources.'[40] Queen Victoria and Prince Albert were Joint Patrons, and in 1850 Sir James Matheson MP was President, with fifty-eight vice-presidents consisting of various dukes, earls, lords and other notable gentleman, including the 2nd Duke of Sutherland. The Secretary was Charles Bond who later became a thorn in the side of Donald's activities. In 1850 Spence wrote two letters to the 2nd Duke describing the success of the 'Crofter System' on Sir Kenneth Mackenzie's Gairloch Estate. Spence explained that 600 crofters had reclaimed worthless land using 'the spade husbandry system' and this system was 'capable of supporting thousands of industrious and happy tenants, and of yielding a good rental to the proprietor,' though was ignored by the Duke.[41] In 1851 MacLeod launched a scathing attack on the society and exposed the hypocrisy of the Secretary consulting 'men whose predecessors and themselves have been ... contriving how to destroy and extirpate the Highland peasantry from the land of their fathers, and reduce them to their present deplorable condition.'[42] Spence died on 22 June 1861 in Edinburgh.

4

Eviction

Donald's mother, widow Ann Gordon, 'completed the improvements and meliorations upon the premises, and did expend considerable sums in improving and ameliorating the said mill, Houses, and Dykes or fences on the premises, in the full confidence, that if she should be removed therefrom, she should be entitled to payment for the full value thereof.'[1]

In March 1841 Donald, his mother, and his uncles John, George and Roderick Gordon, were issued with a Summons of Removing from George [Soper] Dempster and his factor George Forbes.[2] The Gordon brothers were sons of William Gordon and his 2nd wife Ann Forsyth. They were all ordered 'to flit and remove themselves their Bairns, Families, Servants, Subtenants, Cottars and Dependants, Cattle, Goods, and Gear, ... from the Houses, Gardens and Grass ... at and against the term of Whitsunday next to come' and summoned to appear before the Sheriff of Sutherland at Dornoch Court in seven days' time. They immediately appointed George Sutherland Taylor, Golspie to represent them, who was the 2nd Duke of Sutherland's Law Agent and a historian.[3] The case, in one form or another, dragged on for the next seven years and several bundles of papers were lodged with the courts, which are now in the NRS and contain detailed information that would never have been known had they gone quietly.

On 6 April Taylor wrote to Forbes explaining that there were 'certain conditions agreed to by the Proprietor in Writing, and which entitle them to full meliorations' but nothing had been done to ascertain the amount owed. Forbes replied that he had never 'seen the writing.'[4] Taylor drew up Defences which mentioned the letters that the elder George Dempster had written in 1792 to the Miller and other tenants. Dempster replied that the letter to the Miller was only 'in the event of his removal during his life.' However, his Replies were submitted too late so Sheriff-substitute Alexander Gordon dismissed the case and in July ruled that the Defenders (Donald etc) were entitled to expenses. On 6 August John Gordon wrote to Taylor 'Mr. Donald Ross and I came purposely in to Town to day, and succeeded in getting back Mr. Dempster's Process of Removing against us; As we are extremely anxious

One of the bundles of Dornoch Sheriff Court documents regarding the eviction of Donald's family, now in the National Archives of Scotland.

to have the expenses taxed and Decerned for.'[5] In November the Sheriff-substitute approved expenses of £8 11s 3d, however by February 1842 they had not been paid so John Gordon had a Protestation drawn up by the Court of Session in Edinburgh which ordered Dempster and Forbes to pay £10 within fifteen days or they would have 'their readiest goods gear debts and sums of money' seized.[6] However, no further action would be taken until the Court met on 20 May.

On 26 March a second Summons of Removing was drawn up against 'Ann Gordon or Ross' and her sons Donald and John, and a separate Summons was drawn up against Donald's uncles.[7] John failed to appear in court, however he could not be evicted because of his Feu Contract. In their Defences, Ann and Donald outlined that they were entitled to compensation for improvements in the region of £200, and that another Process of Removing was awaiting a decision by the Court of Session. Dempster replied that Ann was the only recognised tenant of 'the Mill and Mill Lands of Clashmugach or Ryre or Rosebank,' that Donald assisted in their management and denied that they were entitled to compensation. He then withdrew the first Process of Removing and paid the expenses due. On 30 May the Sheriff-substitute ruled that Ann and Donald held 'the subjects from which they are sought to be removed, under written conditions granted by a former proprietor of Skibo and binding on therefore as such, whereby the proprietor has to pay to the Defenders meliorations amounting to about two hundred pounds before he has any right to remove them.' Then Ann and Donald pushed their luck. A series of documents were submitted arguing points of law and demanding that the amount of compensation should be established by a third party, but they were dismissed by the Sheriff-substitute. On appeal to the Sheriff, Hugh Lumsden initially agreed with the ruling of the Sheriff-substitute however on 2 September changed his mind and decided that they could be removed. The Defenders harvested their crops at Martinmas (11 November) but refused to vacate the premises.[8] On 21 January 1843, Dempster requested that because Ann, Donald and John had not left by Whitsunday 1842, the Court should issue a warrant to evict them, but not from Rosebank occupied by Donald under Miss Davidson. A Warrant of Ejection was granted which 'Commanded and Charged the said Ann Gordon or Ross, John Ross and Donald Ross, Defenders to flit.' On 14 February Dempster claimed that they 'still retain possession' and requested another warrant to evict them.[9] This was granted four days later and they probably left the house, mill and steading soon after. Losing the mill would have been a blow as they would have lost their main source of income.

On 11 January, shortly before the eviction, a Petition, in Ann's name, was submitted to the Sheriff requesting a valuation of the premises. Alexander Graham, mason at Allardie, presented the valuation on 14 March which came to a total of £218 3s 11¾d, equivalent to about £19,000 today.[10] The valuation provided a very detailed description of the properties. To summarise, the deceased Miller's house was built of stone, with clay mortar. The inside walls were plastered and white-washed, and there was a fire-place and chimney. There was a front stable door with a thumb latch, a back door and three internal doors. The rooms had glazed sash windows, plus a toilet with a glazed window. The roof was supported by twenty pairs of beams and was thatched with straw. There was a loft containing two fixed beds and two glazed windows, accessed by stairs with nine steps and a trap-door. The mill, including the kiln, was built of stone and had a front stable door. Its thatched roof was supported by twenty-four pairs of beams and it had an outer wooden water-wheel. The lower of the two millstones was five inches thick. The steading was built of stone, with a clay floor, containing a stable, byre and cart-shed. It had a front stable door, a back door, doors to the stable and byre, and a thatched roof supported by thirty-four pairs of beams.

On 12 September 1844 a Petition in Ann's name was drawn up by Charles Spence and copied by Donald. It stated that since the eviction, Ann and her sickly daughter (Christy?) had been living in a cold barn at Rosebank and were 'utterly destitute of needful sustentation.' It indicated the Heritors and Kirk Session 'utterly neglect the Petitioners case' and requested that they provide 'needful sustentation and a better place of residence.'[11] On 26 September Rev. Alexander MacIvor, the new Minister of the Parish of Dornoch, replied that the Heritors and Kirk Session had not received an application for relief, so they had not neglected her case: 'the Petitioner is understood to be living in the House of one Son who occupies the farm of Rosebank at a rent of about £10 per annum, and to be residing in the close vicinity of another Son who is a cart and Millwright, and that both these Sons, and other near relations in the neighbourhood of Rosebank are not duly legally bound to aliment and support the Petitioner, but are in sufficient circumstances to enable them to do so.' MacIvor considered the Petition 'premature, informal, and incompetent.' Ann did not appeal so the Sheriff-substitute dismissed the Petition. In 1845 Ann was added to the Poor Roll, drawn up in response to the new Poor Law Bill. Initially she received 1s 6d per week, which was increased to 2s the following year. Dempster was the Chair of the Parochial Board which administered the relief payments.[12]

On 15 March 1845 Dempster had another Summons of Removal drawn up against 'Donald Ross Farmer or Cottar residing at Ryre or Rosebank and Mrs May or Mary Bayne Ross' and it was delivered three days later.[13] This time they did not contest it and sometime afterwards moved south.

Amazingly, on 28 April, Spence drew up a Summons in Ann's name against George [Soper] Dempster of Skibo, George Dempster Hawkins of Dunnichen and Catherine, Charlotte, Helen and Gertude Hawkins, who were Dempster's nieces and residing at Skibo.[14] The Summons requested the payment of £218, 3s, 11¾d, based on Graham's 1843 valuation, plus about £100 for court costs. The Defenders (Dempster etc) were ordered to 'compear before the Lords of Council and Session at Edinburgh' on 27 May.

The Great Hall of Parliament House, Edinburgh in 1847. The statue on the right is of Joanna Dempster's father, Robert Dundas of Arniston.

Eviction

The Edinburgh law courts are situated south of St Giles Cathedral (more correctly the High Kirk), of which the oldest part is the Great Hall of Parliament House.[15] The Supreme Court of Scotland comprised several courts. The Court of Session dealt with civil cases, such as this one, whereas the High Court of Justiciary dealt with criminal cases. At the time, the Court of Session had thirteen judges known as the Lords of Session and was divided into the Outer and Inner House. A case was first presented to the Outer House and heard by one of the five Lords Ordinary, who gave his verdict. If this was not satisfactory then an appeal could be made to the Inner House. The Inner House was divided into 1st and 2nd Divisions comprised of four judges each. The 1st Division was presided over by the Lord President (=Justice-General) and the 2nd Division by the Lord Justice-Clerk. The case would be heard in one of the divisions, however the judges of the other division could be called in if the first lot could not reach a decision. If the verdict of the Inner House was still not satisfactory then an appeal could be submitted to the House of Lords in London.[16]

On 18 June the Defenders pleaded that the 1792 letter and the Miller's will were 'defective' because they were not stamped; that the action should be dropped against George [Soper] Dempster and George Hawkins because 'the former not being the representative of his father, nor the latter [representative] of his mother or grandfather;' that the letter was personal to the Miller, not to his descendants; that the improvements were of a different nature to those outlined in the letter and that the valuations were inaccurate.[17] On 10 July John Cuninghame, Lord Ordinary, dismissed Dempster and George Hawkins from the proceedings, which was odd given that Dempster was the owner of the Skibo Estate as 'heir of entail' and had instigated the eviction. This left his four nieces as Defenders who were only about 16, 9, 7 and 6 years of age respectively.[18] Several documents were drawn up by Spence containing a series of statements, which the Defenders either agreed with or denied.[19]

On 20 March 1846 Lord Cuninghame requested valuations on the improvements to the mill, dams and leads, and buildings on Ryre farm, 1) before the death of Harriet Dempster in 1810, 2) from then until the death of William Soper Dempster in 1830, 3) from then until the death of the Miller in 1838, and 4) from then until the eviction. Surveyor Alexander Lockhart Bauchope visited the premises on 10 June though was unable to value the mill machinery because it was 'a wreck lying in front of the Mill.'

On 27 March Dempster had yet another Summons of Removal drawn up against John Ross, his mother Ann, sisters Margaret and Christy, and John Gordon, who by then were probably all living in John's house. By 1846 William Christie had died and his heir, his elder brother George, was living in Sydney, Australia. The feu duty had not been paid for three years so Dempster repossessed the plot where John had built his house. They were ordered to appear at Dornoch Court in seven days, though did not appear so the Sheriff-substitute 'Holds the said Defenders as Confessed and Decerns against them in absence.'[20] On 18 May they were charged to remove within forty-eight hours before Whitsunday and if they didn't then the Sheriff Officers would 'remove and put forth' them and their effects. On 1 June the Sheriff-substitute granted an eviction warrant. They probably left soon after and John and his family moved to Stirling. Ann and her daughters stayed in the area, but it is not known where they lived.

On 2 February 1847 Dempster's nieces admitted liability for the value of the properties in 1810 when Harriet Dempster died, minus the value in 1792; thus they were prepared to pay £29 16s 6d.[21] On 16 June Lord Cuninghame agreed with this, plus interest since the date of the eviction. This decision was appealed and on 18 February 1848 Spence wrote to the Lord Justice-General stating that 'The Pursuer is a poor person, partly dependent on parochial support for her subsistence. She is at present in a very infirm state of health, and as her case is extremely pressing, she ventures to solicit your Lordship to order the case to be advised during this session at such time as may be convenient.' Sadly, Ann died on 23 April in Clashmugach. It is not known where she was buried as there is no mention of her (or any other family members) on the Miller's tablestone. She had probably joined the Free Church, but there isn't a gravestone in the Dornoch Free Church graveyard either, probably because her children could not afford one. On 31 May Spence stated that 'Donald Ross, Writer in Glasgow, William Ross, Margaret Ross, Merran [sic] Ross, Christy Ross, and Ann Ross or Mackenzie' were executors of their mother's will and were now the 'pursuers in the said Action against Miss Catherine Hawkins and others.'

The case was heard before the 1st Division on 14 June. The four law lords: David Boyle (Lord Justice-General), J. H. Mackenzie, John Fullerton and Francis Jeffrey agreed with the opinion of Lord Cuninghame. They sympathised with the case but emphasised that Ann should have obtained a similar agreement with the later estate owners. Boyle criticised the harsh treatment metered out by Dempster 'For it seems to me that, if the heir of entail saw extensive and praiseworthy meliorations in the course of being made by his tenant on his property under his own eye, it would require very grave deliberations, to decide whether that tenant was not entitled to re-imbursement.'[22] The next day Spence submitted an expenses report which came to £118 8s 9d or £109 1s 8d after tax.[23] On 27 June Lord Cuninghame decreed that the Pursuers were entitled to expenses of £70 to be paid by the Defenders. So, seven years after the first eviction notice was served, they had lost their property valued at over £218 and had spent over £118 on court expenses, though had received back about £100. They had gambled everything on an old letter, but it let them down and Ann didn't live long enough to see the case closed.

Before Donald and his family packed their bags and moved south, he got caught up in other shenanigans.

5

House Breakers

In 1842 Donald and John Ross got into trouble with the law. The year before, four of their uncles: lawyer John, labourer Robert, farmer Roderick and shoemaker George, were living in the house of their deceased father, William Gordon, in Clashmugach. Robert was married to Isabella and had two young daughters. The four brothers had a major falling out which was acrimoniously fought out in Dornoch Sheriff Court. In October 1841, Robert, in a Petition drawn up by his brother John, complained that Roderick had not contributed to the rent since 1838 and accused Roderick and George, among many other things, of breaking down the door of the pigsty and selling a pig, selling a stirk (young bull or cow) and a milk cow, and that they brought 'two young lasses into the House without going even through the ceremony of marriage with them.' George used one room in the house for shoemaking and Robert accused him of bringing in, without permission, two trainee shoemakers, one of whom suffered from measles that had infected many people and some had died. Robert considered that the way he was treated 'became at last so intolerable, that he was under the necessity of requesting a particular favour of the Proprietor to remove them from the premises altogether.'[1] Roderick and George denied most of what Robert accused them of.

On 26 March 1842 a Summons of Removal was served against all four brothers by Dempster. It was indicated that Robert was a 'Tenant at Will' while the others were 'Pretended Tenants.' They were ordered to appear before the Sheriff in seven days. John, George and Roderick were represented by George Sutherland Taylor, however Robert did not appear and 'The Sheriff Holds the said Defender as Confessed.' The three brothers fought against the eviction and submitted several documents, including the 1792 letter to the tenants and a Bond of Caution written by Donald.[2] They considered that they were entitled to compensation before Dempster could evict them. In May the Sheriff-substitute ruled that the Defenders were entitled to expenses, but not compensation as it was not proved that they were the heirs of their father's property. Neither side were happy, so they appealed to the Sheriff.

On 23 July Sheriff Lumsden decided that Dempster was entitled to expenses and said 'the parties have themselves to blame.'

On Tuesday 25 October John, Roderick and George were evicted. All their possessions were removed from the property and Robert became the 'incoming' tenant. The eviction was described in detail, including an inventory of everything that was removed.[3] George Ross, Sheriff Officer, carried out the eviction and John Ross was employed to take down and unscrew some of the bedsteads. Once the contents had been removed the Sheriff Officer put out the fire in the kitchen and put padlocks on four of the doors of the 'lower flat' and one on a door in the 'upper flat.' He then rekindled the fire and gave the keys to Robert. The Sheriff Officer 'made certification to all concerned that if any person or persons intruded into the said House & premises attacked or molested the Proprietor or Incoming Tenant in their lawful possession thereof they would be held liable in the pains of Law.' The removed items were placed in a barn.

The following morning John Gordon met up with Roderick and with 'excited feelings' decided that because they had not received any compensation then they would take away the doors and windows, which they considered were theirs. They went to the mill at about 11am to ask Donald for help, and then on to John Ross's house. John would only help if they paid him, so they agreed to pay 2s 6d. He grabbed a hammer, screwdriver and clippers and

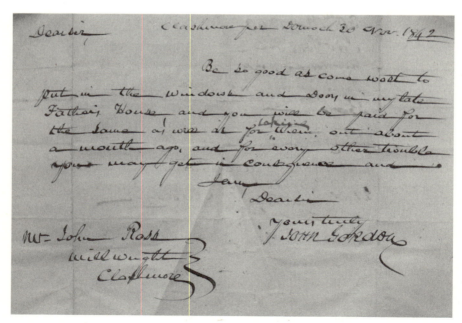

Letter from John Gordon to John Ross, asking him to put back the windows and doors in his deceased father (William Gordon)'s house.

the party proceeded to the Gordons' house accompanied by John Campbell, Pensioner, and Alexander and Neil Mackay who were apprentices of George Gordon. John Ross then proceeded to unscrew the hinges of nine doors and take four window frames out. Robert was out, but Isabella was in a room upstairs and once John had removed the door, she 'threatened to stab any person who would advance into the room.' The party took the doors and windows to the same barn where the other items were placed, however Donald and John Ross later denied they had helped to move them. The party then went back to John's house for a dram.

On 29 October, William Sutherland Fraser, Procurator Fiscal in Dornoch, drew up a petition for a 'Warrant of apprehending' for Roderick and John Gordon, Donald and John Ross, John Campbell and Alexander and Neil Mackay, which was granted by the Sheriff-substitute. Two days later Roderick, John Gordon, Donald and John Ross were imprisoned in Dornoch Jail 'therein to remain until liberated in due course of law.' It is not known why Campbell and the Mackays were let off, however they were later called as witnesses.[4]

Dornoch Court and Jail were in Dornoch Castle, owned by the 2nd Duke of Sutherland and leased to the council.[5] In 1818 the jail was described as consisting of

> ...two rooms or cellars for the confinement of Criminals on the ground floor, which are rough flagged, strongly arched above, and well ventilated; – And of two Rooms for the confinement of Debtors, the lowest of which is two stories high above the cells, which are commodious and neatly furnished, well lighted by three Windows in each Room and sufficiently aired, and are indeed the most salubrious prison Rooms we ever had occasion to see; – All the said apartments are provided with good strong beds, necessary boxes and other suitable accommodation.[6]

The prison wasn't secure and there were regular escapes. At times it was very overcrowded and in the late 1820s was reported to have held eighty prisoners, with men and women forced to share cells. In 1835 two more cells were added that were '16 feet square and 10 feet in height and may be divided by wooden partitions so as to form two sleeping apartments and a day room each, having a spacious window in each, and a fire place in each day Room.'[7] The building of a new jail commenced next door in 1844 on ground purchased from the Duke, however, it wasn't operational until 1850. The new jail closed in 1880 and now contains shops.[8] Today the castle is a hotel and the old cells on the ground floor are used as cellars.

On 30 November 1842 John Gordon wrote to John Ross asking him to re-fit the doors and windows.[9] This indicates that the four defendants had been let out of jail, probably on bail. On 13 December charges of 'Malicious Mischief, Wilful and Riotous Mischief and Breach of the Peace' were brought against the four men. The trial took place in December and was summarised by the *Inverness Courier*:

> On Thursday, the 29th ult., *John Gordon*, and *Roderick Gordon*, residing at Clashmugach, and *Donald Ross*, and *John Ross*, residing at Clashmore, in the parish of Dornoch, were tried before the Sheriff-substitute of Sutherland, and a Jury, accused of the crimes of malicious mischief, willful and notorious mischief, and breach of the peace. The libel charged the pannels with invading the house of Robert Gordon, on the 25th day of October last, and with forcibly and violently removing and carrying away nine doors and four windows therefrom, rendering the house thereby uninhabitable, and putting the inmates into bodily fear and alarm. The pannels rested their defence chiefly on the ground that as the proprietor resisted a claim of meliorations which they alleged was due them, they were entitled to carry away the doors and windows, and that this act did not infer malice or mischief. After a lengthened trial of seven hours, the jury returned a verdict unanimously finding the pannels guilty of wilful mischief and breach of the peace; and after a suitable address the Sheriff sentenced them to pay a fine of £5 each, and failing payment to be imprisoned for two calendar months, also to find caution to keep the peace for six months under a penalty of £10 each, and failing their doing so to be imprisoned for an additional month. The prosecution was conducted by Mr Fraser, procurator-fiscal; Mr D. Stewart, writer, Tain, and Mr Robert Ross, writer, Dornoch, defended the pannels.[10]

The *John o' Groat Journal* added that the two month's imprisonment would be 'with hard labour.'[11] John and Roderick Gordon owed John Ross £7 6s over the trouble caused, mainly for legal costs, but not including the £5 fine.[12] John took his uncles to the Small Debt Court over this on 31 December, only two days after the trial, so presumably they had all paid the fine. On 13 January 1843 John won the case and John Gordon was ordered to pay an additional 7s 7d expenses, though Roderick was absolved.[13]

6
Money Trials and Tribulations

After Donald was evicted from the mill, he found himself in trouble financially. Before then, in February 1841, Donald brought a small debt claim against Roderick Forsyth, Carpenter, Clashmugach for £8 6s 8d and won, plus expenses. In June John Ross, Innkeeper, Bonar Bridge brought a claim against Donald for £5 7s 7d and won, plus expenses.[1]

In February 1843 Lewis Houston, Agent for the British Linen Company Bank, Golspie, received a letter from Donald enclosing a bill for £5 5s drawn upon his brother-in-law, Roderick Mackenzie. The bill was accepted, discounted and £5 3s 8d was sent to Donald. On 10 June the bill became due for re-payment back to the bank and two days later Houston received a letter from Donald enclosing a new bill for £8 8s drawn upon Mackenzie, however the new bill was declined and returned to Donald. On 20 June William Munro, Accountant for the Caledonian Banking Company, Dornoch, received a letter from Donald with the same bill, however he also declined it. Donald then visited the bank in Golspie on 24 June and again presented the £8 8s bill; this time it was accepted and the payment was given to him, discounted by 2s 8d. The bill was due to be paid back in October and Donald was advised that it was being protested but it appears he did nothing about it. The bank then wrote to Mackenzie on 20 November calling for the overdue payments of £5 5s and £8 8s. Mackenzie replied that he had not signed the bills and he was not going to pay them. Donald then called at the bank and paid off the bill for £5 5s; however, the date on the second bill appeared to have been altered from 10 to 20 June, so Houston on 'Finding that the foresaid Bill for eight Pounds eight shillings was a forgery, I, on the twenty seventh November, transmitted the same to the Procurator Fiscal.'[2]

On 28 November a 'Warrant to apprehend' was granted and the next day Donald was arrested by Philip Mackay, Messenger at Arms, at 2am and accused of forging 'a Bill in the name of Roderick Mackenzie, Baker in Tain.'[3] Later that day, Donald was interrogated by Sheriff-substitute Alexander Gordon and Donald declared that Mackenzie had signed the bill for £8 8s but

Inverness Court on Castle Hill and the old Ness Bridge in 1836. Donald was tried in the court for forgery in 1844.

he did not remember changing the date.[4] Four bills and twelve letters were presented as evidence, though only two of the letters have survived, however both were written by Donald.[5] The first two bills were the ones for £5 5s and £8 8s; the third bill was found by Mackay and Alexander Leslie, Clerk to the Procurator Fiscal, who examined 'repositories' of Donald Ross and found a bill dated 16 February for £5 5s, drawn by Donald and signed by Mackenzie. One of Donald's surviving letters was sent with the third bill to Robert Barclay Sangster, Agent for the Aberdeen Town & County Banking Company, Golspie.[6] Sangster accepted the bill and paid the money to Donald. On 19 June the bill became due so Donald went to the bank and offered to retire the bill with 'another Bill for the same amount upon the same party, dated 22nd June, payable four months.' Sangster accepted and discounted the bill and gave the former bill to Donald. The new bill was unpaid by 25 October so it was protested and payment was requested several times.[7]

The fourth bill presented as evidence was drawn up by Donald on 13 May for £12 10s upon John Macdonald and his son James, Sawyers, Clashmore, payable within four months to the Caledonian Banking Company, Dornoch. Munro paid Donald the discounted money that same day. On 16 September the money had not been paid so the bill was protested by Charles Waterston, Manager of the Caledonian Banking Company. On 19 September Donald wrote to Munro 'I will retire my Bill with Mr. McDonald on Thursday. I trust there will be no inconvenience in allowing it remain till that day as I am to be from home tomorrow.'[8] Munro declared that Donald only made a payment of £3 4s 6d, leaving £9 5s 6d still due.[9]

On 30 November, the day after Donald's arrest, Mackenzie, in the presence of Sheriff-substitute Robert Sutherland Taylor, was shown the two bills for £5 5s, but denied that he'd signed them or authorised anyone else to sign them on his behalf. He was also shown a letter, signed by him, though written by Donald just two days before. Mackenzie declared he signed the letter at Donald's 'urgent request as he was at the time in a state bordering on madness for fear of being taken into Custody on the charge of forgery.' John Macdonald declared that he had not seen the fourth bill and had not signed it. James declared 'I cannot say what it is but it is a paper with a stamp in the corner of it; I cannot read it... I cannot write.' Various bank agents, clerks and accountants also provided declarations.[10]

On 7 December Donald, 'Prisoner in the Prison of Dornoch,' was again interrogated by the Sheriff-substitute and Donald declared that the third bill was signed by Mackenzie. With regards to the fourth bill, Donald declared 'these signatures are in my handwriting but I had express authority from both MacDonalds to sign their names for them.'[11] That same day, a 'Warrant to poind' was issued on behalf of Waterston, against Donald and the Macdonalds for the unpaid bill of £12 10s. Mackay on 20 December, after crying three O yesses, seized Donald's property, valued at £11 6s. The items, mostly furniture, were not taken away but remained at Donald's house and became the property of the Caledonian Banking Company until they could be sold to pay off the debt.[12]

On 26 December James MacIntosh, Merchant, Clashmore lodged a claim with the Small Debt Court against Donald for £5 4s, which MacIntosh won, plus expenses. That same day another claim was lodged against Donald and May Bayne Ross by John Sutherland, Merchant, Clashmore for £6 10s, but this case was dismissed. A later claim from William Ross, Merchant, Bonar Bridge for £2 9s 6d was also dismissed.[13]

On 13 January 1844 Donald, in prison, wrote a letter to Alexander Graham, Ardalie, asking him to pay off the bill with the Caledonian Bank and take possession of his 'poinded' furniture. That same day a bill was drawn up for £12 3s 7d, signed by Graham, Roderick Forsyth and William Cuthbert, with four months to pay. Two days later the furniture was removed from Donald's house and taken 'a few hundred yards' to Roderick 'Rory' Forsyth's house.[14]

On 22 February, Donald was accused of 'the crime of Forgery; as also wickedly and feloniously Using and Uttering as genuine any forged writing knowing the same to be forged.' He was summoned to appear before the Lords Justice-General, Justice Clerk, and Commissioners of Justiciary in the Criminal Court-House of Edinburgh on 15 March at 9:30am. They accused him of six counts of forgery, namely forging the signatures of Mackenzie on two bills for £5 5s and using those bills at the Aberdeen Town and County Banking Company, Golspie, and forging the signatures of the Macdonalds and using that bill at the Caledonian Banking Company, Dornoch.[15] Oddly, the bill for £8 8s, the reason for his arrest, was not mentioned, even though it was listed in a Register of Warrants to Imprison.[16] On 19 March the Law Lords set Donald's trial to be held at the Criminal Court House of Inverness on 18 April 1844 at 10am.[17] Mackay delivered the summons to Donald in jail on 25 March. A list of witnesses was drawn up:

Alexander Gordon, Sheriff-substitute of Sutherland
Donald Macleod Smith, Sheriff Clerk of Sutherland
William Sutherland Fraser, Writer, Dornoch
Alexander Leslie, Clerk to William S. Fraser
Roderick Mackenzie, Baker, Market Street, Tain
Philip Mackay, Messenger at Arms, Dornoch
Robert Barclay Sangster, Agent for the Aberdeen Town and County Bank, Golspie
James Brown, Accountant for the above bank
John MacDonald, Sawyer, Clashmore
James MacDonald, Sawyer, Clashmore
William Munro, Accountant at the Caledonian Banking Company, Dornoch

The trial took place in the Court of Justice, Inverness, which is on the site of an old castle on the east side of the River Ness and was built from 1834-6. Immediately north of the court is a prison, built from 1843-9, so Donald may have seen it in the process of being built. Both buildings are called Inverness Castle today. Near to the castle was the old stone Ness Bridge, which was swept away by a flood in 1849.[18] If Donald had travelled by road from Dornoch then he would have crossed the old Ness Bridge, or he could have travelled by boat down the east coast of Scotland. The verdict of the trial was briefly reported by the *John o' Groat Journal*:

> Donald Ross, Dornoch, was accused of forging the names of John and James Macdonald, sawyers, Clashmore, near Dornoch, to a bill of £12, 10s. The case went to proof, and an unanimous verdict of not proven was returned, when he was discharged from the bar. The prisoner's counsel, Mr William Forbes, made a most ingenious and eloquent defence for Ross, who signed the bill at the desire of the acceptors, who acknowledged that he was authorised to sign the bill, but denied that they put their names to it.[19]

It is interesting that only the bill for the Macdonalds is mentioned, so the charges for forging Mackenzie's name must have been dropped. It was later revealed that Mackenzie 'had absconded to America to avoid giving evidence.'[20] It looks like Donald was extremely lucky to be let off and could have faced deportation if found guilty. However, it does beg the question, did he forge the signatures? It does look suspicious that Donald sent two bills, both for £5 5s drawn upon Mackenzie, to two different banks in Golspie in February 1843. Why not to a nearer bank in Dornoch or Tain?

That was not the end of the episode. On 16 May 1844 the bill signed by Graham, Forsyth and Cuthbert became due and was 'lying in the Bank, under protest.' On 20 May Donald wrote to Graham 'If I could retire the Bill in cash, I can assure you that you would not get any annoyance by it, but I am not able to do so, and as you have my property which you can convert to cash to meet the Bill I hope you will not consider it but fair that that property be appropriated by you to meet the demand from the bank.' Graham and Forsyth later stated that they met Donald on 13 June to decide how to pay off the bill. Apparently, Donald said 'that if they would have the goodness to sign a Bill for £7, he would be prepared to pay the other £5 himself ... [and] immediately proceeded on Horseback to Dornoch' to pay the £5. Graham, Forsyth and Cuthbert then signed a bill for £7 which they 'immediately forwarded to the Bank' but it was refused because Donald, 'in place of paying the £5, as falsely stated by him, did not pay even one shilling.' On 28 June another bill was drawn up for £12 12s to pay off the one owed, and Donald wrote to Cuthbert 'I wrote to William Munro in the bank, as I promised and he sent the enclosed bill so that it would be in before 2 o clock tomorrow, you will be good enough to sign it at the x, and I will go with it to Migdol to Rory Forsyth in the morning, Mr. Graham will indorse it when he returns from Helmsdale and Mr. Munro will endorse it after Mr. Graham so that it will be as strong as names can make it.' [21]

On 21 October Donald's landlady, Jess Davidson, fearing she might not receive her rent of £12 15s due at martinmas, had a Petition for Sequestration drawn up. She claimed 'a right of hypothec [security] by law' over property which on 19 October had been impounded by 'the Aberdeen, Town and County Bank and are liable to be embezzled and abstracted by the subtenant himself and by his creditors.' So Donald still owed money to that bank and they had seized his other possessions. Davidson requested a warrant to sell them by public auction to cover her rent, and that the bank, 'and all others,' should be prohibited 'from interfering or meddling with any part of the sequestrated subjects.'[22] Sheriff Officer Alexander Ross made an inventory:

Two stacks of Hopeton oats
Five quarters of oats in the dwelling house
A cart
A white horse
An iron plough
A pair of harrows
About two bolls of oats in the barn
A dresser
A wooden table
A wooden pail
A bedstead
A chaff bed [straw-filled mattress] and three blankets

A wooden table

On 28 October Donald lodged Answers in which he considered Davidson had taken 'such a malicious step but from vindictive feelings, as there is not only a sufficiency upon the Farm to meet her demands but the most satisfactory security would be offered if applied for.' He admitted 'that the Petitioner has a right of Hypothec, but denied that she has a right to use the same for the express purpose of injuring the credit or character of the Respondent.' He also stated that John Murray, Cuthill was ready to give security or payment. Davidson denied all this on 9 November.

Meanwhile, on 31 October, the final bill with the Caledonian Bank for £12 12s became due. Donald was not able to pay if off, so on 15 November the furniture that had been kept at Forsyth's house was sold at auction in Clashmore. A Roup Roll of the sold items was drawn up by John Gordon, and the total amount raised was £16 8s 1d:

A picture, sold to Mr Graham, Ardallie, for 1s 3d
A picture, Graham, 1s 6d
A picture, Mr. MacIntosh, Clashmore, 1s 6d
A picture, William Polsan, Miller, Skibo, 1s 3d
A picture, Donald Murray, Game Keeper, Skibo, 1s 6d
A picture, Murray, 1s 8d
A picture, Graham, 1s 9d
A picture, Murray, 1s 2d
A picture, Graham, 1s 2d
Basin stand, Polsan, 2s 1d
Map of Sutherland, Graham, 1s 11d
Three hardwood chairs, Angus Murray, Clashmore, 7s 4d
Wine cooler, Miss Bell Gray, Clashmore, 3s
Three cane bottomed chairs, Graham, 10s
Six mahogany chairs, MacIntosh, £1 17s 6d
A sideboard, Mr Cuthbert, Skibo, 10s 6d
A mahogany breakfast table, MacIntosh, £2 1s
Hardwood sofa and cover, Graham, £1 18s
Mahogany chest of drawers, Roderick Forsyth, £4 2s
Mahogany bedstead and curtains, Donald Murray, £3
Chaff bed, Gray, 4s
A fender brass mounted, Robert Hall, Evelix, 4s
German clock, James Halyburton, Meikle Ferry, 13s[23]

These are far superior to the items that were seized by his landlady and indicate how relatively well-off Donald and his family were before they were evicted from the mill. The £12 12s bill plus other expenses came to a total of £16 11s 9d, so Donald still owed 3s 8d to Graham, Cuthbert and Forsyth.

On 23 November Donald took out a claim in the Small Debt Court against Graham for £8 6s 8d, however the claim was dismissed.[24] On 27 November Donald may have realised he couldn't afford the rent or wasn't going to win the dispute with his landlady so withdrew 'his answers and all further opposition to the present action.'[25] The Sheriff-substitute granted a warrant for an auction to go ahead on 19 December, though it is not known how much was raised.

On 29 November Donald, in an act of desperation, wrote a Petition against Graham and Forsyth, signed by lawyer Robert Ross. Donald had changed his tune and wrote 'on the morning of the 15th day of January 1844, the said Alexr. Graham, and Roderick Forsyth, demanded entrance to said House of Rosebank, then occupied by the Petitioner's wife and after getting admission immediately began to remove the Furniture ... at a time when the Petitioner was absent, and could not protect his property from invasion or abstraction.' The furniture was taken 'to the House of said Rodk. Forsyth and in doing so the greater part of the Furniture owing to the darkness of the night; had been destroyed ... the Petitioner's wife was not even allowed to empty the Drawers of a Table containing valuable articles or the Drawers of a chest containing some papery.' Graham and Forsyth denied that they had demanded entrance, nor that any of the furniture was destroyed, nor that they prevented Donald's wife from emptying the drawers. They countered, 'the Petitioner's wife applied to every quarter she could think of, to prevent a sale of the Furniture.' On 13 January Graham, Forsyth and Cuthbert 'had occasion to accompany the Funeral of a neighbour to Dornoch, when the Petitioner's wife availed herself of that opportunity to follow them' and gave them Donald's letter from prison. Afterwards,

> ...the Petitioner's wife expressed an earnest and anxious desire that the Furniture should be forthwith removed ... and carried away by the Respondents before Breakfast time on Monday the 15th January ... as privately as possible... Mr. Cuthbert, the Respondent Roderick Forsyth, the Petitioner's Brother John Ross with some Assistants called at Rosebank about seven o clock on Monday morning, where they found the Petitioner's Wife with a lighted candle waiting them, who immediately delivered to them the schedule of Poinding at the instance of the Caledonian Bank, and pointed out to them the various Articles enumerated therein, which they carefully brought out.[26]

According to Donald, Forsyth visited him

> ...on the morning of the day of sale (being the first intimation to the Petitioner that the furniture advertised for sale was his own property) requesting the Petitioner's authority to proceed with such sale, but which request had been indignantly refused... Alexander Graham and Rodk Forsyth proceeded with a sale of said furniture to the Petitioners

serious loss and damage ... under the whole circumstances of the case, the said Alexander Graham, and Roderick Forsyth have, by their illegal proceedings rendered themselves liable in heavy damages to the Petitioner ... to the extent of at least Fifty Pounds Sterling as a solatium for the injury sustained by the Petitioner in taking unlawful possession of his property, appropriating the same to themselves, and for the injury done to him in his character and credit.

In response, Graham and Forsyth claimed Donald had said '"Mr. Graham sell the Furniture to the best advantage, and if there is anything over and above, after satisfying the Bank, and relieving yourselves, give me Credit in your other claims against me", and in short, he appeared quite reasonable and submissive and apparently anxious to do what was right and proper.' Graham posted six adverts in Clashmore 'about eight days before the sale, and public intention of the sale was given by the usual Cries in the churchyard of Dornoch, on Sunday, being five days preceding it ... when the sale commenced the Petitioner appeared and asked under whose warrant the sale was proceeding, when he was informed that it was under his own written authority, which was then exhibited to him and the Purchasers.' If Donald was prepared to pay off his debt to 'the Bank, and the necessary expenses attending the sale, the same would be instantly stopped ... whereupon he unceremoniously walked away.' They denied they were 'liable in Fifty Pounds sterling, or one farthing of Damages to the ungrateful Petitioner,' and 'had no desire to injure the Petitioner's Character or Credit, if ever he was possessed of either.' In the meantime, on 18 December, Graham took out a separate claim against Donald in the Small Debt Court for £8 6s 8d, and won, plus expenses.[27]

Donald lodged Replies on 1 January 1845, again written by himself and signed by Robert Ross. Donald maintained that the furniture was damaged when taken from his house and they, 'at the early hours of three or four of the morning of a Monday, would arrive at the residence of an unprotected female, and boldly demand entrance, and when the same was granted under the greatest terror and alarm ... she positively declares that she dreaded the party would turn her out of the house.' Donald admitted he wrote the letters that Graham and Forsyth had submitted as evidence but denied most of their Answers without presenting any evidence to the contrary. On 3 January the Sheriff-substitute considered 'In respect that the action appears to have been incompetently brought in the form of a summary Complaint, Dismisses the Process ...; finds no expenses due.'[28] So, Donald had not drawn up his Petition correctly, which was fortunate as Graham and Forsyth would most likely have won and Donald would have been liable for more expenses.

Donald and his family probably had a miserable New Year in a house devoid of furniture and in debt, with no source of income.

7

Charles Edward Gordon

In 1843 the *Stirling Observer* published a fascinating series of letters written by 'Charles Edward Gordon,' who was particularly vociferous against George [Soper] Dempster and his factor, George Forbes. On 27 February he wrote:

> On extensive ridges of moor, under his management, is placed a great many poor tenants, who were removed *from more favoured and fertile localities* – and that to make room for sheep. These tenants are pressed to the ground by exorbitant rents, and it may be readily believed, that, in despite their industry, the rent cannot at all times be ready for the Factor. This, of course, soon is the means of setting them adrift from their poor wretched hovels, everything they possess is by the strong arm of the law taken from them; and they are at times turned out of these hovels even in the severest of storms, and middle of winter ... this was the case with *sixteen poor wretches* on the estate of the Christian Laird of Skibo in January last. They were ejected from their dwellings – deprived of every article they had in the world – and are now wandering about among their poor neighbours, getting the shelter of a cot, or barn, for the night – and actually suffering from hunger and starvation... A more murderous and atrocious system than that exercised by the Laird of Skibo and Factor, and a more determined resolution to get rid of the natives, does not exist in Scotland.[1]

On 18 March Gordon wrote about the good times under the elder George Dempster, though 'if you would peep in upon Sutherland, *after a long absence, as I have done, and see the* fruitful and fertile straths where your ancestors and friends lived comfortably, and from where your relations have been expatriated to foreign climes, would it not make the nobler faculties of your nature shudder, to think that the very localities your vigorous, athletic,

The reading of the Disruption Protest in St Andrew's Church, Edinburgh on 18 May 1843.

and loyal predecessors occupied, is now desolate'.[2] His next letter was particularly harrowing:

> ... about the month of August, 1840, a poor female called at the summer cottage of the laird of Skibo with a grievous complaint against the laird's "red factor." The complaint was, that the factor, on hearing that complainant's father was drowned, near Loch Buie, came immediately and turned her and an aged mother adrift, threw down the "bothan," [cottage] and added their crofts to his already large sheep walks; that they then had to resort to beggary; and that she now demanded redress. Redress was immediately resorted to by the laird – a stick being near his hand, he used it in a manner against her that would have graced the agility of a Nootka Sound savage, or an Affghan chief.[3]

One letter, which he wrote on 23 June, was about the Disruption of the church.[4] Long before, in response to increasing populations and people becoming more religious, civil parishes were subdivided into *quoad sacra* parishes. The patrons (landowners) chose who would be the civil parish ministers and their decisions were backed by the Court of Session. The Church of Scotland felt the civil courts had no jurisdiction in spiritual matters; in 1834 it passed the Veto Act so a congregation could reject a minister they did not approve of. This was not accepted by the law which considered that the '*spiritual* authority of the Church should be restrained, as it is restrained and made *subordinate* to Parliament' whereas the Church considered 'that to ordain a minister over a congregation who refused him would be to desecrate the ordinance and sin against the mind of Christ.'[5]

In November 1842, 474 ministers met in Edinburgh for the Convocation – the largest gathering ever seen and it lasted for eight days. The meeting resulted in a split; the Non-intrusionists, aka Dissenters, wanted to separate from state control, however the Moderates, wanted to continue the fight from within. In January 1843 the Court of Session took out an Interdict against the *quoad sacra* parishes and 'more than 200 ordained Presbyterian ministers were stripped of one-half of their sacred functions, [and] more than 200 kirk-sessions were extinguished.' This was regarded as an attempt by the civil courts to 'overturn the whole constitution of the Church.'[6] A petition from the Church was defeated on 7 March and Parliament refused to enter into an inquiry. A Protest was then drawn up and signed by about 400 ministers.

The Disruption took place on 18 May at the General Assembly of the Church of Scotland at St Andrew's Church in George Street, Edinburgh. Dr David Welsh took the Chair at about 2:30 and once the Lord High Commissioner was seated, Welsh read out the Protest: 'We protest that, in the circumstances in which we are placed, it is and shall be lawful for us ... to withdraw to a separate place of meeting, for the purpose of taking steps, along with all who adhere to us ... for separating in an orderly way from the Establishment.'[6]

He then laid the Protest on the table and walked towards the door 'It was a sight never to be forgotten, as man after man rose, without hurry or confusion, and bench after bench was left empty, and the vacant space grew wider as ministers and elders poured out in long procession.'[7] Over 400 left and less than 100 remained. The procession proceeded to a hall at Tanfield, Canonmills, and there was held the first meeting of the Free Church. On 23 May, 474 ministers signed the Deed of Demission pledging to abandon the Established Church. The ministers were photographed by Robert Adamson over a period of three years and the photos were copied for a huge painting of the event by David Octavius Hill, which took 23 years to complete.[8]

The ministers and their families moved out of their comfortable manses and most of the people in their congregations joined the Free Church. By June, 667 ministers and preachers had joined and were preaching in 'Barns and stables, and old mills and granaries, wool-stores and malt-barns, and cart-sheds and saw-pits, and wooden churches and tents ... and when everything else failed, then out in the open air.'[9] With time new churches were built with generous donations from the congregations.

The minister in Dornoch at that time was Rev. Angus Kennedy.[10] Rev. Sage described Angus, who was one of his cousins, as 'remarkable more for the strength of his judgement and shrewd common sense than for the gifts and graces of his ministerial office.'[11] Hugh Miller mentioned he was 'greatly beloved and all attended his ministrations.'[12] Angus wrote the Dornoch Parish entry for *The New Statistical Account of Scotland*. He 'never had any intention to secede' from the Established Church, however his 2nd son, Rev. George Rainy Kennedy had different views.[13] Rev. John MacDonald toured Sutherland to prepare 'the Highland congregations for the approaching Disruption of the Church.' On 25 January in Dornoch he 'Preached in the open air to upwards of two thousand, and after addressing them in Gaelic at considerable length, preached in English in church to a respectable audience.'[14] The immense crowds 'showed the depth of feeling with which the Highlanders view the present contest, and no doubt also their veneration for the "Apostle of the North."'[15] Angus wrote on 9 March 'I have for some months been preparing my mind for coming to this decision ... I need have no more reserve on the subject.'[16] George signed the Protest and his name was read out.[17] Angus wrote to state his 'adherence to the non-intrusion protest' and George signed the Deed of Demission.[18] On 11 June the Kennedy's preached farewell sermons. Angus gave his in English in Dornoch Cathedral, whereas his son gave his in Gaelic, to a congregation of about 400, on 'the links' in a tent which 'consisted of a few rude *cabers* fixed in the ground, and meeting and bound together by a cord at the top – and a Scotch blanket or two, pinned around them.'[19] The following day Angus informed 'the Presbytery that he adhered to the Protest' so he and George were struck 'off the Roll of the Presbytery.'[20] At that same meeting Dempster was elected ruling elder of the Presbytery of Dornoch and said 'I do most deeply regret the afflicting secession which has taken place, and even less on account of its numbers than on account of its having carried from our Church its most eminent members.'[21] On Sunday 18 June Rev. A. Macpherson, Golspie, declared the church vacant and 'the attendance was very small indeed.'[22] That may have been the day that people arriving at the cathedral found an inscription chalked on the doors:

The walls are thick,
The folk are thin;
The Lord's come oot
And the Deil's gone in.[23]

Charles Edward Gordon reported the English service was well attended however the sermon was 'remarkably cold and speculative, and gave general dissatisfaction.' In contrast, George gave a Gaelic service on the links from a 'wooden tent' to an audience of 1,500. Gordon described crowds 'pressing in from all quarters and passing the cathedral, as if it had been a tomb from which emanated the most obnoxious effluvia. This large concourse of people moved on to a green sward, and sat down to hear their minister preach the glad tidings of salvation.'[24]

On 12 July the *Inverness Courier* reported Dempster had 'given the use of a mill at Clashmore to the Free Church people, who used to assemble in the Sabbath evenings on the hill side; but this act of kindness has provided them with a shelter from the storm – wrights are busy fitting up the mill with seats.' If Ann Gordon and her children had joined the Free Church, which is likely, then they had to listen to sermons in a building built by their deceased husband/father that they had just been evicted from. Did John Ross help fit it out with seats? Oh the tormented thoughts that must have been going through their minds. Dempster also provided a site for a Free Church at Migdale, Bonar Bridge for the Parish of Creich, to be ministered by Rev. Gustavus Aird.[25] Dempster wrote 'how deeply I lament the present feeling of so many of my tenants and neighbours to secede from the Established Church of their fathers,' however two years later it was considered that he was 'bitterly opposed to the Free Church.'[26]

Sir George Gunn Munro of Poyntzfield provided a site in Dornoch for a Free Church.[27] Loch initially considered that they could use the 2nd Duke of Sutherland's stone quarry at Dornoch, however the Duke disagreed. There was a heated exchange of letters between the Duke and Rev. Patrick McFarlan, widely publicised in the press, about the Duke not providing sites for Free Churches and manses in Sutherland. Finally he relented and agreed to consider applications and stone from his quarry could be used for the church at Dornoch.[28] It was reported 'the seceding clergyman here has accepted a house and garden, *rent free*, from the Duke of Sutherland, on the condition that he is not to agitate or inflame the minds of the people against his successor.'[29] The church, with seating for 1,100, was completed in 1848.[30]

In the meantime, on 31 August, Dr George Munro, Rector of Stirling Grammar School, handed to the Presbytery of Dornoch a recommendation from the Duke to become the new minister of Dornoch. He preached in the cathedral on 3 September 1843, however on 14 September lawyer William Sutherland Fraser, on behalf of sixty-one parishioners, presented nine long objections as to why Dr Munro wasn't suitable.[31] At the next meeting of the Presbytery on 4 October, Munro was represented by a lawyer from Inverness and Fraser withdrew the objections. However, three days later, Munro resigned.[32] On 25 October Rev. Alexander MacIvor, Minister of Sleat, Isle of Skye was recommended as the next minister and on 22 November was duly appointed.[33]

Rev. George Kennedy took over as the Minister of the Free Church in 1855, after his 86-year-old father died.[34] 'His preaching, both in Gaelic and in English, was frankly evangelical, and it was delivered with great freedom and power.' He remained the minister until 1880 and died in 1899, aged 86.[35] A grave memorial to Angus and George, and their families, is in the Free Church graveyard.

Charles Gordon's last published letter, dated 20 October, was by far the longest. He described the earlier Sutherland Clearances in a similar vein to that of Donald MacLeod; in his first letter, Gordon had referred to MacLeod as 'my friend.' He then attacked Dempster with no holds barred:

> The conduct of the fierce and tyrannical factor, who has the reins of that property, is most nefarious. The swarms of poor Gaels whom he has robbed of their land on the straths, are planted pretty close on the precipices of the neighbouring hills, *and there they are*, his bound slaves – they are obliged to attend to every servile and drudging work he offers them, and the least resistance on their part, or the smallest frown on their countenance, will incur his displeasure, and their speedy removal from their place on the precipice. One after another are they swept away, and this notorious tyrant glories in the *act*.[36]

Gordon went on to discuss a familiar eviction case:

> I had the pleasure of meeting a well-known and highly intelligent individual, who gave me a most amusing account of a law suit that was then pending, at the instance of one or two of his neighbours, against Skibo, for meliorations. The tenants, after a very long struggle in the Sheriff Court of Sutherland, were removed, and, on their removal, they respectfully demanded the amount and value of their improvements... I was greatly delighted with the amusing intelligence of my friend on the subject of Skibo and his tenants. He appeared to be well informed in the matter, and on my pressing him to give me a written statement of the whole proceedings, he declined with a "No, Sir; I am determined, when these two cases are out of court, to publish the whole proceedings in the form of a pamphlet." I replied, "If that is your object, my good friend, I wish you every success." O Skibo! Your cruel treatment of your tenants will soon appear *en masse* before the public.

There is no evidence that a pamphlet ever materialised. Then here's the twist, the *Stirling Observer* on 21 December published an apology:

> We have, besides, now made more particular inquiries regarding the professed author, the party who forwarded these letters to us, one Donald Ross, resident at Rosebank near Dornoch, and find that Ross has recently been apprehended on various charges of forgery, and is now committed to Dornoch jail to stand his trial at the next Inverness

Circuit, and so far as we can discover, there is no such person as "Charles Gordon Stewart."

We deeply regret having been thus imposed upon, the more especially as several of these letters contained improper remarks upon individuals, particularly in regard to Mr Dempster of Skibo. We are now aware that Mr Dempster is a gentleman of the highest respectability, and incapable of acting in the manner alleged in the letters. We now humbly apologise to that gentleman.

The *John O' Groat Journal* added:

This said Donald Ross has been an indefatigable contributor to the public press. We have ourselves received some few dozen pages from his pen, but which we thought proper not to admit into the columns of the *John O' Groat*. His last effusion extended to about four closely written pages, giving a detailed account of a law suit he said he had in the Court of Session with Mr Dempster of Skibo about a meal miln and some ameliorations. In suppressing all Mr Ross's correspondence, therefore, we have not been so unguarded as some people would have us to be.[37]

A subsequent note appeared in the *Inverness Courier*: 'We have received a letter, signed "Donald Ross," and dated from Dornoch, denying all participation in the imposition lately practised on the *Stirling Observer*.' However, there were more than one Donald Ross in Dornoch.[38]

The *Stirling Journal and Advertiser* on 5 January 1844 published a long article about the apology, pointing out the error in referring to Charles Gordon Stewart instead of Charles Edward Gordon. It considered the attacks upon Dempster were 'brutally insulting' and 'are, like the libels against the Duke of Sutherland, unfounded slander.' The *Observer* published a response on 11 January, and thus started a petty war of words between the two newspapers. The next day the *Journal* stated 'Donald Ross, had arrived at Stirling, from Dornoch, three or four days previous to Dr Munro's proceeding to that quarter – and had one or more … interviews with the publisher [*Observer*], had also interviews with several leading Non-intrusionists in town … that some of them were heard to boast that this man had set off for Dornoch with a "pretty budget against the Doctor."'[39]

On 18 January two long articles appeared in which the *Observer* finally admitted to making a mistake over the name. On 25 January it provided yet more confusion, but with another twist:

The *Journal* has for three weeks declared as a solemn truth, that Donald Ross of Rosebank, near Dornoch, who, he thinks, was the writer of several letters which appeared in the *Observer*, bearing the signature of "Charles Edward Gordon," was in Stirling within six months from the time that the *Journal* first noticed said letters… However, a person calling himself John Ross of Clashmore, the brother of Donald Ross of Rosebank, called upon us within the period mentioned. This man we saw frequently, and from the frank nature of the occasional conversations which passed between us we took his address ... we wrote to Dornoch for an explicit account of the matter, and the substance of the reply is as follows:– With John Ross there was in Stirling a Donald Ross, a cousin both of his and Donald Ross of Rosebank... Our information also tells us, that two letters, subscribed "C. Munro," addressed to Donald Ross, Rosebank, had arrived there with the Stirling post-mark upon them, but that Donald Ross of Rosebank had sent them to Donald Ross his cousin, who had been in Stirling, as they were evidently intended for him, though addressed to Rosebank. We learn from this letter, that there are three persons of the name of Donald Ross living in the same hamlet.

The following day the *Journal* had the last word:

Two or three days previous to Dr Munro proceeding to Sutherlandshire, a person called at Mar Place, upon the Doctor, as Donald Ross, and was accompanied by his wife. The Doctor was from home – but was expected to return soon... Now the Non-intrusionist referred to (Mr Ross) and who obtruded himself upon Mr Munro and his relatives – was introduced to us as Donald Ross of Rosebank, near Dornoch... More, we have, at this moment before us, a letter, under his own hand, dated from "Rosebank," addressed to Dr Munro at Golspie Manse – expressing regret that he had not seen him, but that he was kindly received by his relatives...

Since writing the above, we have received information which leaves no doubt on our mind that the Rosses of Dornoch must have been hoaxing our contemporary. There was not a John Ross with Donald Ross when in Stirling. We are also assured that it was the same Donald Ross, styling himself of Rosebank, who called upon Dr Munro, that had an interview with the publisher and proprietor of the Observer. This we are ready to prove by the evidence of respectable parties in town.[40]

There is no doubt from the tone of the letters that Charles Edward Gordon had a personal vendetta against the laird and factor of Skibo. Putting aside the vitriolic remarks, evictions were certainly going on as evidenced by the Rosses and Gordons' cases, and there are other records in existence. Spence led an appeal for the case of Thomas Matheson, aged 73, who was served an eviction notice in 1845 and had a violently insane daughter who he kept in a cage. He 'was plainly told by the Laird on whose property he lived, that he was much to blame for having left the National Church; – as, if he had remained, three hundred persons who left it would have remained along with him.'[41] In 1855 Dempster admitted he had 'removed tenants, though generally only from one part of the estate to another, where their chance location stood in the way of well-considered plans of tillage and planting.'[42] In 1883 a Commission was set up to look 'into the condition of the Crofters and Cottars in the Highlands and Islands of Scotland,' commonly known as either the Napier or Crofters' Commission. The commissioners were informed that Dempster had evicted 95 families and 'twelve went to America, six settled down in the neighbouring parishes, and five scattered over the country, all the rest squatted here and there, chiefly on the moors and fens on the estate.' Rev. Aird provided additional information.[43] In 1892 a Royal Commission was set up to inquire if any land in the Highlands and Islands used 'for the purposes of a deer forest, grouse moor, or other sporting purposes... is capable of being cultivated to profit or otherwise advantageously occupied by crofters or other small tenants,' commonly known as either the Brand or Royal or Deer Forest Commission. William Macleay, Clashmore mentioned that 'within my own living memory there have been removed in some shape or another, within a radius of a mile and a half from the village of Clashmore, 40 families who occupied more or less land, and what they did occupy was either added to large farms, or planted with trees.'[44] There is also archaeological evidence of cleared settlements in the upper Evelix Valley, which was part of the Skibo Estate.[45]

Could the Gordon letters have been written by Donald? Very likely, but not conclusive, as a few articles deny it was him, though given he had been arrested and accused of forgery, he would hardly have admitted it. The letters were certainly written with a mastery of English reminiscent of Donald's later pamphlets and perhaps Donald was frustrated that his other letters had not been published so resorted to using a pseudonym. In his letter of 18 March, Gordon quoted a line written by the elder George Dempster: 'I would not give one little Highlander for *ten* of the highest mountains in Lochaber,' though had changed the wording slightly. Donald used this quote, though correctly, in one of his later pamphlets. Gordon had said he had been away for a long time and certainly Donald had been away before he first appeared in the statue labour lists. All of Gordon's letters were signed with a different address yet the *Observer* stated that they were forwarded to them by Donald Ross of Rosebank. Surely Gordon could have used the existing postal service from wherever he was staying. Donald could have provided the addresses as a smokescreen and when Gordon referred to the 'highly intelligent individual,' he could have been talking about himself. It is uncertain whether Donald went to Stirling. John Ross could have been in Stirling at that time and may have had a cousin named Donald Ross. However, the *Journal* claimed to have had evidence that it was Donald Ross of Rosebank who had visited.

8
Glencalvie Clearance

In 1845 Donald was as listed as a recipient of donations to help the victims of the Glencalvie Clearance. Glencalvie, a north-south trending valley, where the Calvie Burn runs north into the River Carron in Ross & Cromarty, is the site of one of the legendary clearance episodes. It is infamous for the engravings on one of the windows of Croick Church, etched while the victims were camped in the churchyard. The engravings are still visible today, a site of pilgrimage for descendants of people affected by the clearances. For detailed accounts see Prebble, Richards and Fenyő, however additional information has come to light.[1]

The local minister was Rev. Gustavus Aird. His distinctive first name stemmed from one of his ancestors who fought at the Battle of Lützen in 1632 under the King of Sweden, Gustavus Adolphus.[2] Aird's first position was as the minister of the *quoad sacra* parish of Croick. This position was ratified by Queen Victoria on 9 November 1840 and he was ordained on 27 January 1841.[3] The church's previous incumbent, Rev. Robert Williamson, emigrated to Pictou, Nova Scotia, in 1840 along with many of his parishioners.[4]

The neighbouring civil parish was Kindardine and the minister, Rev. Hector Allan, wrote the entry for the NSA in 1840: 'the system of turning whole straths, where formerly peaceful cottages were to be seen, into sheep-walks, is becoming too prevalent; and is productive of the worst consequences, for every succeeding summer sends the finest of our peasantry to a foreign shore, there to seek those means of subsistence which are denied them in their father-land. These evil consequences have not as yet, we are happy to say, been much felt in this parish.'[5] But not for much longer.

In February 1842 the *Inverness Courier* advertised farms to be let in Greenyards and Glencalvie.[6] Aird wrote to the factor James F. Gillanders on 14 March 'understanding that the Glencalvie people have made you an offer for that part which they at present occupy, to the effect that they promise to

Glencalvie Clearance

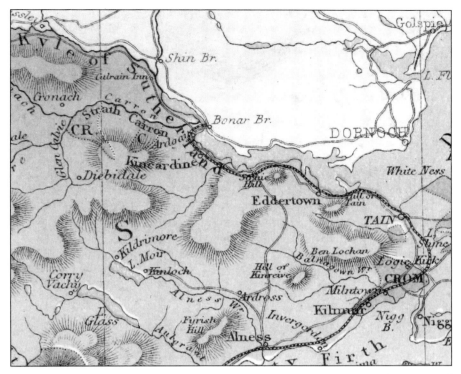

Map of part of Easter Ross showing Glencalvie, Strathcarron, Bonar Bridge, Tain and Alness.

pay as much as has or may have been offered by another, and that they hope that you will give them the preference, and thus be allowed to retain their places.' Gillanders replied to Aird's 'pathetic appeal' on 21 March, saying that the people needed to specify their offer and 'in the event of the present tenants procuring the farm by a higher offer, it will be necessary for them to find security for the due payment of their rents.'[7]

On 25 March 1842 attempts were made to serve Summons of Removal. The *John O' Groat Journal* reported:

> On Friday last, a Messenger was despatched from Tain to execute removings in Glencalvie, a remote and sequestered highland glen in the *quoad sacra* parish of Croick, the property of Major Charles Robertson of Kindeace. On arriving at a foot-bridge which crosses a branch of the river Carron, and which joins the estate of Amat to Glencalvie – the only point at which the glen is accessible – he was met by a crowd of men and women, principally composed of the families to be removed, who were armed with sticks, and who instantly seized his person, and forcibly deprived him of his warrants and relative papers. On this being done, and finding that all remonstrance was in vain, the Messenger

would have returned home, but he was forcibly detained until a fire was lighted, and the papers committed to the flames before his eyes. On this being reported to the Sheriff, he, along with the Fiscal and Mr Aird, Minister of Croick, on Monday [28 March], preceded the Messenger in Glencalvie, with a view to remonstrate with the people, on the folly and danger of their conduct. They were met at the same place by at least a hundred men and women, all armed with sticks, and prepared for action. The Sheriff would have addressed them, but they would not listen for a moment to anything which he had to say, and resolutely refused to permit him to pass the bridge, which he wished to do, in order to speak to the principal tenants. On the Messenger, who carried the warrants, making his appearance, he was again seized by the crowd, and had his papers forcibly taken from him; a fire was instantly lighted, and the whole were deliberately committed to the flames, in the Sheriff's presence. A second and a third attempt to cross the bridge being forcibly resisted, the authorities saw that perseverance was in vain, and at last withdrew from the scene of action, and were followed by the unruly crowd for more than a mile.[8]

Rev. Gustavus Aird, who was the minister of Croick Church, though left to join the Free Church just before the Glencalvie Clearance took place.

Glencalvie Clearance

A longer account in the *Inverness Courier* differed; in the first attempt to serve the eviction notices 'The officer ... was met ... by a few men and women.' In the second attempt, led by the Sheriff-substitute, the officers were met by '50 to 100 persons.'[9] There is no mention of them being armed with sticks. The residents had won this round, but the fight was not over.

The following year Aird joined the Free Church and signed the Deed of Demission.[10] 'When the Disruption actually took place, the minister of Croick, followed by the entire body of the people, with the exception of two families ... joined the Free Church.' Aird moved from Croick manse, 'a very miserable house, situated in a bleak, uninteresting position,' to a farm cottage owned by George Murray of Rosemount who also supplied a large wool shed as a temporary place of worship. Aird was inducted as the Minister of the Creich Free Church on 16 August. His new church at Migdale, built on a site supplied by Dempster, 'was a long, capacious, double-bayed building, with wooden pillars down the centre aisle, and a deep gallery facing the pulpit.' After 37 years it was replaced by a 'handsome church' that opened in 1881.

One of Aird's nephews described him in later years as 'a tall, impressive figure, with light, flaxen hair.' His biographer wrote, 'The pulpit was his place. He stood, with his genial face looking out upon his audience, with a dignity and grace that were more suggestive of a Roman Cardinal than of a Presbyterian minister. His strong voice, his correct enunciation, and his easy conversational delivery enabled him to be heard with ease by the average Church congregation and by the great open-air gathering alike.' It was estimated that he had delivered 'over 10,000 sermons in the course of his long ministry' and when visiting his parishioners, he rode around in 'his little phaeton with his faithful white pony.'[11] In 1888, at the Free Church Assembly in Inverness, he was unanimously elected the Moderator of the General Assembly, and Inverness Town Council presented him with the Freedom of the Burgh.[12] In 1896 he gave his last service in Creich and moved to Manchester for his and his wife's health. Aird died there on 20 December 1898 at the age of 85 and was buried at Migdale Church where he had ministered for 53 years.[13] His coffin was 'of polished oak with brass mountings' and was carried 'shoulder-high for upwards of a mile' to the church from Bonar Bridge Station, accompanied by 'hundreds of mourners from Ross and Sutherland.'[14]

Aird was interviewed in 1843 by the Poor Law Commission and described the people of Croick as having 'small crofts, and have liberty to feed their sheep and cattle on the hill ground attached to these crofts. The old people reside very much with their relations. It is the practice of the younger members of a family to go a great distance to seek employment, in order to pay the rent, and in the meantime the old people keep the crofts. The old people in my parish are not generally well provided for. They are often very ill off. Their food is chiefly potatoes, but also meal and sometimes milk. They are temperate in their habits, and the greater number of the young people can read, but not write.'[15] The population of Croick was 370, an increase of 54 since 1841.

Subsequently, the eviction notices were delivered by deceit, and the residents were told to leave their homes by the 12 May 1845, later extended to 25 May. A public appeal for money to help the victims appeared in *The Scotsman* on 19 April. Aird was quoted: 'Matters have really come to an awful pitch, when beings, possessed of immortal souls, originally created after the divine image, are driven out of their homes and fatherland to make room for *fir* and *larch plants, deer, roes, moorfowl, partridges*, and *hares*.' Five recipients for donations were listed: Aird, Allan, George Kennedy, John Lusk and Co., Glasgow and Charles Spence.

Donald was added to the list of recipients in *The Scotsman* on 14 May:

Glencalvie – Ninety Ross-shire cottagers removed, without houses where to take shelter. The following sums have already been received for the Relief of these Poor People. It is hoped they may yet be saved from the necessity of encamping in the Churchyard, as the aged could not be expected to survive the effects of exposure to damp and cold in such a situation, especially labouring as they are under heavy depression of spirits, produced by expulsion from the land of their fathers, where for centuries they have been located. It is earnestly trusted the Subscriptions will be liberal, and that the sympathy of the public will yet help to cheer the sufferers amidst their cloudy prospects.

Then followed a list of 18 donations totalling £36 2s. Donald was also mentioned in appeals in the *Greenock Advertiser*.[16]

According to Prebble, Spence wrote a letter to *The Times* with the same appeal that was published on 14 May.[17] However, rather than print it, *The Times* sent a correspondent to investigate. The reporter wrote a long sympathetic article, the first of several, on 15 May in Ardgay.[18] In the next article he mentioned 'One man, a respectable miller, whose father, and grandfather before him, had rented a mill of one of the heritors in this neighbourhood … walked 10 miles yesterday to tell me his own case. In the midst of a winter's night, with deep snow on the ground, he and his aged mother were suddenly turned out of his house under a decreet of removal, and his mother is now bed-ridden from the consequences of that exposure to the weather, and her distress of mind at thus being driven out of the place in which she had lived the greater part of her life.' Clashmore is 10.6 miles from Ardgay, so it was probably Donald. He also informed the reporter about 'a poor woman who was ejected from her holding to make room for some improvements, and who on applying to her landlord to do something for her was beaten and driven from the door by him *with a stick*,' like the incident 'Charles Edward Gordon' reported.[19]

The articles in *The Times* led to a flurry of articles in many newspapers in May and June 1845, which often quoted *The Times*. Most of the articles were sympathetic but some accused *The Times* of exaggeration. This was the first Highland Clearance event to be widely publicised in the press, with charity donations being given for the victims from afar. The clearance was brought up at the 2nd reading of the Poor Law Amendment Bill in Parliament, in which the Lord Advocate, with regards to the articles in *The Times*, considered 'great exaggerations had gone abroad.'[20] Revs Allan and Aird responded by declaring that *The Times* reporter's 'statements, so far from being exaggerated, are strictly and literally correct.'[21]

The Times article of 2 June included a detailed description of the conditions that the people endured while camped in the churchyard, which has been widely quoted, however another contemporary description appeared:

Eighteen households, or about fourscore and ten persons, old and young, have just been ejected from a remote Highland strath. They had no foot of land to call their own – no *home* to welcome them in all the green universe – and they went at once to the churchyard of their native parish. There I saw them, … the homeless *living* among the housed and buried *dead*!…

I came upon this strange encampment at the time of evening worship, and the burst of praise which rose from the place of the dead, and was wafted along the hill-side, was almost thrilling. The singing was in Gaelic, and the Psalm most appropriate (the 145th).

There was a large peat fire kindled in the churchyard, with a group of females and children around it – the poor women sad enough and thoughtful; but the thoughtless little ones seemingly pleased with the novelty and variety. Amongst the men were the aged and weak, and the stout, and hardy, and young. A long range of beds lay along the low wall or dyke, roofed over with sheets of tarred canvas, readily furnished by a most kind-hearted extensive sheep farmer in the immediate neighbourhood. In front their tents were closed in with blankets, the whole structure resembling the merchant-booths common at one time at country fairs.[22]

After visiting Glencalvie, *The Times* reporter toured Sutherland and Caithness and wrote a series of long articles on 'The Condition of the Poor in the Highlands.'

Rev. Allan later said 'We divided the money amongst the Glencalvie men – about £150 in all… The people were all highly satisfied with the sum and its appropriation, some of the poorest and most numerous families getting £10 16s 9d. The receivers were exactly eighty in number.'[23] In 1893 William Campbell, Crofter at Amatnatua informed the Royal Commission that he was twenty when evicted and inhabited the churchyard. He recalled that seventeen crofter families and four cottars were evicted and Mr Murray of Tain provided 'tarpaulins for shelter to keep off the rain.'[24]

It is not known when the people vacated the churchyard. Prebble said they left 'within a week,' however MacLeod recalled, 'I have seen myself nineteen families within this gloomy and solitary resting abode of the dead; they were there for months.'[25] Many years later Aird said 'No after-provision was made for them by the evictors, not even the modern panacea – emigration; they had to take up their abode in the graveyard of the locality till they could find shelter throughout the country.'[26]

In February 1846, the 'Grazings of Glencalvie' were again advertised to be let by Major Robertson.[27] *The Times* reported that it and an adjoining district were let 'to a sheep famer named Munro,' and to avoid 'awkward publicity' from evicting all the tenants at once, a clause was included in the lease 'binding him *"to turn away two families every year, until the complement of cottars is extirpated."'* This was not the last we hear of Robertson and Munro.[28]

The appeal article in the *Greenock Advertiser* on 3 June 1845 was the last known record of Donald at Rosebank. In May 1847 he wrote a letter to the *NBDM:*

> In 1845, the proprietor of Glencalvie ejected from that glen 14 families, consisting of 98 persons, and that their farms were handed over to one individual, who immediately converted them into a sheep-walk. Only three families out of the above number obtained small farms – the rest have got no farms, but are resident in wretched huts not far from the glen. Their destitute condition may be collected from the following letter...
>
> '...with the exception of three families who got small crofts, in ordinary years inadequate to supply them with a sufficient crop of potatoes, none of us got a house to which even a bit of a garden was attached ... the subscription-money, which had been obtained through your own kind and noble exertions, to live on, since they had been removed from Glencalvie in 1845, which is now all exhausted.
>
> Though some work is to be had, in some instances, the heads of large families are unable to work to earn a livelihood for them, from the effects of sickness, &c.; others who can work, from the high price of food, cannot earn in two or three days what will be sufficient to supply their numerous young family for one day.
>
> As every other effort has failed us, we avail ourselves of the opportunity of addressing you on the subject, as your former noble efforts had been crowned with such success in forwarding our views and interests, in order, if you think it proper, and likely to be productive of the desired effect, that you will set a subscription on foot, through the public prints, stating our circumstances, and appealing to public sympathy, in order to relieve us from the pangs of starvation, which otherwise will inevitably be the case.'[29]

That was the time of the potato famine.

9

A New Life in Glasgow

By March 1846 Donald, his wife and daughter had moved to Glasgow, Lanarkshire, in the lowland central belt of Scotland. It must have been a wrench for them to leave the rest of their family and friends, but they didn't have much choice. They had been used to living in a quiet sleepy village with lots of fresh air and water, so the move to an overcrowded industrial city would have been a shock. For the 200-mile journey they probably used a horse-drawn stagecoach, at least for part of the way. They could also have taken a steamboat down the east or west coast. A railway line had opened in 1842 to connect Edinburgh and Glasgow, however the first line northwards opened in 1848 and only went as far as Perth, so they wouldn't have used the train to head south.[1]

Glasgow in the mid-1850s, looking east along the River Clyde. The four bridges, near to far are: Glasgow Bridge, Portland Street Suspension Bridge, Victoria Bridge and Hutcheson Bridge. The three main steeples are, left to right: St Enoch's Church, Merchants' Steeple and Gorbals Church.

The River Clyde runs through the centre of Glasgow and was its lifeblood. River improvements in the 17th century allowed larger boats to travel upstream and the building of a quay at The Broomielaw enabled the city to become prosperous.[2] In the 18th century merchants grew rich on tobacco and sugar harvested by slaves in the North American and West Indian plantations, and these commodities were superseded by cotton.[3] Major improvements to the steam engine by James Watt led to the industrial revolution and Glasgow became known as the 'Second City of the Empire' after London, living up to its motto 'Let Glasgow flourish.'[4] The first steam-powered boat on the Clyde was Henry Bell's *Comet* in 1812.[5] This method of power quickly took off and by 1833 there were 61 paddle steamers operating on the river, servicing ports along the estuary and up and down the west coast, to the Hebrides and across to Ireland.[6] Bridges and ferries connected the north and south parts of the city.

The many factories and mills spewed noxious effluent into the waterways and smoke and poisonous gases into the air. Rainy days were common, with an average yearly rainfall of 40 inches, but at least that would have cleared the air.[7] In 1827 it was decreed that the chimneys of steam engines had to be at least 55 feet high if built within two miles of Glasgow Cross (on the north side of the river where the Saltmarket, High Street, Gallowgate and Trongate meet), and 'the chimneys of singeing works, sugar works, lime kilns, flint kilns, biscuit or glass kilns, slip pans, brass foundries, and lead smelteries; of the air furnaces of foundries; of black ash and calcar furnaces used in soap and soda works; of distilleries, breweries, public washing houses and dye works ... shall be constructed ... for the purpose of preventing ... the said works being a nuisance to the neighbourhood.'[8] The chimneys sometimes deposited 'their sooty flakes on the foliage of the trees' in Glasgow Green and presumably on everything else.[9] Hugh MacDonald in 1854 added 'the fine rugged old elms and stately beeches are yearly perishing in scores under the baneful influences of smoke.'[10]

From 1818 onwards the night-time gloom was penetrated by coal-gas lighting from 1,472 street lamps.[11] Gas lights were installed in buildings soon after and by 1850 441 million cubic feet of gas was used per year.[12] In 1834 there were nearly 100 cotton mills; by 1843 there were 16-17,000 steam-powered looms producing an estimated 57,000 miles of cloth per year and by 1850 there were 25,000 looms producing 130,000 miles of cloth.[13] The Charles Tennant & Co. chemical works at St Rollox to the north of the city had become the largest in Europe, producing sulphuric acid, bleach, soda and soap. 'Tennant's stalk' built in 1842, then the tallest chimney in Europe, reached a dizzy height of 436ft (133m).[14] The night sky to the south was lit up by the 'perpetual blaze of fire and cloud of smoke' from the furnaces of Dixon's Ironworks, which 'shed their beacon-glare over the whole city, and for miles around.'[15]

The city progressively grew in size, particularly in 1846 when the Glasgow Municipal Extension Act added the Burghs of Anderston and Calton and most of the Barony of Gorbals, thus doubling in size to 5,063 acres. The population (including suburbs) grew from 202,426 people in 1831, 274,300 in 1841 to

344,986 in 1851.[16] 56% of the inhabitants were not born there however Donald was in a minority as only 0.2% had been born in Sutherland.[17] The increase included influxes of Highlanders and Irish immigrants attracted by job prospects and most of the former were from the southern and eastern Highlands.[18] In 1836 there were over 22,000 people living in Glasgow who spoke Gaelic as their primary language and by 1855 it was estimated there were 45,000.[19] One poor family, originally from South Uist, was reported to have walked all the way from Inverness; so many others probably also arrived on foot.[20]

The wealthier middle classes moved to the rapidly expanding suburbs, while the poorest stayed in the overcrowded, ramshackle, squalid slums in narrow lanes ('closes') around Glasgow Cross. In the early 1840s the Poor Law Commissioners undertook an inquiry into the 'Sanitary condition of the labouring population of Scotland' and the *Sanitary Inquiry: – Scotland* was published in 1842. This led on to the *Poor Law Inquiry (Scotland)*, published in 1844. In the *Sanitary Inquiry*, Charles R. Baird, Secretary of the Glasgow Relief Committee reported that there were over 17,000 people working in the cotton mills, including children who were limited to 10 working hours per day since 1846, earning 2s 6d to 10s per week. 'That many of the operatives in Glasgow live in comfort and are able to clothe themselves and families, and to educate their children, is well known to all who know anything of them, and must be evident even to the passing stranger who sees the thousands pouring along the streets on the sabbath-day, apparently well fed and well clad, to their respective places of worship.'[21] Many families lived in only one room of a tenement building and took in lodgers to help make ends meet.[22] Imagine sleeping, washing, dressing, eating and going to the toilet in the same room as others. Many of the families were large so the parents were procreating in that environment.

Pollution wasn't the only cause of health problems; the combination of poor sanitation with inadequate sewers and dung hills, and contaminated water and milk led to the spread of pestilence and disease.[23] The rapid population increase was even more remarkable given the high death rate. Typhus, tuberculosis and relapsing fever were rife, with measles, scarlet fever, whooping cough and smallpox often being fatal for the young. Cholera first hit in 1832, accounting for 2842 deaths that year, and in 1837 there were 2180 deaths from a typhus epidemic.[24] By 1840 the annual death rate had reached 5.6% (one in every eighteen people) and the following year the rate for the under-fives was 11% (one in nine).[25] The life expectancy of babies born in the slums must have been horrifically low: 'births and deaths follow each other in rapid succession, the death of one child, after existing for a few months, making way for the birth of another, each event increasing the poverty and recklessness of the parents.'[26]

Those without jobs and money resorted to pawning everything they owned, even their clothes.[27] They ended up in the slums and had the stark choice of starving, begging or resorting to a life of crime. Peter Ferguson, Inspector of the Unemployed, informed the *Poor Law Inquiry* that 'when a man has nothing but the horrors of starvation before him – when he sees his children starving, and has nothing to do, he is prepared to do anything ... even acts of violence.'[28] Many, particularly children, walked barefoot in the filthy streets.

Captain Henry Miller, Superintendent of the Glasgow Police described the slums:

> In the very centre of the city there is an accumulated mass of squalid wretchedness, which is probably unequalled in any other town in the British dominions... These places are filled by a population of many thousands of miserable creatures. The houses in which they live are unfit even for sties, and every apartment is filled with a promiscuous crowd of men, women, and children, all in the most revolting state of filth and squalor. In many of the houses there is scarcely any ventilation: dunghills lie in the vicinity of the dwellings; and from the extremely defective sewerage, filth of every kind constantly accumulates. In these horrid dens the most abandoned characters of the city are collected, and from thence they nightly issue to disseminate disease, and to pour upon the town every species of crime and abomination.[29]

In 1857 Alexander Brown aka 'Shadow' wrote a series of graphic descriptions that first appeared in the *Glasgow Argus* and were published together as *Midnight Scenes and Social Photographs* the following year. At 10pm on a Monday night,

> Crossing from Argyle Street into King Street... It looks ... as if hell were let loose. First, and most excusable, we hear the thundering noise of vehicles, as they hurriedly roll along the causeway; then the incongruous cries of apple-women, fish and other dealers. Here again, the idiotical jeer and senseless laugh of the drunkards, who now stand in groups, or stagger their uneven way across the street, in quest of their miserable homes. There, again, are heard the horrid oaths and imprecations of low prostitutes – carrying their loathsome figures about with offensive boldness – flushed with drink, and bloated with disease.[30]

William Logan of the Scottish Temperance League estimated that in 1842 there were 450 brothels and 1,800 prostitutes, of which 300 died every year and had an average survival rate of six years after they entered the profession.[31] Captain Miller said they '"live in a state of great personal filthiness; they have most wretched homes; they are scarcely ever in bed till far in the morning; they get no wholesome diet:" and, in short, are exposed to every evil in the worst forms.' Many were prone to drinking 'strong liquors to drown remorse and shame.'[32]

'Shadow' provided detailed descriptions of squalid overcrowded abodes and lodgings crammed with people who had paid a couple of pence for the privilege of having a roof over their heads for the night. Rev. Sidney Godolphin Osborne described such rooms:

> Small square or oblong places, they were crammed with human life, and the insect life which finds a living on and about our kind when cleanliness and decency are absent. There were dogs, and a few cats; these were, to all appearance, the cleanliest creatures we saw. On the ground as the rule, on rotten bedsteads as the exception, lay human beings of all ages and sexes; some of the children perfectly naked, many, even of the women, nearly so. The bedding black rags, nondiluviated relics of blankets and old clothes.[33]

Captain Miller informed the *Poor Law Inquiry* that poor mothers begged while carrying young children or would send older children out begging and 'consider themselves fortunate in having a cripple child' as they would bring home more money. William Brebner, Governor of Glasgow Prison, informed the Inquiry that the children sent out were 'often beaten at night' if they didn't bring home their quota. It was a small step from begging to stealing. Sheriff Alison informed the Inquiry that if a mother 'is reduced to pauperism; the children are turned out to the streets, and become thieves almost the moment they walk.'[34] In 1840 he reported that serious crime in Glasgow had increased by 500% over the previous sixteen years. 308 policemen patrolled Glasgow and its suburbs, though being arrested and imprisoned was not a deterrent.[35] James Pagan, Editor of the *Glasgow Herald*, reported that 'there are many scores of vile wretches who professedly and constantly live by plundering the public – that is, they pick pockets, and steal "orra things," when out of prison, and they thrive upon the rates when in it. In fact, a few months in prison to these red republicans is like a sojourn in Torquay or Madeira to the invalid. They are compelled to lead sober and orderly lives, and accordingly they come out a stone or two heavier than when they went in – fresh complexioned, and furious for plunder.'[36] 'Shadow' described the police cells:

> On the floor, on a board slightly elevated, are more than a dozen men, several just recovered from the maddening effects of drink. They are lying in all possible postures, variously dressed, and of different ages and conditions... Visiting the next room, immediately adjacent to this, is another pitiful scene. Lying about in a similar manner to the former, are nearly as many women. They are locked up for protection. In one corner, upon the bare boards, is huddled up a poor miserable creature; she looks a bundle of old rags. Near her, and crossways, rests another, all but naked, muttering in low and broken accents some wild raving, and midnight dream. In the centre of a group is an old wrinkled-faced woman, sitting up in an erect posture, gloating as if in pride over her misery, and exposing, with a bold effrontery, her poor withered breasts.

As we leave, she expresses herself in terms which show her to be old in vice as well as in years.[37]

In 1848 a survey of properties in a 'ruinous and dangerous state' commenced and the Dean of Guild Court ordered that if they could not be repaired then they should be demolished.[38] Some of the narrow closes contained timber buildings, though after the great fire of 1677 the council decreed that they should be built of stone.[39] One was Fiddler's Close which Dr Fisher, District Surgeon, described as

> ...a very dirty close, abounding in low Irish Lodging-houses. The floors of the houses in the ground flats are damp and dirty, in fact little better than cellars. The upper part of the close is very filthy. The lower flat of one of the houses here was lately appropriated to the breeding of swine, while several families occupied the flats above. The part of the close at the side of the house is used as a dunghill, which renders access to it by no means either pleasant or easy. I believe every inhabitant of this tenement has had fever.[40]

This 'ricketty property was ordered to be taken down.'[41] The demolition of the old buildings led to further overcrowding as the evicted people needed to find

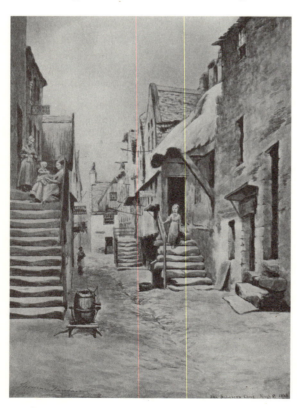

Fiddler's Close, 75 High Street, leading from the west side of the High Street, as seen in 1844 before much of the slums were demolished.

A New Life in Glasgow

somewhere else to live. The new stone-built tenements were just as overcrowded as before, which made little difference to the underlying problems.

Tobacco would have been smoked using the short 'cutty' clay pipe and opium was also available.[42] Alcohol was easy to obtain and for the weak-willed was the path to ruin. William Thomson, Inspector of Sessional Poor, reported:

> Intemperance is indeed the most powerful and the most fruitful of all the causes operating towards an increase of pauperism... Drunken husbands and drunken fathers inflict incalculable misery on innocent wives and families... The pauper drunkard, whatever place he may once have occupied in society, after neglecting religious duties, loses self-respect, and is soon subjected to all the miseries of nakedness, hunger, and disease.[43]

In 1840 there were 2,274 premises licensed to sell alcohol and Alison considered that 'Ten or twenty thousand workmen are more or less intoxicated every Saturday [payday], and for the most part of Sunday.'[44] A member of the Glasgow City Mission visited 'an old woman apparently in the last stage of consumption. Her husband is a very bad man... He not only drinks every farthing of his wages, but has emptied the house of furniture. He had that morning taken the covering that had protected her from the hard damp straw, and sold it for whisky.'[45] William Davie, Clerk, informed the *Poor Law Inquiry* that 'It is an offence for butchers and bakers to open shop on [the] Sabbath, but not an offence to sell spirits... The [grocer's] shop cannot be opened on the one side for the sale of sugar and tea, but it may be opened on the other side for the sale of spirits, before and after the hours of divine service.' Alison informed the Inquiry that some parents 'lead a life of intoxication, living on the earnings of their children.'[46] In the Bridgegate 'Shadow' reported 'Nearly every shop on both sides of the street, is a public house.' He described a pub on a Wednesday night:

> Inside are no less than a dozen poor people scattered about at different parts of the bar. But for one or two better clad of the group, the place might be truthfully designated a shopful of rags... [The landlord has] a welcome cheerful twinkle in his eye to every new comer who enters, no matter how emaciated, ragged or destitute... One young man is leaning back upon a seat, dead drunk; in less than two minutes a wreck of a woman staggers, rather than walks, towards the counter. She presents a broken tea-cup to the landlord, who charges 4d. for the whisky.[47]

By Friday night the scene was very different as the week's wages had been spent and the streets were quiet, though the pawn shops were making a killing from the desperate, of which there were 30 licensed and over 200 unlicensed brokers in 1843.[48]

Sheriff Alison calculated that in Glasgow about £1,200,000 was spent on whisky per year (equivalent to just under £111 million today) and about 1,740,000 gallons were consumed.[49] In the year 1844, 8,841 people were arrested and charged for being 'drunk and disorderly' or 'drunk on the streets,' 46% of all who appeared in court. Alison considered that intoxication was the cause of two-thirds of all crime and Captain Miller considered it was three-quarters.[50] It often led to more serious consequences:

> A mother... of twelve children, under sentence of transportation for ten years... [after having a drink with her brother] 'I stepped into ____'s spirit cellar in Stirling Street, and paid five bawbees for half a gill o' the best whisky. The first thing I recollected after drinking that half-gill of burning stuff – dear knows what was in it – was awaking in the police-office charged with the theft of which I have been convicted.'
>
> ...On Sabbath the 18th December, 1842, C. Mackay was confined in Glasgow Police Office for murdering his wife... [That day Mackay and his wife had] consumed betwixt them, in a public-house in High Street, not less than twenty-eight glasses of whisky. He was hanged in front of the south prison on 18th of May, 1843. On the previous day he dictated a letter... 'When sober we never quarrelled. The fatal act was not premeditated; it was the result of a drunken quarrel.'[51]

Children were also badly affected due to being exposed to drink, neglected by alcoholic parents or becoming orphans due to the parents dying. Two-thirds in the Boy's House of Refuge had 'been precipitated into crime through the habits of intoxication of one or more of their parents.' One teenage pickpocket told Rev. George Scott, Chaplain of Glasgow Prisons 'that he often drank 12 glasses of whisky a-day ... it only made him bolder and more expert; "for," said he, "he had no fear then, and thought nobody saw him."'[52] Some poor children from the Highlands were more fortunate in that several hundred at a time were clothed, educated and trained in various trades for three years by a Highland Society.[53]

Surprisingly, in hospitals the consumption of alcohol was not restricted. In the Royal Infirmary in 1848 the 2,400 patients drank 338 gallons of whisky, 696 bottles of wine, 4,998 bottles of porter and 551 bottles of beer. Alcoholics with severe mental health problems were admitted to The Glasgow Royal Asylum for Lunatics: 'several of our patients have confessed that they had taken a bottle or more of whisky daily for weeks at a time.'[54] Not everyone drank, in 1851 there were 33,500 members of abstinence societies in Glasgow.[55]

In 1853 the Forbes Mackenzie Act made it illegal for grocers to sell spirits, and licensed premises could not sell wines and spirits after 11pm or any time on a Sunday, however inns and hotels could supply their lodgers after 11pm.[56] Although this brought down the numbers of people arrested 'Shadow' asked a policeman if the Act had made a difference: 'No, not a bit; them that canna get drunk after eleven o'clock, get drunk a' the faster before't, but the maist

A New Life in Glasgow

o' them hae their clubs, brothels, and hotels, whaur they get it, an' there's nae preventin' them.' 'Shadow' described several 'low shebeens' or unlicensed drinking dens, which increased from about 'forty or fifty to eight hundred' after the introduction of the Act.[57]

The slum-dwellers did have somewhere to go on a nice day. In the west end of the Green the 'veriest dregs of Glasgow society, indeed, seem congregated here. At one place a band of juvenile pickpockets are absorbed in a game at pitch-and-toss; at a short distance, a motley crew are engaged putting the stone, or endeavouring to outstrip each other in a leaping bout, while oaths and idiot laughter mark the progress of their play.'[58]

So, into this polluted, disease- and crime-ridden metropolis, Donald Ross and his family moved into their new home. Over the next decade they moved frequently, and their movements can be followed in the Post Office directories (Appendix 1), often with two entries for Donald's different home and work addresses. They initially lived at 51 Adelphi Street on the south side of the river, in the Gorbals. They probably rented a room in one of the ninety-two lodging houses in that area.[59]

When they arrived there were three or four bridges spanning the Clyde, from west to east: Glasgow (Jamaica) Bridge, a wooden Timber Bridge, Stockwell Bridge, and Hutcheson Bridge.[60] The Timber Bridge was demolished sometime before the end of 1846 and was later replaced by Portland Street

Glasgow Green in 1848, looking W.N.W. From left to right: Gorbals Church, Hutcheson Bridge, Glasgow Sheriff Court, Merchant's Steeple, Aldephi Theatre and Nelson's Monument. The wooden theatre burnt down in November 1848. In the foreground the women are bleaching cloth at Arns Well.'

Buchanan Street in the 1860s, looking north towards St George's Church. A couple of windows of no. 16, where Donald had an office in the late 1840s, can be seen in the right foreground.

Suspension Bridge, which opened in 1853.[61] Stockwell Bridge was restricted to pedestrian access in 1847 and was demolished in 1850, though a temporary wooden bridge was built just upstream beforehand.[62] It was replaced by Victoria Bridge and Donald and his family may have witnessed the laying of the foundation stone by the Duke of Atholl on 9 April 1851. It was opened by the Lord Provost on 2 January 1854, who headed a procession lined by 400 police officers. He considered the 'orderly appearance of the crowds which thronged the streets this day was a proof that they were not deserving [of] the character which had been given them in some quarters.'[63] St Andrew's Suspension Bridge, situated east of Hutcheson Bridge, opened in 1855.

West of Glasgow Bridge, Donald and his family would have seen the Clyde full of boats, with ocean-going sailing ships moored on the South Quay and paddle steamers moored on the north side at The Broomielaw.[64] The paddle steamers carried day-trippers 'off doon the watter' and Donald and his family may have gone on such trips. Living near the river was not pleasant in the summer as the 'thousands of water-closets pouring their contents into the Clyde' was 'odious in the extreme,' and people were 'sickened from it on board the steamers.'[65]

From at least August 1846 to March 1848 Donald had an office at 16 Buchanan Street which would have been on the east side of the road, not far from the junction with Argyll Street. A gap is shown between numbers 14 and 18 in an 1842 elevation, so no. 16 must have been built soon afterwards.[66] Buchanan Street was becoming fashionable and the existing buildings were

A New Life in Glasgow

Buchan Street in the Gorbals in 1848. Donald and his family may have attended Gaelic services in Kirkfield Church to the left of centre when they lived at Adelphi Street. The spire of Gorbals Church is in the background.

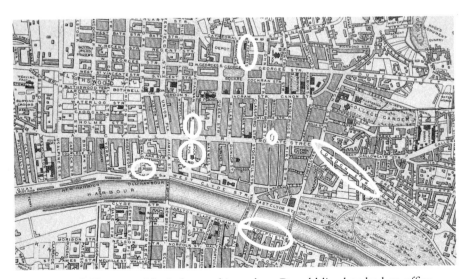

1851 map of Glasgow with circles marking where Donald lived or had an office.

being steadily replaced by elegant shops.[67] Donald could have walked to work across Stockwell Bridge or crossed the new temporary wooden bridge in a variety of horse-drawn vehicles from two-wheeled 'noddies' and hansom cabs, through to four-wheeled mini-buses, cabriolets, coaches and omnibuses.[68]

Donald had a respectable job, however his close contact with poor people probably exposed him to a high risk of contracting life-threatening diseases. In 1847 a typhus epidemic caused 4346 deaths, and cholera epidemics caused 3772 deaths in 1849 and 3885 deaths in 1854.[69] Water was obtained from wells, springs, pumps, streams and the river, though in 1848 Donald and his family would have had access to good quality water supplied by the Gorbals Gravitation Water Company. In 1852 it was estimated that 14 million gallons were used daily for domestic and industrial use.[70]

The working classes were generally eating 'parritch [porridge] for breakfast, with a little milk or small beer; Scotch broth and beef, for dinner, or sheep's head and trotters, or salt herring and potatoes; and supper, usually a thin meal made up of what had been left over.' Donald was on a relatively good salary so he and his family could have afforded a more varied diet including 'rounds of beef, roasted sirloin, mutton boiled and roasted, turkeys roasted and boiled, haggis, and cockie leekie soup.'[71] Although Gorbals Church with its tall spire would have been their nearest church, Donald and his family may have preferred to hear Gaelic services at the old Kirkfield Church in Buchan Street.

By June 1848 they had moved to the north side of the river, where there were four Gaelic churches.[72] Donald lived and worked at 29 Brunswick Place at the southern end of Brunswick Street, north of Trongate Street, which was close to the slums.[73]

Donald and his family probably witnessed the first visit to Glasgow by Queen Victoria and Prince Albert. On 14 August 1849 Victoria's steam yacht *Fairy* moored near Glasgow Bridge and a procession of carriages travelled to the Cathedral, then to the University, and finished at the railway station, from where the Royal couple headed up to Perth by train. Sheriff Alison considered there were more than 600,000 spectators. He rode on horseback on the right side of the royal carriage wearing 'the full-dress uniform of the Mid-Lothian Yeomanry' and had the honour of explaining 'to her Majesty the localities and objects of local interest' along the route.[74]

In 1850 Donald had an office in 31 North Frederick Street and was living in a house in Cathcart, Renfrewshire, which was a village south of Glasgow. In the first half of 1851 he was living and working at 143 London Street, just north of Glasgow Green, described in 1843 as 'a broad and handsome avenue, but sorely bungled, and in a half-built and disgraceful state of dilapidation.'[75] By July 1851 he was working at 20 St Enoch Square at the southern end of Buchanan Street. This remained his office for five years and is where he wrote most of his pamphlets. In 1856 he briefly worked at 28 St Enoch Square, however by June he was working at 1 Oswald Street, which was his office until he left Glasgow.

Donald's pamphlets were sold direct from the publishers and his office, and may have been sold by competing booksellers, 'Cheap Jacks,' who had

A New Life in Glasgow

Trongate Street in 1849, looking east. The tall Tolbooth in the distance marks the entrance to the High Street. Donald lived and worked at Brunswick Place from 1848 to 1850, which led north from Trongate, but is out of view to the left.

Donald and his family may have been spectators when Queen Victoria and Prince Albert visited Glasgow in 1849, here travelling under the 'triumphal arch,' erected for the occasion at the north end of Glasgow Bridge. Sheriff Archibald Alison is on horseback on the far side of the carriage.

Donald Ross and the Highland Clearances

Govan, west of Glasgow, in 1848, where Donald and his family lived in the early 1850s.

barrows outside the Court House.[76] At some point in the late 1840s or early 50s the market moved from Glasgow Cross to St Enoch Square. 'Shadow' mentioned market day on Wednesdays in the square where 'whole armies of poor women, lost and abandoned, have turned out, contrary to general custom, in the blaze of sunlight, to prosecute their pitiable calling. As they pass, flaunting in silks and satins – the vulgar blotches of *rouge* in the place of once glowing health of beauty on the face, attract frequent attention. Thus, these poor creatures, from their desperate condition, prowl like vultures after their prey.'[77] This may have been a familiar sight to Donald from his office.

The 1853-5 directories listed Donald living at a house in Naples Place and then Napier's Place, Govan, though the first is probably a spelling mistake. Meickle Govan was a village to the west of Glasgow, situated on the south side of the river.[78] MacDonald described it in 1854 as

> ...a long straggling congregation of houses, having been permitted apparently to "hing as it grew," each individual proprietor "biggin'" where it best pleased himself, and without the most distant regard for the opinion or convenience of his neighbour... The village itself, as seen from the margin of the Clyde, with its handsome church and elegant spire ... has an exceedingly fine effect, and has often tempted into action the imitative skill of the artist. The church is a chaste Gothic structure, and the church-yard is one of the most beautiful that we know. It is surrounded by a girdle of tall and rugged elms.[79]

A New Life in Glasgow

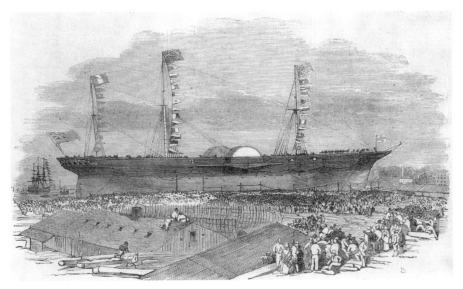

RMS *Persia*, the then largest ship in the world, being launched from Napier's shipyard in Govan on 3 July 1855. Donald and his family probably saw this ship being built.

Brotchie described the cottages as 'occupied by weavers with a strong penchant for gardening... Each cottage formed a picture in itself, being embowered in green creeper, rose-bushes, and many other sweet-smelling flowers.' The weavers had their own society and every year had a parade on the first Friday of June, the day of the Govan Fair.[80] The old parish church was built in 1826 and its spire was a replica of the spire of Stratford-upon-Avon's church. In 1884 it was moved, stone by stone, and re-erected next to Elder Park, though was demolished in 2008. There were also United Presbyterian and Free churches in Govan at the time Donald lived there.[81] Govan became famous for its ship-building, which started to take off in the 1840s with the production of iron steamships, firstly powered by paddles and then by propeller.[82] It is uncertain where Napier's Place was, though presumably it was near Robert Napier's shipyard. The Napier Place on today's maps wasn't built until the 1970s.[83] The shipyards would have been a hive of activity: 'The clang of the hammer drowned the hum of the weaver's shuttle, and in a few years "the iron king" absorbed all that was assimilable of old Govan' and a 'densely populated industrial town has taken the place of the ancient village and well-nigh obliterated every trace of it.'[84]

The ships became progressively larger and in July 1855 the RMS *Persia* was launched, which, at the time, was the largest ship in the world at 390 feet long (118.9m), built for Cunard by Napier.[85] Donald and his family probably saw it being built though were no longer living in Govan when it was launched. Donald may have commuted into the city by taking the horse-drawn omnibus or a paddle steamer to and from The Broomielaw. Passengers

Cathcart, south of Glasgow, in 1842, where Donald and his family lived twice in the 1850s.

boarded the steamer from the Govan Ferry, which was a hand-operated chain ferry.[86]

If Donald and his family were looking for a quiet life, they would not have found it in Govan, which may be why they moved back to Cathcart, probably in 1854. MacDonald described Old Cathcart, which lay on the east side of the River Cart, as 'somewhat irregular and scattered. It consists of some score or so of houses, mostly one-storeyed, and with little patches of garden-ground attached to them. Among these are a handsome farm-steading, a smithy or cartwright establishment, a snuff-mill, and in the neighbourhood an extensive paper manufactory. It has two public-houses, one of which, that of Mr. Mitchell, is an exceedingly neat and comfortable little place of rest and refreshment. The landlord is an amateur florist, and his small garden plot, with its flower-beds and bee-hives, is a perfect model of neatness and beauty.'[87]

There was also a Gothic-style church, built in 1831, though only the tower remains today.[88] To the south lay the ruined Cathcart Castle, which was demolished in 1980. New Cathcart lay on the west side of the river where building commenced after the laying of a new road in 1810. In the 1850s it was 'a quiet little village,' which MacDonald described as 'of modern origin, and possesses but few features of interest.'[89] It is not known whether Donald and his family lived in the old or new village, though either way, Cathcart was the last place they lived in Scotland.

10

Agent for the Poor

In June 1845 a meeting was held in Glasgow on 'behalf of the poor,' chaired by William Campbell of Tullichewan and attended by Charles Spence and Robert Somers. Somers gave a long speech about the findings of the Poor Law Commissioners and that the new Poor Law Bill 'was not calculated to improve the condition of the poor.' Spence talked about the Ceres case and criticised the Board of Supervision; Donald Macleod talked about the Highland Clearances. It was resolved that petitions should be sent to parliament.[1]

On 10 November the Glasgow Association in Aid of the Poor was formed and on 16 March 1846 Donald commenced employment as their one and only agent, for which he was paid a respectable £40 per year.[2] Intriguingly, in 1851, Spence, when referring to the Scottish Association for Protection of the Poor, wrote that Donald had 'long acted as clerk to this association in Edinburgh' before getting the position in Glasgow.[3] So Donald probably lived and worked in Edinburgh beforehand, but this can't have been for long. Spence probably had a big part to play in Donald's appointment as he was acknowledged for legal advice in the 2nd Annual Report of the Glasgow Association.[4] Donald was also listed in the Post Office directories as an agent for the National Friendly Society. An advert listed him as the Glasgow agent who 'will furnish Prospectuses giving full particulars, gratis; and Rules, 6d. each.'[5]

Donald's role in the Glasgow Association was to support and defend the poor to enable them to receive the relief that they were legally entitled to, but which was often withheld by the Parochial Boards. In 1847 the association changed its name to the Glasgow Association for the Protection of the Poor to align itself with the Scottish Association.[6] In the first six months of operation 'no fewer than five hundred applications have been made to different parishes, by the agent, on behalf of such poor persons as were really found to be in want, and unable to earn a livelihood for themselves.'[7] The 1st Annual Meeting was held in the Trades' Hall, Glassford Street on 30 November 1846 at which Donald and the other office-bearers were thanked.[8] The 1st Annual Report was briefly reported in the newspapers, in which a couple of cases were mentioned: 'Fancy an old asthmatic woman, totally unable to work from having lost the use of her right arm, receiving for her entire support 2s. a-month, out of which she has to pay 8d. a-week for the wretched garret in which she resides! or a disabled labourer, 66 years of age, having only 3s. 6d. a-month for food, fuel, and clothing!'[9]

The President of the Association was William Campbell.[10] Campbell was a partner of J. & W. Campbell & Co., successful retailers who built a large store in Candleriggs in 1823, then a much larger wholesale business in Ingram Street in 1856.[11] He was the President of the Glasgow Celtic Dispensary, set up in 1837 to provide medical help to Highlanders in Glasgow, and co-founder and President of the Board of Directors of the Night Asylum for the Houseless, which opened in 1838.[12] Campbell purchased Tullichewan Castle in the early 1840s, which was demolished in the 1950s.

William Campbell of Tullichewan, merchant and President of the Glasgow Association in Aid of the Poor, that Donald was the Agent of in the late 1840s.

Agent for the Poor

In 1846 Donald was briefly mentioned as the 'agent' in a series of communications between John Russell, Secretary of the Glasgow Association and William Smythe, Secretary of the Board of Supervision. On 18 November Russell wrote, 'I am instructed to state, that the directors will be happy to give the Board of Supervision the names and residences of several of the persons to whom they referred, provided that the Board resolves to institute an open investigation into these cases, and is willing to allow the agent for the Association in Aid of the Poor to be present, and take part in the investigation.' The Board declined.[13]

Donald was soon writing articles to the newspapers, the first known one appearing on 28 August.[14] Many of the articles were about court cases in which he had successfully defended people to get them poor relief payments. In December he wrote to the Scottish papers about many poor Irish immigrants arriving because of the potato famine. The *Glasgow Argus* mentioned 'Donald Ross, of the Glasgow Association in aid of the poor, informs us that vast numbers of Irish paupers – old men and women, and young children – have arrived, and are arriving in Glasgow in search of employment.'[15] Donald also wrote to the Irish newspapers and his letter dated 10 December, written in response to an article in *The Times* which incorrectly indicated 'there was a great demand for labourers at the public works in Scotland,' was published by the *Dublin Weekly Nation*:

> During the last three weeks a great number of poor persons from Ireland arrived here, and expected immediate employment at the public works; but not one of them could procure a day's work. They are totally destitute; and in some instances, where whole families of five or six persons have come over, their sufferings are dreadful...
>
> As I am placed in a public situation, these poor creatures daily call at my office, expecting to obtain some aid from the poor's funds through my agency; but as they do not fall under the description of persons entitled to relief in Scotland, I can do nothing for them; and I am grieved to add that some of them are suffering all the miseries attendant on starvation. They have neither means nor money, and their emaciated and haggard appearance tell too faithfully that they had undergone a course of privations before arriving in Glasgow.[16]

He then wrote a much longer letter with more details:

> In one case I observed a man, apparently sixty years of age, his wife somewhat older, and in a frail and destitute condition, with two sons and three daughters, all ragged and emaciated, and after spending a few days in Glasgow seeking work, applied to me, earnestly seeking my aid to procure a free passage for them back to Ireland. This poor family were actually starving, the mother was in very bad health, she had tasted no food for twelve hours previous to calling upon me, and was actually

a victim to sheer starvation. I procured a passage for them, but it was with the greatest difficulty the children managed to convey their dying mother to the boat, where she expressed the words – "If I die let me die in my own country."[17]

In January 1847 he informed the *Glasgow Argus*

...that within the last month from 700 to 800 Irish paupers have arrived in this city, and are now begging in our streets, or dying of slow starvation in our wynds... The last arrivals of Irish with which we have been afflicted are quite different from all previous importations. Formerly men came who could work, but now we see only squalid and debilitated lads, accompanied by frail old men and women, and young children, reduced to the last stage of sickness and misery.[18]

In April Donald submitted an advert requesting 'communications from parties favourable to the establishment of a Gaelic Newspaper in Glasgow.'[19] There is no further mention of this, so he can't have gathered much support.

Donald's first known pamphlet, *Pictures of Pauperism*, was published that year, dated 17 November (see Appendix 2 for a list of Donald's pamphlets). It comprises over 15,000 words and is divided into three sections. The first described the flaws of the Poor Law Bill and the state of the poor in Glasgow. Donald commenced by mentioning that the Poor Law Amendment Act provided the poor with a legal 'right to "*needful sustentation*" on the part of all who are destitute of means, and who by reason of age, non-age, or bodily infirmities, are incapacitated from earning a livelihood.'[20] However, he considered that 'Before the passing of the new Poor Law Act, paupers on the roll were in a much better position, in some respects, than they are now. Defective and improper as were the parish tribunals ... I do think they were, upon the whole, less likely to act severely towards paupers than those constituted by the new act. Their members were not elected by rate payers ... they in many cases chiefly consisted of ministers and elders ... [who] manifest a decided leaning to the side of mercy to the poor.' However, with the new system 'with respect to those who have been admitted on the poor's roll, and who complain that their allowances are inadequate, the Sheriffs are not allowed to review the decisions of the Parochial Boards; the only remedy left to the pauper being an appeal to the Court of session, which he may make – *if the Board of Supervision give him leave to do so* – a liberty, however, which has not been given in any one case, so far as I know.' Donald considered that the Board of Supervision was 'a worse than useless part of the machinery for administering the poor-law. It has done very little for the benefit of the poor, while it stands as a cruel bar between them and their unquestionable rights.'[21] Donald referred to a 'Review of the First Report of that Board [of Supervision] by a Committee of the Glasgow Association in Aid of the Poor.' He probably had a great deal of input into this though unfortunately a copy does not appear to have survived. It was discussed by the *London Daily News* which largely sided with the findings of the association.[22]

With regards to the state of the poor, Donald explained 'that there exists in Glasgow an amount of *unrelieved* destitution, of squalid wretchedness, disease, and misery, fearful to think of, and which must appear incredible.' He had clearly witnessed this first-hand:

> In one miserable-looking apartment I found an aged widow – in bad health – without food, without proper clothing, without fuel, and without furniture. She was allowed 5s. per month by the parish, out of which she paid 3s. per month for rent, leaving 2s. *a month, or little more than three farthings a day* for food, fuel, and clothing! This poor woman had seen better days. She was now confined to bed, if such a name may be given to a small quantity of straw in a corner of her room. *One* dirty-looking blanket covered her emaciated body. There she lay shivering with cold. There was no fire, and not one article of furniture of any description in the abode. I could not help thinking when I left this poor woman (after providing a little food and fuel for her) how much better are the lower animals cared for than this human being has been in the heart of Christian Glasgow.[23]

This description is consistent with other contemporary reports. Donald considered that the 'funds raised for the support of the poor is in most cases utterly inadequate' though he acknowledged that 'enormous expenditure' would be required and that an increase in the Poor Rates would be unpopular. There was also the widespread opinion that 'a *liberal* provision for the poor must necessarily tend to a rapid increase of pauperism, and that the sure way to keep it down is to bring the allowances to "the lowest point at which existence can be supported."' However, Donald considered that 'the allowances to paupers in Glasgow is not only not liberal, but is in multitudes of cases much below the "lowest point at which existence can be supported."'

Donald was critical of the Parochial Boards: 'The members of these Boards are appointed by the parties who are assessed for the support of the poor; and, as is perfectly natural, many of them (and these the persons who take the lead in the management) have been selected chiefly because they are likely to do every thing in their power to keep down the poor's-rate.' He quoted them as saying 'we cannot afford to give more than we do; the rate-payers are already too heavily burdened.' However, it 'may be true that a portion of the rate-payers are unable to bear the burden of heavier assessments; if so, that class ought to be relieved from the burden, and those who can afford it made to bear it; but it will not do to say, in a city so full of wealth and luxury as Glasgow, that the community cannot afford to give to the poor such support as is required both by the divine law and the law of the land.' Donald considered that single women with children were the worst off:

> Relief is often withheld, or only a miserable pittance given on the ground that the poor person has some good furniture which she might dispose of, although when she has disposed of it both she and her family are for ever sunk into hopeless pauperism; whereas, in many cases, prompt and liberal assistance, given but for a short time, would, in all probability, have prevented such degradation. The effect ... is in too many instances that the mothers sink into the deepest degradation and misery, and the children grow up in ignorance and vice.

Then, pulling at the heart strings, Donald wrote: 'What can be more distressing to the heart of an affectionate mother than to hear her children crying bitterly for bread, while she has no means of providing for them? ... I have not unfrequently seen poor, heart-broken widows, with children in their arms, who had tasted no food for 24 hours.'

Donald mentioned three eminent authors. The first was Sir Archibald Alison noted for his many volumes and editions of *The History of Europe*. In 1835 he moved from Edinburgh to Possil House in Glasgow to take up the position of Sheriff of Lanarkshire.[24] Alison wrote *The Principles of Population* which demonstrated that he was sympathetic with the plight of the poor. However, conversely and surprisingly, he was also outspoken against the abolition of slavery.[25] In 1851 Alison became Lord Rector of the University of Glasgow and in 1852 he was made a baronet.[26] He was certainly very popular as his funeral procession, 'from the gate of Possil to the railway station, a distance of two and a half miles, was lined with crowds of the poorest of the population; and all the mill-workers in the vicinity sacrificed half a day's earnings to come and pay, with quiet respectful demeanour, a last tribute or respect to the old Tory Sheriff.'[27] It was estimated that half of the working population of the city turned out, between 100,000 to 150,000 people. He was buried in Dean Cemetery, Edinburgh.

Archibald's brother was William Pulteney Alison who Donald referred to as 'Dr Alison' or 'Prof. Alison.' In 1822 William was appointed a Professor of the Institutes of Medicine at the University of Edinburgh, in 1850 was appointed first physician to Queen Victoria for Scotland and in 1852 he was President of the Royal Patriotic Society of Scotland. In his distinguished medical career he wrote works on fevers, epidemics, physiology and pathology. He noticed the link of the increase of fatal diseases with the increase of pauperism and he was interviewed twice for the *Poor Law Inquiry*.[28] Prof. Alison's views on the poor, which stemmed from the benevolence of his father Rev. Archibald Alison, were certainly similar to those of his brother.[29] Donald wrote to the Prof. about one of his court cases and received two long replies in November 1846. He was 'happy to see' that Donald had 'an Association in Glasgow in aid of the poor,' and had 'no doubt' that his 'cause will prevail.' He agreed with Donald that poor relief payments were inadequate and considered they were 'illegally small.'[30]

Agent for the Poor

The third author Donald mentioned was Daniel Defoe, author of *Robinson Crusoe*, whose 'shrewd common sense and uncommon powers of accurate observation were combined with great genius.' Donald quoted Defoe: 'Begging is a shame in any country. If the beggar is an unworthy object of charity, it is a shame that he should be *allowed* to beg; if a worthy object of charity, it is a shame that he should be *compelled* to beg.'[31] However those words were used by Rev. Thomas Guthrie in his 1847 pamphlet *A Plea for Ragged Schools*, loosely based on Defoe's *Giving Alms no Charity*.'[32]

In the second part of Donald's pamphlet, he published fifty letters 'out of the multitudes of letters and petitions addressed to me by the poor, with some notes explanatory of the cases to which they refer. I have given them just as I received them, without altering either the language or spelling. They afford a faithful picture of the condition of the applicants, their want of education, and ignorance of the laws that define their right, as well as the wretched circumstances in which they are placed.' For example:

No. 9.

The allowance to this man was increased, and continued until he was able to work. It is a short-sighted policy to refuse relief in such cases; the result generally is, that by refusing aid to proper and deserving objects, a whole family are brought to be permanent paupers.

' ... I am a labourer, having 4 of a family all unable to work, about 3 month ago I had a severe attack of Typhus Fever, from which I have never recovered; having nearly lost the power of my limbs; and suffering under a protracted attack of bowell complaint; within that space of time the whole of my 4 children had Fever each in succession – so that I was reduced to nearly absolute want; without the power of getting such nutriment as was necessary for our recovery; the children are in a weakly lingering condition from this very cause, I made application to the Barony Parish authorities for support – and received 3s. p. week – they then reduced it to 2s. and I now only receive 1s. – and let any reasonable man ask himself how that is to maintain 5 persons. They now threaten to withdraw it altogether, and it is this that has urged me to make the present application to you, hoping that your mercy and love of justice may interest you in my case, and that you may have it in your power; to induce the parish authorities; not to leave a Family who has been within their bounds for the last 16 years to absolute starvation; and the blessing of God will attend your endeavours.
Your most humble
& obedt Sert
133 Main St. Anderston 1847. (for) William Devine.'[33]

One person mentioned several times in the letters, with various spellings of his surname, was John Maclaren, who was interviewed twice by the *Poor*

Law Inquiry and became the Treasurer of the Parochial Board for Barony Parish, though he appears to have been miserly.[34]

The third part of the pamphlet entitled 'Suggestions for ameliorating the condition of the poor, and for lessening the burden of poor rates' consisted of a long letter that Donald wrote to the *Glasgow Argus*. He suggested that poor people should be employed in agricultural work and allocated their own plot of land so they could support themselves and their families: 'Many of the poor who are at present thrown out of employment, would be glad to work, and many more who are confined in loathsome cellars and hovels, on pittances of out door relief, would be but too happy to go and avail themselves of the opportunity of admission into a well regulated agricultural workhouse, where they would receive a sufficiency of food, enjoy pure air, and be removed from the fever and contamination of this large city.'[35]

The 2nd Annual Report of the Glasgow Association is hugely informative and demonstrates how successful Donald became at persuading the Parochial Boards to provide relief payments to the poor. The 2nd Annual Meeting was held on 15 December 1847 at the Trade's Hall. At the meeting Somers outlined the same utopian vision that Donald had written about. The last resolution to be approved was 'That this Meeting recommends to the Directors to take whatever steps may be found necessary for bringing before Parliament the unconstitutional, partial, and oppressive proceedings of the Board of Supervision, and to endeavour to obtain an inquiry into the working of the Poor-law under its superintendence.'[36] Donald was mentioned several times in the report and 'the Directors desire to record their entire approbation of the manner in which Mr. Ross, the Agent of the Association, has discharged his onerous and most important duties, in which he has exhibited a combination of unwearied energy, zeal, and prudence, seldom met with in the same individual.'[37]

In two years at least 1,575 people had benefited from Donald's help, consisting of people he helped directly and their dependents. These people resided in the four parishes of Glasgow: Barony, City, Gorbals and Govan. He kept a record book of his cases, however,

> It is impossible to give any adequate idea of the extent of the labours of the Society's Agent during the past year, or of the benefits conferred on the poor through them. Crowds of poor have, every day, received information and advice at the office of the Association; but a record has only been kept of the comparatively small number for whom the Agent made written applications to the Parochial authorities, after having satisfied himself that they were entitled to relief, and that it had been previously refused, or improperly delayed; and even of this class many have not been entered in the record, owing to the number of urgent cases requiring attention.[38]

Out of the 1,575 people, 384 with 277 dependents were helped in 1846. In the following year, only 50 out of Donald's 550 cases submitted to the Parochial Boards failed, thus he had a 91% success rate (the figure '540' is mentioned

Agent for the Poor

but this doesn't add up). Of the 550 cases, 341 had their original applications for relief refused and all of these cases were successful. The remaining 209 were already on the poor roll but were receiving a pittance. Of these, 124 received an increase. The remaining 85 were 'forwarded by him to the Board of Supervision' of which 35 of the appeals were successful. In a report written by Edward Ellice MP, for the year 1847, 34 out of 62 applicants had had their relief increased, which doesn't quite match Donald's figures but isn't far off.[39] In addition, Donald supported applications for 38 women with dependent children whose husbands had deserted them. Either 'the Parishes succeeded in compelling the husbands to support their wives and children ... [or] where the husbands could not be traced, the Parishes afforded relief to the wives and children.' These, plus the 500 successful cases, had 376 dependents. Donald took the unsuccessful cases to Glasgow Sheriff Court.

The 2nd Annual Report included a copy of a letter that Donald wrote to a member of the Barony Parish Parochial Board on 23 September 1847, clearly demonstrating that he must have been a thorn in the side of the boards:

> Agreeably to your request, I send you herewith the documents which I showed you connected with the case of Widow Miller, as illustrating the way in which poor persons are often treated by the officers of the Barony Parish...
>
> I am aware that parties connected with the different Parochial Boards in Glasgow, are in the habit of grossly, though I hope unintentionally, misrepresenting our intentions and proceedings, and of accusing the Association, and more particularly its Agent, of desiring and attempting to put parties not legally entitled to relief on the Parish roll, and thus of causing reckless expenditure in litigation.
>
> In reply to these accusations, I have to state that the purpose and design of the Association for which I act, is simply to cause the law of the land respecting the support of the poor to be executed. We seek Parochial relief for no person but those who we believe not only need it, but also have a legal right to it. Having to pay each our share of the Poor's rate, it is too absurd to suppose that the members of this Association can have any wish to increase these rates unnecessarily...
>
> It has also been both insinuated and said, that I have instituted proceedings for the purpose of obtaining *expenses!* In the first place, it is plain that unless I were fully satisfied of the justice of the claims, I could expect to gain nothing by instituting proceedings – the poor applicants being unable to pay anything; and secondly, I can appeal to Mr. Meek [Inspector of the Poor], whether I have not often made applications to him, *personally*, to obviate the necessity for legal proceedings; and whether, in various instances, I have not, at his request, withdrawn cases, taking *less* than the legal fees for them...
>
> I shall be happy to make arrangements with Mr. Meek for the purpose of preventing, if possible, all litigation between your Board and me, as

acting for poor persons; but this must be a condition, that matters are put on such a footing with reference to *every* poor person who applies for relief, as will insure an immediate attention to their cases, and immediate and sufficient relief, if found fit objects for relief. Unless this is done, I shall not in future withdraw any cases after having presented applications to the Sheriff, but will insist on a judgment in each, as I feel it needful that the Parish officials should know that they run a risk in every case improperly dealt with, not only of having it brought before the Sheriff, *but also before the Board and the Public*.'[40]

A separate article indicated that the inspectors were being hassled by the claimants: 'While giving Mr Ross the fullest credit for the numerous exposures of neglect of the cases of the poor which he has made in the course of his labours... The effect of the indiscriminate taking up of cases by Mr Ross, and the writing of letters and complaints concerning them, is not only to disturb the inspectors in the discharge of their ordinary duties, but to incite the applicants for casual relief or otherwise to attack the inspectors on the streets or in their offices, and to hold out insulting threats of what will follow if their claims are not implemented.'[41]

The 2nd Annual Report mentioned the critical review that the association wrote in response to the 1st Annual Report of the Board of Supervision. 'Copies of the Committee's report may be had at the office of the Association; and the Directors feel assured that no one, after perusing it, can be at a loss to understand how it has happened that so many of the appeals made to the Board of Supervision by their Agent have failed, while his appeals to the Sheriffs have been so uniformly successful.'[42]

Donald acknowledged help 'almost daily' from Robert Baillie Lusk (a Vice-President and a Director of the Association), and help from 'the following medical gentlemen, viz. – Drs. Hall, Thomas Watson, and M'Donald, who, at the request of your Agent, gratuitously examined into, and reported that state of health and physical capabilities for exertion of 129 poor persons.' Donald 'as instructed by the Directors,' complained to the Board of Supervision about the conduct of two of the Inspectors of the Poor. The Secretary of the Board wrote back to say that after investigation the 'inspectors complained of were completely exonerated from the charges made against them' however the Association was not informed 'when, how, or by whom these *investigations* were made!' Later on, Donald was more successful as it was reported 'documentary evidence produced against the inspector ... assisted by the agent of the Association for the Protection of the Poor, together with exculpatory evidence produced by the inspector' resulted in Inspector Cassels being dismissed by the Board of Supervision.[43] The board had investigated Govan Parish and found 'defects in the system of management' and recommended 'the manner in which these defects ought to be removed.'[44] The board wrote to the Directors of the Association stating that 'a great service was rendered to the poor and to the public by the agent for the society, by bringing under its notice the abuses which existed in certain parishes in Glasgow.'[45] However, the parochial boards were being taken for a ride:

> Persons who have sought an asylum for a night in the House of Refuge (a charitable Institution supported by voluntary contributions), or in some other place, present themselves to the Inspector, and demand relief. If the Inspector is ignorant of their circumstances, he is bound by law to provide them with necessary subsistence, till he shall have ascertained whether or not they are fit objects of Parochial relief. This necessary subsistence the Inspectors have hitherto been in the habit of giving chiefly in money, to the amount of 1s. or 1s. 6d. It frequently happens, that the persons who have received these sums do not again present themselves, and are not to be found.[46]

The figures in the Annual Reports of the Board of Supervision give an indication of the success of Donald's activities. In February 1846 there were 6,024 people on the poor roll in the four parishes of Glasgow, which had risen to 14,460 by May 1847, 19,478 by May 1848 and 22,879 by May 1849. Over a 12-month period, the number 'of Poor refused Relief by the Inspector or Parochial Board, but subsequently relieved under Order of Sheriff' was 43 by May 1847, 49 by May 1848 (excluding Gorbals: no data) and 97 by May 1849. 'The Number of Applications which have been made by Poor Persons complaining of Inadequate Relief' was 8 by July 1846, 77 from then to June 1847, 72 by June 1848 and 106 by June 1849; the figures for Barony Parish for 1847 and 1849 were the highest of any parish in Scotland. £32,610 was paid out to those on the poor roll in Glasgow during the period February 1845 to February 1846, £41,147 from then to May 1847, £66,029 by May 1848 and £71,206 by May 1849. In those same periods £383, £705, £418 and £1201 was spent on litigation by the parochial boards.[47]

The increase in payments appears admirable, however what Donald and the Association do not mention is that sadly much of this money was spent on drink. David Maclure, a former member of the Glasgow City Parochial Board wrote in 1848:

> A spirit-dealer in High Street informs me that he draws £10 more on the pay-days of the Glasgow poor than on any other day of the week. Another spirit-dealer says that the paupers regularly come to him and spend in drink what they receive...
>
> Widows, left with children under 10 years of age receive a great deal of out-door relief from this Board, to bring them up. A large proportion of these are dissipated characters, who drink the money which is intended for the benefit of their children, whom they send out to beg, and thus grow up uneducated, and become, if they survive the bad treatment to which they are subjected, pests to society, like their mothers.[48]

11

Glasgow Court Cases

In *Pictures of Pauperism* Donald stated 'I have brought upwards of fifty actions before the Sheriff of Lanarkshire on behalf of poor persons who had been refused relief by the various Inspectors or Parochial Boards in this city, and that *in every one of these cases* the Parochial authorities were found to have decided erroneously, and were compelled, by the judgments of the Sheriffs, to give the relief which they had previously refused.'[1] In 1846, twenty-one cases were put before the Glasgow Sheriff Court and all were found in favour of the poor; in 1847, forty-three cases were submitted and thirty-two were found in favour; the remaining eleven were still pending. Donald acknowledged 'the valuable legal advice he has received on behalf of the poor, from' George Pattison, Charles Spence and Charles and Robert Baird, 'by following which advice, he was successful in obtaining the many and important decisions in the Sheriff Court.'[2] The Glasgow Sheriff Court records are held at the NRS, however unfortunately most of the Ordinary Court records pre 1858 have not survived. Therefore, most of what is known about Donald's cases has come from contemporary newspaper reports, most of which he wrote.

The first known case he reported appeared in several newspapers at the end of August 1846. Donald was the agent for Sarah Inglis versus the Inspector of the Poor for the City Parish of Glasgow.[3] Inglis 'was a poor woman in extreme poverty, and burdened with two helpless children, both under five years of age.' The Inspector had withdrawn her relief payments until he had the opportunity to examine her circumstances. In May 1846 an action was brought against the Inspector and this was heard at the Sheriff Court on 2 June. Sheriff-substitute Henry Glassford Bell agreed that her relief of 2s 6d per week should not have been withheld. The Inspector appealed against the decision, twice, and both times the appeal was rejected, the second time by Sheriff Alison. Alison concluded 'This is the most important case that has yet occurred, in this Court, under the New Poor Law Act.'

Above left: Henry Glassford Bell, who, as Sheriff-substitute, made the first decision on many of the poor law cases that Donald took to court. Bell later became the Sheriff, as shown here.

Above right: Sir Archibald Alison, Sheriff of Lanarkshire and author, who decided on the appeals against the decisions made by Henry Glassford Bell. Donald quoted Alison's writings and Alison was praising of Donald.

Other successful cases reported to the newspapers were Ann Hunter (or Scobie) v. John Meek (Barony Parish), Donald Ross v. William Howatt (Gorbals Parish), Mrs Rogers v. John Cassels (or Cassells, Govan Parish), Ms Gallacher v. Meek, Widow Gemmill v. Cassels, Mr Spreul v. Cassels, William Johnstone v. Barony Parish, Widow Hope v. Meek, Ms Graham v. Cassels, Widow Mackirdy v. Meek and Mr Mackenzie v. Meek.[4] The cases of Rogers v. Cassels, Johnstone v. Barony and the one immediately below, were also outlined in a *Poor-Law Manual*.[5]

The case of Masson v. Cassels demonstrated how far Donald was prepared to go to see justice done. 'The pursuer is upwards of 72 years of age, and in a very frail and debilitated state of health. Application for parochial relief was made on her behalf to the defender, the Inspector of Govan, on the 4th November, 1846, who merely supplied her, from time to time, with pittances of relief amounting to 13s, 6d' up to 15 February 1847. On 2 June Sheriff-substitute Bell ruled 'that she is a proper object for parochial relief' and ordered Govan Parish to determine the 'amount of relief to be afforded to the pursuer.' Cassels appealed, arguing 'that she had no right to be placed on the roll' until it was proved she had 'legal settlement in the parish of Govan.' Bell refused the appeal, so Cassels appealed to Alison, who concurred with Bell. By 2 July the Parochial Board had done nothing, so Donald wrote to

Cassels warning him that if he did not determine the amount of relief by 10am the following morning 'a warrant will be obtained to imprison you, and the Parochial Board individually, for contempt of the orders of Court.' The board met early the next morning and agreed to give her 8s per month.[6]

One case 'raised at the instance of the *Association in Aid of the Poor*' had a different outcome. In the case of 'M'Kenzie v. City Parish', Mackenzie was described as '70 years of age, that he is frail and quite unable for any manner of work; that his wife is unable to do anything from paralysis.' However, Bell, on 2 February, found that 'so far from being unable for any manner of work (he is a tailor by trade, and has for the last year, and up to the date of the institution of the action, been regularly employed); that his wife is not so disabled as to be bed-ridden, but on the contrary, is able to dress herself, and to prepare her own and he husband's meals; and that in addition to his pension [3s 6d per week], the pursuer's average receipts as a tailor ... for three months immediately preceding said date were 3s. 6½d. per week' and considered the pursuer 'was not entitled to parochial relief.'[7] Donald immediately complained 'I have never felt it right to publish any case until the decision became final... The case is still before the Court, and when a final judgment will be pronounced, it will be published in the usual form.'[8] So it was probably appealed but wasn't subsequently reported, so it looks like Donald lost that one.

The case of Widow Rice v. William Thomson, Inspector of the Poor for City Parish was widely reported in the newspapers and featured in the *Poor-Law Manual*.[9] In this case a bundle of twenty-three court documents

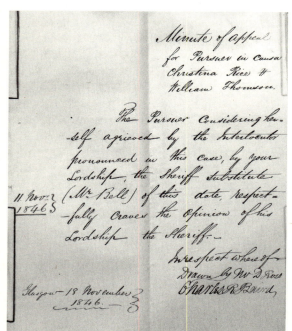

Donald's appeal to Sheriff Alison in the Christina Rice v. William Thomson case.

have survived, which prove how skilled Donald was in arguing his side of the case.[10] They also provide the biggest batch of hand-written documents by Donald known. Interestingly the first one is a printed Petition in which the blanks have been filled in by Donald, but Spence's name and address was crossed out on the cover, so clearly Spence had supplied Donald with the proforma. It is dated 14 July 1846, so was one of Donald's early cases, but took nearly two years to be concluded.

Irish-born Christina Spruel (or Spruell), aged twenty-eight, living at 31 Weaver Street, had lived in Glasgow for eight years and had two young children, Jean (or Janet), aged four years, two months and Peter aged one year, ten months, and she was heavily pregnant. Her Irish husband, Patrick Rice, died at a brickworks in Glasgow on 18 June. Two days later she submitted her application for relief to the Parochial Board. Donald later explained her application was on behalf of her Glasgow-born children and that she had received some interim relief. However, the Parochial Board informed her 'that if any further application for relief would be made by her, that a warrant would be instantly obtained to remove the Petitioner and her children to a remote district in Ireland.' On 31 July Bell ruled that the pursuer was entitled to relief and appeals by Thomson were dismissed by Bell and Alison.

On 7 September J. Macdonald, Commissioner, drew up a Pursuer's Proof in which he questioned Robert Lusk, Thomson and Richmond Willock (or Willox), Assistant Inspector of the Poor for City Parish. On 26 October, Bell considered 'that the Pursuer has failed to prove that she was refused parochial relief,' so changed his mind and sided with the defender. In response, Donald, on 31 October, wrote a 29-page Reclaiming Petition in which he quoted extensively from previous documents and his language was more assertive. He pointed out that the children were entitled to relief and that this 'is not in one single instance denied by the Defender ... the Pursuer was not only illegally threatened to be sent across to Ireland if she renewed her application for relief for her children; but she was also actually deprived of the weekly allowance of 2/6 due to her for the maintenance of her children.' He pointed out that a weekly payment of 1s 6d was reinstated on 16 July, after the first Petition was submitted to the Court. Donald rounded off by remarking on 'the great consequences to a poor person in her peculiar circumstances, resulting from a discontinuation of the weekly aliment for her two helpless orphan children. Nothing but the evil arising from this refusal, forced the Pursuer to seek redress from the Court.'

The defender's Answers contained convoluted arguments and disregarded most of the contents of Donald's appeal as 'there is much irrelevant matter in the Petition which is not necessary to notice at length' and that 'the settlement of the Pursuers children is altogether irrelevant.' Bell was not persuaded to change his mind so rejected Donald's appeal. Donald, on 18 November, appealed to Alison, who decided that 'the Pursuer is entitled to legal relief for her Children.'

The case was then appealed to the Court of Session in Edinburgh on 17 December. Later Richmond Willock reported that Thomson had died and requested that he take his place. The hearing was on 29 June 1847 and Spence was the agent for Christina Rice. On 9 July Lord Cuninghame sided with Alison and considered that 'the Parochial Board ought not to bring a question into this Court with a pauper, unless their Case rested on much more clear grounds than are to be found in the present Case.' Willock then appealed to the Inner House and on 9 June 1848, Lords Boyle, Mackenzie, Fullerton and Jeffrey agreed with the judgement of Cuninghame.[11] Mackenzie considered the threat of being sent to Ireland was 'the most offensive of all refusals' and Jeffrey added it was 'very reprehensible behaviour of [the] Inspector of poor.'[12] The final account of expenses, drawn up by Spence, was for £28, 16s, 6d after tax, payable by the City Parish.[13]

Two other cases became entwined and dragged on a lot longer. The first, initially titled Lindsay v. Balderston, Donald reported was 'the most important decision under the Scottish new Poor-law.' William Lindsay was a cotton-spinner who had been unemployed for five weeks. He had four children, aged 3-10 and his wife was ill in hospital and subsequently died. Lindsay applied to the Parochial Board of Gorbals Parish for relief for his children but given he was 'able-bodied' Inspector Balderston refused. Donald took the case to court and Bell ordered interim relief on 5 January 1848. Balderston appealed and even though Alison considered that the Poor Law did not 'confer a right to demand relief on able-bodied persons out of employment,' he referred to acts going back to 1579 and agreed with Bell.[14] In February, Gorbals Parish, fearing a 'flood of claims' from 'every [unemployed] able-bodied Tradesman or Labourer' with children, sent a circular to other parish boards, including a copy of Donald's report and they requested financial assistance to take the case to the Supreme Court in Edinburgh.[15]

The case was subsequently submitted to the Court of Session, this time titled Thomson v. Lindsay.[16] In addition to Donald, the counsel for Lindsay comprised John Shank More, George Pattison, Charles Spence and Charles and Robert Baird. The counsel for Thomson included George Ross who, confusingly, was often referred to as 'Mr Ross' in the proceedings. A long account was submitted to the *NBDM* by Spence and published over two days.[17] The case was considered at length by the Lord Ordinary, Patrick Robertson, who referred to acts going back to 1424 and gave his verdict on 9 June. Even though Lindsay had only applied for relief on behalf of his children, much of Robertson's musings was whether an able-bodied unemployed person was entitled to relief. He considered 'if the inability to work and the right of relief be co-existent, How can it be the law, that a person who is sick, and so cannot work, must not be allowed to starve, – but that a person not yet sick, but equally unable to work, because he can get nothing to do, shall be allowed to starve, or at least be allowed to become sick and wasted, – and thus more likely to continue a permanent burden, – before the time arrives when he shall be entitled to relief?' He concurred with the judgement of Alison.[18]

Meanwhile, at a meeting of the unemployed of Glasgow, an address was proposed for Donald: 'deeply impressed with the ability, firmness, and talent which has characterised your conduct during the severe struggle with the Parochial Boards, in the case of Lindsay and the Gorbals Parish, [we] take this opportunity of returning you our heartfelt thanks and gratitude for the benefit which you have gained to humanity.'[19]

The case was appealed and went before the First Division in July. George Ross and Dean of Faculty M'Neill presented the Thomson side of the case and More and Pattison presented the Lindsay side. The case was discussed by the four Law Lords and reported at length in three issues of the *NBDM*.[20] Given that the discussion involved not only the right of the children of the unemployed to relief but also the unemployed themselves, the Lord President decided that all thirteen judges should be consulted and meanwhile Lindsay's children should continue to receive interim relief. Unemployed persons with dependents then circulated an appeal to 'Friends and Fellow-Workmen' for money to 'secure able counsel in Edinburgh for the discussion of the case before the Supreme Court... A committee of the unemployed, and others interested in their case, has been formed.' The cause was supported by Prof. Alison and Donald had 'undertaken to receive contributions.'[21]

In the meantime, another case went before Glasgow Sheriff Court, that of M'Williams v. Adams. William McWilliams was an able-bodied man, aged thirty-eight, a boilermaker by trade who had been unemployed for three months. He applied for relief which was refused by Dr Alexander Maxwell Adams, the Inspector. Bell dismissed the case, however it was appealed and on 11 October 1848 Alison overturned Bell's decision and awarded McWilliams interim relief. Alison was 'well aware that the present judgement goes to the question of *interim* relief only; but, as well observed by Mr. [Donald] Ross in his able pleading, the question of *interim* relief, decides the whole case ... for if the present applicant is not a fit object for relief under the poor-laws, no *interim* order for relief should be pronounced; if he is, it should at once be granted and enforced.'[22] Alison subsequently added that the relief was 'only so long as he shall remain in destitute circumstances, and unable to find employment' and 'does not apply to persons who are either idle, and won't seek work, or have *struck* work for an advance of wages.'[23] This case and the Thomson v. Lindsay case were then combined and went before all thirteen judges of the Court of Session in Edinburgh. The case was discussed *ad nauseum* from 5-8 December.[24] Nine of the judges submitted written opinions in February 1849, of which eight considered unemployed able-bodied persons and their children were not entitled to relief. The ninth, Robertson, stuck to his original decision. The issue was discussed by the four Law Lords of the First Division on 27 February. President Boyle and Mackenzie agreed that they were not entitled to relief; Fullerton considered children were entitled and Jeffrey considered both the unemployed and their children were entitled. Boyle announced that 'in conformity with the opinion of a majority of the judges' neither were entitled to relief and dismissed the case.[25] Donald had lost these cases but that was not the end of them.

Before the Supreme Court had reached its verdict, Donald supported other cases of able-bodied unemployed men, though clearly had become complacent. Alexander McKean, cotton spinner, convinced Donald that he had been out of work for twelve months so Donald wrote a letter on 30 October 1848 to the Inspector of the Poor for Gorbals Parish, John McTear, stating 'Alexander M'Kean, an able-bodied man, out of employment, is entitled to relief *ad interim*; and I request that you afford him relief accordingly'[26] The Inspector gave McKean one shilling and made enquiries into his circumstances. McKean had been working for Joseph MacLean, master spinner in Muirhead Street for several years and had left voluntarily the previous Monday. Several newspapers reported that McKean turned up at the Inspector's office 'being covered with cotton as if fresh from work,' thus he was arrested and charged with 'falsehood, fraud and wilful imposition.'[27] He also had a recent certificate of character from his previous employer, which Donald had seen. In response to an article in the *Reformers' Gazette*, Donald wrote it was 'a most erroneous report' and 'I mean to put the public in possession of the full circumstances,' but it doesn't appear that he did. The *NBDM* added that Donald had received a letter and had informed McKean's wife 'that if a certificate as to her husband's character could be got, something might be done for her.' Donald 'despatched one of his office-lads to make personal inquiry into the circumstances of the family. The messenger reported that the interior of their residence, at Main Street, Gorbals, betokened extreme poverty and privation. Under these circumstances, he had no doubt that the statement made to him was correct, and hence the reason of his addressing a note to the Inspector, requesting him to give M'Kane [sic] instant relief.'[28] McKean was found guilty on Friday 3 November and given the maximum sentence of sixty days imprisonment in Bridewell Prison to set an example. Donald was given a ticking off:

> Baillie Smith – Mr. Ross; my first impression here, when I heard of this case yesterday, was that you should have been placed at the bar along with the prisoner, as aiding and abetting him in his designs. I thought the society for whom you act was of benefit to the poor; but, in place of that, it is one of mischief leading to the grossest frauds.
> Baillie Orr – Yes. Your letter to the Inspector was an encouragement to the prisoner to follow up his fraud, and to fasten himself on the Parochial Board; and it would have succeeded but for the praiseworthy inquiry of the Poor-rate Inspector...
> Court – You had better take care of issuing such letters again.[29]

That was not the end of the episode. It was reported 'Mr. John Dougal, the assistant inspector of Gorbals ... suspecting that something was wrong, prosecuted his inquiries, and it now turns out that M'Kean's mother-in-law is a pauper on Gorbals; his sister-in-law is a pauper on the same parish... Dougal's investigation, however, got the old mother of the race of paupers sent 30 days to prison on Friday.'[30] An appeal was subsequently made against Alexander McKean's sentence though the High Court of Justiciary 'refused unanimously' and mentioned that from 'a letter threatening prosecution from Mr. Donald Ross, the inspector was induced to give interim relief.' The article concluded 'We understand the decision of the Court in this impudent case has had a very salutary effect upon the able-bodied, who were accustomed to regard the parochial funds as fair game.'[31]

On 2 December Donald found himself in hot water again, this time with the Central Police Court. 'John M'Afferty, a labourer to appearance, was placed at the bar, charged with having, on the false and fraudulent representation that he had three deserted children to support, obtained from the Rev. Dr. Murdoch, Clyde Street, the sum of 2s. 6d.; as also with having fraudulently imposed on Alexander Pearson, poor's-inspector within the Town's Hospital, on the 18th of November last.'[32] McAfferty pleaded guilty and was sentenced to sixty days in prison. McAfferty had gone to see Donald with a certificate of character from a Mr Gordon, but apparently Gordon had thought he was writing it for another person with the same name. Donald then sent McAfferty to see Sheriff-substitute Skene. McAfferty subsequently presented Pearson 'with a letter from Mr. Donald Ross, enclosing an order from the Sheriff for interim relief.' Richmond Willock went to see Donald after the fraud was discovered and 'requested him to withdraw the threatened action against the parish, as the man had been found to be an imposter. Mr. Ross, however, declined to do so, and ... sent in an account for the sum of 14s. 6d., being his expenses in the case.' Bailie Dreghorn said to Donald 'If this statement is correct, it is a very serious matter for you; and I can assure you that, if a similar case comes again before the court, you will find it to be so.' Donald 'declared that he would make no more applications to the Sheriff.'

Willock then wrote a detailed article about the case, including a copy of Donald's letter, dated 18 November, that was sent to Inspector Adams. 'Dear Sir – Sheriff Skene having issued an order for relief for the bearer, John M'Affray, for three deserted children presently in his house, in 101, Saltmarket, you will please give immediate relief.' However, 101 Saltmarket was a shop and the imposter had taken the name of John M'Affray, who was 'a decent working man.' Willock asked Donald 'did he not consider it to be his duty, before he instituted any action which might involve the rate-payers in considerable expense, to make personal inquiries as to the truth of the statements made to him. His answer was, that he had nothing to do with that. Thus the public will at once see that they are at the mercy of every unprincipled scoundrel who chooses to employ this agent.'[33] Donald responded:

As I feel that I am most unjustly censured by many who should know better, for the proceedings lately adopted on behalf of some of the poor; and as I observe in a pamphlet lately published (evidently for electioneering purposes), entitled, "Remarks on the present mode of assessment," a most unjust and untrue statement, that the "Association for protecting the rights of the poor have been enabled through the aid of local judges, to force upon the poor rates every idle vagabond who locates in the city," – I trust you will allow me ... to express publicly that I am willing and ready to submit the whole proceedings I have adopted on behalf of the poor, to any member of the Board of Supervision, or to any other respectable intelligent gentleman disinterested in the question; and should such member of the Board of Supervision or other gentleman to be fixed upon, declare that I have done anything illegal or improper, I will not only cease from such proceedings in future, but also make a public apology.[34]

However, it wasn't long before another fraudulent case was reported in the press.

A blackguard Irishman was brought before the sitting magistrate in the Gorbals Police Court, on Saturday [17 February 1849], and clearly convicted of falsehood, fraud, and wilful imposition upon the Poor's Inspector for the Gorbals Parish. The name which the fellow gave to the Police was Thomas Hardy or Hardigan, or Harigan, and it would appear that by misrepresentation he had got interested in his case, Mr. Donald Ross, agent for the poor, the Rev. Mr Gordon, Roman Catholic clergyman, the Honourable Sheriff Alison, and other respectable parties, through whose interference on his behalf he obtained the sum of 9s. from the funds of the parish of Gorbals, he having no claim to title thereto... Bailie Smith dismissed the case, after admonishing the party, and strongly expressing himself as to the conduct of the parties. The Sheriff having ordered interim relief, the magistrate, after consulting with an eminent writer, considered that imprisonment might lead to legal proceedings. The magistrate, however, is as much opposed to these cases of Irish imposition as any one, and but for the intricacies of law would have sent the above offender to prison.[35]

One poor error of judgement could be considered careless, but three, that close together, would certainly have appeared suspicious and hugely embarrassing to Donald and the Association, particularly as Alison was also duped. After then it all goes quiet in the newspapers. No more letters from Donald and no more mentions of the Glasgow Association for the Protection of the Poor. It was later revealed that the Association stopped paying Donald in November 1848 and found it 'necessary to discontinue its operations for want of funds.' Even after all that Alison was praising of Donald, as on 13 July 1849 he wrote 'I have very frequently, within the last eighteen months, had occasion to consider and determine cases, many of them of great difficulty and importance, which have been conducted by Mr. Donald Ross, before the Sheriff Court of Lanarkshire, on behalf of applicants for parochial relief; and I have been much struck in them all with the industry and ability which he displayed in conducting them, as well as the zeal and humanity evinced by him in the management of so many cases.'[36]

A couple of articles later that year indicate that Donald was still helping the poor, but he must have been keeping his head down. The only other known case reported that year, for which Donald was the agent, was that of Mary McIntyre or Neilson, v. Dr Adams, which was also outlined in the *Poor-Law Manual*.[37] Mary wanted relief for her two children who she could no longer afford to look after because her husband had left her. Due to the decision of the Supreme Court both Bell and Alison, with 'much regret,' considered that the children of an able-bodied man had no right to relief, even though their father was absent.

There are a couple more extracts in the surviving Glasgow Sheriff Court records. Donald may have been in financial difficulty again since the association had stopped paying him. On 19 December 'Donald Ross, Agent and Writer in Glasgow' was ordered by Skene to pay Daniel Ogg, Furniture Dealer, the sum of £12 12s plus expenses, for an unpaid account dated 9 April 1848.[38] On 9 September 1850 Bell ordered Donald to pay £9 9s 11d to Joseph Taylor, Writer, plus expenses, but it doesn't say why. Fascinatingly, at the hearing of a case brought by the Faculty of Procurators of Glasgow against Donald on 14 August 1850, Bell 'hereby Interdicts Prohibits and Discharges the said Donald Ross Defender from pleading and practising before the Commissary Courts of Glasgow and of [?] or before the Sheriff Courts of the County of Lanark held at Glasgow or before the Town Courts of the City of Glasgow or any of the Court or Courts of law held or to be held in the said City ... so long as he is not a member of the said Faculty of Procurators in Glasgow.' On 20 September Bell ordered Donald to pay a fine to the Faculty.[39] There is no known evidence that Donald obtained any formal legal training or had any qualification in law. It appears you had to be a member of the Faculty of Procurators to practise law in Glasgow, which Donald wasn't and he had been found out.

Before then, on 16 April, a meeting of the Working Men's Poor-Law Reform Association was held in the City Hall, Glasgow.[40] The meeting was chaired by William Campbell and Donald was one of the people on the platform. This included resolutions for 'a legal claim to relief for the able-bodied poor in a state of destitution' and 'a scheme of emigration be devised and kept in constant operation.' Donald moved 'That a committee be instructed to carry out the foregoing resolutions, and prepare petitions to Parliament in consonance with them, and that the petition to the House of Commons be entrusted to Edward Ellice, Esq., M.P., and that to the House of Lords, to the Right Hon. The Earl of Carlisle.'[41] Donald was a recipient of donations on behalf of the Poor-Law Reform Association to raise money to support an appeal of the Lindsay and McWilliams cases to be heard before the House of Lords.[42] In March 1851 it was reported 'Donald Ross, the persevering and energetic agent for the pauper, has succeeded in obtaining the services of the Hon. Stuart Wortley, and Mr Hope as counsel.'[43]

The cases were 'partly heard before the Lords on the 1st' of July and 'Donald Ross, the agent for the appellants M'Williams and Lindsay, received intimation, per telegraph from London, last night, that the Lord Chancellor appointed the above cases to be further heard on Monday next.'[44] Another article added 'Mr Ross attended the discussion at the Bar when the cases were heard on the 1st inst., and we understand he is to leave again for London this night.'[45] So even though Donald was banned from appearing at any court in Glasgow this didn't stop him from appearing before the House of Lords! He probably travelled there by train and it must have been a great adventure. The hearing on 1 July was reported widely in the newspapers, however Donald wasn't mentioned.[46] Wortley and Palmer presented the case for McWilliams and it was discussed by Lord Brougham and the Lord Chancellor, who discussed acts and cases going back to 1579. The hearing continued on 14 and 15 July when lawyers for Inspector Adams, including George Ross, presented their side.[47] Mr Rolt, for Adams, summed up the case but denied '1. That able-bodied men generally who cannot get employment are entitled to relief; 2. If so, then their children are so also; but 3. If able-bodied men are not so entitled for themselves, still they are entitled to relief for their children.'[48] The Lindsay case, now titled Lindsay v. McTear, was also discussed and on the final day of the hearing on 21 July the 'Lord Chancellor said their Lordships would take time to consider the case.'[49] Before the judgement was given, Donald referred to the case in his pamphlet *Scottish Highlanders*.[50] On 26 March 1852 Lords Brougham and Truro discussed the cases at length and 'affirmed the judgement of the Court of Session,' *i.e.* decided that able-bodied unemployed weren't entitled to relief.[51] It can be imagined that after six years of supporting these cases, Donald must have been very disappointed with the result.

The last known mention of Donald in the surviving Glasgow Sheriff Court records is an extract dated 6 February 1857. He appeared in court on 5 November and 9 December 1856 for not paying for work carried out by 'W. G. Blackie and Company, Printers, Villafield, Glasgow,' from June 1855 to March 1856. This must have been for printing his pamphlets. Donald was ordered by Sheriff-substitute Archibald Smith to pay the sums of £15 14s 2d and £5 15s 11d to the printers, plus 6s expenses.[52] It is surprising that he had not paid for this work because he wasn't short of money at that time.

12

Strathaird Evictions

While Agent of the Poor, Donald had received letters from impoverished Highlanders. One was from a 76-year-old man on the Isle of Mull being evicted from a barn he had lived in for four years, even though he was on the poor roll.[1] In 1850 Donald took a closer interest in what was going on in the Highlands and Islands, and this decade was when he wrote most of his pamphlets and newspaper articles. Most of the Scottish newspapers were printed in the lowlands and generally either treated the Highlanders with contempt, sympathy or had a more romantic notion.[2] Donald generally wrote to the sympathetic papers, such as the Glasgow-based *North British Daily Mail* edited by Robert Somers, though many of his articles were reprinted, either in full or abridged, in other papers. Another sympathetic paper was the *Inverness Advertiser*, which published articles by Thomas Mulock. Mulock was another outspoken critic of the Highland Clearances, however he was only active for a couple of years. In January 1850 Donald wrote to the *Advertiser* praising Mulock for his 'efforts on behalf of the poor' in the Highlands and as an 'excellent correspondent,' though the previous month Mulock had become the editor.[3] Two newspapers that were particularly hostile to Donald were the *John o' Groat Journal* and the Glasgow-based *Reformers' Gazette*.

The Isle of Skye is the largest island of the Inner Hebrides and in 1841 the census recorded a total of 23,082 people living in its seven parishes, which was the highest number ever recorded and has not been surpassed.[4] In the Parish of Strath, including the town of Broadford and the Strathaird Peninsula, the population was 3,150, though about 200 had emigrated to Australia a couple of years before.[5] In 1840 Rev. John Mackinnon wrote:

> The great increase of the population is to be attributed to the lotting system, by which tenants are supplied with small portions of land

inadequate for their support. But this is not all, for the possessions which were originally too contracted, were subsequently subdivided by the parents among the various members of the family as they got married... This evil (for evil it must be called, when three, and in many cases four families are to be found occupying the lands which were originally barely sufficient for the support of one family,) has been, and will continue to be productive of the worst effects here, as well as over a great part of the Highlands. And unless some method be devised to provide for the superfluous population, and to check its increase in future, the most disastrous consequences may be anticipated.[6]

Mackinnon considered the people of Strath were sober but spent too much money on tea and tobacco. The Highlander's main source of food was potatoes and when the potato blight, *Phytophthora infestans*, devasted the crop in 1846, Mackinnon's prophecy came true.[7] In August it was reported 'the potato disease is rapidly spreading throughout the whole of this island.'[8] That winter the situation was desperate and in some parts of Scotland the shortage of food led to rioting.[9]

Although Donald was not involved at that time, he would certainly have been aware of the situation, which was much worse in Ireland where from 800,000 to over a million people died of starvation.[10] In January 1847 a fundraising meeting was held in Glasgow, which was attended by William Campbell and Charles Baird. Rev. Norman Macleod gave the main speech, who had witnessed the calamity unfolding in the Hebrides in August. He estimated that nearly a million pounds was required to supply meal and stated that £1,000 had been donated by the 2nd Duke of Sutherland.[11] In February the government set up a Central Board for the Relief of Destitution in the Highlands and Islands, to administer the Highland Destitution Fund and to supply meal in exchange for labour. The board set up the 'destitution test' whereby the unemployed able-bodied were expected to work an eight-hour day for 1lb of meal.[12] The work included the building of roads, piers and walls, and trenching to drain land, however some of the inhabitants of Strathaird were too weak to work from 'defective nourishment.'[13] The Central Board was divided into Glasgow and Edinburgh sections and Charles Baird became the Secretary of the former.[14] However, Donald MacLeod considered 'Never was there a more fatal failure, than in the mal-administration of that magnificent fund intended for the relief and welfare of the afflicted Highland population ... rapacious Highland proprietors ... pocketed two-thirds of the whole: in the first place, they got three-fourths of the meal bought for the people, to improve their estates, and they exacted ... ten hours labour for every pound of adulterated meal.'[15]

Somers visited Skye that year via stage-coach from Inverness, which took twenty hours. He crossed onto the island using the ferry from Glenelg to Kylerhea, which still operates in the summer months and is the last manually operated turntable ferry in Scotland. The parish minister informed Somers 'that the families of the cottars, or persons without holdings, amount to 800 souls in Strath alone; and these are scattered over the large farms of the tacksmen, or huddled among the already impoverished and overburdened crofters.' That year the Central Board supplied 2,000 bolls of meal to the parish. Somers concluded that in 'Skye the rich monopolise all profits and emoluments, while the reins of social oppression are tightened to the utmost stretch of endurance over the necks of the poor.'[16] Some of Somers' opinions were echoed by Donald in his pamphlets.

Most of Skye was owned by successive clan chiefs of the Macdonalds and MacLeods, and the former had the title Lord of the Isles. The chiefs valued their people and were popular with them. Godfrey, the 20th Chief and 4th Lord Macdonald, led an extravagant lifestyle whereas Norman, 25th Chief of the MacLeods, spent a lot of money helping the people suffering from the famine.[17] Both ended up heavily in debt and their financial problems led to their entailed estates being taken over by trustees, whose only interest was to make money.[18]

In 1850 it was announced that the Central Board would cease to operate on 30 September. The inhabitants of Skye were warned by the deputy inspector not to expect any more aid after this date and 'to use every exertion to sow or plant their crofts this season, and to acquire habits of persevering labour, as I solemnly warn them that, after this year, they will have to depend solely upon their own industry and exertions for the support of themselves and their families.' That year the crofters on Skye planted 1297 barrels of potatoes but in July it was reported that the potato blight had re-appeared.[19] Fearing the cessation of government support and that the impoverished population would become an increased burden due to the Poor Law, some proprietors commenced a new phase of clearances.[20]

On 25 May 1850 Sheriff-substitute Thomas Fraser of Portree wrote to the tenants of Elgol and Keppoch in Strath:

> It was intimated to me yesterday, by the factor on the estate, that the proprietor is firmly resolved to have the removings obtained against you carried into effect by ejectment, and that, as it was feared from your not having hitherto made any preparation to remove, that there might be opposition on your part, I would be called upon, as the Sheriff of the district, to take the necessary steps for putting the law in force against you...
>
> I have been informed that you and your families amount in number to upwards of 600 souls; that the rental of the lands you occupy is not more than £150 a-year; that there is an arrear of rent against you of almost £450; and that the whole value of your crops and stock will not much exceed £400... He is, however, willing, if you consent to emigrate to Canada, not only to forgive you all arrears of rent and allow you to dispose of your crop, stocking, and effects for your own advantage, but also to advance to you a sum of £1200, to be divided among you according to your necessities, for the purpose of helping to pay your

passage and providing your outfit. This offer appears to me to be very liberal and most highly advantageous to you.²¹

Mulock explained that 'Strathaird is divided into eight farms – namely, Camismary, Glasnakelt, Kilmore, Kirkibost, Elgol, Keppoch, Arinacraig, Feolin. The population of the whole district is about 620. It is the people upon the four last farms that are under notice to remove – the number of persons, exactly 477.'²²

Donald was planning a visit to the northern counties so that those who had written to him would 'have an opportunity of further stating their complaints to him personally.'²³ However, on hearing about what was going on in Skye he 'felt very desirous to ascertain the real state of matters' and travelled there in August.²⁴ He reported on what he found in a series of five letters which he compiled as a pamphlet, *Letters from the Mountains*. The only known copy, in Edinburgh University Library, is addressed 'To Proffessor [sic] More' in Donald's handwriting. This was Prof. John Shank More who held the chair of Scots Law at the University of Edinburgh from 1843 to 1861.²⁵ Prof. More does not appear to have left much of a trace in the annals of history, though his name does appear in a couple of court cases with Charles Spence, including the Ceres case, and with Donald in the William Lindsay v. Gorbals Parish case.²⁶

It is uncertain exactly where Donald commenced his sojourn on Skye as in his first letter he wrote 'The traveller, on his road from Kyleakin to Broadford,

John Shank More, Professor of Scots Law at the University of Edinburgh, who was part of the defence with Donald in the William Lindsay v. Gorbals Parish case, and to whom Donald sent a copy of *Letters from the Mountains*.

Broadford Hotel, Isle of Skye, where Donald probably stayed in August 1850.

after he ascends the hill, near the inn at Kyle.'[27] Donald could have landed at Kyleakin as it has a pier, however the land from there to Broadford is fairly flat. More likely the hill was the one leading from Kylerhea Inn near the ferry landing.[28] Either way, Donald probably took a paddle steamer, such as the *Duntroon Castle*, from The Broomielaw up the west coast of Scotland to the east coast of Skye, which would have taken about thirty-six hours.[29] He was accompanied by 'Baillie B., from Glasgow' and once on the island they travelled to Broadford, where Donald wrote his first letter on 19 August. He referred to Broadford Inn (now Broadford Hotel) and this was probably where they stayed the night.[30]

To get there they passed through the crofting townships of Ashaig, Breakish and Harrapool. The last two were substantial and clearly marked on the early OS maps; the croft boundaries can be seen on satellite images.[31] These were not cleared and there are many houses there today. Donald described this area as 'well adapted for growing all kinds of grain and green crops, being so near the sea; the climate is mild, and this combined with great humidity, tends to make it a desirable spot for a class of tenant-farmers or crofters.' However, he went on to describe their lots as 'in a wretched condition; they have bad houses, bad fences [walls], and their fields are run over with weeds.' There were a few 'neat clean' houses but most were 'black huts – the thatch tied down with ropes, and to the end of every rope a large stone is tied to keep it firm. The interiors of the huts are very dirty and wretched, and the cow, pig and hens share with the crofters in the occupancy.'[32] At Breakish Donald encountered a boy who he described as

... a fair specimen of what may be called "the starvation process on a Highland estate." Every hair on his head (for it was never under cover) stood out erect as bristles. His cheeks are hollow and pale. He appears tall of his age (14 years), but this is entirely owing to his leanness. His legs are like long pokers; and his knees look enormously large – just as they are seen in a skeleton... One thin woollen covering was wrapped round his body. It had a numerous lot of frills at the lower end of it, which clearly indicated that it was long in use.[33]

He went on to say that the crofters did not have leases and were regarded as 'ignorant and indolent,' which he actually agreed with, but this was because they had no incentive to improve their lots. 'A crofter told me here that he had no encouragement to use lime or anything else for improving his lands, as the rent would be increased, or he would be removed.'

From Broadford Donald travelled south-west through Strath Suardal, rented by a sheep farmer named M'Kinnon, who's shepherd was the only inhabitant. The people had been 'cleared away to make room for sheep – some to America, some to large cities – to swell the lists of paupers there; and the remainder were placed on small lots – portions of the lots of other tenants in the neighbourhood.' In the centre of the strath 'The roofless church, with its sash-less windows, viewed from the road, as I approached, formed a sad spectacle ... the sheep have the run of the burying-ground ... clearly shewing [sic], that sheep and shepherd's dogs have trampled not only on the living, but also on the dead.' The derelict Cill Criosd (Kilchrist) church is still there today. It fell out of use in 1838 though the graveyard is still used.[34] Continuing along the road Donald would have encountered the township of Torrin, though he did not mention it.[35] Donald then crossed the ford at the head of Loch Slapin and warned travellers to be careful 'otherwise they may have an unlooked-for cold bath in the loch.' Today a bridge crosses the stream though the route of the ford can still be seen.

Donald explained that much of the Strathaird Peninsula was owned by Alexander Macalister of Torrisdale Castle, Argyll who left the management of the estate to a factor 'or commissioner, [who] ordered the whole tenants at Keppoch, Elgol, and Arinacraig, to remove from their houses at Whitsunday last,' on 19 May.[36] Donald found four families living at the small township of Arinacraig. Ruins can be seen today next to the shore of Loch Slapin below a house named Arincreaga, and croft boundaries and lazybed strips can be seen lying just to the north on satellite images. Keppoch was further south, clearly marked on the first detailed OS map, surveyed in 1875, as 'Capach.' For 50 years some of the ruins were obscured by a forestry plantation which was felled in the spring of 2017.[37] Donald described Keppoch as 'divided into twenty lots; the rent is from three to eight pounds per annum per lot. The land is of excellent quality, but the

Strathaird Evictions

A Skye blackhouse in 1853.

The inside of a Skye blackhouse in 1853.

rent is by far too high. The cottars are so hemmed in on every side by sheep farms, that they have no hill pasture.' In a twist, Donald reported that the evictions had been given a stay of execution because 'The proceedings adopted against the tenants in the Sheriff Court of Portree are not of that correct nature, nor in such strict conformity to the rules of the law, as to warrant ejectment for the present.'[38]

His third letter was written in Elgol on 22 August and explained that there were about fifty-three families living there. The land was 'well adapted for producing crops of corn, potatoes, turnips, carrots, and other vegetables' however 'their lots are too small' and their hill pasture 'was seized upon by the neighbouring sheep-farmers.' The crofters 'fully resolved to quit possession in peace ... however, before the term of Whitsunday last, the "Commissioner," accompanied by the Inspector-General of the Highland Destitution Fund, in Skye, made their appearance in Elgol, and pleaded hard with the people to leave the country and go to America.' The crofters objected and the 'meeting was consequently adjourned from the roadside at Elgol, to Broadford Inn, next day at 12 noon.' The next day the crofters travelled thirteen miles to the inn where the factor and Inspector-General 'renewed their arguments as to emigration with double their former force and energy. A proposal was made to provide some of the most destitute people – paupers, & c., with a sum of money to assist them, and that the crops on the ground would be taken at a valuation. The cottars, on the other hand, pointed out the absurdity of removing them to America, by showing the vast quantity of land laying waste in Skye, and their willingness to pay any reasonable rents for it or their present holdings.' Sheriff-substitute Fraser then issued the people with a document which threatened 'the poor, ignorant crofters with bands of sheriff-officers, scores of constables, and constables' batons, with regiments of military, and in short, "with the whole force of the country!"' This was probably the letter written by Fraser on 25 May, though Donald had exaggerated the threat. Donald then argued how ridiculous this was and wrote 'In any farther opposition to the removings, no other weapon stronger than the pen will be necessary. This weapon, in the hand of a good counsel in Edinburgh, will, in my opinion, answer their purpose at present.' Donald then described his visit to the residents on a stormy day:

> When approaching near one of the houses, I distinctly heard the words "*Shin am maor*" (that is the officer) – coming from some men working in a barn... The disagreeable idea soon got wing. Little bare-headed and bare-legged messengers passed me as swift as roes, sounding the alarm at every door – *Shin am maor! shin am maor...* On entering the house I found a good fire blazing on the hearth. The crofters are well supplied with peat, and on cold rainy days they test the merits of them. The inmates were all engaged, with the exception of two men of sombre visage, who sat near the fire holding a discussion upon matters relative

Strathaird Evictions

The derelict church of Cill Criosd in Strath Suardal, which Donald visited.

The ford at the head of Loch Slapin that Donald crossed, with Blàbheinn (Blaven) in the left background.

to the fishing. The females were engaged at knitting and spinning; and one young man was busily engaged mending a net. The females suspected at once that I was the *maor*; and they, therefore, did not fail to state their opinion in low whispers, to the effect that it was a "cruel business to come to turn people out on such a day." ...I speedily announced in Gaelic the object of my visit. The inmates immediately saluted me with a thousand welcomes; and everything that could be devised was done to make me comfortable. Boots were pulled off, and warm dry stockings were supplied. Coats and plaid were put up on a screen near the blazing fire, and everything that good will and humanity could dictate to the kind mountaineers was done to make me happy ... they were well pleased that I was ready to listen to their own simple annals and to note down their grievances. Warm milk from the cow, and oatcakes were supplied, which I relished well after a long travel... When leaving, the crofters, (all in a row,) with their strong horny "paws" gave my poor fingers a terrible (but kindly meant) squeeze, whilst one after another they exclaimed – *beannachd leibh* – (blessings be with you) – the sound of which reverberated in my ears until I was several hundred yards away from the place.[39]

Donald ended the letter by criticising the clearances: 'Unless some stop be put to the now general system, nothing will soon be heard but the bleating of sheep and the barking of dogs, throughout the length and breadth of the land.'

Donald's fourth letter was written back in Broadford on 26 August: 'I did not fail to observe with regret sufficient to convince me that the poor law is a dead letter in the Highlands, ... and that the new-fangled machinery, called "Inspector of the Poor," "Parochial Board," and "Board of Supervision," are, at best, but wretched, official obstacles, placed in the way of obtaining relief, and much calculated to deprive the pauper of his right.' He provided examples of people who were 'shamefully neglected':

Catharine M'Kinnon, aged 80 years, residing at Broadford ... is very frail; she cannot walk, and is bowed to the ground with general infirmities. The Parochial Board of the parish of Strath, the principal heritors of which are Lord Macdonald and Mr Macallister, of Torrisdale, allow this helpless indigent person only the miserable *dole* of 16 lbs of meal every 21 days. Nothing whatever is allowed to her for fuel, clothing, or lodging ... and there she lives, pining away in misery and want, on a dole of meal, scarcely sufficient for sustaining life in a dog. The hut occupied by this poor creature is of the most wretched kind. The apartment is so small that a person must creep into it, and through it. The roof is low, and not watertight, consequently the rain oozes through the turf and straw, and mixing in its descent with the sooty incrustations that are glued to every part of the humble hut, makes everything in the house as black as pitch… Her face is small, and as she crawled "on fours" through the hut to speak to me through an aperture in the wall, which she calls "a door," I was startled by her singularly emaciated and unearthly appearance. She has no bed: she sleeps (if, indeed, such a person can sleep with cold and hunger) on a sort of turf mound in the side of the hut, with scarcely a rag of bed-clothes to cover her.[40]

Donald encountered 'insane persons roaming about at perfect liberty, no one caring for them. One woman, Ann Robertson, at Broadford, who is aged 67 years, is quite insane.' On receiving her meal allowance 'she immediately sets off through the district treating the natives to a "puckle meal" until all is done.' Donald explained that the Inspector of the Poor for Strath was 'Lord Macdonald's ground officer, or bailiff. He was only fixed upon by the proprietors for his efficiency in hunting down poachers, and for his stern firmness… The system of starving the poor is pursued with impunity; and, in a country where no legal recognition is taken of the cause of sudden deaths, and where the officials are all deeply interested in "hushing up" cases of death by starvation, little or nothing respecting the real condition of the poor, and of their sufferings, find their way before the public.'[41]

In Donald's last letter, dated 28 August from the Parish of Sleat, the southernmost promontory of Skye, he considered the best way to help the people would be 'to teach and induce men to help themselves.' If they were granted leases they would 'have every incentive to exertion, in order to improve their own condition and also the condition of those around them.' They needed to be taught methods of agriculture as manure was 'just thrown out of the byre and stable, by a hole on the wall near where the cows or horses stood inside' and thus lost its 'fertilizing power.' He suggested a 'Highland Improvement Society' should be formed to help the people. He finished his letter by suggesting tourists should go to Skye. While visiting Elgol, it appears he had taken time to visit Spar Cave 'with its sparry incrustations – brilliant as diamonds – with its stalactite ornaments,' and Loch Coruisk, which 'has far more terrific grandeur about it than Glencoe. The loch is deep and black below, and closely surrounded by rocky mountains and needle-pointed hills at great height.'[42]

On 14 October the people of Strathaird wrote to Donald 'We have to inform you that our potatoes have almost entirely failed … we have no prospect at all how to sustain life during the next six or seven months… We feel this loss now as we are on the brink of starvation… What can we do but apply to you to take up our cause and plead it, and by doing so the blessings of them that are ready to perish will rest and remain with you for ever.'[43] Donald was 'glad to correspond with any person who may feel interested in the condition of the people of Strathaird, and to take charge of any aid that may be offered to alleviate their distress.'

At a meeting in Edinburgh in December, Donald reported he had 'failed to find any writer willing to act for the people of Strathaird, who, to the extent of 620 persons, were about to be turned out of their cottages, and deprived of their land; and yet of that number he had found 100 to be proper objects of parish relief. Upon his arrival, he immediately took steps to enforce the right of the aged and infirm to parochial assistance; and the result was, that, rather than undertake so heavy a burden, the people were allowed to remain.'[44] The 1851 census showed that the population of the parish had increased to 3,243, including twenty-six households of 124 people living at Keppoch and four households of twenty people living at Arinacraig.[45] Donald subsequently received a letter from a resident of Keppoch:

> The reason I write to you is to let you know that we lost 600 long lines and our herring nets with the storm we had lately. We have no lines nor herring nets now, and it is with the long lines we supported our families. We are now in great want and have nothing, and what we can do is to let you know. The Keppoch people are much obliged to you Mr Ross, for what you was doing for them this year past; we may have died but for you; but we must speak to you again to take us out of our trouble. If there is any way at all that you can get nets and long lines for us to make up our loss, we pray to you to write us soon. Our wives and children are starving and we cannot go to sea for anything. You will have our blessing for ever Mr Ross, if you mind on us and get what will put us to sea again.[46]

In June 1852 Macalister took thirteen tenants of Keppoch to the Small Debt Court in Portree, presumably over rent arrears.[47] So they were still living there then, but not for much longer. On 3rd October eight households of forty-six people from Keppoch and two households of fifteen people from Arinacraig embarked on the *Ontario* from Liverpool to Sydney, Australia, under the auspices of the Highland and Island Emigration Society.[48] In 1883 Donald Mackinnon, crofter in Elgol, informed the Crofters' Commission that in 1852 from Keppoch 'forty-four families were removed, and sixteen of them were sent away to Australia. Five of these were placed among us in Elgoll.'[49] The 'forty-four families' appears to be an exaggeration as it is much higher than the twenty-six households recorded by the census. Donald Nicolson of Torrin informed the Royal Commission in 1893 that twelve crofts were cleared from Keppoch and 'Arinacreige' was cleared at the same time.[50] Elgol wasn't cleared.

13

Barra Exodus

Barra is one of the southernmost islands of the Outer Hebrides. In 1840 the Estate of Barra, including the surrounding small islands, was purchased by Colonel John Gordon, the 'richest commoner in Scotland,' for £38,050, who's only interest was to make money.[1] Most of the population were Catholic and lived in houses 'of a most miserable description.'[2] The population was 2,097 in 1831 and even though 'emigration to Cape Breton and Nova Scotia carried off the island a great many almost every year' it had reached 2,363 by 1841.[3] A resident of the neighbouring island of South Uist wrote to a settler in Prince Edward Island: 'Colonel Gordon, who is now sole proprietor of all South Uist, Benbecula and Barra seems to be a very hard and selfish man and the opinion generally entertained of him is that the sooner people are quit of him, the better for them.'[4]

The local Catholic priest, Rev. Donald Macdonald, informed the *Poor Law Inquiry* in 1843 that 'the poor over the country are in a very distressing state' and received no aid from the kirk-session. The schoolmaster, Hugh Macdonald, added that many of the poor people 'have only one bedstead with a little straw in it, and one or two plies of covering – some only one, and that very probably a worn out blanket originally made in the country. A whole family sleep in the same bed… Some of the children are half naked, wearing an old flannel shirt and nothing else.'[5]

The potato famine exacerbated the problem. In March 1847 William A. Peterkin of the Board of Supervision visited Barra to investigate four 'reported deaths from starvation' and concluded two of them had received meal allowances though for the other two, applications were not 'made to the Inspector for relief,' one of whom was a four-year-old boy. Peterkin considered the Inspector of the Poor, Archibald Macdonald, was 'in utter ignorance of his duty' and 'unsuited for the important office which he now holds.' John Fleming, the Factor, defended the Inspector and quoted Sheriff Shaw who considered he 'was the most efficient one in the whole of the Long Island.' Fleming pointed out that Gordon had distributed food to the value of

£4940 in South Uist and Barra. However, much of this was probably supplied by the Central Board and had been supplied to the people on credit. He considered the people squandered their money on tobacco and whisky and in 'several instances when they were directed by the Factor to work at roads, and kelp manufacture, for the supplies of food advanced to them, they either openly disobeyed the order, or excused themselves on the most frivolous pretences.' £6000 of rent was due plus the £4940 for food, yet only £651 had been received.[6] In 1849 Gordon wrote to the government pointing out that there was no employment for the population, most of whom were destitute, in rental arrears, were 'a burden too great on the property' and he accused them of stealing sheep. He appealed to the Government to 'immediately apply the remedy of an effectual emigration.'[7]

In 1850 it was reported that the potato and oat crops in the Outer Hebrides had failed.[8] In May some people from Barra went in boats

> ...to a small island – that on which the Barra Head Lighthouse is situated – to carry away the eggs of sea-fowl from the cliffs of the precipitous environing rocks. After reaching the place they had to descend 1200 feet in the face of tremendous crags. Desperation had caused several of them to venture so far down that they lost their lives. Their weakness from want of food was such that they could not hold on by the shelves of the rocks, and were precipitated into the raging surge.[9]

132 families, totalling 660 people, were evicted from Barra and by the time of the 1851 census the population had dropped to 1873.[10] On 3 December 1850 the first party of fifteen Barra refugees arrived in Glasgow. They were initially lodged in the Night Asylum, then the hospital. Donald MacLean recalled that after 'my house was pulled down I took shelter with my family under an old boat, turned bottom upwards' and fed on shellfish.[11] They had travelled to Dunoon but could not obtain employment so were put on a steamer and landed at The Broomielaw. Their plight was debated by the City Parochial Board who feared that these were just the first of many and the board could not provide relief to the families of able-bodied men.[12] Mr Hannan, Chairman of the Glasgow Section of the Central Board 'was surprised at the heartless manner in which these people had been driven out from their homes at this season of the year. By means of the Relief Fund ... the man who, after getting a year's work out of them, should dismiss these people, and send them to Glasgow at a time when there was no employment for them, had acted in ... a most unchristian part.' At the next meeting of the Parochial Board Hannan reported that:

> The former proprietor was Colonel M'Neill, who had established a kelp or barilla manufactory, and this had been the cause of bringing large numbers to the island. These works did not succeed in consequence of the duty being taken off foreign kelp, and the estate was sold to

Colonel Gordon. The majority of the people were thus left in poverty and had never been able to get out of that state. Their only resource was fishing, which was not sufficient to support them. Then followed the total destruction of the potato crop, and but for the Relief Fund many hundreds must have perished... Col. Gordon had done much for the people, and co-operated with the Committee in many ways. One year he had given no less than £1000. But the island was a dear loss to him.[13]

On 14 December Donald wrote to Colonel Gordon, who replied four days later:

> Of the appearance in Glasgow of a number of my tenants and cotters from the Parish of Barra, I had no intimation previous to the receipt of your communication; and, in answer to your inquiry, 'What I propose doing with the people?' I say – *Nothing*.
>
> In the *Mail* newspaper of the same date as your letter, I observe a notice under the head 'The Cruelties of Cluny,' initialled D. R., which I take to be *Donald Ross*, and in it you pretend to say that I am 'legally and morally bound to do something for the people I have so unmercifully turned out.' I take leave to inform you, sir, that I am neither legally or morally bound to support a population reduced to poverty by the will of Providence and Acts of the Legislature; and that neither man, woman, nor child have been turned adrift from Barra either by my orders or with my knowledge.[14]

Initially, Donald only published the first part of the letter and ended his article 'The above is conclusive, as showing that no help need be looked for from the Colonel.' The full version was published later with the accusation that Donald, 'while professing to publish a true copy of a letter addressed to him by Colonel Gordon of Cluny, has suppressed an important portion of it.'[15]

Before Donald received Gordon's reply he travelled to Edinburgh with a party of refugees. It was reported 'Our city on Tuesday last [17 December] witnessed the melancholy spectacle of twenty-three natives of the Island of Barra, including men, women, and children, wandering our streets, in a state of extreme destitution.'[16]

> The females and children were shivering of cold, as the rain was pouring at the time... On arriving opposite Cluny's door, Mr Ross made the necessary inquiry after that gentleman, and was informed by the housekeeper that the Colonel, *i.e.* Cluny, was from home. A gentleman who stops in the house in Cluny's absence put his hand out at a window in the second flat, and enquired the meaning of such a desperate company of beggars coming to any gentleman's door, and Mr Ross quietly informed him that they were not beggars, but Cluny's tenants, who came to visit him at St Andrew Square, because he removed them

from his property in Barra, and that lodgings must be got for the whole of them in Cluny's house, or elsewhere, at his expense...

Mr Ross, after remaining with the people for about an hour at St Andrew Square, proceeded with them up to the Parliament House, and after getting a further supply of food for them, he soon collected a most respectable deputation, who inspected the people...

Mr Ross has done his duty faithfully by them, and the poor creatures were deeply sensible of this, and expressed their gratitude in the strongest terms.[17]

Hugh Miller described the people as having

...generally black hair cut short, sparkling black eyes; the men of square, compact forms and faces, in stature shorter, it struck us, comparatively, than the women... Here is a black-eyed, merry looking girl of six, clinging at the end of a form to her mother. The matron has spare features, with a strong intelligent expression; a high *mutch* fastened close round her face with a spotted handkerchief, whose knotted ends fall over her care-worn brow. She is looking anxiously, but softly, on another child nestling under her plaid, – a fine boy of some two years old, with dark, peering eyes, and cheeks already tanned. In front is a bashful high-cheeked lad of some eighteen, with his hands in the pockets of his cotton jacket; and beside him the hard-featured father, with coat somewhat in need of the gudewife's needle.[18]

That same day, Donald, Prof. More, Spence, Rev. Begg and others appeared at a meeting of the Edinburgh Council. Donald reported that

...he had been in the island of Barra some months ago, when he found the people in a state of great destitution. In the month of September the Highland Destitution Board suspended relief, when Colonel Gordon immediately ordered a large number of his poor tenants to be removed, which was accomplished by demolishing their cottages, and then, after they were cast out desolate on the fields, getting them shipped off the island. About 132 families were sent in this way to Tobermory. Of these, 37 families had made their way across to Ardrishaig, and from that to Glasgow.[19]

The Lord Provost considered that 'if Col. Gordon was made fully aware of the miserable and distressing case of these poor people, his humanity would induce him to do something for them. He (the Lord Provost) would be glad to subscribe towards providing for the present necessities of the poor people.' The twenty-one people 'were afterwards lodged in the Night Asylum, Old Fishmarket Close' and a list of names was published[20]

That day it was reported that 'another importation of destitute people from the same island was landed yesterday within the limits of the Barony Parish.'[21] The following day another meeting was held in Edinburgh, chaired by Sheriff Monteith, and also attended by Prof. Alison. Donald expanded on his previous report. After being evicted,

> The wretched people then erected tents, with their blankets hung on posts, and some of them took refuge in caves, and others lingered about their old haunts. They passed their time thus till the relief operations ceased, and the officers again warned them to remove. They said they had nowhere to go, and could not remove from the island. The officers then procured warrants from the Sheriff Substitute, and demolished their tents and shipped all the inmates in a steam-boat to Tobermory, here they were left to wander on the mainland, to beg or starve. Several of the expatriated families had reached Glasgow, other were on their way there, wandering over Argyle and Dumbarton shires... Unless something was done for the poor exiles many of them would die of starvation.[22]

It was decided that a new committee should be formed, composed of the gentlemen mentioned above, and 'the Lord Provost, Sheriff Monteith, and Mr Ross should wait on Colonel Gordon, and report the results to a future meeting.' There were three attempts to visit Gordon in Edinburgh that day, though at the time he was staying on his estate at Cluny, Aberdeenshire.[23] Charles Baird also wrote to Gordon, who replied 'They must have left Barra of their own free will, and I am not sorry they did so; for it may be expected that they will tell their story as favourably as they can for themselves ... they have uniformly thwarted all my efforts to put them in the way of maintaining themselves and their families by their own industry, and have rendered that property of no value, but rather a heavy incumbrance.'[24] Gordon provided evidence that he had received £1273, 16s, 5d over the previous three years, though had spent £3117, 6s, 3d, and had recently sent a cargo of Indian corn meal for the poor people. In a later twist it was declared by Charles Bond that Baird 'in my presence, at Col. Gordon's house in Edinburgh, in the spring of 1849, recommended an extensive clearance by emigration of the people on the Colonel's estate.'[25] In response to the reply from Gordon to Baird, Donald wrote that the people had not left Barra of their own accord,

> ...and in a few days they will satisfy the gallant colonel of this fact, and of what is done in Barra in his name. They are to start for Aberdeen on next week, and will present themselves before him at Cluny Castle, with all their poverty and rags. The colonel will know them at once, for no other proprietor in Great Britain can boast of cottars so well furnished with rags, and with every other symbol of misery and want.[26]

Another small party of two widows and five children, arrived in Glasgow 'in a state of such extreme misery, that, on their arrival at the Town's Hospital, Mr Willox had to consign all their miserable articles of wearing apparel to the flames ... they appear to have been driven from the island by absolute privation. Being widows, they were on the pauper roll, but all they were allowed for themselves and their children was about a peck of oatmeal for each family weekly; and for this the women were obliged to assist in breaking stones for the repair of the roads.'[27]

On 26 December the refugee committee met again in Edinburgh. Donald mentioned the two letters from Gordon and with regards to him denying the evictions Donald 'stated that, so far from this being the case, he had numbers of people who could swear to the evictions having taken place under Col. Gordon's direction.'[28]

The Secretary of the Night Asylum received donations and 'provided under-clothing to the whole of these destitute families, and also material sufficient to supply all the females with a change of dress. We understand that the articles ... are now being made up by the women of the party, who are both expert and industrious in this coarse sort of needlework.'[29]

A few newspaper articles were critical of providing charity to the destitute as it encouraged begging and the 'other thing to be deprecated is the mischievous counsel given by a Mr. Donald Ross ... it is intended that the destitute refugees from Barra shall "start for Aberdeen on an early day and present themselves at Cluny Castle with all their poverty and rags." This may annoy and humiliate Colonel Gordon, but it can do no good to the poor people. It will subject them to a long journey in the dead of winter, will obtain no relief for them, and may bring them into awkward collision with the law.'[30] However, they were offered employment by 'William Dunn, contractor, East Calder, who has undertaken the management of extensive draining and trenching operations on waste land, on the estate of a nobleman in the north... The able-bodied men, seven in number, will leave Edinburgh with their families, in all twenty-three individuals, early tomorrow morning for the scene of their labour.'[31]

Of the twenty-three, ten were under the age of thirteen and one was over seventy.[32] The men were provided with 'a suit of good working clothes, some underclothing, a pair of shoes, and a spade.'[33] However, their plight was not over as it was soon reported they 'were not only totally unfit for work, but among their followers (sixteen women and children) there were some bad cases of small-pox.'[34]

Dunn sent them back to Edinburgh on 7 January 1851 and the following evening they were placed in the Victoria lodging-house.[35] Another account reported that the people of Laurencekirk Parish, Aberdeenshire, feared that the Barra families would become chargeable upon the poor's fund, so 'they seized the opportunity of the small-pox breaking out, to despatch the whole party from the neighbourhood.'[36] It was later reported that 'several bad cases of small pox have broken out ... so that although we have got rid of the people ... they brought that most loathsome disease with them, and left it behind them.'³⁷ It was also reported that the men could have stayed on working there, though 'the whole of them are to be conveyed back to Glasgow.'³⁸

The refugee committee held their last meeting on 11 March. They had collected £31 13s 6d of which £3 10s 8d had been paid to Donald for 'sundry expenses connected with bringing the Barra refugees to Edinburgh.' Most of the money had been expended on travel to and from Laurencekirk, supplying the refugees with spades etc and looking after them after they got back to Edinburgh, except for those with smallpox, who had been taken to the hospital. It was reported that most of the people had left though three families had stayed in the Edinburgh Workhouse 'and were getting parochial relief, which, of course would be charged against the Board at Barra.'³⁹

Those that returned or had just arrived in Glasgow were reported as 'prowling about, begging, and taking shelter in sheds, or near public works, where they are warmed by the heat of the furnaces.'⁴⁰ In February another party of sixty-one turned up in Inverness on a steamer and after a few days headed 'eastwards towards Moray and Banff shires' seeking employment.⁴¹ Another report said that there were fifty-six of them who had believed a 'false report that employment might be readily obtained in the Highland capital.'⁴² They had not been evicted but had left voluntarily without 'a penny to purchase a morsel of food.'⁴³ Another group arrived at Fort William and one or two families made their way to Inverness who were 'vagabond in the extreme.'⁴⁴ Subsequently, thirteen men with families found labouring work in Inverness and Nairn. The Parochial Board of Barra was inundated with requests for relief payments from other parishes and if 'claims continue to pour in, the board will be involved in difficulties beyond their powers of extrication.'⁴⁵

As part of a tour of the Western Highlands and Islands, Sir John McNeill visited Barra and had a meeting with the Parochial Board in April. Immediately afterwards he wrote a letter reminding the board of their responsibilities and 'should any applicant who has been refused relief perish for want of food, you would subject yourself to be indicted by the public prosecutor on a charge of culpable homicide.' At their next meeting, the board considered 'that means for carrying out the provisions of the Statute for alimenting ordinary paupers, are becoming every day more difficult to realise, and how they are to be supplied during the ensuing year, involves an alarming anxiety.' They put this down to a 'dearth of food,' the low value of cattle and the 'population are quite disinclined to seek labour elsewhere in Britain, or when they migrate, do so in such a manner which increases our parochial burdens.' The board disagreed with statements given by refugees to the newspapers. They referred to Donald MacLean as 'an indolent man, who never did much work even when wages could be earned.' They considered 'that the eleemosynary relief ... has induced many to misrepresent their circumstances with a view to participate in it.'⁴⁶ Three migrants responded

'Donald M'Lean was not indolent, as is falsely reported; but, the poor man was quite incapable of standing fatigue or hard labour, as he was for a long while labouring under the consumptive disease' and had since died.[47]

McNeill reported that the inhabitants on Gordon's estates were 'convinced that emigration to the colonies affords them the only prospect of extrication from their difficulties and sufferings, that petitions signed by heads of families, representing nearly three thousand individuals, have been transmitted for presentation to Parliament, praying for aid to enable them to transport themselves to Canada.'[48]

Two more groups of refugees, totalling twenty people arrived in Inverness in the summer of 1851.[49] In the meantime it was reported that those employed in Nairn were doing well and that some of their children were attending school and learning English. They still loved Barra 'but they feel that they must be contented wherever they can find a living.'[50] The Inspector of the Poor of Barra wrote to his counterpart in Inverness requesting that the people return as 'a free passage to Canada will be provided' however most did not want to return nor to emigrate.[51]

At the beginning of August it was reported 'Colonel Gordon is now sending batches of emigrants from his Barra and Uist estates to North America. Two ships left these islands last week, carrying about 1000 emigrants. A third is now loading, and two more are expected forthwith; altogether, we think about two thousand will leave the Colonel's Highland estates this year... The cry of starvation will then we trust cease to be heard from these lonely isles.'[52] However, an eye-witness described the duplicity used was 'worthy of the craft and cunning of an old slave-trader... The poor people were commanded to attend a public meeting at Loch Boisdale where the transports lay, and according to the intimation, any one absenting himself from the meeting was to be fined in Two Pounds. At this meeting some of the natives were seized and in spite of their entreaties were sent on board the transports.'[53] Another eye-witness recalled 'I have seen the big strong men, the champions of the country, the stalwarts of the world, being bound on Loch Boisdale quay and cast into the ship as would be done to horses and cattle.' Rev. Beatson, the new protestant minister, was complicit in the coerced emigration of the population.[54] At least 1,681 people from Barra and South Uist left on five ships for Canada that year.[55]

In November Donald wrote a long letter to the *NBDM* which included two articles from the Canadian press. The first, from the *Dundas Warder*, reported that emigrants 'of the poorer class who arrive here from the Western Highlands of Scotland, are often so situated, that their emigration is more cruel than banishment. Their last shilling is spent possibly before they reach the upper province – they are reduced to the necessity of begging.' The second article, from the *Quebec Times*, included a statement from seventy-one emigrants. Most of the 413 people

...proceeded voluntarily to embark on board the Admiral, at Loch Boisdale, on or about the 11th August, 1851, but that several of the people who were intended to be shipped for this port, Quebec, refused to proceed on board, and, in fact, absconded from their homes to avoid embarkation. Whereupon Mr. Fleming gave orders to a policeman who was accompanied by the ground officer of the estate in Barra, and some constables, to pursue the people who had run away among the mountains, which they did, and succeeded in capturing about twenty from the mountains, and from other islands in the neighbourhood; but these only came with the officers on an attempt being made to handcuff them; and that some who ran away were not brought back, in consequence of which, four families, at least, have been divided... [They were promised work and land, but are now] so destitute, that if immediate relief be not afforded them, and continued until they are settled in employment, the whole will be liable to perish with want.[56]

Hector Munro, a former Captain living in Hamilton, Ontario added that 'the emigrants from Barra and South Uist, amounting to between two and three thousand, were the most destitute I ever saw coming into this country. They were actually in a state of nudity on their arrival here, and were utterly helpless.'[57] Subsequently the chief emigration agent in Quebec sent Colonel Gordon a bill for £152 10s, but given that it was addressed to his factor, Gordon refused to open it.[58]

Nine families had remained in Inverness, and by January 1852,

...many of the sources of work on which they were dependent have become to a great extent exhausted, and consequently the Barra refugees now depend entirely on the charity of the public. We regret to learn that the poverty of the poor creatures is so extreme that several families are compelled to live together in a single miserable apartment. They have nothing but straw to lie upon, scarcely a blanket to cover them, and, worst of all, scarcely a morsel of food to eat. Many of them have neither shoes nor stockings, and their clothes are perfect rags.[59]

Rev. James Mackay returned 'most cordial thanks to the ladies and gentlemen who have so kindly sent him contributions of clothes and money for the relief of the destitute families.'[60] Five pounds was 'transmitted through Mr Donald Ross, of Glasgow, whose persevering exertions in behalf of his countrymen are well known.'[61]

14

Highland Destitution

Donald wrote general articles about destitution in the Highlands; the first was written on 24 December 1850:

> It is impossible, by any written description, to give an adequate idea of the great destitution that prevails at this time throughout the Western Highlands and Islands of Scotland... The severe storm of the 19th, 20th, and 21st August last, which ran over the whole of the Outer Hebrides, Skye, Small Isles, and the whole of the west coast of Inverness and Ross-shire, did great injury to the corn-crop, destroying more than one-third of it over the entire country. In the month of September the potato crop began to show symptoms of decay: and, by the latter end of that month, the disease spread over the whole country, destroying that valuable root as it went along.[1]

He listed twenty-six parishes with a total population of 60,980 people of which 25,329 (42%) had been in receipt of relief from the Central Board. Also, Skye contained a population of '21,000, and no less than 13,000 ... in a state of great destitution.' He continued:

> With 38,000 of our fellow-creatures on the outskirts of the Highlands in a state of destitution bordering on starvation, and without any legal provision for their relief, it is high time the public should become alive to their anomalous position... I do not expect a relief fund such as the last; but I am sure that a fund on a smaller scale would be of immense benefit.

In January 1851 Donald returned to Skye 'to obtain legal redress for those entitled to it... Any sum will be thankfully received for this purpose by Charles Spence, SSC.'[2] On 3 February Donald wrote to Spence from Broadford Inn:

> Herewith I send you a petition to parliament on behalf of the poor people of Durinish and of Bracadale in Skye...

Highland Destitution

I left for Portree on Saturday, and came up through a number of districts inhabited by a tenant and cotter population. The people are in the depth of misery, they have nothing to eat, and they have no employment, and no prospect whatever before them but death! ... The most destitute districts in all Skye are Roag and Kilmuir Moss, in the parish of Durinish; Conordan, Achnahanait, Sconcer, and Luib in Portree; and Breakish and Harpool in the parish of Strath. There are here about 400 persons this night without 400 ounces of meal among them all. Many of them are actually starving...

At Roag I found the family of a Rory Campbell in actual starvation. The wife in bed unable to rise from pure want. Four children, ragged, lank, and lean. The oldest fourteen years, the youngest three and a half years. Their father, a poor dejected man, strong enough in bone, but without any other necessary. For four days, this family lived on 3lbs. of oatmeal. The meal being exhausted, a small hen, belonging to one of the children, a boy of six years, was their only remaining property. The father proposed to kill the hen for food to his sick wife; but the little owner decidedly objected, and ran out with "poor chuckie" to the hill-side. The father followed, took the hen from the boy, and killed it in presence of his children, who all cried bitterly for their poor favourite hen. The hen was soon eaten up, and the family were again in want... I was just in time to save the life of the poor mother by providing some food for her at my own expense, and by getting the parish doctor to prescribe some nourishment...

If you succeed in getting anything for these poor people, you can remit to me to the Post-office, Broadford, Isle of Skye.[3]

The petition was signed by 255 heads of families, representing 1,057 people. It called for an 'immediate inquiry, by commission or otherwise, into the extent and the causes of the present alarming destitution.'[4] Spence and Prof. Alison set up a committee in Edinburgh for the 'Relief of the famishing poor in the Isle of Skye' and the Free Church in Edinburgh also set up a Highland Destitution Committee.[5]

From 3 February to 17 April Sir John McNeill toured the Western Highlands and Islands on HMS *Comet* and investigated the conditions in twenty-seven parishes. This was in response to numerous letters sent to the government, including letters from Spence. McNeill submitted a long report to the Board of Supervision dated 7 July and the letters were included in an Appendix, including the one that Donald wrote to Spence.[6] At each parish McNeill met with the local parochial boards and informed them of 'the obligation imposed upon them by statute, to give adequate relief to all disabled and destitute persons who, from want of sufficient food, ceased to be able-bodied, and had a right to relief.' He also interviewed two or three persons in each parish selected by the inhabitants, who often only spoke Gaelic and their statements were translated into English. Alexander Macpherson, ground officer to

Lord Macdonald in Portree, stated 'a Mr Ross has been amongst the people promising them assistance; and I have heard from some of those who were in communication with him, that they were confident of obtaining it. I have also heard that he collected the people of this place and of Sconser, and induced them to sign a paper, but I do not know its contents, and I do not believe that the people who signed it knew what it contained.'[7]

McNeill met the Parochial Board of the Parish of Duirinish on 27 February and laid before them Donald's account of Rory Campbell's starving family. 'Dr Ferguson, the medical officer of the board, stated ... that the above representation is utterly incorrect, and ... he had not been called to see the parties in question... The inspector, and Mr John M'Pherson, schoolmaster at Roag, say that Campbell's wife was not confined to bed.'[8] William Peterkin, one of McNeill's officers, reported:

> I visited Rory Campbell in his house, on Saturday the 1st of March, at about nine o'clock A.M. I found him and his wife and three children sitting around the fire, and a fourth child lying in bed...
>
> Having made inquiry as to the means by which this family had yesterday had their food, I was told that they had received a stone of meal in charity, – that it would last them to-day and to-morrow, and that they would have some fish. The wife and the whole family are able to go about, and Rory has every appearance of being able-bodied...
>
> I made particular inquiry in regard to whether or not he [Donald] had ever been in the house, or had seen these poor people, or whether or not they had received the relief from him, which had been administered in time to save the life of the wife. In reply to my inquiries, I was told that Mr Ross had never been in the house – that the family had never received relief from him – that the wife had no occasion to be in bed while Mr Ross was in the neighbourhood, as she had nothing the matter with her – that as she had never required the doctor's assistance, she had never asked for it – that the family were in good enough health... They killed their last hen seven weeks ago.[9]

In another house Peterkin was told 'there was nothing ... in the third box I opened, my hand, when thrust down, was buried in flour.'

McNeill considered 'the general condition of the inhabitants of all of those districts in regard to health, continued to be at least as good as it had usually been, and better than appeared to be compatible with suffering from insufficiency of food,' *i.e.* the people weren't starving. There were a 'number of persons, capable of maintaining themselves by labour, who were unable to find employment in their own parish or district, and who were therefore subsisting partly upon fish and shell-fish, caught and collected by themselves and their families, and partly upon parochial and private charity.' He considered charity aid had done more harm than good: 'it induced them to misrepresent their circumstances, with a view to participate in it; and caused them to relax their exertions for their own maintenance ... that a people who some years ago carefully concealed their poverty, have learned to parade, and, of course, to exaggerate it.' He concluded 'If emigration is necessary to the well-being of the population, and to their extrication from their present difficulties, there can be no doubt that the sooner that measure is put in operation, the better for all parties.'[10] McNeill's report led to the passing of the Emigration Advances Act in 1851, which supplied loans to proprietors to financially assist their tenants to emigrate.[11]

Before McNeill's report was published, Donald submitted an advert appealing for help for the people on Skye:

> Many of the small Crofters have consumed the small quantities of corn they had for seed, to keep themselves and their poor neighbours alive. They are now without corn for seed, and without the means of getting it; and the result will be, that large tracts of land will be left untilled this year, just because the poor Crofters have no corn to sow it with.
>
> Contributions of Oats, Bere, and Barley, for seed for the Crofters, and of Meal for the relief of the destitute Cottars, will be received at the premises of Mr James Steel, Grain Merchant, 11, Jamaica Street.[12]

Donald then attacked Treasurer Wemyss of Edinburgh Council for making derogatory comments about Highlanders at a council meeting on 20 May:

> You are reported to have said – "that when the Highland Destitution Board commenced their labours, some two or three years ago, a large number of Highlanders had left their work, both in this neighbourhood and in other parts of the country, to proceed to their own districts, on the presumption that they would either get the oatmeal of the Destitution Board for nothing or for working very little for it." ... I should like to know from you upon what authority you made the statement referred to.

On not receiving a reply Donald wrote to the newspapers, including the above letter, and mentioned that 200 Highlanders were working on railway construction at the Bridge of Earn. The contractor, Mr Oldham, had reported that 'they were giving him *entire satisfaction*, and conducting themselves in a most exemplary manner.' Donald also quoted the 1847 report of the Central Board: 'The committee have likewise taken great pains to trace the reports regarding Highland labourers leaving their work, and returning home; and they are happy to say that they have found little foundation for it.'[13] At the next council meeting on 17 June Wemyss said 'I received another sharp note from this same "Donald Ross," threatening me that "if he did not hear from me in receipt," he would be obliged "to make public notice of my conduct;" and, accordingly, out he comes forthwith with an advertisement containing his letter to me, and some other documents, preceded and followed up by a great deal of vulgar abuse.' Wemyss then provided quotes to back up his statement, including James Bruce who visited Skye in 1847: 'I certainly could, on respectable authority, have mentioned cases in which in destitute districts men had refused work ... not even alleging short wages as their reason, but that the work was too troublesome, and their backs were "sair wi' loutin;" and that in some cases they had not sneaked away from their employment, but had marched off proudly, with a piper performing in front.' Wemyss went on: 'I had no wish to rake up these damaging proofs of the laziness of many of Donald Ross's countrymen, and if the result shall be to injure the subscription now being raised in behalf of the destitution in Skye, on him alone must the responsibility rest.'[14] Donald immediately responded:

> Mr Wemyss attempted to throw dust in the eyes of the Council, by referring to speeches and paragraphs in the newspapers, dated some months before the Highland Relief Board publicly investigated those charges which Mr Wemyss, unfortunately, for his own credit, so foolishly resuscitated ... however much he may feel vexed for his own reckless blunder, the best thing he can do under the circumstances is to admit his error.[15]

An article Donald wrote in May included two letters from Skye: 'I have distributed, in meal, the amount of cash you was pleased to send me... Dreadful are the cries of the poor people ... and, unless some door of mercy is opened, and that immediately, death must ensue.' In the other letter, 'One man came up after the whole [quantity of meal] was divided, and he told me he was obliged to go and gather shell-fish on *Sunday*; his son, aged twelve years, died last night. He was crying like a child, declaring he had nothing.'[16] In another article Donald quoted three more letters, including two from Skye: 'Many have not an *ounce of food this night*, and have nothing between them and death but a few shellfish.' The third letter, from North Uist, considered 'the destitution is even worse than it is in Skye... *Think of a man walking fifty miles for a stone of meal!!*'[17] However, the *Reformers' Gazette* considered 'the statements of Donald & Co, '"to reach the pockets" of the kind Christians in the Lowlands, are a tissue of gross exaggerations. There is food and plenty of fish in Skye, if the (robust) destitute would only get their hands and work in right good earnest, in place of snuffing and chewing tobacco, and loitering away their time in indolence or idleness.'[18]

At the end of June *The Witness* reported 'death by famine has now been judicially ascertained to have occurred in the Isle of Skye' and it was subsequently reported that John Macrimmon had died of starvation.[19] Donald mentioned that he and Prof. Alison had received letters from the Hebrides reporting famine, including one from Rev. Angus Martin of the Parochial Board of Snizort, Skye, who had been interviewed by McNeill. Another, from a Sheriff-substitute, stated there was 'more distress in my district for want of food, than has existed at any time since failure of the potato crop in 1846.'[20]

Highland Destitution

Donald wrote in July 'That famine exists in the north-west of Scotland, among thousands of our fellow subjects, is now a truth made palpable to all by the written testimony of ministers and others residing in the famine-stricken districts.' One letter provided details of seventeen families 'who have nothing to support themselves and families except shellfish.' Also, a sixty-six-year-old woman who 'without tasting food that day' had walked twelve miles to Portree to try to sell a few oysters and fainted when she got there. A correspondent in South Uist wrote 'No supplies of meal, adequate to meet the wants of the people, reached here this season; consequently, there is great suffering among the poor, and many are in danger of perishing.' Rev. Martin mentioned 'several deaths have occurred in Skye from want of food' and a minister from Long Island believed 'deaths have occurred in Benbecula, and in South Uist, all from the same cause.' Donald went on to mention that gentlemen in London were collecting funds to help the poor Hebrideans and he appealed to the people of Glasgow for help.[21]

Donald wrote a long letter to the 2nd Marquis of Breadalbane on 21 July:

A poor Old man applied to me here this day stating that he is a native of Kilninver [Argyll], and that he resided almost all his days until Whitsunday last on your Lordships property in the parish of Kilbrandon, but that he was removed there-from by your factor about six or seven weeks ago.

This poor mans name is Duncan Graham and he is now ninety years of age – consequently he is frail and helpless. He occupied land on the Estates of Breadalbane for about 60 years, and during a period of 20 years he paid regularly £150 Sterling per annum for one farm. Latterly he occupied farms at a lower rate of rent; but bad seasons – bad markets – the potato blight, and other causes – pressed severely upon him, and threw him into arrears of rent to your Lordship for his holding – consequently his circumstances became embarrassed and your factor in order to secure all he could for your Lordship seized upon his effects – stock and crop – as well as debts due to him, and at Whitsunday last turned him adrift out of his house without food or shelter and without a farthing in his pocket.

...Old Duncan Graham was obliged to leave Kilbrandon with his staff in his hand, and make for a city of refuge. He is now in Glasgow – without means of support – almost totally destitute of English and without friends able to assist him...

I can scarcely believe that your Lordship will permit that this poor old Highlander be allowed to starve in Glasgow. He was not only well known but he was very useful on your Lordships Estates. He was a cattle dealer for the long period of 40 years – and no one rich or poor ever lost one farthing by Old Duncan Graham in his transactions.

If your Lordship should decline to interfere and leave poor old Duncan Graham to the mercy and to the charity of the public, I will feel it then to be my duty to let the public know and that in the most public manner that this application was made to your Lordship on Old Duncans behalf; and as a public meeting is to be held here with reference to the famine in the Highlands – and with a view of devising measures for mitigating the sufferings of parties who are subjected to cruel eviction, I will not only bring old Duncans Case before the meeting, but I will bring up before the meeting Old Duncan himself, and I will let those present see the old man whom your Lordship turned away from Kilbrandon, and now refuse to shelter or support.

I am sorry to say that this is not the first case, nor yet the first time when I had to direct your Lordships attention to reckless eviction from your property – and that of aged and respectable men, but as the system is pursued in face of all remonstrance, and as many Highland Landholders seem to suppose that, if they turn over on the Streets of Glasgow – their aged, worn out or broken down tenants they will get free of them, I beg to inform your Lordship most distinctly that the inhabitants of Glasgow will not any longer tolerate such conduct as has hitherto been pursued. It remains therefore for your Lordship to say what should be done for Old Duncan Graham, – for his case is urgent, and requiring immediate attention.[22]

There does not appear to be any mention of this case in the press so perhaps the Marquis helped Graham. The 2nd Marquis, John Campbell, appears to have been a clearance landlord who has received very little criticism. In 1853 Breadalbane admitted that at Loch Tay the population had decreased and the farms had increased in size from the consolidation of 'some of the smallest possessions.' However, this was done gradually 'to produce as little inconvenience as possible to those whom it was necessary to remove ... [and where] practicable, those who were removed were offered other houses.'[23] Alexander Robertson of Dundonachie, writing under the pseudonym 'R. Alister' accused him of evicting 'since 1834, no less than 500 families!! ... I believe that your Lordship has done more to exterminate the Scottish peasantry than any man now living; and perhaps you ought to be ranked next to the Marquis of Stafford in the unenviable clearing celebrities.'[24]

At the end of July 1851 McNeill's report was summarised in the newspapers. Some of the articles included Donald's and Peterkin's contrasting accounts of Rory Campbell's family, which would have been embarrassing to Donald and his fundraising efforts.[25] Donald responded that Peterkin 'could not understand one single word the people said to him, neither did they understand his *broad Scotch*.' With regards to Peterkin's account of Campbell, 'there is not a single word of truth in it, excepting the latter portion of it,' that they killed their last hen. Donald continued 'I was not there for the purpose of relieving any one, but by economy, and much exertion, travelling on foot to save the expense of conveyances, I was enabled, out of my travelling allowance, to give a portion towards relieving urgent cases of distress. It was while so engaged that I relieved the family referred to by Mr Peterkin.' Donald published two letters by witnesses. Ewen McLeod wrote 'I saw you, and walked with you for several days among the destitute people in Skye and went with you into their houses, and in several instances I saw you giving some money to poor persons who were in great distress.' Divie Bethune wrote 'I saw you in *several instances giving relief to very poor people who felt very grateful to you for it.*'[26] Donald then quoted a letter from Mr Nicolson, schoolmaster: 'At the meeting which he [McNeill] held here, the only thing advocated by the sheep farmers was Emigration... At Broadford ... Rev. Mr M'Queen, Baptist minister, and Mr F. Mackenzie, along with many of the poor, sought admission to speak to Sir John about the state of the people of Strath, but they were told that "he held no open court, and could receive no further information."' Donald added, 'This was the "impartial" investigation made into the sufferings of the poor Highlanders of Skye.' From a subsequent letter, Rory Campbell denied 'that he made the statements alleged by Mr. Peterkin in his Report ... the interpreter chosen by Mr. Peterkin must have either misunderstood or misrepresented what was said, and, therefore, Mr. Peterkin has been found reporting what is grossly untrue.'[27] In another article Donald emphasised that there had been deaths by starvation, backed up by Dr Alexander Macleod, Portree. Fired up, Donald wrote:

> We now see through the miserable report prepared by Sir John M 'Neil, aided by Mr Peterkin, *his clerk* ... we find Peterkin, like a Bow Street officer, entering houses when the inmates are asleep – searching boxes, bags, and pots, to see if he could find any meal in them; and, on discovering a "handful" of "*charity meal*" in one house in a district, he started away from that district, exclaiming, "No distress here! no distress here!!" ... The charges of misrepresentation and exaggeration brought against some of the clergymen of Skye, and against me, by Mr Peterkin, are now more than sufficiently answered ... I had no wish whatever to exaggerate the evils under which the people suffered.[28]

Donald curtailed writing articles to Scottish newspapers for a while, perhaps due to the bad publicity, however he was still receiving donations from England. 'The Rev. Mr Kennedy of Stepney Green, London, has ordered through Messrs Dryden & Lamb, corn merchants, Glasgow, £25 worth of oatmeal to be sent to such places in Long Island, Hebrides, as may be considered most destitute by Mr Donald Ross.'[29] Donald praised Rev. Kennedy's fundraising efforts and 'took charge of seeing £21 worth of oat meal sent away to Barra and Lochmaddy.'[30]

Donald found a sympathetic ear in the Oxford newspapers: 'Subscriptions, however small, will be most thankfully received at the Old Bank, Oxford, and by Mrs. Pearce, 12, Beaumont street; and will be forwarded, with as little delay as possible, to Donald Ross.'[31] The article quoted a letter from Donald dated

14 August: 'Hundreds of the cottars of Long Island and of Skye went to seek employment at the herring fishery on the east coast of Scotland, and travelled about 2000 [sic, actually 200] miles on foot in search of work, but failed. They at last arrived at Thurso, near John o' Groat's and Sir Geo. Sinclair ... divided seven barrels of good oatmeal among them, and got them on board a vessel for their own native islands... I fear that many of them went home to starve!' Subsequently it was reported 'The following subscriptions are most gratefully acknowledged, and have been the means of sustaining many who were "ready to perish,"' and listed fifteen people who had donated a total of £15 16s.[32] Donald also wrote to John Davies, Rector, who had publicised Donald's appeal in *Berrow's Worcester Journal*: 'The severity of the famine will soon pass over, for some of the sufferers will have corn and potatoes; but it will take six or seven weeks yet before the corn will ripen for the harvest.'[33]

In September, Donald's next pamphlet, *Famine in the Hebrides*, was published. He sent a copy to Rev. Prebendery Oxenham, who forwarded it to the editor of the *West of England Conservative* newspaper, who published a review. This was fortunate as it appears no copy of this ephemeral pamphlet has survived. Donald outlined the problems caused by the combination of the potato blight, storms destroying the crops, the cessation of the Central Board, the two major proprietors of Skye going bankrupt and the clearances. 'In the Island of Skye alone, there are no less than 1765 families, amounting to 9817 persons, wo have no land, no trade, and who can find no employment. In the Island of Mull, 514 families have no land. In the Islands of Barra, Uist, Benbecula, and Harris, there are no less than 819 families who have not one inch of land.' To counter the accusation of the Highlanders being lazy, Donald quoted Robert Brown, Commissioner to the Duke of Hamilton who could 'speak from experience of their praiseworthy industry and perseverance whenever they had an opportunity of finding work at home.' Dr Macleod of Portree described 'Cases of low typhus have appeared for the last four months, and are now daily increasing ... some of the deaths that have taken place from typhus have been occasioned by the previous *want of proper nourishment*... Of late diarrhoea has appeared extensively throughout the country, and this I attribute solely to the poor having *to live principally on shellfish, such as mussels, wilks, and limpits, and latterly on watery new potatoes*.' Similar statements were received from Dr Lachlan Matheson of Portree and Dr Norman M. Macalister of Strath. Donald continued: 'Hundreds of poor Highlanders are accused of laziness, when they are at this moment, with blistered feet, empty sporans, and impaired constitutions, depressed minds, and exhausted and hunger bitten stomachs travelling up and down through Scotland seeking employment.' He mentioned the court case pending before the House of Lords and went on to thank 'the benevolent public in England and in Scotland' for their donations.[34]

In November an article in the Oxford papers mentioned Rev. McLeod had received £10 worth of meal from Donald and 'Had it not been for the kind supplies sent me from time to time, when most needed, I should have lost hopes of seeing the people preserved from the ravages of famine.'[35] A further £12 1s had been received and another two pounds was sent by Rev. Willis from Toronto, Canada.[36]

In December, Donald mentioned the Glasgow Committee was about to distribute '1000 yards of warm clothing, £50 worth of excellent Meal, £5 worth of good-sized Blankets, for the aged.'[37] So Donald wasn't operating alone. Then followed a list of twenty-nine donations totalling £106. The article ended 'An excellent Pamphlet can be had gratis, just published, "A Voice from the Hebrides," on application to Donald Ross.' Unfortunately, this pamphlet hasn't survived either. The lists of donors usually provided their names and where they lived. Most were willing to have their names published as this was a sign of social status, demonstrating a level of financial independence as well as generosity to a good cause. For the wealthy Victorian, donating to charity was expected of them.[38]

At the end of the year Donald placed a long advert in the newspapers. It included a letter from Rev. David Ross, Tobermory, Isle of Mull, who had been interviewed by McNeill: 'At present measles and small-pox rage to an unusual degree, and I much fear that typhus fever has made its appearance. The village is overcrowded by the ejectments unfeelingly going on in the rural districts. Mothers are seen barefoot at this cold season, surrounded by a helpless offspring almost in a state of nudity.' Rev. Adams of Skye wrote 'Yesterday I received by the steamer the grey cotton and the tartan sent by you to be distributed amongst the most needy in this place ... it is now delightful to be able to clothe so many of these poor sufferers.' Frank H. Mackenzie, who McNeill had refused to see, added 'Fifty-one boys got [j]ackets and trowsers [sic] with cotton lining, and twenty-seven girls got frocks and less or more of grey cotton.' Donald listed the donations from Oxford and a further nineteen donations totalling £63 18s. He appealed for more contributions to help 'about 15,000 in a state of want' and listed addresses in London, Oxford and Glasgow where donations would be collected, and parcels by Messrs. Pickford & Co.[39]

The London-based *Quarterly Review* published a long article about the McNeill report and considered that earlier reports were 'much exaggerated' and 'the existence of actual suffering from want of food; though generally believed, eluded all proof... Donald Ross, of Glasgow, is distinguished, as having carried embellishment beyond the bounds permissible even to the best cause and most fertile imagination.'[40] The article included both Donald's and Peterkin's accounts of Rory Campbell. This was more bad publicity for Donald, which was lapped up by the *Reformers' Gazette*.[41] Donald wrote a long defence to the *Morning Advertiser*: 'the whole story is revived and dressed up by the learned reviewer with the avowed purpose of impugning my veracity.' He included the two letters by Ewen McLeod and Divie Bethune though had changed a few of the words. Donald went on 'I had no reason to exaggerate nor yet to embellish, and no statement of mine regarding the distress in the Highlands contained one single sentence but what was strictly correct.'[42]

15

The Hebridean Benevolent and Industrial Society

Towards the end of 1851 Donald set up The Hebridean Benevolent and Industrial Society. On 5 November it was reported:

> Interesting specimens of the domestic industry of Skye were shown to us yesterday by Mr Donald Ross, in the shape of knitted woollen socks and drawers, and knitted stockings of lint grown upon the island. These articles display marked superiority in the art of knitting, and we understand that this kind of work is executed with great expertness by the women and girls of Skye, so that they can make a pretty fair income by it.[1]

In January 1852 Donald advertised 'a large quantity of Socks and Stockings, Knitted by Poor Destitute Females in the Hebrides. The Socks and Stockings are of most excellent quality, and some of the Ladies' Merino and Spanish Wool Fancy Stockings are beautiful.'[2] A subsequent article noted:

> Nearly 200 persons, we are informed, are at present engaged in this way in Skye alone ... the articles thus produced, which are generally of a very superior description, and reflect considerable credit on the ingenuity of the knitters. Some of the stockings for ladies, which are of fine merino yarn, are indeed ornamented in an exceedingly tasteful manner.[3]

This idea was not new. In 1849 William Hogg of Aberdeen established a wool spinning factory on Skye. He employed ten women at the mill and over 1,000 knitters, who produced nearly 16,000 pairs of stockings that year.[4]

Donald's next pamphlet, *Scottish Highlanders*, was dated 12 February and 'Published by order of the Hebridean Benevolent and Industrial Society.' It included quotes from Burns' poems and from other authors including Prof. Alison and Somers.[5] It commenced:

> We do not like always to parade the indigence, and the actual poverty of the inhabitants of the Western Highlands of Scotland before the public. We are well aware that the condition of persons in a state of positive and constant mendicity is a condition which often exhibits very little virtue, and promotes only a feeble amount of bounty or patriotism in the rich ... the destitute in the Highlands have at least a moral claim on the charity and the bounty of the rich; and, that in the case of the poor Hebrideans for whom there is no legal provision made, appeals to the public are at present the only practical means by which a starving people can be saved from the evils of famine.

Donald discussed the able-bodied unemployed being unable to claim relief and attacked the clearances with gusto:

> ... we are no avowed enemies of sheep; altho we are aware that a very large portion of the Highlands have been most cruelly dispossessed of human beings to make way for the wooly [sic] tribes. We are, however, avowed enemies of the "clearance system" in the Highlands, where such scenes were enacted, by fire and faggot, in the extirpation of honest, peaceable, and loyal subjects... By this system thousands upon thousands of happy peasantry have been brought into a state of irretrievable indigence and beggary... Many of the descendents of the men who stood nobly in Egypt, in India, on the Peninsula and at Waterloo, in the service of their King and country, were torn from their homes, and put across the seas – to chop timber or hunt beavers in the back woods.[6]

Donald reproduced several letters received in January still reporting the dire situation in the Hebrides. Dr Norman Macalister, Strathaird wrote 'The bales of clothing for the poor came safely... I never heard stronger or more frequent cries for food among our starving poor. There are many families in this district who have not a particle of human food to appease the cravings of hunger.' Frank H. Mackenzie, Harrapool, wrote: 'The state of the poor in this island is deplorable. The weather has been very bad for some time past, and to day it is terribly so. The poor creatures cannot stand for a moment on the shores to collect shellfish. The sea is running mountain high, and the spray is carried far inland, so that fishing or shell gathering is out of the question ... I sent to Kyleakin, for the 10 bolls of meal you sent, and forwarded 4 bolls to Strathaird, which were carefully distributed by Mrs Dr Macalister ... Mr M'Queen and myself distributed the other 8 bolls here, after considerable trouble, not with the people, but to make the quantity reach them all. They were very grateful and thankful.' Malcolm Morrison, schoolmaster, Harris, wrote that the people 'have nothing to depend on, and were it not for a few fishes (called 'sprats,') they would actually have starved ... I am glad that you sent us a quantity of meal and clothing.'[7] Donald considered the future was bleak:

> The cottar population in great distress – many of them on the verge of famine. No employment to be found – the cultivation of the soil debarred – the landlords bankrupt – sheep-farmers cold and indifferent, and the very energies of the people benumbed. The ordinary resources of subsistence exhausted – and no means existing, whether in the shape of labour or otherwise, to supply the want of them. A cold and stormy season staring them in the face; and very large numbers of the population destitute of food and clothing.[8]

Donald quoted Mackenzie of Gairloch, who valued the people living on his land, and mentioned 'Macculloch's Account of the British Empire,' who considered there were 170,000 Scotch acres of arable land in the Hebrides, though Donald considered there were 180,000 aces and 'upwards of *one million* of acres for pasture!'[9] He continued:

> ... we know what farming is, for we have tried it, and that successfully too. We wrought hard with the spade, and handled the plough as well as the pen, and, therefore, we can write from experience. Our firm conviction is that if the crofters in the Hebrides were properly instructed in the most approved systems of agriculture, and their lots secured to them by leases, that a decided improvement would be soon visible in their social condition.

He also considered 'A great boon would be conferred on the West Highlanders were friends to aid them in getting boats and nets, and in this way enabling them to support themselves and their families permanently by their honest industry.' In the conclusion Donald mentioned 'We have in former pamphlets shewed the worthless and useless character of the Report prepared by Sir John M'Neill on the state of the Highlands.' These were probably the elusive *Famine in the Hebrides* and *A Voice from the Hebrides*. More information was provided on the stocking knitting venture as well as other plans:

> We have about 260 females constantly employed; and the work done by them is giving entire satisfaction. We are now to open two Schools for teaching young females the sewing of Muslin, and when this is accomplished a constant supply of work will be furnished them by Merchants in Glasgow ... We have been anxious to establish model crofts in Mull, Skye, and at Fortwilliam, where crofters would receive information regarding the best system of agriculture; but hitherto the funds at our disposal were so limited that we could not accomplish this. We have, however, arranged as to one model croft, and have commenced operations... We have provided nets and other materials for many poor families, and in this way enabled them to earn a livelihood by fishing.[10]

An Appendix included four more letters. Alexander MacLean, Missionary in Glasgow and former Free Church Minister in Barra, referred to a family of seven, originally from South Uist, who had walked all the way from Inverness to Glasgow; they were living in an old-rag store and were starving. A 'most benevolent, and highly respectable lady in Oxford' wrote, 'I rejoice to find the wicked falsehoods in the Quarterly are sent back to the source from whence they came. I hope you will "go forward" in this good cause: and I rejoice to send you Twenty pounds for our poor friends in the Hebrides to be distributed among them at your own discretion.' The pamphlet ended with an account of the money received and spent 'under the direction of the Hebridean Benevolent and Industrial Society, from 12th November 1851, to the 12th Feb. 1852.' In only three months Donald had raised £370 7s 6d, of which he had spent £180 19s 7d on meal and clothing, £9 6s 10d on transportation and £30 4s 4d on other items such as postage, printing, paper and advertisements. This left £149 16s 7d remaining in the City of Glasgow Bank. The account was verified by four gentlemen – John Finlay, Robert Forbes, D. McLennan and Dr W. Macdonald. It ended with an appeal for more contributions.

An article on 26 February indicated that Donald would be 'in Edinburgh to-morrow and Saturday, and will gladly meet with parties in town, who take an interest in the extreme destitution at present existing in the Islands and West Highlands. He will be found at Mr Allan's office, 4 St Andrew Square.'[11] Robert Allan provided insurance for train passengers 'against loss of life, with compensation for personal injury, by railway accident.'[12]

In March, Donald submitted an appeal to the *Manchester Times* which included a list of twenty-three donations, mostly from people in England, totalling £96 18s plus nine bales or parcels of clothing. He indicated 'The Hebridean Benevolent and Industrial Society disbursed about £400 sterling in relieving the wants of the Hebrideans since the 12th November last, and now, when the funds at its disposal are exhausted, the cries of the poor creatures are more heart-rending than ever.'[13] Several addresses were provided in London, Oxford, Manchester and Glasgow (mostly banks) for donations, and clothing to be sent to Donald. On 26 March it was reported Donald 'sent yesterday by the Duntroon Castle steamer, 16 bolls of meal for the poor cottars in Mull; 8 bolls to Broadford, in Skye; 8 bolls to Portree; 12 bolls to Harris, and 8 bolls to Moidart.'[14] However, the following article appeared in *The Times*:

> Mr. Dond. Ross, of 20, St. Enoch's-square, Glasgow, (up stairs) having for many months past advertised in the English, though not in the Scottish, newspapers, requesting contributions to be sent to him for the relief of the destitute Highlanders, and more recently in connexion with what he terms the Hebridean Benevolent and Industrial Society, some friends of the Gael, having been unable to find out any existence in fact of the said society, nor to discover any list of the contributions

received by him, and from whom, nor any account of the receipts and disbursements, except for four months, viz., from 12th November last to the 12th Feb., 1852, request all parties who have Forwarded directly or indirectly Contributions intended for the destitute Highlanders to the said party, to Send Particulars of the amounts and dates of such remittances to the Secretary [Charles Bond] of the Royal Patriotic and Industrial Society of Scotland, 47, King-street, Parliament-street, London.[15]

Donald quickly responded: 'The advertisement in *The Times* of the 22d inst., with reference to me and my labours to relieve distress in the West Highlands, is a tissue of gross falsehoods and wicked insinuations ... my whole conduct in this, as well as in every other act of humanity and charity, can bear the strictest investigation,' and he republished the accounts from his pamphlet.[16] Bond then wrote that Donald was 'enraged at being required to "give an account of his stewardship," as a self-constituted receiver of contributions for the destitute Highlanders ... on personally calling upon three out of the four gentlemen in Glasgow whose names are appended to his limited statement ... they intimated that they had merely consented to audit these transactions for Mr. Ross, and not as the transactions of the "Hebridean Benevolent, &c., Society," which I repeat has no existence in fact; no treasurer, secretary, or member being discoverable.'[17] The *Reformers' Gazette* made fun of this: 'The society must have been very unanimous... Who proposed a vote of thanks to the chairman for his able conduct in the chair? This duty, of course devolved on Mr. Donald Ross himself, and we have no doubt it was performed sincerely.'[18] That appears to have been the end of The Hebridean Benevolent and Industrial Society.

In April and May Donald submitted an appeal to the newspapers listing twenty-seven donations totalling £60 4s 6d, plus £35 10s 'for employing destitute females at knitting' and eleven bales or parcels of clothing.[19] 'Within the last five weeks, there was upwards of 150 bolls of good meal sent from Glasgow to relieve the wants of the poor sufferers in the Hebrides,' followed by the names of ten ministers or other gentlemen in the Inner Hebrides or on the west coast, 'to the most of whom was also sent clothing, medicines, and other necessaries for the sick.' Robert Allan of Edinburgh was added to the list of recipients of donations. There do not appear to be any further appeals submitted by Donald to the newspapers for the rest of the year.

Two years before, it was suggested 'that there should be a public friendly subscription raised among the admirers of Mr. Ross's disinterested labours, for the purpose of presenting him with a token of respect, by referring to many high testimonials of the most respectable gentlemen in Glasgow ... for his benevolent, able, and valuable services to the helpless.'[20] On 11 June 1852 in Mr Sinclair's Hotel, St Enoch Square, Donald was presented with a 'most valuable' gold watch and 'massive gold chain, enclosed in a beautiful morocco case,' and a purse of sovereigns by Dr C. R. McGillivray. The watch was inscribed 'Presented to Mr Donald Ross, by Highlanders and others in Glasgow, as a token of their gratitude for his labours on behalf of his Countrymen.'[21] McGillivray gave a speech:

> We have all observed his progress through life – rising step by step through the force of his talents and integrity of character alone. You know how highly Mr Ross is esteemed by his professional brethren; and all of you recollect the high terms in which he was spoken of by the Historian of Europe [Archibald Alison]; and how he adorns his station by many estimable and amiable qualities, both of head and heart. (Hear, hear)... And in his transactions he has shown a zeal and intelligence, together with prudence and courtesy, which has gained for him the approbation and gratitude of his countrymen.

Donald replied and

> ...disclaimed having been actuated by any selfish motives in the course he had taken; and declared that he had sought to better the condition of his poor countrymen, by finding food and employment for many of them – by seeking to elevate others – and by promoting their moral and physical improvement. (Hear, hear)... He called upon them, in conclusion, to accept his heartfelt thanks, and begged to assure them that he was as proud of that splendid gold watch and appendages, as if he had been put in possession of the largest sheep farm in the Highlands.

George MacLeod 'gave an account of Mr Ross's first introduction into Glasgow as the agent of the Poor Law Association, the directors of which consisted of the most influential citizens, all of whom, to his knowledge, were highly pleased with his labours in connection with that Association.' Several gentlemen 'expressed strong indignation at certain attacks which had been made lately upon Mr Ross; and, as proof of the contempt with which these attacks were regarded by the public, referred to the testimonial that had just been presented to Mr Ross.'[22] This was rare evidence that in some quarters he was still held in high esteem and clearly had been given the green light to continue his endeavours. The comment about the sheep farm was an odd thing for Donald to say. A misguided attempt at humour perhaps?

Donald found another sympathetic outlet in *The British Friend: A Monthly Journal, chiefly devoted to the interests of the Society of Friends*. This was published by William and Robert Smeal, merchants in Glasgow, who also became recipients of donations for Donald's cause. In July Donald reproduced extracts from more letters, such as from Rev. John Fletcher, Bracadale, Skye: 'I now beg leave to thank you for the last supply of meal, and I hope, and most earnestly beg of you to send me more without delay. Destitution has come to a most fearful height in this parish... People come here a distance of thirteen or fourteen miles, and are thankful if they get half a stone of meal.'[23] Donald listed another twenty-six donations amounting to £85, 9s 7d. In September he acknowledged receiving another £15 and the Smeals later forwarded another £6 10s enabling Donald to send 'A small supply of meal and molasses to one of the districts.'[24]

The venture to manufacture hosiery appears to have been ticking along in the background. In November Donald advertised 'Several *Thousand* Pairs of Excellent Socks and Stockings, well fitted for winter use, and all knitted from the best Yarns by Destitute Females in the West Highlands of Scotland.'[25] However, this appears to be the last mention of this activity, so perhaps it didn't continue for long.

The situation was still bad in the Hebrides, and in February 1853 John Davies wrote to the editor of the *Worcester Journal* quoting several ministers on Mull and Skye who had written letters describing *'extreme misery.'* They 'kindly take a share in distributing the meal, clothing &c, which may be placed by the benevolent in the hands of Mr. Donald Ross, 20, Enoch Square, Glasgow, the indefatigable friend and agent for the poor inhabitants of the Hebrides.'[26] The *Reformers' Gazette* didn't let up and in April wrote:

> It appears, that Mr. Donald Ross, the celebrated Hebridean philanthropist, is still pursuing a profitable traffic in famine, and driving a flourishing business in charity, by levying extensive contributions in the south, for the management and dispensation of which he appears to be responsible to nobody except Mr. Donald Ross himself... Nobody in Glasgow is fool enough to think or believe that Mr. Donald Ross labours in such an agency for nothing... And yet this curious specimen of Christian integrity and charity still continues to levy his benevolent black-mail in the south. Why do none of his advertisements appear in the Scotch papers?[27]

That same month *The Witness* reported that people on Skye had received 'twenty bolls of oatmeal, some molasses and clothing' from Donald.[28] Subsequently, Rev. David Ross of Tobermory, Mull, received twenty bolls of meal and a bale of clothing and said he had 'never witnessed' destitution 'greater in this village than during the late cold and wet spring.'[29]

16
HMS *Hercules*

Ships were regularly leaving from Scotland or northern England full of emigrants desperate for a better life, and most of the ships made it to their destination without incident.[1] But not all, such as the *Annie Jane* which ran aground in Vatersay Bay, Barra, in the night of 28 September 1853, with the loss of at least 326 people.[2]

In August 1851 a meeting was held in Portree, Skye, where William H. G. Kingston from the Australasian colonies 'on a mission from her Majesty's Colonial Land and Emigration Commissioners' provided information on emigration. As a result, a committee was formed to investigate further, chaired by Sheriff-substitute Thomas Fraser and it became the Skye Emigration Society.[3]

In February 1852 a meeting was held in Edinburgh 'to consider the means of facilitating the emigration of some thousands of poor persons in the Isle of Skye who have applied for aid to enable them to go to Australia.' It was chaired by the Lord Provost and the gentlemen present included Sir John McNeill and Sheriff-substitute Fraser. Another committee was formed to raise funds to 'enable these poor people to emigrate.'[4] Later that month a meeting was held 'to promote measures for aiding persons in the Island of Skye, who desire to emigrate to the British Colonies.' Most of those present were supportive, except for Donald MacLeod who considered it would be better 'to put the Highlanders in the possession of their land.' It was resolved that a public subscription would commence; £150 was raised at the meeting and McNeill was put in charge of the funds.[5] Queen Victoria and Prince Albert subsequently gave £370 and £105 respectively to the Skye Emigration Fund.[6] The committee soon became a branch of the Highland and Island Emigration Society, chaired by Sir Charles Trevelyan of the Treasury in London.[7] In July, Donald Ross wrote 'Emigration is found to be inadequate, as well as a tardy measure of relief. As yet only 510 poor persons are provided with passages for Australia from the island of Skye alone.'[8] However that was just the start, from 1852-7 the society assisted nearly 5,000 people to emigrate to Australia.[9]

One of the assisted emigrant ships caught the widespread attention of the press: Her Majesty's Ship *Hercules*; a 74-gun, Vengeur-class ship of the Royal Navy, built in Chatham Dockyard and launched in 1815. In September it was reported that the *Hercules* 'now mounting only 10 guns, has been commissioned ... for the purpose of conveying emigrants to Australia.' It was subsequently fitted up for their comfort but there was concern about it being due to set sail in the winter.[10]

That same year the Emigrants' Lending Library Association was formed to supply such ships with adequate reading material. On hearing that the *Hercules* was going to transport 'a considerable number of Scotch immigrants ... Charles Gilpin ... obtained one of the "Libraries," also some Friends' tracts... The whole were then sent to the care of Donald Ross, Glasgow.' The Society of Friends gave Donald a further supply and he acknowledged receiving 'a large number of books, pamphlets, and valuable tracts and papers, from benevolent Friends in England... The books consist of thirty-three valuable volumes, enclosed in a portable neat library, with lock and key.'[11]

The *Hercules* arrived at Campbeltown Harbour, Argyll & Bute late November and the following month the *Celt* steamer transported people from the Hebrides to board the ship.[12] It was reported that at Harris 'the attachment of some of the more elderly to their native soil was so strong that they could not be induced to leave it... Aged sires ... were here and there bathed in tears, and bidding a last sad farewell.'[13] On 9 December it was reported:

> ... it has been our high satisfaction to welcome to our town Mr. Donald Ross, of Glasgow, a gentleman well and deservedly known for his philanthropic exertions in behalf of the suffering Highlanders...
>
> Mr. Ross has collected, in all, upwards of 8,400 publications for the emigrants, consisting of every variety of valuable reading, from Sir Archibald Alison's *History of Europe*, consisting of twenty volumes, down to the *Dairyman's Daughter*, and other small publications for the instruction of children. In the collection there are 600 Gaelic publications of great value.[14]

McNeill also visited the ship and wrote to Trevelyan 'It would have given you great pleasure to have seen the emigrants in the *Hercules* this morning. Cheerful faces met me everywhere. They are surprised and delighted with the accommodation, the bedding, the diet, the kindness they receive – in short with everything.'[15]

On 26 December the *Hercules* departed with 756 emigrants on board, plus 160 officers and crew.[16] The ship, with Captain Benjamin Baynton at the helm, was towed out of Campbeltown Loch by the *Duke of Cornwall* steamer.

> The passengers were mostly from Skye, Uist and Harris, of both sexes, and of all ages, from infancy upwards. They were divided into classes,

HMS Hercules

HMS *Hercules* in Campbeltown Harbour from where it set sail on 26 December 1852 with 756 emigrants on board, destined for Australia. Donald supplied 8,400 books and pamphlets for them to read on the journey. Half of the passengers had to be left behind in Ireland due to outbreaks of small-pox and fever, and some died.

and each class had its own department of the ship partitioned off from the rest. The married parties, with their families, had one compartment; the young unmarried females another, under superintendence of a matron, evidently suitably selected for this office. The young unmarried males had also their own quarter, in another part of the ship... The emigration commissioners have secured the services of the Rev. Mr M'Tavish, formerly minister of the Free Church at Killean, as chaplain... A department of the ship has been fitted up as a school, and a schoolmaster and assistants have been appointed to instruct the youths during the voyage. The whole party will have the benefit of excellent medical care from Surgeon Carey, and assistant Surgeon Stewart.[17]

On 1 January 1853 the schoolmaster, Alexander Nicholson, wrote to Donald:

After we left Campbelton, on Sabbath last, and proceeded to sea, the wind blew from S.W., directly against us. We hovered about Ailsa Craig the whole of Sabbath night and Monday... On Tuesday, as the wind moderated a little we made some progress towards the Isle of Man. On Wednesday it blew a perfect gale from the S.W., and we drifted along to the coast of Ayr. On Thursday morning we were close to Arran, and as there was no prospect of a change of wind, it was deemed advisable to put in here (Rothesay). The Hercules suffered some damage in her sails, &c., and they are busy repairing them. I cannot describe the scenes of sea sickness that prevailed during the storm... In the midst of the storm a poor woman was safely delivered of a child, and both are doing well. The emigrants are now quite as buoyant as ever. It is gratifying to see amidst all the turmoil that prevails, the regard they have for reading... Send me as many newspapers as you can, they will be interesting to us on board.[18]

Donald 'complied with the latter request; and should any of your readers have on hand English or Scotch newspapers, may I ... suggest the propriety of addressing them to Mr Alex. Nicholson, teacher, on board H.M.S. Hercules, Rothesay.' Nicholson subsequently thanked Donald for the receipt of books and newspapers:

I do assure you the newspapers were duly appreciated by all on board, and the other periodicals were received with great pleasure... The emigrants are all quite well, and are resigned to their lot; they get excellent food, and are kindly treated. Nothing could excel the kindness and urbanity shown by Commander Baynton and the whole officers and crew towards the passengers since they came on board, and particularly during the terrible storms we encountered before coming here... Dr Carey's conduct during the storm was highly meritorious. His attention, civility, and superior medical abilities have gained for him the universal esteem of the emigrants.[19]

Donald added 'a number of the emigrants are very ill off for clothing... I intend to send them on Monday afternoon a bale of clothing; and should any friend send parcels here before 1 P.M. on Monday, they will be enclosed with the bale.' Subsequently,

Huge bales of old, and but partially worn clothes, have been gathered under the special superintendence of the Free Church Ladies' Society, and already the comfort arising therefrom is sufficiently evidenced in the grateful expressions of the recipients... Besides the clothes sent out, there have also been sums of money contributed, with which decided cost price bargains are being regularly had at the shop of Messrs. Munn and Stewart...

Loaves to the extent of about 400 each day are being sent off to them; butcher-meat to an enormous amount is regularly supplied; potatoes also of excellent quality have been shipped on board the vessel...

Notwithstanding the small-pox and mitigated fever have broken out in the vessel, we are glad to learn that the magistrates have not

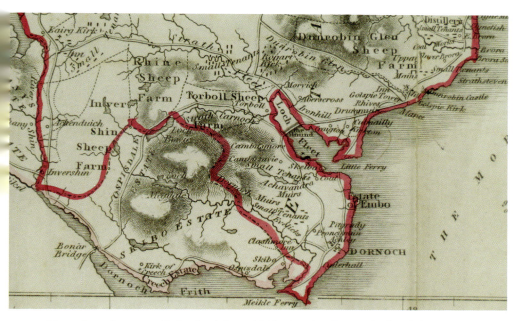

Map of south-eastern Sutherland from 1820, showing Dornoch, the Skibo Estate and the boundary of the Sutherland Estate.

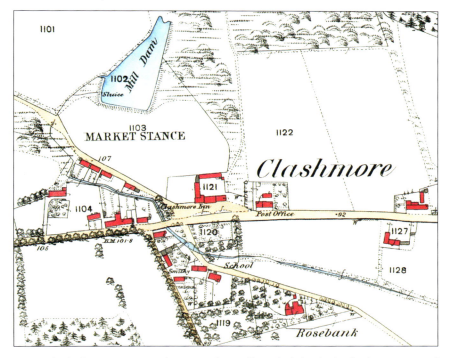

Map of Clashmore, surveyed 1874. The Miller of Skibo built the house S.E. of '1104;' his son John Ross built the house immediately west of the burn on the north side of the road, and son Donald Ross lived at Rosebank.

Dornoch in 1818 showing the cathedral and Dornoch Castle. The ruined west aisle of the cathedral is in the wrong place, it should be perpendicular to the spire. Donald Ross was baptised and married in the cathedral.

Dunrobin Castle based on a sketch by the Countess of Sutherland. The memorial statue of the 1st Duke of Sutherland can be seen on Ben Bhraggie to the right.

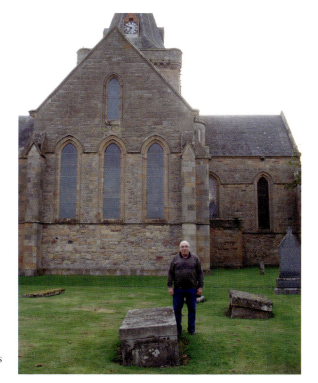

Right: The author's father, Malcolm Ross, next to the tablestone of his great-x3-grandfather, Donald Ross, the Miller of Skibo; in St Barr's Churchyard, on the east side of Dornoch Cathedral.

Below: The inscription on the Miller of Skibo's tablestone.

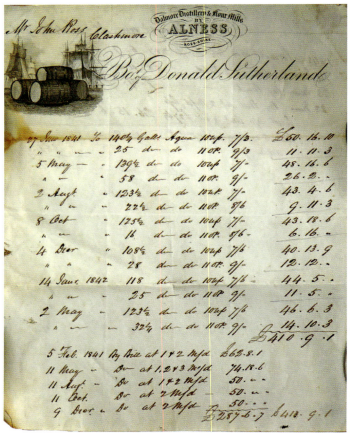

Above: St Andrew's Church, Golspie, where Donald's brother, John Ross was married to Catharine Sutherland in 1833.

Below: Part of John Ross's account with Dalmore Distillery, from January 1841 to May 1842.

The ruin of the old Golspie Flour Mill, looking east across Golspie Burn; where John Ross probably worked.

Above: John Ross's gravestone, in the old graveyard of the Church of the Holy Rood, Stirling, situated just to the west of the church tower.

Right: A Stirling Town Officer, late 19th century. John Ross was a Town Officer in the mid. 19th century and wore the same red uniform and black hat.

Above: Tibbermore Church, Perthshire, where May Bayne was baptised in 1796. May became Donald's wife though was 16 years older than him.

Below: Edinburgh in early 1850s, looking up Princes Street from Calton Hill; with the old town on the left and new town on the right. Foreground, right: Dugald Stewart Monument; skyline, left to right: Tron Church, St Giles Cathedral, Assembly Hall, Edinburgh Castle, St George's Church, St Andrew's Church; mid.-ground, left to right: Bridewell Prison, Martyrs' Monument, Scott Monument, Melville Monument.

Above left: Lord Cuninghame of the Supreme Court in Edinburgh, who decided against Donald's family in their eviction case, though awarded them nearly £30 in compensation and £70 expenses.

Above right: Old postcard of Dornoch Castle, which served as Dornoch Court and jail in the first half of the 19th century. Donald was imprisoned there twice. The newer jail, on the left, opened in 1850.

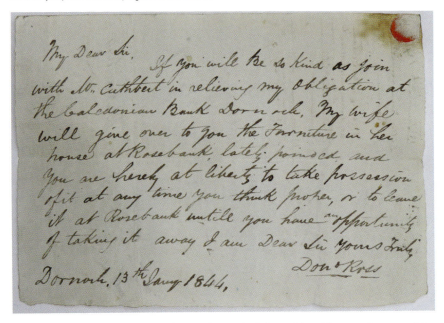

Letter from Donald to Alexander Graham, Ardalie, asking him to take away his furniture. Donald wrote this while in prison in Dornoch Castle.

Left: A later depiction of the Disruption procession from St Andrew's Church, Edinburgh on 18 May 1843 looking along George Street to the Melville Monument. The bank with the statues on the roof at the far side of St Andrew Square wasn't built until 1850.

Below: The grave memorial to Revs Angus and George Kennedy and their families, with the Free Church of Dornoch behind.

Above: Croick Church, N.N.W. of Glencalvie, where the victims of the Glencalvie Clearance camped in 1845 and scratched messages on the window.

Right: Grave memorial to Rev. Gustavus Aird at Migdale Free Church, Bonar Bridge, where he ministered for 53 years.

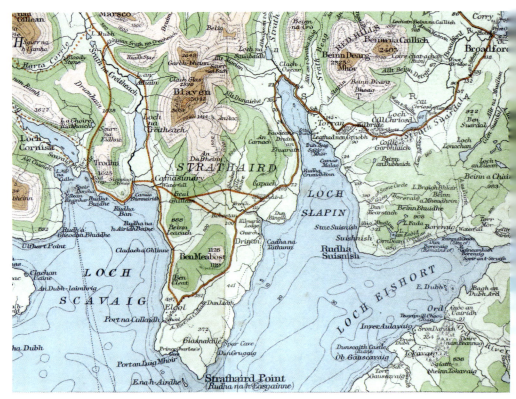

Map of the Strathaird Peninsula, Isle of Skye, showing the route that Donald took from Broadford to Elgol in 1850 and places he visited. He later wrote about evictions at Suishnish and Boreraig.

The ruins of Arinacraig next to Loch Slapin. Four families lived here when Donald visited in 1850.

Ruins of a blackhouse at Keppoch, Strathaird, cleared in 1852. Some of the ruins were obscured by a forestry plantation for 50 years until the trees were felled in 2017.

Loch Coruisk, Skye, which Donald described as having 'more terrific grandeur than Glencoe.'

Looking east from the Skye mainland towards the harbour of Isle Ornsay, where the *Sillery* left on 9 August 1853 with 332 people from Knoydart on board, destined for Canada.

Ruins of the cleared township of Niag-àrd, Knoydart, looking N.N.E. towards Inverguseran Farm.

Ruined blackhouse at Suishnish, Isle of Skye, looking west.

Entrance to a ruined blackhouse at Boreraig, Isle of Skye, with the door lintel still in place.

The River Carron, looking east from the mouth of Allt Greenyard, near where the Massacre of the Rosses took place.

Above left: Ann Ross of Langwell, victim No. 16 in the *Massacre of the Rosses*. Ann was beaten and jumped into the river to escape. She was rescued by her husband and later they emigrated to Australia where this photo was taken.

Above right: Lieutenant-General Sir Colin Campbell, who commanded the Highland Brigade in the Crimean War and ordered the 93rd Sutherland Highlanders to form 'The Thin Red Line' at the battle of Balaklava. Donald invited Sir Colin to attend a public dinner in Glasgow, but he declined.

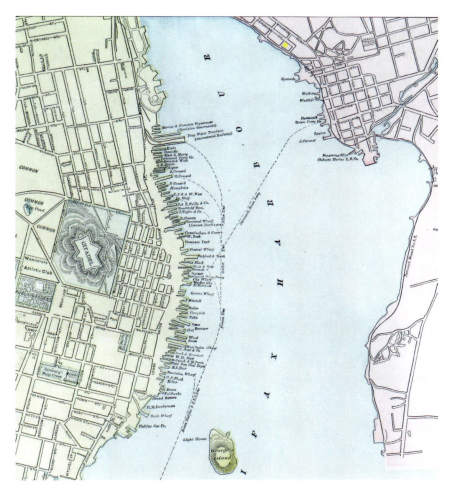

Above: Map of Halifax and Dartmouth, Nova Scotia. Donald was the bookkeeper for merchants Bauld, Gibson & Co., situated next to the ferry wharf in Halifax, and Donald would have used the ferry to commute. The position of his house in Dartmouth is marked in yellow, top right.

Right: John Stuart Blackie, Professor of Greek at the University of Edinburgh, to whom Donald wrote in 1865 praising him for his defence of the Gaelic language.

Above: The spectacle of the Marquis of Lorne and Princess Louise arriving in Halifax in 1878. In the lower view, from Dartmouth, Donald's house would have been just out of view on the right.

Left: Donald and May's gravestone in Dartmouth Common Cemetery.

been kept back from boarding her; but, on the contrary, have shown a well-timed and courageous zeal in ameliorating the condition of our less fortunate fellow-mortals.

...that never-failing friend of the Highlanders, Mr. Donald Ross, has been acting his part in a most creditable manner; for not only has he sent them donations, received from the benevolent in Glasgow, but on Monday [10 January] last he actually came down to this place, bringing with him a miniature mountain of cotton and woollen fabrics, suitable for the emigrants. He visited the vessel, and as was to be expected, received as welcome a reception as the kind-hearted sons of the Gael ever gave to one whom they knew to be their long and well-tried friend.[20]

The *Hercules* was stuck at Rothesay for over two weeks and finally set sail on 16 January. Donald wrote the following day:

I visited the Highland emigrants on board the Hercules a second time last week, and found many of them very ill off for clothing. Through the kindness of a few friends, I was enabled to provide for them upwards of 400 yards of good cotton for shirts and shifts, and several hundred yards of check derrys, and other suitable fabrics for frocks, gowns, trousers, &c. A number of ladies and gentlemen in Rothesay also contributed clothing for them; and although not last, not least, the Most Noble the Marchioness of Bute gave a considerable quantity of clothing to the poor emigrants.[21]

The British Friend added:

The poor creatures were exceedingly grateful for this timeous supply of clothing, and when they got their friend, Donald Ross, on board, it was no easy task for him to get away from them. It was only after many a firm shake-hands, and "*Beanachd leibh*" (Our blessings be with you), that this was accomplished. He also supplied the children with five dozen primers and six dozen second books, for their school on board.[22]

In response to Donald's article, James Chant of the Birkenhead Emigration Depot wrote to McNeill to say that the emigrants had been supplied with sufficient clothing.[23] '*Every person*, whether child or adult, had, when they went on board, Two *complete suits of exterior clothing, and* Six *changes of linen and stockings*, besides sheets, towels, soap, and new bedding. The beds and bedding were supplied by the Commissioners. The average amount of aid for outfit granted by the Society was 30s. per head.' Donald retorted 'I further assert, and offer to prove, that, either from neglect or mismanagement, the clothing referred to by Mr Chaunt [sic] was not given to the emigrants up to the time the Hercules left Rothesay... I could not be deceived with regard to them; for they stood before me, many of them literally in rags.'[24] However, McNeill ascertained that

> ...the emigrants embarked in the Hercules were supplied by the Society with clothing to the value of above £1000, in addition to all they had of their own, and were further supplied with a very considerable quantity, – three large boxes full, – sent to them from Brighton by ladies who had a bazaar there for the purpose... But it is true that at the moment of their arrival there [Rothesay], the greater part was not immediately accessible to them, for it was in their chests in the ship's hold, and could not be got at during the storm to which the ship had been exposed for the five days she had been out....
>
> After a day or two, the chests were got on deck, and were found to contain the quantity of clothing which, with what they had on and in their bags, made up the regulated outfit.

Sheriff-substitute Fraser added:

> By the regulations of the Emigration Commissioners, it is necessary that each male emigrant shall have at least two complete suits of exterior clothing, six shirts, six pairs of stockings, and two pairs of shoes; and that each female shall have six shifts, two flannel petticoats, six pairs of stockings, two pairs of shoes, and two gowns; while three sheets must be provided for each berth, and four towels, and two pounds of marine soap for each person...
>
> But, *in addition* ... they were supplied by our Society with materials for 150 nightgowns for children, 100 women's caps, and 100 pairs of stockings, to be made on board; besides an additional supply of materials, sent by the Emigrants' Friend Society.[25]

Nicholson wrote to Donald from Queenstown (now Cobh), County Cork, Ireland, on 20 January:

> On Wednesday morning it blew hard, with rain, and very little progress was done. Towards night it became worse, and about 12 o'clock it blew a perfect hurricane. We were by this time a considerable distance beyond Cape Clear. The sea was dreadful – rising mountains high; and, when she would give a lurch, it was with the greatest difficulty that the emigrants remained in their berths, by laying hold of anything they could get to support them... About 1 P.M. on Thursday morning a tremendous sea struck her and damaged her bows, and some of the females, imagining that she had struck on a rock, rushed upon deck with only their shifts on. It was then deemed prudent to put in here, which we managed about 3 P.M ... shortly before we left Campbelton a man died very suddenly on board, and just at the time we were leaving

HMS Hercules

Rothesay, on the 16th instant another man died equally sudden. Both men belonged to Sleat, and have left families; but these will be looked after... We have several cases of sickness on board, both among the emigrants and sailors, and the patients are all kindly attended to by Dr Carey, whose conduct towards us all deserves great praise.[26]

On 25 January it was reported that there were fifty to sixty cases of smallpox on board.[27] Two days later they were 'removed in large boats covered in with sails, which were towed' to 'the Naval Hospital at Haulbowline [Island] ... Dr Dunn, the Royal naval medical officer, had made every preparation to receive his patients.'[28]

After being at Queenstown for three weeks, on 11 February it was reported 'only one case of typhus has occurred, which proved fatal at the hospital... A great many cases of smallpox have appeared ... out of 70 and more attacked ... three of these, I am sorry to say have died since they landed at Haulbowline.'[29] By the 18 February 'they had on board 4 births, 1 marriage, 14 deaths, 130 cases of small-pox, and 3 cases of fever.'[30] On 11 March the *Cork Examiner* added that the ship was

> ... *cleansed* or *fumigated* with the remainder of the passengers on board... Up *to the present day* the healthy passengers have not been landed, numbering perhaps over 600. It is proposed to land them at the barracks or military hospital, but this place not possessing sufficient accommodation, a large shed is in course of erection for the purpose. About 140 persons have been removed from the vessel since she came into port, the fever patients to the hospital ship, and the small pox do. to Haulbowline.[31]

After being stuck at Queenstown for over six weeks Rev. John McTavish wrote:

> We wished to have a day of thanksgiving ... but were not able for nearly a fortnight. Meanwhile fever, of which we had one case early, made great progress, and our day of thanksgiving, when it came, was a day of humiliation ... for some days after both diseases increased, and two of the officers were seized... I am glad to be able to acknowledge that our sick were received into hospital, though the fever patients with difficulty. These latter are for some days sent on board of an old rotten hulk, which has been hired and fitted up as an hospital at a heavy expense. Some of its timbers are so decayed that I took pieces off with my hand, and so moist, that I could squeeze the water out by pressing them gently between my finger and thumb. This is deemed good enough for us, while large storehouses, under the control of the Admiralty, lie empty. We hear they would not suit, as they are damp!!!!...

One family, parents and child are dead. We have widows and orphans; sorrowing parents, brothers, and sisters. Our list of deaths includes twenty-six persons, or three per cent of our number. The fever and small-pox patients amount to about one hundred and fifty, or one in six. The painful feeling of anxiety and sorrow, with the watchings and fatigues undergone, have produced many cases of hysteria; and it is only wonderful to see the quiet, resigned, and generally cheerful disposition of the people amid all these trials.[32]

The remaining emigrants 'were all landed on Monday last [14 March] and quartered in a newly erected shed, and adjacent is an old building, for many years occupied as a military barracks or hospital. The arrangements are that they sleep only in the building, which is composed of a number of small rooms, and mess together in the shed, at the end of which there is a kitchen, and as the building will not afford sleeping-room for more than 400, about 250 will have to sleep in the shed.'[33] Dr Lawrence Carey died of fever, presumably typhus, on 30 March, aged 35 and was buried in the Old Church Cemetery in Cobh.[34]

The *Hercules* set sail from Queenstown on 14 April and after having 'had a fine passage ... lengthened by a succession of calms' it landed at Simon's Bay, Cape Town, South Africa, on 14 June.[35] Nicholson wrote a long letter while on board which was sent to Donald from the Cape.[36] He considered that if action had been taken sooner then there would have been less people taken ill 'and it seems to me a wonder that more were not affected by it.' Bringing the remaining people ashore had not helped as in the barracks 'there were upwards of 600 souls cooped up in them, and there was scarcely a room without fever in it.' He criticised Mr Chant who was keen to get the *Hercules* to re-embark. The symptom-free people were put back on board however several new cases of fever quickly broke out and five families had to be taken back to the barracks, but their luggage was left on board. 'Then a great many families were separated. Young lads and girls are on board here, while their parents and friends are in Ireland... I remonstrated with Mr Chant against going to sea so speedily, without waiting for a week or so on probation to see if the people were clear of fever or not.' McTavish was one of those who had caught the fever. 'This was a heavy stroke for us for we feel his absence very much, and all regret his staying behind... Although we have no minister, we are not without the means of grace. We meet twice a-day on Sabbath, and twice through the week for prayer meeting and devotional exercises.' Fever was 'still prevailing' when the *Hercules* arrived at the Cape. Nicholson provided a detailed list of the forty-seven people who had died.

Chant subsequently defended his actions by explaining that he had received 'an order from the Admiralty for the ship to proceed immediately' and where families were split up 'it was with the full consent of the parties concerned.'[37] 337 people had been left behind though were later put on other ships to Australia.

HMS Hercules

The *Hercules* set sail again on 20 June. After arrival in Australia, Baynton wrote to McNeill on 5 August:

> I have the honour to acquaint you with my arrival here on the 3d inst., from Adelaide, where I landed 192 emigrants [on 27 July], including two sappers and miners with their families; and at noon to-day the remainder were landed at Melbourne; amounting to 183 souls...
>
> You will be pleased to hear that our passage has been favourable – to Adelaide 102 days, and omitting seven days at Simon's Bay, Cape of Good Hope, only 95; during which time only seven deaths have taken place – one of an emigrant cook hired in London; and during the same time four births, one still-born. Sickness was prevalent during the third part of the passage, but we only lost three by death before our arrival at the Cape, and one during our stay there, and one woman and child since...
>
> I landed with the married people and single men at [Adelaide]... the single women having landed the day before under Dr. Duncan's charge, all of whom (the single women) I saw at Adelaide at the Depot quite well, and in good spirits. Almost all of them had got good places, from £20 to £25 a-year; and parties from the country had already arrived seeking for the married and single men, so that by this time few are without employment; but it was a great drawback their not speaking English.
>
> During the passage... In the afternoon the married women and children had the quarter-deck to themselves, where games of every kind were carried on without fear or restraint; and the officers deserve great credit for their forbearance in carrying on the duty without disturbing any one.
>
> Again, in the evening the quarter-deck was promenaded by the single women after their work; for none were idle, thanks to your supply of worsted, cotton, trimmings, &c. &c., which lasted until we made land near King George's Sound. The women were likewise engaged in making their own clothes, besides making white frocks for the seamen, trimmed with blue collars and rows of white tape, for which they received payment in shoes and money. During the whole time the emigrants have been on board, a friendly feeling has existed between them and the crew, and I think I can safely say no improper freedoms have taken place during their sojourn on board...
>
> After making the land, all the presents of books, &c., were impartially bestowed on the most deserving... All the emigrants had some little remembrance given to them before leaving the ship.[38]

The entire journey had taken just over seven months.

17
Weeping in the Isles

In 1852 the *Reformers' Gazette* published a letter from William Livingstone, Glasgow, who reported that on 20 May 'eleven young girls, whose names are under-noted, arrived here from Skye; and as it happened took up their quarters, by direction, where I at present lodge.' He asked them, in Gaelic, why they were there: 'Donald Ross, that noted philanthropist, sent for them, and that they are to be sent to Manchester to be educated. Q. What kind of education? – A. Reading, sewing, and other things, and that Mr. Ross is to conduct them thither... I asked them if any of them could write: one of them acknowledged that she could read and write both languages tolerably. Upon that declaration, I took their names and ages as follows:

Marion M'Crae, 14 Strath
Christian Nicholson, 16 Sleit [Sleat]
Mary Robertson, 14 Strath
Catherine Munro, 15 Strath
Marion Robertson, 15 Sleit
Catherine Robertson, 13 Sleit
Mary M'Kinnon, 12 Sleit
Mary Nicolson, 14 Sleit
Ann M'Kinnon, 14 Sleit
Isabella M'Donald, 14 Strath
Ann M'Nicol, 12 Sleit'[1]

Livingstone asked them other questions that they refused to answer, which he considered was suspicious. The *Gazette* added 'one of the girls, having mentioned Mr. Ross's name, apparently by inadvertence, seemed to check herself immediately, as if she had done something wrong, and then, like the others, maintained an obstinate silence... We cannot help thinking that some extraordinary game is going forward, and after the affair of the "Hebridean hen," and the "Industrial Benevolent Society," we must confess that our suspicions and apprehensions are of the worst kind.'

The episode was exposed the following year by Rev. John Forbes, Minister of Sleat, who published a book entitled *Weeping in the Isles*. A long section entitled 'A consoling address to bereaved parents' reads like a sermon and in the last section entitled 'Remarks on the industrial character of the Highland people,' Forbes argued that they were not 'indolent and lazy.'

This episode is a tangled web and out of three pamphlets that Donald wrote about it, only one has survived, and that was written in Gaelic. Forbes wrote 'Eleven young girls, varying from fourteen to eighteen years of age, four from the parish of Strath, and seven from the parish of Sleat, in the Island of Skye, were, with the consent of their parents, taken away to England in May, 1852, and placed in the factory of Messrs. W. and C. Walmsley, at Marple, near Manchester.' This was arranged by Donald and Francis ('Frank') Humberston Mackenzie, Broadford, who was one of the distributors of meal and clothing supplied by Donald. The village of Marple is nine miles S.E. of Manchester and four miles E.S.E. of Stockport. The factory was a cotton mill called Hollins Mill, which at that time was run by brothers William and Charles Walmsley, who lived with their mother Betty nearby at Hollins House. In 1851 the mill employed eighty people, most of whom were teenagers taken from workhouses around the country, though

The gravestone of Rev. John Forbes in Kilmore Churchyard, Isle of Skye. Forbes wrote the *Weeping in the Isles* and criticised Donald for taking eleven girls to work in a cotton mill in Marple, near Manchester, where one of them died.

children as young as six were also employed.[2] Only nine of the eleven girls were named in Forbes' book and their details differ from Livingstone's list:

Marian, 18, and Catherine Robertson; daughters of Ewen and Catherine Robertson, 'Tarskveg' (Tarskavaig), Sleat, who had two sons and six daughters, including Alexander ('Sandie').
Christina, 17, and Mary Nicolson, 15; daughters of Angus Nicolson, 'Drimfern' (Drumfearn), Sleat, who had five children.
Mary M'Kinnon, 15; daughter of widower Miles M'Kinnon, 'Tarskveg.'
Anne or Ann M'Kinnon, 15; daughter of widow Flora M'Kinnon, 'Tarskveg.'
Catrina Munro, Strath.
Isabella Macdonald, daughter of Donald Macdonald, 'Sculamus' (Scullamus), Strath.
Sarah Macrae, Broadford, Strath.

Forbes mentioned that their parents 'thought themselves very fortunate at first in getting such an opening for their children; they regarded it as a great favour, and were thankful for it.' However,

> On the 23d August last, Ewen Robertson and his wife, Miles M'Kinnon, and Widow Flora M'Kinnon, residing in Tarskveg, in this parish, called upon me at the manse here, and told me that they had bad accounts from their daughters at Marple ... they came to get my advice as to the best way of getting back their children, stating at the same time, that the parents of the girls from Strath were equally anxious to get their children brought home. I stated to them at once that I was very unwilling to interfere in the matter, and advised them to apply to the party to whom they had intrusted their children...To this the parents answered, that they had applied to Mr. F. H. M'Kenzie, and that he refused to restore the girls. Then, said I, your best plan is to apply to the persons who have charge of them at present... I do not wish to have any thing further to do with the matter. The parents having, after hearing this, got greatly excited, began to weep bitterly for their absent children, and urgently besought me to write on their behalf to Messrs. W. & C. Walmsley...
> On the 7th of September, I received a letter from Mr. F. H. M'Kenzie, this cottager at Broadford, in which he says – "On Saturday I received a letter from Messrs. Walmsley of Marple, in which they enclose a letter written to them by you on the 24th ult, making a peremptory demand on them to return immediately four young females from Sleat, now in their employ. These girls, and seven others who accompanied them, volunteered to go with the consent of their parents..." When the parents called again, and they called very frequently, I told them all that Mr. M'Kenzie said in his letter to me, and advised them not to be rash in demanding the girls. But his explanation did not satisfy them; they said, that they must hear from the employers of the girls themselves.[3]

Forbes wrote a second letter to the Walmsleys on 17 September: 'I have told them what Mr. M'Kenzie says in his letter to me, that you offer to defray the expense of any suitable person whom they may choose to send to see how their daughters are treated; and that he has a letter from one of the girls from the parish of Strath to her father, to this effect, "that they are all well and comfortable." ... but it appears that the only satisfaction which the parents of the girls from this parish require, is to have their daughters returned to them.' On not receiving a reply Forbes wrote a third letter on 13 October: 'I am directed by these people to acquaint you, that unless their daughters are sent back to them, or satisfactory reason given for detaining them, within a fortnight of this date, it is their intention to petition the Secretary of State for the Home Department for his assistance in this matter.' The Walmsleys replied that they had forwarded the letter to Donald 'as the only party we know in this matter.' Forbes pointed out that Donald could not be 'the only party' as they had sent his first letter to Mackenzie.

One of the parents, Miles Mackinnon, 'was preparing to go to Australia; and being desirous of taking his daughter [Mary], along with him, and the emigrant ship being daily expected, the parent was very uneasy, fearing that he would be obliged to go away without his child.' The Inspector of the Poor for Sleat Parish wrote to the Walmsleys on 16 October asking for her immediate return and offering to refund her travel costs. Forbes received a letter from Donald dated 23 October: 'You may therefore inform the parents, that the girls will be delivered up to them at Marple when they choose to call for them, or when they send a person duly authorized to receive them; and no further notice will be taken of their *silly paper kites*, nor yet of your inflated threat of petitioning the Home Secretary.' Forbes replied that he would 'communicate its contents to the parents.'[4]

Meanwhile, Marian Robertson died on 21 October. Her sister, Catherine, wrote to their parents at the beginning of November: 'I am not well, but I hope and trust in God I soon shall be better. Marian is dead, I am sorry to tell you; but I hope she is better off than any one in this world. I should like to see you very much, dear father.' She requested money so she could return home.[5]

In November there appeared a long article in the *Gazette*, which included mentions of the various letters:

The girls were all young – from thirteen to eighteen years of age – and their emigration to England occurred at a time when a very disreputable traffic was known to exist between certain parties in England and others in France, leading to the degradation and ruin of hundreds of unfortunate victims like the Skye girls...

We think he [Donald] might carry his philanthropy just a little farther. Why not send them a little money to help defray the expenses of the "duly authorised agent," and likewise the travelling expenses of the girls back to Skye? ... the agitated state of the poor people in Skye, who are now imploring the restoration of their children, and the earnest solicitations made with that object in view, are treated by Mr. Donald Ross with contempt.[6]

Forbes reported that Mackenzie had gone to Marple and in 'his opinion they all appeared to be well pleased; and he does not say that any of them expressed a wish to return to Skye.' Apparently, before he went, the parents of four of the girls asked him to bring them back, but he didn't. Neither did he mention that one of the girls had died. Messrs Walmsley wrote to Donald and stated 'that Alexander Robertson had with their consent taken away three of the girls, and that he said, "if he had known how kindly the girls were treated, he would not have come from Skye for them, had they been his own children."' Another letter to Donald, dated 6 December, was from James Hibbert, Marple, who, along with Rev. J. B. Dickson 'visited the children at Marple, and found them in a very healthy condition.' Yet another letter to Donald was from Rev. Alexander Munro, Manchester, dated 8 December, who visited Marple 'In consequence of certain representations made in a Scottish newspaper, as well as in letters from ministers and others chiefly in Skye.' Forbes mentioned that Munro gave 'a favourable report of what he had seen.'[7] However, the *Gazette* demurred:

> They were kept working like slaves – for what are the factory girls but *white* slaves? ... The person who was sent to take them back to their parents states that he found them suffering severely from hard treatment, and that in respect of food and other matters they could not have been worse off in a prison. One of them had actually pined and died under the severe ordeal; another had lost one of her fingers... The individual above-mentioned took three of them away... He desired the Messrs. Walmsley to send them all home, but they refused to do so. They declined also to pay one penny for the passage home of the three, and even demanded back the clothes with which the girls had been furnished.[8]

Forbes mentioned that a pamphlet was circulating in Skye

> ...dated Glasgow, 16th December, 1852, and signed "Donald Ross." It contains a series of letters, vindicating the character of Messrs. W. & C. Walmsley and their establishment, with a tissue of abuse, a tirade of the lowest personal invective and most vulgar language against individuals in Skye, who had simply written a few respectful letters at the request of the parents of the girls to Messrs. W. & C. Walmsley...

> The *first letter* in the poor pamphlet before us is by Mr. Donald Ross himself. He submits it as copy of the letter which he wrote to the minister of Sleat on the 23d October, 1852, from which it differs in several points. For example, he says, in the copy which he published, "I am assured by parties who have seen the girls, one of them a minister, that the treatment which they have received was very good." In his letter to the minister of Sleat, the above sentence runs thus – "I am assured by parties who have occasionally seen the girls, that the treatment which

they have received was very good." ... Perhaps he thought the people of Skye are so obtuse, that they cannot detect egregious blunders, or so simple, that they will believe any thing, seeing he denominates their letters as "silly paper kites."[9]

Donald's pamphlet was entitled *The Skye Girls in England* and included the letters mentioned above from Mackenzie, the Walmsleys, Hibbert and Munro. Forbes indicated that the sixth letter was from Donald and wrote:

> Is it not the fact, says the writer of this pamphlet, "that the editor" [of the *Gazette*] ... or a "notorious speculator in twaddle and slander," as he is called in a preceding clause by the same foaming writer – "at first darkly hinted, that the girls were sent to England for immoral purposes, and that from England they were likely to be conveyed to France, to be disposed of there? ... and a great deal more of palpable untruths." O writer, have a care what you say. Is it a palpable untruth, that Marian Robertson died and was buried at Marple, and that her sister's finger was made useless there? Is it a palpable untruth, that the sister came home broken-hearted, and was unable to leave her bed till she died a few weeks after her return to Skye? These are melancholy facts, and not "untruths" or "slander."[10]

On 17 December Donald wrote two letters to the newspapers, though neither were mentioned by Forbes. One was to the *Gazette*:

> The Skye girls were not sent to Marple, as you allege, to learn "sewing, knitting, &c." They were sent to learn to earn an honest livelihood under the care of the Messrs. Walmsley, and the conditions on which they were received were fully explained to the girls, and to their parents, by the Rev. Mr. M'Queen of Haripool, in Skye, and by Mr. Mackenzie of the same place.
>
> It is not true that the girls *"were kept working like slaves."* They only wrought nine or ten hours a day, and they had the rest of the time for instruction, amusement, or recreation...
>
> It is grossly untrue that any of the girls from Skye, in Messrs. Walmsley's employment, were found by any one "suffering severely from hard treatment," or from want of food, as is stated in your paper. The whole girls were most kindly treated – their work is exceedingly light, and their food, which they have in abundance, is of the best description...
>
> It is not true, as you allege, that one of the girls died in consequence of *hard treatment*, and defective food, and "pined away," as you say, "under the severe ordeal." The girl died of *synochus*, *i. e.* of fever of the *very worst* kind, and this is certified by the medical gentleman who attended her during her illness...

> One of the girls had got her finger hurt (not *"lost,"* as is stated in your paper), by incautiously handling a mangle...
>
> Three of the girls have been brought home by their parents and the parochial authorities – not on the ground of any ill treatment the girls received at Marple, but because their parents are going to Australia...
>
> The Messrs. Walmsley were not bound to send the girls home to Skye at the bidding of the Sleat minister, or at the request of any other busy body; and, the parents were duly informed that if they wanted to remove their children without assigning any reason for doing so, that they must just remove them at their own expense.[11]

The *Gazette* defended itself by stating 'we published the statement he complains of on the authority of information transmitted to us by the parish minister of Skye, and other competent authorities.'

Donald's second letter was to the *NBDM* with copies of Munro's and Hibbert's letters, 'containing a complete refutation of the wicked and calumnious allegations with reference to the treatment of Skye Girls at Marple,' which he asked to be published. Hibbert's letter was short, Munro's was long and detailed:

> I found that three of the girls had been removed and taken home by the authority of their parents and others – also that one who, it appears from the statement of her friends, was naturally consumptive had died. She died however of *fever*, having received the best medical care. She was decently interred, and her sister put into a becoming suit of mourning. Five of the girls were pointed out to me employed with a number of other young persons in the winding room. The apartment was ample in dimensions, well aired; and with a temperature as agreeable as that of a family parlour. Their employment was light, consisting merely of placing and displacing bobbins, and preserving the continuity of the threads. The Skye girls, as well as all the rest, were well and sufficiently clothed, with pinafores worn over while at work. Instead of being pale and thin, as is often the case in town mills, the girls, with their bright washed faces and smoothed hair, in some instances put up in silken nots or fancy handkerchiefs, looked ruddy and plump. I saw the sixth girl who was older and stouter than the rest, working in the carding room, which was scrupulously clean and well aired...
>
> I desired the six girls to be taken up to the house, where they are lodged and kept, which is about three hundred yards from the mill, and as far from their employers' dwelling. The house is formed of a set of two storey cottages. It contains a kitchen with suitable conveniences; a large hall where all the girls take their meals, with sleeping apartments on the second floor. A respectable, kind, and intelligent person as Matron, assisted by several servants, takes charge of the whole. My friend and I had an interview with her and the Skye girls in her own

room. I questioned her closely as to the management and treatment of her charge, and took a note on the spot of the following particulars, namely – that the girls go to work at 6 o'clock – that they then receive a large morning piece of bread – that at 8 they come in to breakfast, consisting of as much flour bread as they please, with a pint of the best sweet milk, and bread and cheese, or butter, afterwards. That at 12 they come in to dinner – bread and beef with potatoes, sometimes also broth – and on Sundays a pudding. That they leave the mill at 6 o'clock, when they have coffee with bread and butter, and at 9 they retire to bed – that on Saturdays the mill stops at 2 o'clock – and that their appetite is always excellent. The Matron showed us specimens of their week day shoes and stockings, and clothes, with their Sunday cloth boots and dresses, consisting of Merinoes, Alpacas, and such stuffs, all of good material and workmanship.

We ascertained likewise that when these girls came to Marple several of them could scarcely speak a word of English – that the Master of Marple Grammar School attended regularly to give them lessons every Monday evening – that on Sunday they statedly attend Church – that on Sunday evenings one of the brothers of Messrs W. & C. Walmsley, a member of the University of Cambridge preparing for the ministry, kindly instructs them with the other girls in the Holy Scriptures, conducting with them suitable devotional exercises; and that, as one consequence of all this care, they now speak and read English with moderate ease...

I examined their sleeping apartments. These are whitewashed, well-aired, and sufficiently commodious. The beds and bed clothes are scrupulously clean and fresh. The girls as they sat before us appeared in the best possible condition – healthy and vigorous in frame, with clear complexions and easy, untroubled aspects. On being questioned, they said they were well treated and comfortable... The seventh girl we saw at Messrs Walmsley's own dwelling, into which she, as the most tractable and alert of the group has been taken, to wait at table and perform other light work, and who looks fresh and strong, distinctly stated that she was quite happy, and had no wish to return to Skye.[12]

In January 1853 *The Glasgow Sentinel* considered Donald's pamphlet 'set at rest the charges brought against Mr Donald Ross in the case of the Skye girls.'[13] Conversely, another article in the *Gazette* questioned Donald's and Mackenzie's philanthropy; 'But how did it happen that the Messrs. Walmsley never condescended to inform the parents of the girl who died at Marple of their sad bereavement?'[14] Forbes published a statement from Alexander Robertson:

> I went to Marple in November last, to take home my sister Catherine, Mary M'Kinnon, and Anne M'Kinnon... William Walmsley led me to

the doctor, who said to me that my sister Marian died of fever. After that, one of the servants in Messrs. Walmsley's cooking-house told me that my sister was putting out blood, and that she had no fever... He took from them their new frocks and shoes, and sent them away with old dirty frocks and old shoes, but his mother kindly gave a black frock and bonnet to my sister. I never said to Mr. W. Walmsley, or any other person, that 'if I had known how kindly the girls were treated, I would not have come from Skye for them, had they been my own children.'[15]

Mary Mackinnon, along her widowed father Miles and six siblings, boarded HMS *Hercules*. Miles was 'Found dead in his Berth on the 26th of December, & interred at Campbeltown,' which was the day it set sail. He was the first person on the list of those who had died sent to Donald by the schoolmaster.[16]

Forbes wrote: 'The remaining Skye girls who were sent to Marple in 1852, were taken home by their friends in the beginning of January last, except one [Sarah Macrae], who has been employed as a domestic servant; and that one has since come home, in consequence of bad health.' He included declarations made by the parents and girls, most of which 'were made before a Justice of the Peace.' Catherine Robertson declared on 26 January 1853 that Mackenzie had

> ...promised that a woman was to accompany me and others to that place; that when there, I was to work four hours every day, and during the rest of the day was to be in school learning reading, writing, knitting and sewing; that I was to receive three shillings every week; and that I was to be sent home at the expense of my employers whenever I and my parents might desire it... While we remained in the steam-boat at Glasgow, Mr. Donald Ross came to us and took charge of us... He gave us lodging, and food, and some clothing, and took us to Manchester, from which he sent us forward to Marple, saying he would follow us thither; but this he did not do. While there, I went to work at six o'clock in the morning, and left off each evening at six o'clock. When at work, I was frequently and severely struck. This was done with a thing that was like a stick,* but was not a stick; it also resembled leather, but was not leather (* This instrument is supposed to have been made of *gutta percha*). A stroke of it caused very great pain. As, though I understand a good deal of English, but cannot speak it much, I could not defend myself by telling that girls near me were putting their *waste* among mine, and I suffered much on this account. After we succeeded in getting intelligence sent home of our unhappiness, and it was known at Marple that we had done so, I and the rest were punished much more severely. My sister Marian was violently struck on both sides of her head, and cried out that she was done for. She was immediately taken unwell, and from that day grew worse, and at last died... When I came away, all my best clothes were taken from me, but Mrs. Walmsley gave me a bonnet

and a frock. The masters refused to give any money to help me home; and during all the time I was in the factory, I received only 11d. in all. I reached home in great weakness, and do not expect to recover, or to live many weeks.[17]

The day after giving her declaration, Catherine was 'worn down to a mere skeleton, lying on a small couch at the fireside.' The other declarations were in a similar vein. Ann Mackinnon, and Christina and Mary Nicolson declared 'William Walmsley came to us, and seeing us in distress and very sad, he warned us not to be thinking of getting home, for that he would get our heads cut off if we attempted it.' Mary Nicolson died on 11 February 'a few weeks after her return home' and Catherine Robertson died eight days later. Forbes indicated there were rumours 'that Ewen Robertson's daughters have died of consumption, and that this disease has been hereditary in their family. We are credibly informed, that none of the girls has died of such a disease.'[18] Sarah Macrae, the last girl to return, declared on 7 April:

I continued at Marple till the 30th of March last, having been employed in the house of my employers till the last fortnight... I wrote to my father to take me home, for I had become very unwell. When my father applied to Mr. Ross at Glasgow, that gentleman gave a letter, and I was sent home. I was sent to Glasgow, when coming home, at the expense of my masters; and in Glasgow, and coming from thence home, my expenses were paid by Mr. Ross... I received as wages not 2s. 6d., but only 1s. a-week, and with the money I thus got I bought clothes. When I came away, part of the clothes I had thus bought was taken from me, and also all I had got from Mrs. Walmsley. If I had known how I was to be when at Marple, I would on no account have gone.[19]

Forbes added 'There is no account in her declaration of such hard usage as the other girls give in their declarations. She was sent home, and her expenses paid, as soon as her return was demanded... Why did they not treat the other girls in the same way?' Forbes declared 'we are fully prepared to bear all the reproaches which any designing man may fabricate against us for faithfully and fearlessly discharging our duty to our country.'[20]

In August several reviews of Forbes' book appeared. The *Fifeshire Journal* wrote:

We do not know how much Messrs Ross and M'Kenzie pocketed on the transaction, or what the Messrs Walmsley paid for this petit cargo of mill-workers; but we are told that the girls got no education, that they were kept like slaves, wrought like slaves, and beaten like slaves, and that in six months one had died, and others were in such a condition, as if not soon released, they might be expected to die too... Messrs Walmsley stripped these poor girls of their clothes and sent them half naked in *mid winter* from Marple to Skye – where another died shortly after reaching home... It would be interesting to know whether or not a willing Lord Advocate could not bring Messrs. Ross and M'Kenzie to account for this transaction.[21]

The *Church of Scotland Magazine and Review* considered 'the excellent author deserves high credit for his kind-hearted efforts' on behalf of the girl's parents. The *Elgin Courant* concluded 'a very strong case has been made out against the parties implicated,' and the *Montrose Standard* hoped the book would 'draw the attention of those in authority to the iniquities sometimes perpetrated under the mask of philanthropy and benevolence.'[22] The *John o' Groat Journal* wrote that Forbes' book contained

> ...a full exposure of a system of white slavery suffered by young girls allured from their homes in Skye, in consequence of false promises made them of good wages and easy work in England... "Donald Ross," *alias* "Scotus," is mixed up with the affair... This is the patriot who is to emancipate the Highlands from thraldom. The old adage "Save us from our friends," may well be used by the deluded islanders.[23]

A correspondent on Skye wrote to the *Inverness Courier* and referred to the episode as a 'pamphlet war.' He had not seen Donald's first pamphlet but was informed that

> ...a regular onslaught was made on the minister of Sleat, for reasons I cannot conceive... Within the last few days copies of the title-page of a Gaelic pamphlet, in reply, have been sent to this quarter from Glasgow; and if the pamphlet, which is said to be "in the press," comes up in its matter and spirit to the title-page, it will prove one thing at least, that the Gaelic language, which is well known to be remarkably well adapted to the purposes of poetry, devotion, eloquence, reasoning, and rhetoric, is also as suitable for the purposes of sarcasm, scorn, and criticism of the severest kind.[24]

Donald's Gaelic pamphlet was entitled *Am Ministear air "An lair mhaide,"* literally translated as 'The Minster on the cross-pole,' and included quotes of lines by the Gaelic poet Rob Donn. The title page features a cartoon of the minister 'riding the stang'– sitting astride a long pole being carried aloft by two Highlanders. This was an old punishment of Scandinavian origin.[25] The English preface of *Am Ministear* stated:

> From the interference of John Forbes, Minister of Sleat, Skye, along with a few others, the poor girls who were so kindly treated, had plenty of food, and the prospect of soon earning 8s. or 9s. a week, were brought home to the cold and poverty stricken island of Skye, where two of

them died – it is said from the effects of a sudden change from strong, wholesome English food, to shell-fish and poor potatoes. The other girls, who, no doubt suffered much poverty during winter and spring in Skye, are now ... most anxious to get back to Marple, and are asking the Messrs Walmsley to send money to take them back. Mr John Forbes Minister of Sleat, having written a most calumnious and senseless Pamphlet about the Skye girls, alleging they were ill-treated in England, the following publication in Gaelic is given to the poor people of Skye to meet that charge; and also that they may know who are really their friends.

The Skye correspondent was not wrong about the use of Gaelic. Translated, Donald considered Forbes' book to be

> ... composed of lies, abuse, quarrel, malice, treachery, idle talk and as much corruption and ignorance as could be mustered...
> I would not like to hunt down any minister, but this hypocrite is worth of having his hide skinned and having his lying mouth shut. His black cassock or the '*poloni*' (his suit of armour) will not save the minister's back from the punishment whip, and his '*position*' (his situation) will not free him from his lies being returned to his own door.

Donald expanded on his version of events and added that he informed Forbes that if any of the parents wished to travel to Marple, he would pay their travel expenses plus food and drink for the whole week, but none of the parents took him up on the offer. He reproduced, in Gaelic, a substantial part of Munro's report and,

> Mr Forbes was aware of all of this, but he continued without regard on his self-righteous path, stirring up the children's parents against the people who employed them in *Marple* and against both myself and Mr Mackenzie in Broadford ... which he continued until he got the poor girls back to the Isle of Skye which resulted in their deaths from malnutrition!! ... The honest and respectable gentlemen of *Marple* who employed the girls on the Isle of Skye can treat the minister and his friend's malevolence with contempt and we are more than ready to prove him a liar in any Court of Law.

Donald was highly critical of Forbes' 'consoling address':

> A godly person will accept anything that is offered as spiritual comfort but the first thing they will do after reading the "Address of Condolence" is to throw it in the fire...
> Oh, John, John, you are the one that needs a sermon that would reach your vile black heart. You were previously a member of the

Donald Ross and the Highland Clearances

Temperance Society, and when you broke your pledge of sobriety, you would certainly relish the glass-full that would gladden your heart. You would greedily partake a scoop of the best Ferintosh, Glenlivet or Talisker and how you would lick your lips thereafter! ... Recently, we asked a very devout man what he thought of the minister's "*Consoling Address*" and he was of the opinion that the publication was evil and akin to the author... He further states that it was a satanical attempt to corrupt the minds of Christian people with his noxious work.

Donald criticised Forbes for not standing up when the people were suffering:

John, if you are so affected by grief, why did you not shed a tear for the scores, indeed the hundreds of poor Gaels who were evicted from their land on the Isle of Skye and who were brought to the brink of death by famine... You were aware, John, that many other people that you knew on the Isle of Skye died on board the *Hercules*. However, you did not weep then.

Donald then counteracted some of Forbes' statements:

(1) He states that the girls were promised a weekly wage if they went to *Marple*. That is false, as no wage was offered until they became competent at the work appointed to them.

(2) He states that the girls were not given good care in *Marple* and that their overseers treated them harshly. That is another lie. The girls were given ample food and drink plus clothing and they were treated very kindly by their overseers...

(3) The Minister states that their overseers kept them working for ten hours daily for months and finally sent them home without any money for travelling costs (without a "bawbee" as he put it.) That is another lie. The girls were not working for months on end for ten hours per day and when Mr John Robertson came to take them home, the masters gave both him and the girls provisions plus thirty shillings for their travel costs... On our table is a receipt from Mr Robertson for the money and acknowledgement in regard of the girl's good condition...

(4) The minister further stated that one of the girls died at Marple through neglect. That is a lie so evil that it is worthy of Satan's own fabrication. The girl died of fever after being ill for three weeks and had she been a member of high society, she would not have received better medical care and attention...

(5) The minister stated that another two girls died a few weeks after returning home from *Marple* to which he attributed their demise to the poor conditions they had suffered there. This is another lie. When the girls left *Marple*, they were in excellent health and the letter which Mr Robertson gave regarding the reasons why they

left *Marple*, he attests to their good health and that they were getting plenty food and clothing...

(6) The minister states that the girls were kept working like slaves for months and the masters would bully them without mercy and that one of them even threatened to cut their heads off... This is another blatant and senseless lie. The girls were far better off than if they were living within the Sleat Minister's own house...

Donald said that the girls wanted to return to Marple and included letters in English from and to Sarah Macrae.

Broadford, 20th April, 1853.
I am glad to let you know that I arrived safe at home, and this place not pleasing me so well as Marple – my sister says that she will go out with me to Marple if she will get work in the house or Mill, and I will go with her, when I told my mother the place I was in she was sorry for taking me home...

Marple, 17th May, 1853.
Messrs. Walmsley are agreeable to receive Sarah M'Rae, her sister, and Isabella M'Donald; but they will not take the responsibility of bringing them back to Marple.[26]

Donald then went on to criticize the girls' declarations:

Forbes does much boasting about the *Declarations* within his book, but we are putting it to you that they are totally without credit. The words which the Minister and his genial friends are putting in the girl's mouths are betraying their author. Reasonable people are aware of how easy it is to persuade naïve children to sign a document when asked to do so by someone in authority. The girls are now writing of their own accord to *Marple* in the hope that their masters will take them back; this merely highlights the fabrications within the *Declarations*, which the girls were made to sign.

Donald ended the main text with reference to 'riding the stang':

The Gaels ... will lift you on to their shoulders, and from there the Gaels will be able to verify your precarious position and the vulnerability of your *poloni*. But John, I won't keep you any longer as the men are coming with the Cross-pole and Murdo says that you will be shortly lifted upon, but keep in good spirit John as it is flexible, and the bearers are strong.

Then followed a fictitious conversation between three men and Forbes. This was a pop at a book that Forbes had written about English and Gaelic.[27] In the conversation Forbes is the 'Grammatist.'

> *Grammatist*. And what is your opinion of the book?
> *Ewen*. I can inform you that your Gaelic is poor and full of errors.
> *Kenneth*. It is so full of mistakes and drivel that no adult or child can understand it. Academics will denounce it at first sight and the uneducated will remain so after wasting their time in reading it in the forlorn hope of finding new information about English and Gaelic.

Am Ministear ended with a long poem of 18 stanzas written by a 'friend' which again mocked Forbes. Translated, the second stanza reads:

Since you went horse riding,
On top of the Cross-pole;
Try and reach Marple,
Where you'll be made aware of your slander,
And the foul-mouthed lies,
You told about the girls;
And you'll see your deceit.

An English version of the pamphlet was advertised at the end of August, to be published shortly:

> Humanity Defended and Calumny Refuted; Being a Review of, and Reply to, a very Fallacious Pamphlet recently circulated by John Forbes, Minister of Sleat, Skye, entitled, "Weeping in Isles," with important Documents, showing the Mis-statements and Slanders in the Minister's Pamphlet; as well as a thorough Exposure of his ingratitude. By Scotus.[28]

When published it was advertised as being authored by Donald Ross.[29] Apart from the mention in the *John o' Groat Journal* above of Donald using the alias 'Scotus,' the *Inverness Advertiser* reported 'Donald Ross (writing under the signature of Scotus),' and the *JOGJ* also wrote 'We have ever deprecated the blind manner in which many evictions have been carried out in the Highlands; but had the people listened to sound advice, instead of to the counsels of such demagogues as Donald Ross *alias* "Scotus," they would, in nearly every instance, have averted the calamities which befel [sic] them.'[30] So what else had Donald written using this pseudonym? This is hard to ascertain as there were at least three other people using this alias in the 1850s. Articles that could have been written by Donald are of course those that are on the same subjects that he was writing about under his own name and at the same time. Even then it is by no means certain. A letter in *The Times* from 'Scotus' about Skye triggered follow-up articles, however this 'Scotus' referred to the 'principal proprietor' of Skye as 'my relative.'[31] The *Glasgow Free Press* reviewed a pamphlet entitled 'The Poor Man's Guide to Parochial Relief... By Scotus. Glasgow: Archibald Sinclair.'[32] This must have been by Donald as he was experienced in this subject and given that he had been banned from the courts it is understandable why he had not used his own name. It is no coincidence that the same publisher published *Am Ministear* and *Humanity Defended* that same year. Unfortunately, this is another ephemeral publication that does not appear to have survived. The review commenced 'This is a lucid, concise, and well written pamphlet, and contains much useful, and, in many respects, necessary information regarding the poor and their legal rights, and is calculated to do much good, by enabling the pauper to become his own lawyer.' Corroboration can be found in Donald's later pamphlet *Real Scottish Grievances* where he quoted a Highland Sheriff: 'I beg to thank you for the pamphlets. The "Poor Man's Guide" will be very useful here, for I have seen more than enough to satisfy me, that many of the Parochial Boards are grinding the faces of the poor.'[33]

Humanity Defended was extensively reviewed by the *Fife Herald* and quoted additional letters, however the reviewer had not seen a copy of Forbes' book:

…it is for this mass of misrepresentation and calumny that Mr Ross makes the minister "ride the stang." There may be a lack of literary refinement in Mr Ross's style; but he is evidently a man of very great ability, and we have seldom, if ever, witnessed a severer punishment than that which he inflicts on poor Mr Forbes…

The cruel "bondage" to which the girls were doomed at Marple is entirely a fiction. Mr Forbes attempts no proof. Mr Ross, on the other hand, gives copious evidence that the labour was in all respects light and pleasant. Two letters, from the girls themselves, when in the midst of the "inhuman oppression," express full contentment. We give one of these from Neil Nicolson:–

"Dear father and Uncle … This place is very good, and plenty trees in it and plenty houses in the town. We are keeped very clean, and *must* wash our face and hans always before meat and at night too, and we go to church two times on Sabbath day. Master go first, and then the servants, and we go with the England lasses, and all very clean Sabbath frogs [frocks], and bonnets and bots [boots] on all of them and on us. Sarah was take to the house as servant. Plenty meat here, coffy, an bread an butter, and chese, and white bread, and good dinar, bef and potatus, and broth, and other meats. Bella Macdonald she is very fat, and al the girls is strong too… I is very well just now, and all the girls is very well, and good health…"

[Sarah Macrae on 8 March] wrote to her father describing her comforts, and urging him to send back her sister to be "happy like me." His reply, however, shows that he was in the hands of designing men:–

"Broadford, 14 the March 1853.
My Dear Daughter:– I send you these few lions [lines] to let you know that we had the fefer [fever], thank god that we are getting beter and

hops this will find you the same... I thought your mother would Dy and now let you tel me of you are for coming home ... plenty die here Cirty Fowls is dead and got the fefer, and Bel Mac Donald hes got the fefer ... John Macrae."

...the punishment, due to the calumniator, has been so vigorously inflicted by Mr Donald Ross, that the offence is not likely to be repeated or imitated. The prospect of being made to "ride the stang," will deter the boldest minister.[34]

The *Glasgow Sentinel* considered 'Mr Ross has furnished a satisfactory and complete answer to his accussers [sic], and in several essential particulars turned the tables fairly against them.'[35] The *Northern Ensign* considered Donald's pamphlet to be 'without exception, the most complete, satisfactory, unanswerable, and triumphant defence we have ever read... The pamphlet is 42 pages, each of which mangles and crushes the statements of Mr. Forbes, and leaves him not only without a leg to stand upon, but without even the shadow of a crutch on which to lean.'[36] The most thorough review was by Hugh Miller in *The Witness*, which was similar to the *Fife Herald* article, though more guarded and with additional quotes. Miller compared Sarah Macrae's declaration from *Weeping* with her two letters to home, quoting more from her letter of 8 March: 'I am very well, I like this place very much. Mrs Walmsley is very kind to me. She a very nice lady, master is the same.' Also quoted was a final letter from Messrs Walmsley: 'We have suffered so much annoyance and loss from the Skye people, that we are not disposed to have anything more to do with them in any shape whatever. How a minister should dare get the girls to put their names to declarations to contradict the statements in the Rev. Mr Munro's report, and their letters to us wishing to get back, we cannot comprehend.' Miller concluded:

> The Rev. Mr Forbes seems to have been the moving spring of the whole, and it is certainly not often that we find the saying of the wise old king better illustrated, – "One sinner destroyeth much good." ... Alas for the poor people of Skye! When famine again visits them and sharp hunger gnaws their vitals, we know not what else will be left them than just to deal by the Rev. Mr Forbes as the people of Caithness once dealt by their bishop [Adam of Melrose]. According to the description of one of the Marple girls, they found the sleek ecclesiastic "very fat," and, being sore pressed by appetite, they *boiled* him.[37]

In a Presbytery of Skye meeting in October:

> The Rev. Mr Lamont of Waternish observed, that the time had not yet arrived when the Presbytery could competently take up this case; but that the charges brought against Mr Forbes were of a very serious

character. That the facts which he attempted to prove were supported by very loose and irregular declarations and unsatisfactory evidence, whereas Mr Ross's reply, so far as the testimony of parties went, was able and business-like, and most damaging to Mr Forbes's statements. He [Lamont] had the honour of being personally acquainted with the Rev. Mr Munro of Manchester, one of the four clergymen who certifies the kind treatment of the Skye girls by the Messrs Walmsley, and a more respectable clergyman he did not know. However, as this was a matter of controversy, he thought the Presbytery should not interfere at present.[38]

The Skye correspondent for the *Inverness Courier* provided the only balanced review and the final word on the subject. He considered Forbes deserved 'very little blame' though 'all those concerned in taking the girls to England are handled with considerable, and, I think undue severity; for I really cannot see what these parties had in view but to enable the girls to maintain themselves in a better way than they could in Skye – at the same time, of course, not over-looking their own business interests in the matter.' He considered in *Am Ministear* 'ridicule and scurrility have but too prominent a place, and which was evidently meant to minister to the coarser conceptions of the common people.' By contrast, in *Humanity Defended*

> ... with reasoning and argument, and a great deal of sarcasm, he [Donald] issues a perfect shower of affidavits from clerical, medical, educational, and menial personages, showing that the Skye girls were well used while in England; and this pamphlet is, I perceive, considered by a number of editors in the south quite conclusive on the subject. Whether it will be allowed to continue so is another thing; for his neighbour sometimes comes after a man and "searches him out," which may be the case also in this instance.[39]

18

Knoydart Evictions

Knoydart is a peninsula in the Parish of Glenelg, in Lochaber, opposite the Isle of Skye, bounded by Lochs Nevis (Heaven) and Hourn (Hell) and was formerly part of the lands of Glengarry.[1] Knoydart is not easy to get to – you cannot drive there. The main way is by ferry from Mallaig to Inverie, though it can be reached by adventurous hikers.

From 1773 onwards there were a series of emigrations from Glengarry lands, destined for North America.[2] In 1836 Rev. Alexander Beith explained that emigration was 'of necessity and not of choice. The letting of large tracts of land to single individuals caused the original banishment of the hardy and numerous race, who had for so many generations possessed the soil.'[3] Many settled in Nova Scotia, in the aptly named Glengarry County and by 1852 nearly 10,000 of the county's inhabitants had Highland scots surnames.[4] It is estimated that about 2,000 people, predominantly Catholic, emigrated from Knoydart from 1773 to 1852.[5]

In 1847, during the potato famine, Andrew Fraser, Sheriff-substitute of Fort William, found the people in the region 'bordering on starvation' and in Knoydart 'destitute both of meal and money.'[6] In 1852 the laird, Aeneas Ranaldson, 16th Chief of Glengarry, died and his widow, Josephine Macdonell of Torquay, spoke to Sir John McNeill to try to persuade the Highland and Island Emigration Society to support the emigration of the inhabitants to Australia.[7] This did not materialise so Josephine and the other trustees of her son, Alexander, the under-age hereditary chief, took advantage of the Emigration Advances Act and on 11 August 1853 the Inclosure Commissioners agreed to loan them £1,200 'for defraying the expenses of the Emigration of certain poor persons.'[8] This was retrospective as two days before the *Sillery* had set sail for Canada with 332 people from Knoydart on board.[9]

Early in September an advert appeared for the letting of farms at 'Neugart,' 'Samadallan' and Doune in Knoydart.[10] At the same time the *Inverness Advertiser* reported 'It is with intense pain that we announce the carrying out of a large number of evictions on the property of Glengarry.'[11] It later added:

Some 300 persons left peaceably, taking advantage of the opportunity for emigration which was presented to them. About one-fourth of that number (exclusive of several infirm and sick persons, whose forcible removal was thought dangerous) persisted in remaining, had their habitations tumbled down about their ears, and are now living in the shelter of the rocks. All of them, we believe, were much in arrears of rent; and Mrs Macdonell behaved liberally as respects their proposed transportation.[12]

The *Inverness Courier* added:

The managers of the property offered to remit all arrears to such as should emigrate; a ship was engaged to take people either to Australia or Canada; and an outfit was provided – each person who applied receiving clothes, blankets, shoes, &c. The people were also allowed to sell their cattle and stock, and to retain the proceeds for their own use... When the time of departure arrived, 15 or 16 families refused to emigrate... Ejectments were served on them, and last week the work of eviction was carried out, and the huts pulled down – a most distressing spectacle. No resistance was made to the officers employed on this task; and the people retreated to the hill-sides, to gravel-pits, and other localities in the neighbour-hood, where they remain, altogether about sixty in number.[13]

A similar article in *The Times* added that the ship had left from Isle Ornsay.[14] The ship probably moored in the harbour between the Skye mainland and Ornsay.[15]

'An observer' added more information, including the names of some of those evicted:

The failure of the potato crop was felt in Knoydart with as much severity as in any locality of the Highlands... As long as Glengarry lived, he displayed more anxiety for the lives and interest of his poor crofters than for procuring payment of his rents...

Last spring all the crofters on the Glengarry estate in Knoydart received legal warning for removing at Whitsunday... The ship came to Isleornsay in the beginning of August, to convey the people to Canada. Mrs Macdonell paid a visit to the country to arrange matters personally for the departure of the emigrants. She ... paid their passage – supplied every article of clothing they required – and allowed each of them 10lbs of meal after arriving in Canada until employment was procured... It can no sense be called a voluntary emigration. For the people said, "we will go because we cannot remain."

...About the 22nd of August, Mr Grant, the factor of Mrs Macdonell of Glengarry, with some servants and law officers, traversed the estate of Knoydart, pulling down the houses of the remnant who did not accompany their neighbours to Canada. Eleven houses, forming so many different homes, were pulled down, and the families that occupied them turned out, and left to live day and night in the open air...

The factor who superintended this business, commanded the paupers* (*Those on the poor's roll receiving parochial relief) not to shelter, even by night, any of the outcasts, or if they did their own houses would soon be pulled down.[16]

It was subsequently stated 'that of the sixteen families evicted all but four or five have obtained shelter or dwellings, chiefly through the kindness of Mr Macdonald, Scothouse [Scottas]', near Inverie. 'A Constant Reader' disagreed with some of the articles:

At Martinmass 1852 many of the crofters paid the rent, and they all paid what they could... When the people wrote Mrs Macdonell of Glengarry, begging of her to allow them to remain, and promising to pay the rent for the future, as times were improved, they were told in answer that Sir John M'Neill was to take them to Australia; that they would emigrate without resistance, their arrears would be remitted, &c.; that if they did not go, she would at all events turn them off her property. The people choosing the least of two evils, made up their reluctant minds to go to Australia. Very soon after, when Mrs Macdonell found, as I suppose, that it would be more expensive to send the people to Australia than to send them to Canada, she wrote home saying that they *must* now go to Canada... Only about forty of the "four hundred" were crofters or heads of families; consequently about forty only had to pay rent. I have seen the receipts of many to them... [Of the evicted] families only four were crofters.[17]

The factor, Alexander Grant, responded:

In 1847 a list of the population was taken, and it stood as follows, viz., males of all ages, 288; females, do. do., 318; in all, 606 souls ... living on a small corner of the estates the yearly rent of which is only £300 – rent which the crofters were bound to pay, but which they had failed to do, and in January last the arrears outstanding and due by these crofters was £2375, 12s, 5d...

There were four large boats hired to carry the emigrants from Knoydart to the vessel at Isleornsay. These boats were employed from early on Thursday morning until Saturday evening ferrying the people to Isleornsay.[18]

In response to 'An observer' Grant also wrote:

I then stated to them that I was not sure whether they would be sent to Australia or America. They almost, with one voice, preferred being sent to America, because the most of them had friends in that quarter. This desire I communicated to Mrs Macdonell, and shortly thereafter I received a letter from her, saying she would charter a vessel and pay their passage to Canada. I lost no time in conveying this information to the parties, who, with one exception, seemed entirely pleased with this arrangement...

There was no instances of harshness or ill treatment during the whole of the ejectments. Every possible kindness was shewn, and where any serious consequences might be dreaded from rendering the aged or infirm houseless, the parties were left in possession of their huts.[19]

An accompanying editorial in the *Inverness Advertiser* questioned his account based on two letters written by Mrs Macdonell. If the people agreed to leave quietly 'every assistance will be given them... But I must tell you that those who may imagine they will be permitted to remain after this are indulging a vain hope, as the most stringent measures will be taken to effect their removal... *Sir John M'Neill has promised that they shall all be removed in one ship to Australia.*' The second, dated 10 May, indicated 'the destination of the Knoydart crofters has been, for good and efficient reasons, changed from Australia to Canada.'

Early in October Donald travelled to Knoydart to see the situation for himself. A long article was submitted to the *Northern Ensign* by 'Scotus,' the *Advertiser* revealed it was written by Donald.[20] It included detailed accounts of the plight of six families and formed the basis of his subsequent pamphlet *The Glengarry Evictions*. The local Catholic minister, Coll Macdonald, had written to Donald on 11 October:

Christy Kennedy, the wife of Alexander M'Donald, Doune, and Ann M'Kinnon, the wife of John M'Kinnon, had a miscarriage two or three days after their houses had been thrown down. The terror and hardship they experienced on that occasion they declare to have been the cause of it. One of these women lay for some time *during her sickness* at the side of the *bush*; she was afterwards brought within the walls of her former house, where she lay for three days so ill that her recovery was doubtful. The other woman M'Kinnon is very unwell as yet. It is not at all unlikely that this cold weather will put an end to her sufferings and life together... May Almighty God strengthen and encourage you, in your exertions for the poor people of Knoydart.

Donald also wrote to *The British Friend*:

When I visited Knoydart a few days ago, I was shocked at the treatment these poor Highland people received. The scene was melancholy to behold. For a long stretch of seven or eight miles, once studded with houses, all was *ruins*, and the people burrowing in holes, beside ditches and rocks, as if they had been a lot of savages. Every hut, or shelter they put up, the factor's party came round and demolished; and no mercy whatever is shown to them.[21]

Donald ended his letter with an appeal for 'watertight tents, blankets, and clothing; as well as some food and nutritious diet for the destitute and the invalids.' Appended was a second letter from Macdonald:

To-day, Saturday the 22d Oct., is the stormiest day we have seen this year, and the servants from Inverie are after making their round, destroying the shelters of the outcasts. All those poor creatures are out then, exposed to the raging elements. They have broken their huts now six times with the first warrants. Is this legal! O! do not, I beseech you, lose sight of the poor who are living outside in this dreadful weather.

On 28 October Donald finished writing *The Glengarry Evictions*. A quote on the title page was from the 3rd Edition of Major-General Stewart's *Sketches of the ... Highlanders of Scotland*, however Donald had swapped the sentences around.[22] Donald reiterated what had already been reported in the papers and explained that Mrs Macdonell's residence was Inverie House, but she was largely absent. He had travelled by boat from Loch Hourn Head, along Loch Hourn to Airor, the only place along that stretch of Knoydart that had a stone jetty, erected in 1847 during the potato famine by the local people, who were paid in meal to build it.[23] Donald incorrectly referred to Knoydart as being on the right when sailing down the loch.

The wind was very favourable when we started, and, having our little bark fairly balanced, we hoisted sail and glided along in beautiful style... We had not proceeded more than 5 miles when both wind and tide appeared against us. A strong current like a powerful river rushed up the loch, boiling and raging, and had our bark the power of any ordinary streamer it would baffle her to make head against such an element. We had to change our course, ply our oars, and soon got into smooth water again, and a gentle breeze soon starting, filling our unreefed sail, we steered along under the shadow of the high hills of Knoydart, rounded several rocky points, and reached the pier at Arar by seven o'clock at night, after a voyage of four hours and a half.[24]

When he arrived,

As far as the eye could see the face of the strath had its black spots, where the houses of the crofters were either levelled or burnt. The ruins of these habitations of men, and the silence and solitude that prevailed, rendered it unnecessary for any tongue to tell me that here humanity was

Knoydart Evictions

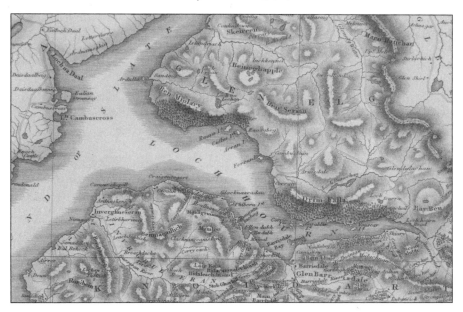

Map from 1830 showing the route that Donald sailed from Loch Hourn Head to Airor, Knoydart in October 1853. Also shown are Isle Ornsay and the coastal townships (from south to north) of Sandaig, Doune, Samadalan and Niag-àrd, though with spelling variations.

Airor jetty where Donald landed in October 1853. It was originally built in 1847 during the potato famine by the local people, who were paid in meal to build it, though has since been re-built.

most cruelly sacrificed to the god of sheep-farming and expatriation. The blackened rafters lying scattered among the grass, the couple-trees [main roof supports] cut through the middle and thrown far away, the walls broken down, the thatch and the cabers mixed up together, and grass beginning to grow on the threshold and hearthstone, ... most of the highlanders of Knoydart were put on board the *"Sillery"* at Isle Ornsay, and packed off to North America like so many African slaves to the Cuban market.

Donald could have been mistaken about the houses being burnt, as peat fires in a blackhouse without a chimney coated the rafters with soot, however if the central fire was still alight when the roof was brought down, then it could have caught fire.

After the ship sailed from Isle Ornsay with her living cargo of highland people Mrs. M'Donell's factor, an old gentleman of the name of Grant, returned to Knoydart and commenced the work of destruction on the houses of the crofters and cottars. Not only the houses of those who had left the country, but also the houses of those who refused to go, were pulled to the ground. The factor was accompanied by some servants and law officers who had axes, crowbars, iron levers and picks. The uninhabited houses were levelled first, then the houses of those who refused to go on board the ship to Canada. There was no mercy shown, no delay given. The inmates were ordered out, and their articles of furniture were thrown out after them; beds, chairs, tables, pots, stoneware, clothing, were all thrown topsy-turvy down the hill. The thatch was pulled off, the picks were stuck into the walls, the levers removed the foundation stones, axes cut the couple trees, and then roof, rafters and walls fell in with a crash. Clouds of dust rose to the skies, while men, women and children stood at a distance completely dismayed. What took them years to erect and collect was destroyed and scattered in a few minutes.[25]

Donald then provided details of twelve families, plus others who had stayed, totalling ninety-two people. Three of the cases are worth quoting as their stories continue.

5th, Archibald M'Isaac, crofter, aged 66; wife 54. They have a family. [Eight children, aged 10-27].
Archibald's house, byre, barn, and stable, were fit subjects of attack, and were levelled to the ground. The furniture of the house was thrown down the hill, and a general destruction then commenced. The roof, fixtures, and wood work were smashed to pieces, the walls razed to the very foundation, and all that was left for poor Archibald to look upon was a black dismal wreck...

His wife and children wept, but the old man said, "neither weeping nor reflections will now avail, we must prepare some shelter." The children collected some cabers and turf, and in the hollow between two ditches, the old man constructed a rude shelter for the night, and having kindled a fire and gathered in his family, they all engaged in family worship and sung psalms as usual. Next morning they examined the ruins, picked up some broken pieces of furniture, dishes, &c. and then made another addition to their shelter in the ditch. Matters went on this way for about a week, when the local manager and his men came down upon them, and after much abuse for daring to take shelter on the lands of Knoydart, they destroyed the shelter and put old Archy and his people again out on the hill.

I found Archibald and his numerous family still at Knoydart and in a shelter beside the old ditch. Any residence more wretched, or more melancholy, I have never witnessed. A feal, or turf erection, about 3 feet high, 4 feet broad, and about 5 feet long, was at the end of the shelter, and this formed the sleeping place of the mother and her *five* daughters! They creep in and out on their knees, and their bed is just a layer of hay on the cold earth of the ditch!

9th, Donald M'Donald, aged 50 years, married and has a wife and family. [Five children, aged 6-16].

Donald M'Donald was a cottar; he was deprived of his land more than 12 years ago; his wife was very sick when the levellers arrived, and yet, notwithstanding of this ... they pulled down every inch of the house except *a small bit of it immediately above the sick woman's bed*. The father and the five children were rendered completely houseless, but the sick mother was allowed to remain under a *mere* fragment of the roof... The poor woman is not only still in bad health but without the smallest prospect of recovery. Anything more cruel and, I may add, more atrocious than this conduct towards a sick female I question much cannot be found in the annals of slavery.

13th, Catharine M'Kinnon, aged about 50 years, unmarried; Peggy M'Kinnon, aged about 48 years, unmarried; and Catharine M'Phee ... also unmarried; occupied one house. Catharine M'Kinnon was for a long time sick, and she was confined to bed when the factor and his party came to beat down the house. At first they requested her to rise and walk out, but her sisters said that she could not rise that she was so unwell. They said, "Oh, she is scheming;" the sisters said that she was not, that she had been ill for a considerable time, and the sick woman herself, who then feebly spoke, said she was quite unfit to be removed, but if God spared her and bestowed her with better health that she would remove of her own accord. This would not suffice; *they forced her out of bed, sick as she was, and left her beside a ditch from 10 a. m. to 5 p. m.*, when, afraid that she would die, as she was seriously unwell, they removed her to a house and provided her with cordials, warm clothing, &.c... Peggy and her half sister M'Phee are still burrowing among the ruins of their old home. When I left Knoydart last week there were no hopes whatever of Catharine M'Kinnon's recovery.[26]

In the 1851 census 'Archy McIsaac' of 'Dunn' (Doune) was aged 61; Donald Macdonald was not listed, presumably away, though his wife, 'Ann McDonald' 44, and children were living at Samadalan; 'Cathrane McKinnon' 52, 'Margaret McKinnon' 50 and 'Cathrane McPhee' 29 lived at Inverie. Catharine MacPhee was the niece of Catharine Mackinnon and the daughter of Margaret ('Peggy') Mackinnon and the outlaw Ewen MacPhee, who's story is in a book about Glengarry place names.[27]

Some of the evicted people took shelter in a store-house at Doune:

Orders, however, were immediately given to burn it to the ground! The conflagration was terrible – the couples and rafters were of old mountain pine, full of rosin – the cabers dry as tinder – the thatch of moss divot, and, from frequent repairs, more than a foot thick – then the turf above the walls, and the straw and heather covering over the thatch all dry, all combustible, blazed away magnificently![28]

Donald wrote to W.R. Baillie, the lawyer for Glengarry on 25 October:

I shall thank you to inform me if you will allow canvas tents to be erected on the grounds at Knoydart for the use of such families until the severities of winter are past. I need scarcely say that, at this inclement season, the lives of many of the poor evicted people are endangered in the wretched holes or hovels which they at present occupy.[29]

At the end of his pamphlet Donald appended the 2nd letter from Macdonald, though had changed a few of the words. *The Glengarry Evictions* was reviewed by the *Belfast Chronicle* which considered 'The crofters of the Highlands of Scotland, or small occupiers of land at will – almost cotters – have had an unceasing, enthusiastic, and resolute advocate in Mr Donald Ross, of Glasgow ... he never can be repaid for the labour he has expended, and the sacrifices he has made in behalf of that class.'[30]

Much that Donald wrote can be corroborated by two articles that appeared in *The Scotsman*. The newspaper had 'procured the services of a gentleman well qualified by experience' to investigate, who arrived on 16 October and 'visited the evicted people in their nests' the next day. He was assisted by Macdonald, Grant and the local manager, John Cameron, to give an 'impartial view', which included additional information:

They were located in the various little bays between Scotus on the one side and Inverguseran on the other, a distance say of five or six miles, along the shore of the Sound of Sleat, and they formed the little townships of Doune, Rhiddarroch, Airor, Samadalan, and Niugart...

On the 2d of August the removal of the people was commenced; by the 6th all who would go had been ferried over to Isle Ornsey; and on the 9th the ship sailed for Montreal. She had on board 331 men, women, and children...

On the 22d of August the ejectments commenced, and the work lasted three days ... in five cases, the occupiers were permitted to retain their houses from motives of humanity... It is sufficient to say here that sixteen families were evicted.[31]

The reporter referred to the building at Doune that was burnt down as a 'small boat-house.' To use the present spellings of the townships, from south to north, in the 1851 census their populations were: Reidh an Daraich 96, Doune 132, Airor 101, Samadalan 92 and Niag-àrd 84. By 1861 these had dropped to 4, 6, 83, 12 and 0 respectively.[32] The Airor figure probably stayed high because it had the jetty. Some habitation of the first four has continued up to the present day and many of the old cottages have been re-built or re-purposed, with ruins nearby. Old croft boundaries and lazybed strips can still be seen on satellite images. Niag-àrd was completely abandoned and the ruins can be clearly seen today.[33] Just to the north of Niag-àrd is a small, overgrown and forgotten graveyard where 'DIED 1805' can still be read on one stone.

The second *Scotsman* article provided information about the people themselves, but not in as much detail as by Donald, though it does indicate which townships they lived in.[34] The reporter concluded that although Mrs Macdonell had 'behaved most liberally to those who left her estate ... she has been guilty of gross inhumanity in her treatment of the miserable and helpless remnant of the people who remain.' He went on to state that the emigrants 'arrived safely in Canada, after a rapid and pleasant voyage of about twenty-eight days' duration' and reproduced a letter from one of them, who was doing well.

In the meantime, Baillie had declined Donald's offer of tents, however he believed the trustees 'would willingly agree, not only to pay the expense of conveying the parties with their families to the County Town of Inverness, or to any town in the Lowlands, where work is abundant, but also to supply them with the means of engaging suitable lodgings for the earlier months of winter.' Donald then wrote to George Anderson, Inspector of Poor for Inverness, who replied 'I have conferred with the chairman of our Parochial Board, and some of the Magistrates of Inverness, and am desired by them to protest in the strongest manner against these poor people being sent to squat themselves down here... Their presence would just entail a repetition on us

Ruined blackhouse at Doune, looking north towards the vitrified fort of Dùn Bàn.

of the expense and annoyance to which our community was subjected by the sudden arrival about 18 months ago of a large influx of poor crofters from the Island of Barra.' Donald also wrote to Ebenezer Adamson, Inspector of Poor for the City Parish of Glasgow and received a similar response. However, Donald received a letter from Coll Macdonald who 'most kindly offered permission to erect the tents for the poor outcasts on an acre of ground belonging to him, and adjoining his chapel. Mr Munro, wright and builder, 100 Holm Street, is now busy preparing the tents.'[35]

The Parochial Board of Glenelg met on 17 November:

Mr Macrae, the chairman, called the attention of the Board to the case of the evicted crofters in Knoydart, and stated that after visiting that district of the parish, he had written to Mrs Macdonell of Glengarry, the acting trustee on the estate, representing to her the miserable condition of these people from the want of shelter from the elements ... he had a letter from Mrs Macdonell, in reply, expressing much commiseration for the sufferings of these people ... declining to pay *again* the passage money to Canada of those who refused to emigrate in August, but offering to take their crop at valuation, and to give them assistance towards removing to any port of Scotland to which they might go for work...

> Mr Campbell, the Inspector, then gave a detailed report ... of six families which are still houseless, three are those of able-bodied tenants, or having some of the members fit for labour, and a fourth consisting only of a middle-aged widow, whose children have left the kingdom with the exception of one married son; that these four families are in no immediate want, some of them having money, and the whole of them [having] crop enough to serve them for the next six months...
> The Board ... unanimously found that they cannot interfere in the case of such of these crofters as are neither infirm nor destitute; but they agreed ... to furnish ... two persons with parochial relief, including house accommodation.[36]

On 21 November Donald wrote an article to say the tents 'were forwarded by me on Monday last, and they are water-tight and substantial.'[37] They were erected in the grounds of St Anthony's Chapel, Sandaig, where Macdonald preached. Other newspapers added:

> The tents were immediately erected under Mr Ross's superintendence and direction. They afford a comfortable accommodation to five families. These dwellings, simple though they be, are considered a paradise by the poor people, contrasted with the wretched holes in which they have been burrowing since their ejectment. They have no language adequate to express their gratitude to their kind benefactors.[38]

> These tents are made of strong couples, covered over with waterproof canvass, and divided into regular divisions, according to the number of each family. While Mr Ross and his assistants were erecting the tents, the outcasts, young and old, collected round them, and we may safely say that their gratitude was beyond description... We understand that in April or May next, Mr Ross will remove this "remnant of the clan" to Canada. In the meantime he has provided them with clothing and food.[39]

Donald wrote an appeal on 16 December, entitled *Highland Clearances*, which included a letter from Macdonald:

> The tents answer admirably... They are water-tight, warm, and commodious, and the poor people are so thankful, that they have no words to express their heart-felt gratitude. Poor old M'Isaac, whom you pitied so much, says he is as happy as if he had got a farm!... The meal and clothing are given out according to the need of each family, and are all contented and thankful.[40]

Donald provided a list of sixty-nine donations and their donors, totalling £133 16s 6d, plus two bales of clothing. Three days later Donald had finished his next pamphlet, which was an expanded version of the appeal and with the same title. He added that a correspondent, probably Macdonald, had written 'Nothing now remains but to have them removed to Canada, and I send you a list of the poor people who are most desirous of emigrating.' Donald added 'The list contains the names and ages of the members of 17 families, numbering nearly 120 individuals, young and old.'[41]

Meanwhile, the fight to help the remaining people of Knoydart was taken up by Edward Ellice MP. Ellice was perfectly placed as his father had purchased the nearby Glenquoich Estate from the Chief of Glengarry in 1838.[42] Ellice had been interviewed by the Poor Law Inquiry in 1843 and considered the people in the area were 'very ill off.'[43] He was particularly interested in the case of Catharine Mackinnon and in November commenced writing a series of letters to the Board of Supervision and the Home Secretary about the situation.[44] The Home Secretary was Henry John Temple, 3rd Viscount Palmerston, who became the Prime Minister in 1855. In January 1854 the *Northern Ensign* announced: 'We are glad to learn that the attention of the Government has at last been fully directed to the heartless clearances carried on in Glengarry and in Skye; and that one of the most prominent members has ordered certain inquiries and reports to be furnished to him, preparatory to the matter being brought before the legislature.'[45]

St Anthony's Chapel, Sandaig, where Donald erected tents for the evicted people of Knoydart to live, since re-built.

Sir John McNeill investigated and received a Memorandum from Baillie that justified the events on behalf of the Trustees:

> When the late Glengarry died in the Summer of 1852, the Curators on entering upon the management of the Estate of Knoydart devolving on his eldest Son, found it burdened with a very heavy debt...
>
> On reviewing the Rental ... only a very small portion had been paid during eight or ten years preceding & that an arrear of upwards of £1500 had accumulated ... and in supplying work of all kinds for both sexes, they had shewn themselves utterly ungrateful for it all and they had gone on from year to year, making no improvement in any respect & getting farther and farther behind with their rents. Many of them had sublet their Crofts to others or had permitted others to squat on their land so that these districts were fast becoming converted into a Nursery of paupers ... tho' almost all able-bodied, they were lazy, idle in abject poverty and otherwise good for nothing...
>
> In place of 400 the number of souls who had signed or otherwise given reason to expect that they would emigrate and for whom passage money was paid, only 332 were prevailed on to go on board, many remained behind ... and some of them had the assurance to sell the clothing which they had received for the voyage. And the curators well recollect at the time how deeply mortified Mrs. Macdonell felt after all the personal trouble she has had and all the expense to which her Son had been put which exceeded £1700...
>
> There then remained on the ground twenty six families, one half of whom from the age or infirmity of their members, or from other causes the Curators did not desire to remove but Mrs. Macdonell ... found that the others who were quite well able either to have emigrated with their friends or to have removed from the ground were obstinately determined to do neither ... on the 14th August a Sheriff Officer went from Inverness and in the cause of the ensuing week served Notices of ejection on these parties and on these Notices being disobeyed he in due course of Law ejected the parties from their possessions and pulled down their houses...
>
> They all after being removed from the ground returned to it and set up out of the fragments of their former houses such temporary Shelter as they could contrive. But it was obvious they could then be only looked on as Strangers forcibly intruding themselves on the property, and the Ground Officer or Bailiff, who was resident in charge of the Estate warned them off as soon as he heard of it and removed the huts which they had erected...
>
> But at last in the middle of the Month of November the Curators ... directed an Offer to be made to the parties to send them and their families to Inverness, Glasgow, or to any other town in the South where

work could be had and to provide suitable lodgings for them there till first of April – all at the expense of Glengarry. This offer was made accordingly and refused by every one of the parties...

The Parish and the County at large have been freed from a number of useless hands while the great body of the poor people themselves who have gone to Canada are enjoying the improved prospects.[46]

McNeill accepted the contents of the Memorandum and reiterated much of it in a long letter he sent to Palmerston on 3 February. He considered 'There can be no doubt as to the legal right of the Trustees to compel the removal of those persons.' However, the condition of the remaining people 'had exacted much sympathy.' McNeill concluded that the trustees 'have acted with great liberality; but that the arrangements were not so skilfull [sic] or judicious as they might have been.' They 'committed themselves to a contest, which might, by more skill and foresight, have been avoided... For this mistake the manner in which the Trustees have been treated by the public press has inflicted more than a just measure of punishment.' He pointed out that other clearance landlords 'by more dexterous management or because less is expected of them than of Highland Gentlemen have escaped the censure to which the Trustees in Knoydart have been subjected.'

In parallel, the *Inverness Courier* reported 'By the direction of the Lord Advocate, Sheriff Fraser of Fort-William was recently sent to investigate judicially the administration of the poor-law in Knoydart... Mr Fraser passed eleven days in visiting the paupers' houses and examining them, as well as other parties, regarding their circumstances, and the treatment they received from the Board... Some of the cases have been found of so very serious a nature, that the Inspector of poor for the parish was judicially examined on a charge of criminal neglect of duty; and the Parochial Board has been ordered to afford relief to about a dozen individuals, whose application they have hitherto rejected.'[47] The farms at Niag-àrd, Samadalan and Doune were still being advertised, so presumably the bad publicity had put potential farmers off.[48]

Donald returned to Skye and Knoydart in February 1854 and afterwards wrote:

I have just returned from the distressed districts, after having prepared forty petitions to Parliament for the poor sufferers.

The examination ordered by Lord Palmerston and the Lord Advocate goes to show that matters are worse than described in my pamphlet; and the Inspector of Poor for Knoydart is committed for trial for criminal neglect of duty towards the poor. He will be tried in Edinburgh.[49]

This was accompanied by another appeal: 'The past winter was exceedingly stormy and cold, and ... meal is at a famine price – just double what it was in the spring of last year... Fever of a bad type, also cholera, has broken out in some of the districts, owing to the poor creatures subsisting upon unwholesome food, such as shell-fish.' He went on to list a further 103 donations totalling £179, 12s, 4d, plus several bales of clothes. On 25 February Donald wrote 'I am glad that Mr Fraser, the Sheriff of Fortwilliam, has been entrusted with the recent inquiry at Knoydart... I have a letter this moment from London, from a distinguished M.P., who says, "the report by the Sheriff is even worse than your pamphlet – it at any rate more than confirms the statements you have made regarding the state of the poor."'[50] On 6 March Donald was thanked for sending 'meal to the poor *outcasts* in Knoydart and the quantity on this occasion was not less in all than twenty bolls.'[51]

Donald's next pamphlet, *Real Scottish Grievances*, was probably written in March 1854 and published early April. This was one of his longest pamphlets at over 15,000 words and the only one to include pictures. It demonstrated Donald's most creative use of the English language with vivid descriptions of places and the terrible experiences of the victims, designed to pull at the heart-strings, bring a lump to the throat and tears to the eyes. Various quotes from the likes of Scott and Burns are dispersed within it, including three stanzas from *The Raid of Albyn*, a long poem written by William D. Campbell who was about 28 years old when he died on 10 January 1854 'an hour or two previous to the last sheet having been sent for revisal.'[52] After visiting Skye, Donald had taken a boat from Isle Ornsay to Knoydart:

> I proceeded at once in the direction of the *"Refugees,"* in the tents which I erected for them in November last, and found them quite contented. The tents were not in the least injured by the stormy weather, and the occupants looked twenty-five per cent. better ... the poor people were delighted to see me, and that they gave expression to their grateful feelings in loud and long-continued blessings and thanks for what was done for them...
>
> I was horror-struck on finding at Neagart, in Knoydart, Donald M'Donald, who last year was a decent, steady, industrious man, now going about a raving madman... [After his family were evicted] The poor man's mind was immediately unhinged, and from that period until now he was getting worse. He is now declared, by medical authority, to be a fit subject for a lunatic asylum... The parochial authorities recently built up a portion of the house which M'Donald occupied, and which they formerly demolished; but, alas! this was but wretched reparation. No patching of the old house can restore reason to her seat; and the poor maniac still goes about looking for his children among the ruins of the burnt and broken down cottages. They are near him, still he imagines they are not; and, in his melancholy aberrations, he cries aloud for them, and travels many a

mile seeking for them amid the ruins of levelled houses, and in the rocky caves of Knoydart...

But this is not a solitary case... One boy in particular, ever since the memorable night when the emissaries of the factor set fire to the storehouse belonging to the evicted tenants at Doune, in Knoydart – as the poor outcasts had taken refuge in it – is so deranged that he will require to be placed in confinement. He jumps out of bed crying "Fire! fire!" and assures those near him that there are men and children inside the burning store-house.[53]

A section entitled 'Aunty Kate's Cabin,' was an updated account of Catharine Mackinnon. A longer version was published in the *Northern Ensign*, which provided a few additional facts. Donald referred to the local manager as 'a very stout fat gentleman, with enormous whiskers encircling a large red face.'[54] Donald, accompanied by Macdonald, visited Catharine's 'cabin' on 18 February.

It is situate[d] near the base of a huge mountain, and not fully half a mile from Inverie House, the residence of Mrs. M'Donnell of Glengarry. On nearing the cabin I thought it was a huge mole-hill! It had not the smallest appearance of being the residence of a human being, for it was an unshapely mound, covered with snow. A small current of smoke, about the thickness of a man's arm, issued from one end of it; and this alone indicated that it was inhabited... On going to the other side we perceived a sort of door – just like the entrance to a rabbit hole in a warren. An old empty sack, doubled up and put across a rope at the

The eviction of Catherine Mackinnon of Inverie, as depicted in *Real Scottish Grievances*. The man is probably the local manager, John Cameron.

top, and fixed in at the bottom with two stones, closed up the entrance. There were two or three branches thrown across outside, signifying that one of the inmates was out. Mr. M'Donald, seeing the door shut up, went to the leeward side of the hut, and after removing some snow with his stick, he lifted up one of the old earthen divots in the roof, and cried – "*A Cheit, ciod an doigh air am bheil sibh an diugh?*" – (Kate, how do you find yourself to-day?) – when immediately a little wrinkled, withered hand appeared through the hole, and which the poor inmate offered to the kind-hearted clergyman, informing him that she was "*not better but worse.*" ...through the opening in the roof, I applied my eye to it in order to see the appearance and dimensions of the cabin inside; and I solemnly declare I never, on the face of the earth, saw such a scene. The pillow on which the sick woman's head rested was just thirteen inches from the top of the roof, and there was no space within except that occupied by the bed on the bare earthen floor... Aunty Kate appeared to me to be labouring under severe indisposition. She was pale and thin, and had a bad cough. She had plenty of bed-clothes, thanks to Mr. Ellice, M.P., and to his kind lady...

The fire-place consisted of two stones 9 inches apart, and over them was a pot, and some embers under it. A person could sit two-folded between the floor and the roof, but that was all. There was no furniture in the cabin, and although divided into two divisions, the cooking and sleeping divisions, it presented a most unearthly appearance... Sometime after they were evicted, the Inspector of the Poor removed Margaret to the end of a dark, wretched, damp, and dismal cave-looking hut occupied by another pauper – as she was, he said, "in danger of perishing," but he made no provision for Aunty Kate. The niece ... said that the Inspector did offer a house once to her aunt: but on reaching the spot she found it in ruins! ... the Inspector never provided a lodging or dwelling-place for Aunty Kate; and all the relief afforded to her was a few shillings since the month of October last.[55]

Donald quoted six letters and articles, including three from Ellice, however the wording differed slightly in his pamphlet and newspaper versions. One was from Dr Alexander Macleod of Sleat, who had visited Catharine in January:

I got into this miserable hole on my knees, with my hat and coat off. On examining the poor woman I found her in a state of great debility, with a weak fluttering pulse. She complained of pain about the region of the heart, and swelling in her body. She appeared to me to be naturally of a weak frame. My opinion of her present state is, that her complaint was mainly if not entirely brought on by cold and exposure to the late inclement weather, as she lay for upwards of twenty days, during the recent snow storm.

The doctor died two months later, on a dark night, 'being unacquainted with the rough and intricate foot-path between Kilchoan and Kyles, [he] strayed among the rocks, and fell over a perpendicular precipice, of at least 150 feet.'[56]

The *Northern Ensign* considered *Real Scottish Grievances* was 'perhaps, without exception, the most sorrowful and telling chapter on Highland Evictions which has appeared from the same or any other pen.'[57] Donald's involvement with the plight of the Knoydart people diminished beyond March due to a more serious event at the end of that month in Strathcarron.

Sheriff-substitute Fraser's report was not released until late in the year. He considered the make-up of the Parochial Board of Glenelg to be 'quite irregular' and explained there were thirty-eight paupers in Knoydart on the poor roll, most of whom were female and twenty-four were over sixty-nine. Their homes were 'of the worst description' and the 'wretched inmates are scantily and miserably clad.' Fraser used four cases: Mary Cameron, Reidh an Daraich, 90; Mary Macdonald, Doune, 91; Angus Mackinnon, Doune, 78, and Mary Macdonald, Niag-àrd, 93, to charge the Inspector of Poor for Glenelg, Ewen Campbell, with 'neglect of duty, in not providing these poor old creatures with the necessary means of subsistence.' Fraser confirmed that Donald Macdonald had 'become deranged.'[58] In September he was 'in custody as a Dangerous Lunatic' and on 3 October was 'committed to Montrose Asylum.'[59]

The Board of Supervision was asked to write a report. When McNeill had visited Glenelg Parish in 1851, he had reported matters to be 'in a perfectly satisfactory state' and in the new report considered 'there is no reason to suppose that they are now in a worse state than then.' In response, in March 1854, Ellice wrote to the Home Office 'demanding a full and impartial inquiry.' He requested that Fraser's report, which he had not seen, should 'be laid before parliament.'[60] Henry Fitzroy MP, Under-Secretary of State, replied 'Inquiries which have been ordered by the Lord Advocate in regard to those matters are not yet concluded, and in this state of things it appears to Lord Palmerston that it would be objectionable that any papers on the subject should be laid before parliament.'[61]

The Scotsman reported that on 11 May seven families in Knoydart were given eight days' notice to leave before their 'houses would be destroyed.'[62] A medical officer, Dr Manford, decided whether they were fit enough to be evicted. The *Inverness Courier* added that when Catharine Mackinnon and her niece were evicted from their 'wretched hovel ... a brood of young rats was found in Kate's bed.'[63] *The Scotsman* also reported that Fraser, along with the Procurator-Fiscal and Sheriff-Clerk on 13 May 'proceeded to examine the chairman and other members of the board of that parish. On his way home, the Sheriff passed through the rugged district of Knoydart, where he examined a number of witnesses connected with the same proceedings.'

Fraser wrote another report which again was not released until December.[64] He reported that the Parochial Board of Glenelg increased the pauper's weekly relief payments by three pence, supplied some blankets and made some temporary repairs to their houses. With regards to the four cases of neglect, Fraser reported that Mary Macdonald of Niag-àrd had died, Mary Cameron had been moved to a crofter's house and Mary Macdonald of Doune had been moved to a house in Reidh an Daraich, inhabited by two other paupers and attended by a nurse who had 'carried the old woman on her back across the hill, a distance of two miles' for which she was paid a shilling. A 'Sheriff Officer from Inverness, with a party' went to Catharine Mackinnon's 'place of abode and conveyed herself and furniture from thence to Ann M'Phaill's house [at Scottas, where her sister Margaret was living], but the tenant of the farm objected to her being placed in that house, and the poor woman (a pauper on the roll) lay that night and the succeeding one at the roadside.' The Parochial Board produced a statement in which Macrae confessed he only knew of the cases of Angus Mackinnon and Catharine and Margaret Mackinnon: '*I did not visit them*. These people are of a different communion from me, and have their own priest to attend to them.'

It was subsequently reported that total poor relief given to the thirty-eight Knoydart paupers was '34s., or about 10¾d. each' per week.[65] However, the parochial board stated that the 125 people on the poor roll in Glenelg Parish were receiving 1s 4½d. per week each.[66] They admitted this was lower than the average for Scotland but argued that their paupers had free fuel and food from the sea, grew potatoes, kept chickens and 'are able, with few exceptions, to earn something by their labour, most of them being employed in weaving, knitting, sewing, net-making, or light field work, occupations by which many of them can realise 6d. a-day.' This implies that the Protestant poor in Glenelg were much better off than the Catholic poor in Knoydart. The board referred to Catharine Mackinnon as 'not a pauper, and refuses to be considered or relieved as such ... she finds her voluntary exposure in the tent far more lucrative than any allowance that this or any other parish could afford to give her. On her being lately removed from the tent it required eight trips of a cart to carry the whole of her property.' However, Fraser had reported that the two sisters only had two cart-loads of possessions. The board also considered 'among the names of those who did not contribute their just share to the Parochial funds, that of Mr Ellice of Glenquoich, as the chief defaulter.' The *Inverness Courier* considered this statement to be 'extraordinary,' so wrote to his factor Niel Maclean who replied 'I confidently state that nothing can be more untrue than this invidious allegation... I may add, that of all the men I ever met in my life, Mr Ellice, junior ... is the most anxiously alive to the condition of the poor, and the most solicitous to have their wants duly attended to, without regard to expense.' Then appeared a series of articles in the *Courier* arguing moot points over who had received relief payments and for how much, and that if the paupers of Glenelg were getting paid for work then they should not be on the poor roll.[67] In the first article, the Inspector reported that after Catharine Mackinnon was 'turned out of her tent, the

Inspector sent a boat and men to convey herself and luggage to a very snug house in Dune, but she would not go; proposed the schoolhouse at Airor – it had been made up for paupers – she refused; offered her niece accommodation in the inn at Airor, which she also refused.' Inspector Campbell's yearly salary was increased from £45 to £70, nearly as much as the thirty-eight Knoydart paupers received put together.

With regards to Fraser's case against the Inspector, on 19 July the Solicitor-General decided that 'Although the condition of the paupers disclosed by this precognition is distressing, and although there must have been, in some quarter, defective administration of the Poor-law' it would be difficult to prove neglect, as old and infirm witnesses could not be brought to Inverness, so he concurred with 'the Advocate-Depute, that a criminal prosecution is not necessary.'[68] Another case between the 'curators for Glengarry' v. 'certain families in Knoydart' went before Sheriff-substitute Colquhoun in May, who found in favour of the trustees. It was appealed and Sheriff Young ruled that the families, 'who were tenants-at-will, had not established any right or title to the possession of the houses occupied by them.'[69]

On 7 August Ellice wrote to Palmerston 'The local authorities are but agents acting under the inspection of the Board of Supervision... But if ... it is further intended to refer the matter simply back to the Board of Supervision, with orders to institute the inquiry it has all along refused, that is a course against which I feel it my duty to protest ... the case now before us is not a singular one – that it is only an instance of that system of starvation which, depriving the poor of their legal sustenance, is protected in the Highlands by the Board of Supervision.'[70] This fell on deaf ears as it was announced that 'the Board of Supervision has resumed its investigation into the management of the poor in the Glengarry country and other Highland districts... The inquiry will be prosecuted by Sir John M'Neill, chairman of the Board, in person.'[71]

On 20 September a 'sheriff-officer from Inverness, accompanied by servants from Inverie, commenced again to demolish the houses of the few poor cottars left on the estate of Knoydart.'[72] Macdonald wrote to Donald that 'Alexander Cameron, with his wife and family were turned out of their father's house, the father being confined to bed at the time... Cameron's wife refused to leave her father-in-law, but the officers struggled with her, and tore the clothes off her back in forcing her out. The parish is to remove the old man to a Poor-house... Some of the outcasts went across Lochnevis to Moidart, to Lord Lovat's property, where they take shelter in large caves... They were in bad health, and could not be removed along with the rest, and were unfit for the passage, when the outcasts or "Refugees," in the tents left for Canada last Summer ... one of their children died, a few days ago, owing to the cold.'[73]

Towards the end of the year Palmerston released both of Fraser's reports and the Solicitor-General's decision, and they were printed together in January 1855 with the summary title *Poor in Knoydart*.[74] Ellice wrote to

Palmerston on 4 December: 'The one admits, the other proves beyond all controversy, the existence of a system which I have properly designated to your Lordship as one of starvation. The Sheriff's Report goes in detail into cases surpassing in misery any that I had previously been aware of. The facts are thus established, notwithstanding the endeavours of the poor-law authorities to suppress them.' Part of Fraser's first report was reproduced by Donald in his later pamphlet *A Plea for the Famishing* and in January 1855 Fraser acknowledged receiving £5 and six bolls of meal from Donald. Macdonald added 'You have no idea how much good your charity has done here. The Sheriff personally distributed the meal, and bought coals with part of the money... Sheriff Fraser's *Report on the Condition and Treatment of the Poor in Knoydart*, now published, does him great credit... Matters are not getting better with us, but worse.' Macdonald wrote an article for the *Glasgow Free Press*, also reproduced by Donald, which acknowledged '10 bolls of meal to be distributed among the remaining outcasts at Knoydart' and praised Donald's activities.[75]

Ellice compiled selected correspondence, newspaper articles and Fraser's reports to form a pamphlet entitled *The State of the Highlands in 1854*, which was published at the end of January 1855. A review by the *Fife Herald* concluded that 'the sooner the Board of Supervision is dispensed with altogether the better' and the *Scottish Guardian* considered 'Mr. Ellice deserves the love and esteem of every true Highlander and the gratitude of the whole country for bringing their case before the Home-Office.'[76]

McNeill's final *Report on the Administration of the Poor Law in the Parish of Glenelg* was appended to the *Ninth Annual Report of the Board of Supervision*. Extracts appeared in the newspapers in February, and it was later serialised in the *Glasgow Herald*. McNeill pointed out that Ellice's complaint was the only one that had been received, and the case of Catharine Mackinnon was the only case that had been put forward by Ellice. McNeill described Catharine and Margaret Mackinnon, and their niece 'of eccentric habits and questionable character, maintained themselves partly by working for wages at field labour, and partly, it appears, by the illicit sale of whisky. Kate M'Phee, described as a smart young woman, occasionally travelled the district alone, hawking tobacco. They had also a large flock of poultry, and contributed to their maintenance by selling eggs.' He went on to say 'they had six or eight chests, some of them of large dimensions, as well as several casks containing property, the nature of which they refused to disclose. Altogether, the furniture, chests, and casks belonging to the two sisters amounted to not less than ten or twelve cart loads.' After summarising Mackinnon's case and that she had refused relief he concluded 'the whole evidence, and all the circumstances, fully confirm the accuracy of the inspector's statements.' McNeill questioned Ellice who 'had no knowledge of any [other] case which he desired to bring to my notice with a view to its investigation.' McNeill was informed by the local manager, John Cameron, that four crofters had been evicted. One of them, Archibald McIsaac,

I examined at the tent in which he had been living. He states that when turned off his croft in August, 1853, he was several years in arrear with his rent, which was £3 per annum; that he had two cows and a stirk, which he sold for £12; and straw for which he got 16s.; that he had debts amounting to £4, which he had paid; that he was allowed to retain the price received for his cattle as well as the crop of his croft for his own use, payment of his arrears not having been exacted or demanded. That his crops supplied his family with food till the beginning of summer, 1854 – that he had also a boat and half a barrel of nets; and that since he had been ejected he had not asked for a house.

McIsaac revealed that he and his family had received from Donald one boll of meal, two blankets, four shirts, two gowns, a light bed-cover and linen for a bed-sheet. Then McNeill stuck the knife in: 'It only remains to be stated, with reference to Mr Ellice's charges against the Parochial Board, that he has himself a seat at that Board – that intimations of its meetings appear to have been regularly sent to him, and that he does not appear to have objected to any of the proceedings, or to have been present at any of the meetings of the Parochial Board. He has not, it is stated, given any assistance in the administration of the Poor Laws in Glenelg... Fortunately the minister, Mr. Macrae, happened to be a man of more than ordinary ability, information, and capacity for business ... to undertake the duty which three of the four heritors altogether neglected.' Inspector Campbell was 'twice examined' and four gentlemen, including Macrae, gave 'a very favourable opinion' of him. McNeill 'discovered nothing that could lead me to doubt the justice of the honourable testimonies to his personal character, and his conduct as Inspector.' McNeill recommended that the Parochial Board should build at Airor 'houses in which the paupers of Knoydart can be collected together under proper superintendence.'[77]

McNeill's report attracted some criticism from the press. *The Scotsman* pointed out that McNeill had ignored Fraser's report and the *Inverness Courier* considered the evictions at Knoydart 'were disgraceful to our country, and cannot be justified by any increase of rent to the proprietor.'[78] Ellice wrote to the new Home Secretary, Sir George Grey: 'Sir John M'Neill's report is an evasion of the real facts, calculated to induce false inferences, and tending to mislead the Government as to the actual state of the administration of the Poor-law.'[79]

The Estate of Knoydart was put up for sale in 1857.[80] Gillies 'Mackissock' of Inverie, aged 54, was interviewed by the Royal Commission in 1894. He had been mentioned in *The Glengarry Evictions* as a son, aged 15, of Archibald McIsaac. Gillies revealed some of those evicted had lived in tents supplied by the people of Glasgow and Edinburgh for three years, set up 'on a small bit of ground that was attached to the Catholic Chapel at Sandaig.' He mentioned that there were still crofters living at Airor, but confirmed that Reidh an Daraich, Doune and Samadalan were cleared and 332 people were sent to America.[81]

19

Boreraig and Suishnish Clearance

In October 1853 the *Inverness Advertiser* mentioned 'a series of very ruthless and inexcusable ejectments has been made on the property of Lord Macdonald.'[1] This happened at Boreraig and Suishnish in the Parish of Strath, Skye. The *Inverness Courier* added that three of the Suishnish tenants had been arrested.[2] Suishnish lay three miles south of Torrin, and Boreraig was one a half miles east of Suishnish. Ruined blackhouses can be seen there today. Those at Boreraig are well preserved and some still have door and window lintels in place. Those

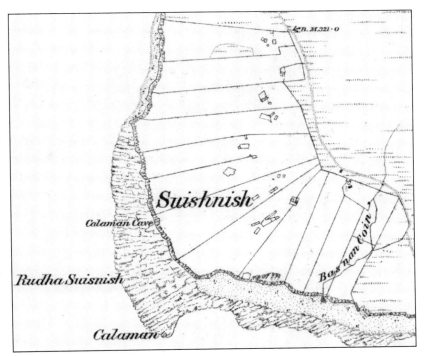

Map of the cleared township of Suishnish, Isle of Skye, surveyed 1876.

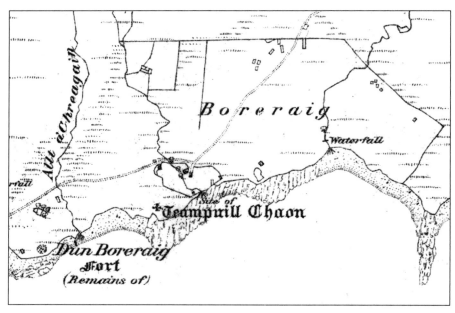

Map of the township of Boreraig, Isle of Skye, surveyed 1876. A few of the houses near the shore appear to be roofed and were possibly still in use, though are all derelict today.

cottages were not demolished after the evictions. When the first OS map was surveyed in 1876, a few near the shore still had roofs, and one of the ruins has lime mortar, so probably remained in use. According to the 1851 census there were 27 households with 145 people living in Suishnish and 22 households with 120 people living at Boreraig. Donald was preoccupied with what was happening in Knoydart, though soon became interested in what was going on here. He provided the background in *Real Scottish Grievances*:

> Boreraig and Suishnish are situate [sic] on the east coast of Skye, and are bounded on the south and east by lochs Slapin and Eishort, and on the north and west by high ridges of mountains, – affording excellent shelter to the sheep and cattle grazing on the slopes below. The arable lands are near the shore; and the houses of the tenants are about a mile from the sea, commanding a fine view of the lochs and the romantic scenery around. The Cullin Hills are in the immediate neighbourhood, having their base at the head of Loch Slapin; yet, rising up to an immense height, with ragged projections, jagged ridges, and gigantic pinnacles – in the utmost irregularity – form the most wonderful cluster of rocks and mountains in Britain.

Boreraig and Suishnish are actually on the S.W. coast of Skye and bounded on the south and west by the lochs and north and east by hills, and most of the houses are about ½ km from the sea. Donald also described the geology:

[Boreraig] is two miles from Suishnish, yet there is a footpath beside the shore from the one place to the other, and that through very romantic scenery. The rocks, which crowd in here upon one another, rise to an amazing height. They are composed of gneiss, greywacke, felspar, trap tuff, amorphous, and decayed layers of quartz, interspersed with veins or dykes of granite, porphyry, limestone, and coarse marble.[3]

However, his description is largely fanciful. The rocks here consist of mudstones and siltstones of the Lias Group of Jurassic age, capped by a thick unit of basalt. Igneous dykes of dolerite and porphyry cut through the sequence. Marble occurs a few miles away and is quarried today. It appears Donald had read some geology and tried to use as many words as he could without understanding what he was writing about. He wrote:

In 1851-52 Lord Macdonald and his trustee commenced to clear away a portion of this people, on the alleged ground that there were too many in the district. Ten families were summoned out that year, and passages were obtained for some of them in the ill-fated "Hercules."... Scarcely had the season for serving warnings of removal on tenants again come round, than the whole of the Boreraig and Suishnish tenants were warned to quit; and on the 4th day of April last year [1853], decrees of removal were obtained against them...

Subsequently they were told that some of them would get lands in another part of the parish; but these were portions of barren moors, exposed to all the storms that blew, and without any shelter wherein to put their heads! Some again were promised lots of land in other distant parts of the island; but this was altogether a mere trick to get rid of them.

Matters went on this way till the middle of September last, when, all of a sudden, Lord Macdonald's ground-officer and constables arrived at Boreraig and Suishnish, and proceeded at once to eject the unfortunate people – in all thirty-two families. In many instances the male heads of the families were away at work; and the wives and children – with, in some cases, aged dependents – were those in possession of the houses... The chief officer directed how the furniture, &c. should be turned out, and then gave orders as to the removal of the aged and the infirm, and such as were unable to move. The scene was now truly heart-rending. The women and children went about tearing their hair, and rending the very heavens with their cries. Mothers, with tender infants at the breast, could do nothing but look on, while their effects and their aged and infirm relations were cast out, and their doors locked in their faces! ... All the appeals to the factor and officers were unavailing, for no mercy whatever was shown to age or sex, – all were indiscriminately thrust out and left to perish on the hills.[4]

The passenger list confirms that some had left previously on the *Hercules*.⁵ The *Inverness Courier* added 'The arrears of rent are said to have been trifling, and with the present improved prices for stock, a good potato crop, and excellent herring fishing, the men were in comfortable circumstances – able and willing to pay rent.'⁶ The geologist Archibald Geikie was a witness and later wrote:

> ... as I was returning from my ramble, a strange wailing sound reached my ears at intervals on the breeze from the west. On gaining the top of one of the hills on the south side of the valley, I could see a long and motley procession winding along the road that led north from Suishnish. It halted at the point in the road opposite Kilbride, and there the lamentation became loud and long. As I drew nearer, I could see that the minster with his wife and daughters had come out to meet the people and bid them all farewell. It was a miscellaneous gathering of at least three generations of crofters. There were old men and women, too feeble to walk, who were placed in carts; the younger members of the community on foot were carrying their bundles of clothes and household effects, while the children, with looks of alarm, walked alongside.⁷

Donald wrote his first letter to the newspapers about this episode in November 1853:

> Four or five of the evicted were above eighty years of age, and there were others sick, and many young children. The scene was heart-rending. Six young children, whose father had gone to work in the south, and whose mother was recently dead, were thrust out by the officers and constables, and left to perish on the hillside. At Boreraig, a woman, aged 88 was brought of a sick bed, and was placed in a chair about 20 yards from her house, and there left totally unheeded. A sick man, aged 83, was brought out on a blanket. At Suishnish, a very old woman, aged 96 years, with her son and four grand-children, were thrust out, and the house was immediately shut up, and they dare not enter it. They took up their abode in an old sheep-cot, 9 feet by 7 feet, with the roof so low that they could only creep in, and the floor so damp that they could not rest on it. They could not take their furniture inside, and there it is still exposed and destroyed by the elements. The son took ill on Wednesday, owing to the cold and damp of the hut; his limbs swelled dreadfully, and he lingered on in painful agony until Sunday morning, when he died. Two of his children lay sick at the time, and the aged grandmother was so ill and so frail that, although her son lay dead aside her for more than four hours before the neighbours called in, *she was quite unable to move*!
>
> Those who visited the hovel in which poor Wm. Matheson lay dead, declare it was *"the most heart-rending sight they ever beheld."* There,

his aged mother and motherless children lay, with the dead corpse in the same bed with them. A coffin was speedily procured, and the remains of poor Matheson were hurried to their final resting-place, from where no trustee or factor can eject them. That Matheson's death was caused by this eviction admits of no doubt whatever.[8]

A similar report appeared in the *Inverness Advertiser* from 'O.P.Q.' corroborating Donald's account, though it referred to the deceased man as 'Sandy Matheson' and before he died his 'aged mother was to be seen seated beside him, vainly attempting, with her attenuated frame, to shield him from the blast which swept at the door.'[9] In the 1851 census 'Alexander Mathison' was aged 48 and his mother was 89. A much longer and more florid account appeared in *Real Scottish Grievances* and Donald also provided detailed descriptions of the evictions of six other households from Suishnish and five from Boreraig. Donald continued in his first letter:

It may now be asked, "But where are the parochial authorities? Where is the inspector of the poor? He should look after such cases." Well, will it be credited that the inspector of the poor is the very official who ejected everyone of the tenants, cottars, and paupers at Suishnish, Boreraig, and Heast? ... Ranald M'Donald is ground officer for Lord Macdonald – acts as sheriff officer and constable for the trustee and factor, and he is inspector of the poor for the Board of Supervision...

Ranald M'Donald, had seven assistants in carrying on these evictions, and such was the wanton violence they used in throwing out the furniture of the poor people, that almost all of it was destroyed.[10]

There are no other mentions of evictions at Heast, so this may be incorrect. In *Real Scottish Grievances* Donald added:

John M'Rae, Duncan M'Rae, and Alexander M'Innes, were, by the orders of the factor, apprehended on the alleged charge of "deforcing and obstructing" the Sheriff's officers when evicting the people of Suishnish. These men, all with helpless families depending on them, were made prisoners, and were dragged along more than thirty miles, and then lodged in the district jail. After being there three days and three nights, they were liberated on bail. Mr. Ross, innkeeper, and Mr. Nicholson, merchant, Portree, kindly offered themselves as cautioners, and the poor men were set at large. Shortly after this they were indicted to stand trial at Inverness, the county town, distant about one hundred miles from them; there they had to proceed, travelling every inch on foot, and reached the Highland capital two days before that fixed for their trial.[11]

The trial took place on 31 October at Inverness Sheriff Court. Alexander Macinnes, Duncan Macrae and John Macrae, all from Suishnish, were 'charged with the crime of deforcing officers of the law in the execution of their duty, inasmuch as, on the 4th of July last, they threatened, intimidated, and violently pushed from the door of the said Alexander Macinnes, two sheriff-officers and a constable who had come to serve on him a decree of removing.' The three men pleaded not guilty. Four summonses of removal had been issued to the tenants at Suishnish and nine at Boreraig, though many of these had families and sub-tenants. The inhabitants had not left by 26 May so, on 21 June, Ranald Macdonald told them they had to leave within 48 hours. Mr Ballingal, the factor, then instructed Macdonald to evict the tenants. On 4 July Macdonald took another sheriff-officer (also named John Macrae), a constable (John Robertson) and two 'assistants' to Alexander Macinnes's house. He spoke to Macinnes in Gaelic but he refused to leave. Macdonald testified that:

> They then proceeded to eject him and put out the furniture. They took hold of a chair and a stool, but no sooner had his assistants done this than Macinnes and his wife said that these articles would not be allowed to be removed ... but his assistants carried them out... No sooner did Macinnes find his assistants out of the house than he cried out that they would not get in again. Before they could turn to go in again, Duncan Macrae and John Macrae were between them and the door... [Duncan] Macrae took hold of his assistants, one after the other, and kept them back... We were pushing to get in and they to keep us out, and in the struggle the side of the wall gave way. He was quite satisfied, from the conduct of these people, he would be unable to perform his duty, except at great personal risk.[12]

Macdonald added that the tenants and families were to be provided with houses or lots at Sleat, Torrin, 'Schomus' and Scullamus. He considered Macinnes was about £2 in arrears and Duncan Macrae about £4. Sheriff-Officer Macrae testified that there were eighteen people at Macinnes's door and 'it was impossible to put the people out, they were so violent' though when cross-examined admitted 'The people might well be peaceable... There were no sticks or stones used; no threatenings to strike, nor angry words. He was not afraid of his life, nor that they would hurt him at all.' Mr Rennie, the lawyer for the defence, mentioned 'It was one of a fearful series of ejectments now being carried through in the Highlands... Here were thirty-two families, averaging four members each, or from 130 to 150 in all, driven out from their houses and happy homes.' When Sheriff-substitute Colquhoun addressed the jury, he quoted Sheriff Alison's definition of deforcement and it was up to the jury to decide whether the 'interference' was 'sufficient to constitute the offence.' The jury then retired and after 20 minutes returned a verdict of not guilty. Donald added that when the men were acquitted, they 'were cheered by a very large crowd of people outside.'[13]

In Donald's *Highland Clearances* the section on Boreraig and Suishnish was similar to his first letter, with this addition:

Many of the evicted people in Skye are sheltered in old sheds, sheep-cots, and other wretched buildings belonging to their poor neighbours. Many of them are suffering severely from cold, and the majority of them are wretchedly clad... Supplies of clothing and other necessaries had to be forwarded to them; and steps have been taken to render their miserable habitations more safe for them.[14]

A long 'Memorandum' was written defending the evictions:

These farms consist of 30 crofts of enclosed arable ground from 6 to 9 Scots acres in extent, with grazing in addition, upon Swishnish for 3 cows and 1 horse, and on Borreraig for 6 cows, 1 horse, 1 stirk, and 16 sheep to each croft, and for which the landlord was entitled to receive a rent, from the Swishnish tenants of £5 11s 8d each, and from those in Borreraig of £11 12s 6d: these rents are, unfortunately, however for the proprietor, only nominal, for he has never yet been able to realize them.

In the year 1849, considerably over one year's rent (£169 18s 3d) was remitted by the Right Hon. Lord Macdonald to the tenants of these farms, in the hopes that, by doing so, the tenants might receive a stimulus to exertion, and for the future prove more punctual in their payments.

This, however, did not prove to be the case; and we find that, in the course of a couple of years, their united arrears amounted to no less than a sum of £239 0s 10d, with no prospect of improvement... 8 of them emigrated to Australia, with their families, and several others left the place for more eligible situations ... the most indigent and idle remained on the farms, and from their reduced circumstances, were found quite unable to stock and manage their own crofts and holdings, far less to take possession of and stock those left by the emigrants.

Under these circumstances the trustees upon his lordship's estate had two alternatives left him, namely, to offer for the acceptance of the remaining 18 crofters (not the 32, as stated in the *Inverness Courier*), that they should follow their friends to Australia, or that they should remove to the vacated lots left by emigrants from other townships on the property...

The first proposition was universally declined, but not so the second, for, with a few exceptions, perhaps 8 or 10 out of the remaining availed themselves of the offer of crofts and dwellings, in localities which they themselves seemed satisfied had been chosen for them judiciously...

A few continuing obstinately to remain upon the ground, obliged the trustee for his lordship to give orders for their ejection by the officers of the law, who, meeting with opposition from the two Macraes and Macinnes, gave rise to the criminal prosecution...

A clearer case in favour of a landlord ejecting his crofting tenants can scarcely exist or be imagined, for here we have a class of people located on

Donald Ross and the Highland Clearances

The eviction of Duncan and Flora Macrae from Suishnish, as depicted in *Real Scottish Grievances*, however the scenery is more like that at Boreraig and they were not forced to emigrate. Duncan was arrested for 'deforcing officers of the law in the execution of their duty' though was found not guilty.

> two farms on the shores of one of the finest, we might almost say without any exception, the most productive loch in the West Highlands for white fishing, at easy rents – none to be found more so anywhere in the West Highlands, with perhaps the solitary exception of those on Glengarry's property – good sizeable crofts, abundance of grazing for stock, and an indulgent landlord ... a community being reared up in poverty and Ignorance, far removed from the means of attending on the ordinary ordinances of religion, or the means of educating their families. Grown up men and women are found, on inquiry, to be unable to read or write; several have never been within the walls of a church. There exists no roads by which they can send their children to school, at a distance of nine miles...
>
> Feelings of humanity, pity, and benevolence actuated the trustees upon his lordship's estates in the removal of these people to a more favoured locality ... the factor went beyond his duty in cautioning the officers of the law to use on no account violence, or even words tending to irritate or annoy the parties against whom proceedings had been taken...
>
> A few of the most obdurate and ungrateful of these tenants continued on their crofts, still declining to remove, and by their inflexibility have deprived themselves of lands which had been set aside for their use.[15]

In response, 'Scotus,' presumably Donald, wrote to the *Northern Ensign*:

> I noticed in the *Inverness Advertiser* a document styled, '*Memorandum regarding the Boreraig and Suishnish Evictions*,' &c., in Skye, dated 'Portree House, Dec. 29, 1853,' and evidently issued by the present

occupant of the '*Portree House*,' the factor for the trustee on the M'Donald properties in Skye...

The 'Memorandum' is one of the most wretchedly imbecile documents I ever perused. It is a tissue of disjointed sophistry and hypocrisy – incorrect in its narrative of facts, and most ridiculous and inconsistent in its conclusions... The famine, it is well known, commenced in Skye in 1847... For the subsequent arrears, which were a mere trifle, Lord M'Donald received ample consideration from the Highland Relief Board, besides having got several thousand acres of ground trenched and drained at the expense of the Highland Relief Meal of 1849-50, given, I believe, on the understanding that his lordship would grant leases to the tenants, but up to this day no leases are granted...

In 1852, and in 1853, the tenants not only paid their rents in *full*, which is £180 sterling per annum, but they also wiped off some arrears that had remained since 1851; and they improved their houses considerably, and built fences round their gardens and fields...

Since the people were deprived of their lands, a sheep farmer has offered £100 of rent for the lands and grazings for which the tenants paid £180, and it is understood that, as he is a friend of the factor, he will have the two townships at this offer. Does not this shew a disgraceful system of management of property, as well as of people? ... the M'Raes and M'Innes's, who remained on the property, had not only been thrust out, but were kicked and struck, and afterwards made prisoners of, and yet the 'Memorandum' holds that these people were properly treated, and that Lord M'Donald and the trustees on his property are most indulgent and exemplary in their conduct as landlord and managers... When Matheson, one of the evicted tenants, died a few days after in a sheep cot ... there was no inquiry from 'Portree House,' nor from Armadale castle, whether these things were true or not, – no steps taken to rescue these families from death...

Who ever heard of Lord M'Donald's or of the trustees' zeal for religion until now? Is it not a fact that at and subsequent to the disruption in 1843, his Lordship would not grant one inch of ground to the adherents of the Free Church, to build churches or schools on, although they formed nine-tenths of the population on his extensive estates? ... And yet this is the new-fledged zeal for religion that dictates the eviction of the people, the levelling of their houses, and turning them adrift on the moors, in order to bring them nearer to schools and kirks! All fudge! Common sense would dictate sending the schoolmaster to the people where they were... And as for the people being far from church, (only nine miles), who ever heard of a Highlander being too far from church? We have seen them walking ten, twelve, or fifteen miles across the hills, to hear sermon...

The people of Boreraig and Suishnish, indeed, had for some years been favoured with periodical visits from a Baptist minister, who preached to them, and whose labours for their spiritual good were highly appreciated. These visits were made five or six times a year.[16]

From Geikie's account, the Suishnish people certainly knew their local parish minister, John Mackinnon, who lived at Kilbride. Geikie added that 'Not only the people of the parish, but numbers of others from adjacent parishes, tramped many a long mile to attend the services' at Broadford Church.[17] More evictions followed. 'O.P.Q.' wrote on 2 January 1854:

On Friday last [30 December], Ranald Macdonald ... accompanied by two other sheriff-officers, the policeman of the district, and a private individual of the neighbourhood, went to the house of Niel Macinnes, a lotter in Suishnish, and proceeded to evict him...

Among those to be ejected was a young wife, the daughter-in law of old Niel, and her infant not four weeks old. She had never crossed the door from the time of her confinement; but not to give offence, she went to the well and brought a drink to the officers of the law. Yet she and her infant were turned out to all the horrors of the fearful storm.

Another of the ejected persons was a woman of about 60 years of age – a very good natured and harmless person. She was subjected to exceedingly rough usage at the hands of one of the party... The woman gave him no sort of molestation or offence, yet he kicked her severely.

On Saturday the whole party proceeded to evict Alexander Macinnes ... on that day, every whit as stormy and cold as the preceding one, with snow lying deep on the ground and drifting fearfully in the wind, he and his were driven from their house. From this house three very young children were ejected.[18]

Donald visited Skye in February, just before his third visit to Knoydart, and provided a similar account in *Real Scottish Grievances*. Donald Macinnes was Neil's son and the father of the infant mentioned above:

Donald's wife had a child only twelve days before, and she was not in a fit state to be removed. Still the officers persisted in her removal, and then she came out of bed, with her child in her arms. Her husband was not in at the time; and the officers forced her out of the house with nothing on but her petticoats and a bedgown. The snow and drift was now terrible; and the poor creature, moving on before it, took shelter beside a fence, closely clasping her tender infant in her arms. In a few moments her back and head were completely covered with snow; and it was her movements, in trying to shelter her child from the drift, that caused her husband to notice her as he was coming home. He immediately lifted her up and took her to the house from which she was evicted, and found his furniture put out, and the officers trying to close the door. He pushed open the door, and took his poor wife and infant in under shelter... The ground officer was now afraid at Donald's appearance, and called in the district policeman, giving him instructions to apprehend Donald and convey him to prison; but when this official saw Donald armed with a formidable oak cudgel, which he promised to bring with all his strength over the head of the first who would meddle with his wife, or with himself while protecting her, the policeman skulked away. It now appears that this recent eviction was illegal from beginning to end. No fresh warrants were granted against the people, and the old warrants were exhausted with the first evictions...

Donald M'Innes's wife became seriously unwell. Her breasts dried up, and she could not nurse her child. A nurse was brought from a distance, and the mother was relieved of the child; but for several weeks after her health was not improving, and when I was in the district on the 15th February, she was far from recovered; and although only in the 24th year of her age, she looked prematurely old, and was evidently much depressed in mind as well as in body.[19]

The *Northern Ensign* considered 'The course of conduct pursued by the trustees on Lord M'Donald's property, – who, so late as 30th Dec. last, and when a fearful snow storm prevailed, turned adrift on the hills of Skye about half a dozen families, leaving them to perish of cold and exposure – loudly calls for Government interference.'[20]

On 25 February Donald wrote: 'During my recent visit to the Western Islands, I have witnessed such scenes of suffering, of want, and of misery, among the paupers, as could scarcely be credited.' He gave two detailed examples, including an update on the mother of the late Alexander Matheson:

I found Flora Robertson or Matheson, a widow, aged *ninety-six years*, at Swishnish ... suffering from the infirmities of old age, and only allowed by the parish the sum of *two shillings and six pence* per *month*. Anything more wretched than the appearance of this old woman I never yet witnessed. Her bed, a pallet of straw and some pieces of old blanket, was on the bare floor. Her appearance, as she lay on this collection of straw and rags, with a thin threadbare dirty blanket over her, was enough to have excited pity in any breast. Her face and arms had the colour of lead – she was evidently starving...

[After sheltering in the sheep-cot] The old woman was subsequently removed to where I saw her – a more comfortable place, certainly; but her physical state was most shamefully neglected... There she lay – her voice feeble and her speech stammering ... I asked her what was the state of health – what was it she complained of most? She tried to raise herself up, and then replied, 'I complain of nothing, but general weakness or debility, *all arising from want of food*.'[21]

A letter dated 6 March acknowledged that Donald had

> ...sent a quantity of meal for distribution among the most needful in the parishes of Sleat and Strath, the same having been distributed in the former parish by the Rev. Mr M'Phail of the Free Church, and in Strath by Messrs George R. M'Phail and F. H. Mackenzie, Broadford, who are requested to convey the grateful thanks of the recipients to Mr Ross for this and many former favours of a similar kind...
>
> Mr Ross has sent a bale containing a considerable quantity of ready made clothing, together with several hundreds of tracts and other popular periodicals, to be distributed in Sleat by Mrs M'Phail, and in Strath by Mr F. H. Mackenzie, and Mr Hector M'Kinnon, schoolmaster at Torran, chiefly for the benefit of the children attending the school.[22]

In June a 'A Bill to promote the more regular administration of the Poor-law in certain parishes in Scotland' was presented by Edward Ellice and read before Parliament. It called for 'a more regular inspection of the administration of the law' in 'the more remote and comparatively inaccessible parishes' by 'special inspectors.'[23]

It was not until the May 1855 that the second reading of Ellice's amendment to the Poor Law (Scotland) Bill went before Parliament. It was widely reported in the newspapers though the reports varied. Hansard reported that Ellice said that his bill 'did not propose to interfere with the operation of the existing law... His sole object was to enforce the better carrying out of the present law, and to secure to the poor of Scotland those benefits which the Scotch Poor Law Act professed to give them, but of which they were in fact deprived.'[24] Ellice pointed out that the appeal process was flawed and there was a lack of regular inspections. With regards to evictions in Strath, presumably Boreraig and Suishnish, Ellice had received a letter from Lord Macdonald:

> ...the evictions had been in direct opposition to his feelings and wishes, and that he had repeatedly written to the trustee on his estate representing to him the cruelty of the measure he had in view, and begging him to send orders not to proceed with it, or, if he insisted upon such a measure, to delay it till spring, when the people would be better able to provide for themselves. His wishes had not been attended to, and these cruel proceedings had been carried out to the utmost extent of harshness.

With regards to the evictions in Knoydart 'their houses were pulled down over their heads. Two women nearly died under premature labour caused by the hardships they suffered.' Ellice provided information from Fraser's reports and said that the Board of Supervision had sent a commissioner to investigate: 'Sir John M'Neill was the last person who should have been intrusted with that inquiry, and his Report must of necessity be looked with suspicion.' Ellice continued 'What, then, was the House to think of the two reports...? They could not leave those two men in responsible situations, remaining under a doubt as to which of their statements was true. Either the sheriff should be removed from his situation, or Sir John M'Neill should be dismissed from the post of Chairman of the Board of Supervision.'

The Lord Advocate, James Moncreiff, believed Ellice 'had considerably exaggerated the present condition of the districts in question.' He had 'sat as Solicitor General for a time on the Board of Supervision, and he could bear testimony not only to the exceeding ability and unwearied industry of Sir John M'Neill ... but to the many hours which he devoted to the consideration of appeals from paupers in all parts of Scotland.' He considered the new bill 'was not in the slightest degree required, as the powers contained in the present law were quite sufficient to accomplish the purpose aimed at by this Bill.' With regards to McNeill's report, Moncreiff did consider that 'although there was no application for relief, there was distress which was known to the inspector and to the local Board, and which, he thought, they ought to have remedied ... and he would suggest that the hon. Member, who had done good service in bringing the question under the consideration of the House, should content himself with that proceeding, and refrain from persevering with the measure ... if his hon. Friend would leave the question in his hands, he would promise to procure for it an early and careful consideration.' Other MPs agreed with aspects of Ellice's reading though also agreed with Moncreiff's offer. In response Ellice said 'after the assurance which had been given by the Government with reference to the subject with which his Bill proposed to deal, he had no difficulty in at once consenting to withdraw it.'

Evictions on Skye continued and in the 1880s things came to a head when the people of the Braes on the east side and Glendale on the west violently resisted attempts to evict them. The marines were called in but the people accepted them passively and not a shot was fired. The events resulted in the government setting up the Crofters' Commission in 1883, which led to the Crofters' Act 1886, giving the crofters some rights but was not wholly satisfactory as it did nothing for the landless cottars.[25] The Commission was informed that some of the Suishnish people had been moved to Scullamus, Breakish and Sleat. Donald Macinnes, 75, one of those evicted from Boreraig, confirmed that Alexander Matheson of Suishnish had died 'caused by his being evicted in bad weather.'[26] The people were re-settled on plots vacated by *Hercules* emigrants or on subdivided plots, additionally at Isleornsay, Drumfearn and Tarskavaig.[27] Farquhar Kelly, who was mentioned in *Real Scottish Grievances* as aged 11, informed the Royal Commission in 1893 that his father, Neil, was one of the last to be evicted, from Boreraig.[28] James Hunter and David Craig interviewed descendants of those evicted, one of whom was teacher Peggy MacKinnon, a grand-daughter of Farquhar Kelly.[29]

20

The Massacre of the Rosses

The pamphlet for which Donald is best known was originally titled *The Russians of Ross-shire or Masscacre of the Rosses*. It had 'Russians' in the title because the Crimean War had just commenced and was getting a lot of attention in the press. The first edition sold out very quickly and no copy appears to have survived. A second edition was issued soon afterwards, which included an additional essay, *The Clearing of the Glens*, and was his longest pamphlet at forty-three pages and over 20,000 words.[1] A third posthumous edition was published by Alexander Mackenzie in which 'Russians of Ross-shire' was dropped from the title and the English had been improved. The first twenty-nine pages of the second edition were reproduced in 1977 for the *Radical Reprint: Series 1*, by The Journeyman Press.

Donald's pamphlet was the main published account of the police brutality and has been widely cited, along with a few newspaper articles and letters.[2] However, numerous court documents have also survived, including many witness statements, prisoner declarations and a medical report, which corroborate much of what Donald wrote.

The 'Massacre' took place at Greenyards on the southern side of the River Carron, to the east of where the Glencalvie Clearance took place a decade earlier. Strathcarron was described as a 'beautiful vale' with 'an excellent river for angling;' the fishing rights were owned by the 2nd Duke of Sutherland.[3] On William Roy's mid-18th century military survey map of Scotland, Greenyards was marked as 'Er.' and 'Wr. Gruniard.'[4] In 1854 the principal tenant clarified that 'Easter Greenyard' and 'Wester Greenyard' together make up 'Greenyards.'[5] They are clearly marked on the first detailed OS maps, surveyed in 1875, however, on modern maps they are marked as Easter and Wester 'Gruinards.' In the 1851 census the inhabitants of 'Greenyard' comprised twenty-seven households and 127 people.

In 1852-3, there were five attempts at evicting the people of Coigach in Wester Ross, which the people resisted. Eventually the landlord, Lord Stafford, later 3rd Duke of Sutherland, gave up trying.[6] It is likely that the people of Greenyards heard about this and decided to follow suit.

The Massacre of the Rosses

Donald in *The Russians of Ross-shire* explains:

> The proprietor of these lands is one Major Robertson, whose residence is in Kindeace, in Easter Ross. He is now close on 70 years of age, with nothing remarkable in his history, excepting a strange hatred of human beings as occupiers of his land, and an inordinate love of sheep and sheep farmers... There were removed from Glencalvie thirty six families, from Eidan twelve families, and now it is contemplated to remove twenty-four families from Greenyard; and when this is accomplished the whole lands belonging to Major Robertson, in the parish of Kincardine, will be under sheep. The present Tacksman of Glencalvie, Eidan, and Greenyard, is one Mr Munro, a very old man, with scarcely any good qualities to recommend him... In his neighbourhood there lives twenty-two families occupying land. They pay rents, varying from £8. to £14. each, to him as the principal Tacksman, – he paying so much to the proprietor for the lands which they occupy. These tenants are not one penny in arrears of rent: they bear a very excellent character: no complaint is made against their conduct in the district; and yet, Munro with (as is alleged) the "consent and concurrence" of Major Robertson, the proprietor, applied recently for warrants of removal against them.

Alexander Munro, the principal tenant, was listed in the 1851 census as aged 68, with his wife, Margaret 35, and two children. He lived at the farm at Easter Greenyard, which is still there today.

Before the 'Massacre,' incidents took place which inflamed the situation. On 20 February 1854 an anonymous letter declared Munro 'will be Burned to Hell' if he evicts 'the poor of Grinyards.'[7] Shortly afterwards Major Charles Robertson visited his agent 'Donald Stewart [in] Tain, along with Alexander Munro ... for the purpose of instructing him to serve a summons of removing against certain subtenants of Munro's... Though four persons were included in the Summons, one of them was to remove voluntarily.– viz John Munro who is the brother of Alexander Munro.' Alexander Munro stated 'There are about twenty subtenants on the farm, who occupy houses and lots of land. They held their said possessions before I became tenant of the farm, but I got right to their holdings, and their sub-rents were made payable to me. I have been tenant of the farm for about thirty years. I obtained my present lease nine years ago, and it endures for nine years yet. The Proprietor stipulated in my lease that he should have power to remove two of the subtenants each year, after which their lots would fall to be occupied by me.' Stewart confirmed that Munro had given him the names of the four subtenants.[8] Stewart was one of the two lawyers who had defended Donald and John Ross at Dornoch Sheriff Court for removing the doors and windows from Robert Gordon's house.

A Summons of Removing was drawn up ordering John Munro of Acre-Dhu; George Ross, pensioner, of Balmeanach; John Ross alias Bain of Rein-Rhiach, and Ann Ross alias Taylor of Rein-Rhiach, 'to flit' by Whitsunday.[9] Donald

Ross alias Mackinlay of Langwell was asked to drive Sheriff Officer William Catharine Macpherson, who was to serve the summons, to the area. Ross later stated 'I had come to Tain in a gig along with William Ross Kincardine, and we agreed to drive Macpherson as far as Ardgay... We all had a dram together in the Inn at Ardgay, and Macpherson there told us that he was going to Greenyard... On reaching that part of the road from Ardgay to Greenyard which is situated from 60 to 100 yards to the east of the march between Greenyards and Dunie, and on the lands of Dunie, we were met by a crowd of women, some of whom took hold of me, and others took hold of Macpherson, and drew him off my horse, on which he was riding... I got from the people and followed the horse, but was caught by the people in a potato field, and they threw me down and searched me.' On 10 March Macpherson lodged a statement with Tain Sheriff Court:

> We reached Greenyard about 8 o'Clock in the evening of the 7th of March ... I was met by a crowd of people within about two hundred yards of Munro's house. The crowd consisted of men and women, and their number might amount to I think Sixty or Seventy. I think the number of women preponderated. There was a cry among them "Now he is come". They surrounded me, and on my asking what they wanted, they said they wanted my papers. I was immediately laid hold of by the females of the party, and they took the summons and service copies, with some other papers which I had in my pocket, from me, and they pulled off my coat and searched all my pockets. They then lighted a fire, and some of the men having examined the papers, they returned to me all except the said Summons of Removing and service Copies, but burnt them in the fire... After searching me they allowed me to rise, and I then saw that part of the crowd had laid hold of Peter Mackenzie one of the County Police who happened to be there ... the whole crowd escorted us away from Greenyard and brought us to Bonar Bridge a distance of about four miles where they gave us our liberty. I was not hurt by the proceedings.[10]

Mackenzie provided a similar statement, adding that Greenyard

> ...is within my beat as a Police Officer. For about a week before the 7th of March, persons were assembling at Greenyard for the purpose of preventing the service of summonses of removal ... it was arranged among them, that on the arrival of an officer with summonses, a signal should be made by the discharge of a gun. I was in the house of Alexander Munro the Farmer at Greenyard, between eight and nine o'clock in the evening of the said 7th of March, and then heard a shot. I immediately went out... I saw that William MacPherson, a preceding witness, was in their hands, and that they had stripped him of his whole clothes (leaving him quite naked), and were searching his clothes and

taking papers out of his pocket ... some of the crowd caught hold of me, and tried for my pockets to search for papers, but they were unable to find the pockets in my uniform. They however laid me down on my back, and took off my shoes and stockings. After taking the summonses from MacPherson, the crowd allowed him [to] put on his clothes...

[Fourteen people were listed] In particular the following persons were engaged in taking the summonses from the officer and burning them viz; Ann Ross Taylor; Ann Ross McKinlay; Donald Ross Bain & Peter Ross Bain. The said Ann Ross was one of the persons against whom a summons was to be executed, and so were George Ross father of the said Betty Ross; & John Ross Bain father of the said Donald, Peter and Charles Ross Bain.

Munro later confirmed that Mackenzie was in his house: 'I had asked him to watch my house, being afraid of violence from the mob.'

On 9 March Sheriff-substitute Robert Sutherland Taylor wrote to Sheriff Thomas Mackenzie, 'It would be worse than useless to go through the form of attempting to serve the summonses without having an adequate force to ensure the executions; and I think that at least 20 or 25 regular policemen will be required for that purpose... It is certainly I think high time to put an effectual stop to these lawless deforcements.'[11]

The next incident happened two weeks later. Dugald McCaig, Excise Officer, Inverness, stated:

On Wednesday, the 22d March 1854, I was at Greenyard in the Parish of Kincardine along with John Docherty and Alexander Macleod Preventive men. We were surveying the grounds to see that there was nothing wrong. As soon as I approached Greenyard a number of people began to collect and gathered round me... When I had reached the place on the farm of Greenyard and near the house of Alexander Munro the tenant of the farm, I was laid hold of by some women of the party, who took off my weekcloth and muffles, and my shoes, and opened my waist-coat, and attempted to take off my coat and waist-coat and trousers but on seeing them proceed so far I took out my pistol and stood before them holding it in my hand, and I told them that I would have to put the law into execution against the first person that would touch me thereafter. One of the men, whose name I have since learned to be Peter Ross Wester Greenyard then came forward to me with a pistol and said that it would be life for life. I had before this told the people assembled who I was, and had shewn them my Commission and explained that I was in the discharge of my duty. Considering that it would be useless, in consequence of the number of the people to resist them farther, I replaced my pistol in my pocket, and they then proceeded to search me. This was done by the women. They took my papers out of my pocket including my Diary and Commission and also took my pocket book containing my money. On my demand they returned the money, but some of the women disappeared with the papers and pocket-book, and in about a quarter of an hour afterwards they brought them back to me... After restoring them they insisted on me and my said assistants returning by the way we had come ... and I in consequence was obliged to go back to Ardgay. My clothes were slightly injured by the people but I was not personally hurt.[12]

McCaig returned the following day and obtained the names of some of those present. Docherty and Macleod confirmed they were also searched and that McCaig had drawn his pistol. Docherty added 'I cannot say whether Peter Ross's pistol was loaded, but I observed that the cap was on the lock.'

The first newspaper article appeared on 28 March:

About three weeks ago a sheriff-officer appeared in the parish with summonses of removal against some of the tenants on the Estate of Major Robertson of Kindeace, and was met by large crowd of men and women, who stripped him naked, burnt the summonses, and conveyed him unhurt to the boundary of the parish, where they parted with him on friendly terms. Encouraged by their success so far, they have resolved to prevent the execution of any fresh summonses, and have since watched day and night the appearance of other officers, and are ready at any time ... on a certain signal, to summon to their aid upwards of 300 persons, comprising many of the inhabitants within an area of 15 miles. We understand the proprietor and authorities are determined, however, to vindicate the majesty of the law, and a smart contest is anticipated.[13]

Two days later the *Inverness Courier* added 'thirty-five Ross-shire constables and fifteen of the force of this county, are to muster to-morrow with a view to enforcing the removals.'[14]

For the deforcement of Macpherson, Harry Munro Taylor, Procurator Fiscal, requested a warrant from the Sheriff to apprehend 'Donald Ross alias Bain, Peter Ross alias Bain, Charles Ross alias Bain, Neil Matheson, Peter Matheson, Simon Ross, David Ross, Donald Mackenzie, Ann Ross and Ann Ross alias Mackinlay and to bring them before you for examination; and thereafter to Commit them prisoners to the Prison of Tain.' For assaulting McCaig, a warrant was requested to apprehend 'Peter Ross alias Bain, Hugh Ross and Donald Ross.'[15] The warrants were granted by Sheriff-substitute Taylor, who was Harry Taylor's cousin. Another Summons of Removing was drawn up and entrusted to Sheriff Officer David Mitchell, and early on 31 March he proceeded to Greenyards, accompanied by a police force led by Sheriff-substitute Taylor. Later that day Taylor wrote to Sheriff Mackenzie:

I am very glad to be able to announce the successful termination of our expedition to Greenyards this morning. The arrangements for the junction at one point of the 3 parties from Dingwall, Invergordon and Tain at 5 o clock were well carried out and after swearing in the Inverness-shire men as Special Constables and reproaching the men we all proceeded direct to within two miles or so of Greenyards in the carriages. We had then to walk, which we did at a quick pace in the expectation of surprising the people; but we soon heard shots from different quarters, which we knew were fired as signals of our approach. At the same time we saw numbers of men and women running towards Greenyards from the various scattered cottages along the strath; and on approaching the place, we saw a mass of people principally women collected and intercepting the path. On getting up to them, they raised quite a clamour of voices, all vociferating at once. I tried to obtain silence, told them who we were, and required them to allow us to pass and to disperse quietly; but my voice was quite drowned, and the crowd made towards us in a menacing way,– when the police were ordered to clear the road, and then began a regular skirmish, in which the women used their sticks and were assisted by a number of the men. But the police likewise used their batons vigorously, and seeing and feeling that we were in earnest, the mob soon gave way and began to make their escape in all directions. We had thus the way open, and proceeded without farther molestation to the cottages, and had the citations duly served. This effected, the police gave chase to several persons who kept watching at some distance with the intention of making prisoners; but the men got off from their superior knowledge of the ground which is a series of swelling hills intersected by deep gullies; and we were obliged to content ourselves with five of the principal ringleaders among the women. One of these women had been so very badly hurt by the batons that it would have been cruelty to drag her along with us, and we left her at Mr Munro's house, sending an express for the nearest Doctor to come and visit her & dress her hurt... We take the four prisoners to Tain along with us.

I think the people have had such a lesson today as will effectually prevent a recurrence of the lawless deforcement of officers of the law in this quarter.

We estimate that there were fully 200 women assembled to receive us and 100 men... None of the Police force has been hurt. They are a fine active body of men, and did their duty with good courage and spirit.[16]

Taylor's statement, dated 1 April, added,

...a Police Force of twenty four men was procured, to assist the Sheriff Officers in getting the Citations delivered, and in apprehending the ringleaders in the deforcement.– I accordingly proceeded to Greenyards in official charge of that Force (27 men in all)... On reaching a point, about 4. or 500. yards in a direct line from Greenyards farm house,

> we found that the pathway, which had the river on the right hand & high ground on the left, was blocked up by a large mob of people... I called out for "silence", and said "I am the Sheriff Substitute,– these are officers of the law on duty,– & I require you to allow us pass." But my voice was completely drowned in the clamour. I had the Riot Act in my hand, which I was about to read: But saw that the attempt was useless from the continued noise & violence of the mob:- So, without further parley the Officers were ordered to clear the way.[17]

Other witness statements by officers present were similar in stating there were 200-300 people in the mob and that most of them carried sticks. Superintendent George Cumming later added 'The sticks were of various degrees of thickness, some of them stouter, and others less stout than a walking stick.' It was also reported that stones were thrown. Mitchell thought 'there were some men in women's clothes' but no-one else said this. Donald Ross alias Mackinlay who was 'merely looking on,' subsequently stated that Sheriff-substitute Taylor said '"I am the Sheriff – Clear the road", and without giving any time, said "Knock them down," and immediately the police officers rushed on the women and knocked many of them down with their batons... Some of the women carried small sticks.'

The statements are inconsistent in exactly where the incident took place. Cumming later stated 'It was arranged that we should reach the ground shortly after the appearance of day light... On arriving within about a quarter of a mile to the east of the Greenyard farm house we found that a crowd of men and women were assembled on the road or pathway and ground on both sides of it and they occupied the whole space extending from the river on one side to high ground on the other, this space forming a narrow pass by which alone we could proceed.' Peter Mackenzie said it happened 800 yards east of Munro's house, however, both he and Mitchell said it happened on the Greenyards side of the boundary between Greenyards and 'Dunie.' The boundary between Greenyards and Dounie (Downie) is clearly marked on the early OS maps along the Alltan Doirein. Donald, in *Russians*, said it happened 'in the pass where the road led to Greenyard' and 'the policemen emerged from a wood.'[18] A living descendent of one of the victims explained that the 'Massacre' took place at Fearnich field (or Fernich, Fearniach or Fearnaich as it was never written down) near a burn called Ault Dorain or the 'burn of pain.'[19] Just to the east of the burn is the Fuaran na Suileig wood, which was probably the one Donald was referring to. So, the most likely site of the 'Massacre' was near the river just west of the Alltan Doirein and 200m N.E. of Easter Greenyard farm. At some point 'Greenyard murder was in the year 1854 March 31' was added to the Glencalvie scratchings on the window of Croick Church.

Harry Taylor immediately asked Surgeon William Gordon to visit the injured people, who wrote a report later that day:

The Massacre of the Rosses

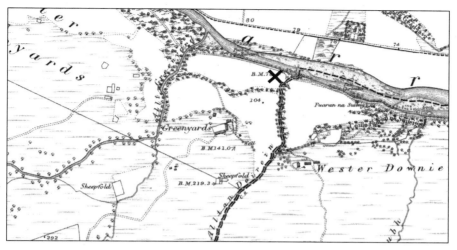

The likely site of the Massacre of the Rosses at Easter Greenyard, Ross & Cromarty, which took place on 31 March 1854.

1st Case. of Elizabeth Ross Amat, and found her in the house of John Ross Greenyard.– she is about 22 years of age and unmarried.– she is Wounded severely above the left ear – 3 inches long – ¼ inch deep – scull [sic] exposed + bleeding profusely – pulse 90 – there are several marks of blows on her right arm and other parts of her body – and I consider her dangerously ill – I have dressed her wound and gave her medicine.

2nd Case. of Grace Ross – Ca-derg – she is about 20 years of age and unmarried – I found her in bed wounded on right temple – 2 inches long + scull exposed – vomiting incessantly – pulse 92 and intermittent – I consider her in a very precarious state – I shaved about the wound + dressed it – also gave medicine.

3rd Case. of Christina Ross Greenyards – she is about 48 years of age + unmarried – wounded on left temple 1½ inch long scull exposed, pulse regular – I dressed her wound + gave medicine.–

4th Case. of Margaret McGregor Wife of William Ross Wester Greenyard – wounded on left temple ¼ inch long + bleeding from right ear – it is my opinion the scull is fractured and the injury seems to have been inflicted from the point of a sharp weapon – she was in such excited state from pain – fainting + vomiting that it was with difficulty I dressed her wound – I consider her in a very dangerous state – I gave her medicine.

5th Case. of Ann Ross Langwell – she is about 56 years of + unmarried – wounded above right ear 2 inches long scull exposed – left elbow joint cut open – all the fore part of that arm bruised + discoloured – right shoulder much swollen + discoloured + unable to move it – I dressed her wound and gave medicine.

6th Case of Naomi Ross Langwell – she is about 24 years of age + unmarried – I found her in bed – wounded above the right ear 2 inches long – about the wound much swollen and almost all her body marked with bruises – pulse 105 – feverish + convulsive – I dressed her wound + gave medicine.[20]

Harry Taylor then asked Dr N.B. Ross to visit, who, on 3 April, reported 'I found that the greatest number had received slight injuries' though three of the women had severe head injuries: Marrion Ross of Langwell, Margaret Macgregor or Ross of Wester Greenyard and Elizabeth Ross of Amat.[21]

The four women who had been taken to Tain Jail were Margaret Ross of Amat, Margaret Ross of Amatnatua, aged 18, daughter of Thomas Ross, Christy Ross of Rein-Rhiach, 50, wife of John Ross alias Bain, and Ann Ross alias Taylor of Easter Greenyard, 35. John and Ann were two of the subtenants in the Summons. The four were interrogated on the day of their arrest in the presence of Sheriff-substitute Taylor and gave declarations in Gaelic, which were translated by Burgh Officer Hugh Mackay, written up by Clerk Andrew Ross and witnessed by Peter Mackenzie. With regards to the deforcement of Macpherson, the first Margaret wasn't present. Christy declared 'I held Macpherson by the coat while others searched him for his papers' and Ann admitted that she was in the party that escorted Macpherson and Mackenzie to Bonar Bridge. None of them admitted stripping Macpherson or burning his papers. With regards to the assault on McCaig, only Christy and Ann were present. Christy declared 'I did not do any harm to him, nor did I put my hands into his pockets. He presented a pistol at my breast three times.' Ann declared 'I did not myself put a hand upon him. The Excise Officer drew a pistol from his pocket which he presented close to my breast.' With regards to the events of 31 March, the first Margaret declared 'I had no stick in my hand at the time. I did not strike any of the Officers or Policemen, nor throw stones at any of them.' The second Margaret declared 'I had not a stick in my hand at that time. I received a blow in the scuffle on the shoulder.' Christy declared 'The Sheriff told the people that he was the Sheriff Substitute and to clear the way on which I was moving off, when I received a blow on the head from one of the Policemen, which knocked me down and he afterwards struck me a blow on the arm.' Ann declared 'I had no stick. I received a blow on the head from some one I do not Know, and another person seized and held me till I received three blows on the shoulder... Our object was to prevent the service of the Summons of Removing on me and others at Greenyard so that we might Keep our places for another year.'[22]

From seeing the women in prison, Macpherson 'had a strong impression that Ann Ross was one of those who led me away from Greenyard to Bonar.' Mackenzie stated that Ann lived at Wester, not Easter Greenyard and 'She was particularly active in stripping the officer Macpherson of his clothes, and she was one of the first who laid hold of me. The prisoner Christy Ross ... was very active in the deforcement of Macpherson.' With regards to the events of 31 March Mackenzie stated 'The prisoners Christy Ross, Ann Ross, Margaret Ross and

Margaret Ross were all among the mob... They all carried sticks, and had them raised up in a threatening attitude' and 'Christy Ross took hold of the Sheriff.' Mitchell added 'I observed Ann Ross Taylor to be one of the most prominent. She carried a stick.' Cumming stated 'I am sure the tallest of the prisoners Ann Ross Taylor was one of the mob, as I saw her in front where she was one of the active parties. She carried a stick.' Petitions for bail for the four women were lodged with Tain Court on 1 April, which were granted by the Sheriff-substitute on condition of 'finding sufficient Caution and Surety.' William Ross, Shepherd, Glenmore, signed Bonds of Caution on the same day and the four women were released.[23]

On 12 April Peter Ross alias Bain, aged 21, was arrested and taken to Tain Jail. He declared he was present when Macpherson went to serve the summons, though did not strip him or burn his papers. With regards to McCaig 'The Excise Officer took out a pistol three times, and said that he would fire it, on which I asked him what warrant he had for shooting anyone, and that if that was what he meant to do that we could get pistols as well as himself, and that there would be life for life. The Excise Officer's pistol was in full cock that last time he presented it. I had a pistol in my pocket and I took it out and had it in my hand by my side but I did not present it at the Excise Officer. There was powder in my pistol and there was a cap on, but there was not shot or lead in it.' Peter was released on bail two days later. Regarding the events of 31 March, he later declared he was at Ardross at the time.[24]

Sheriff Mackenzie sent a copy of Sheriff-substitute Taylor's letter to the Lord Advocate, James Moncreiff, in London on 1 April and three days later wrote 'I regret to learn from a report sent by Dr Ross of Tain to Mr Taylor, that two women who were engaged in the scuffle with the police have been very badly hurt, and are in a precarious state from wounds on the head... When I wrote to you last week I was under the apprehension, that the police would be defeated, and that a military force would be required to vindicate the authority of the law. To avoid this necessity, peremptory instructions were given to the Sheriff Substitute to act with vigour, and if he met with resistance to repel force by force.' Moncrieff requested a report, so Mackenzie sent him one on 8 April (incorrectly dated '8th March'), similar to previous accounts, though included the note the Sheriff-substitute had sent him on 9 March and mentioned that Robertson and Stewart had 'applied for the aid of the Constabulary force to enable the officer to execute new summonses against the four small tenants.' Mackenzie wrote to Moncreiff again on 9 April:

> ...it was the women, who, according to custom, maltreated the officers sent to execute the summonses by stripping them naked and burning their papers; and who violently obstructed the police in the execution of their duty... If the police had not acted with great energy and promptitude, the people from the surrounding county would have assembled in still greater force and could have easily over-powered them in this remote mountainous district, and the consequences might have been much more serious to all concerned.[25]

On 12 April, on hearing that the events were 'likely to be made a question before the House of Commons,' Sheriff-substitute Taylor sent Moncreiff a report, though played it down. Taylor wrote that the summons was executed 'against three Subtenants' not four. He mentioned 'one of the men on one occasion drew a pistol & presented it at a Revenue Officer' but didn't mention the officer had pulled out his pistol first. 'I regret most sincerely that in the scuffle which ensued, so many of the people both men & women received hurts from the Constables batons;– and personally I did all I could to try & restrain both parties.– But I am satisfied that if the Police had not used their batons to force a passage, in the manner they did, our party would have been deforced & maltreated ... the police ... being more expert, warded off in a great measure the blows aimed at them, & so comparatively escaped from being injured. I have no hesitation in saying that the Police acted strictly within the line of duty,– and that they used no more force than was necessary to save our party from deforcement & maltreatment.'

The first newspaper report appeared on 4 April, which was similar to the statements, with additional details:

> At six o'clock Sheriff Taylor proceeded at the head of several sheriff-officers and a police force of about 30 men... A detachment of the Inverness-shire police was led on by Mr Mackay, one of their inspectors, and the Ross-shire police were under the superintendence of Mr Cumming ... the sheriff endeavoured to reason with the crowd on the impropriety and illegality of their conduct; but he was immediately laid hold of, and struck by some of the women. Mr Cumming then urged them to give way, but they refused, on which he led the whole police force into the heart of the crowd, and after a brisk combat of five minutes duration, dispersed them, leaving on the ground one or two dozen women and men, who were knocked down almost insensible by the blows inflicted by the police with their batons... The police officers broke several batons in the fray, but escaped themselves almost unhurt. It fared differently, however, with the rioters. We understand several of the women are very seriously injured, and some of the men have broken heads. Next day a gallant friend of one of the female prisoners came forward and became bail for the four women, and they are now at liberty.[26]

The *Northern Ensign* exaggerated the events: 'One day lately a preventive officer, with two cuttermen, made their appearance on the boundaries of the Estate, and were taken for Tain Sheriff officers ... the poor fellows were taken and denuded of their clothing, all papers and documents were extracted and burnt, amongst which was a purse with a considerable quantity of money. In this state they were carried shoulder high off the property, and left at the braes of Downie.' On the day of the 'Massacre' the force 'were surrounded by four to five hundred men and women. Sheriff Taylor first remonstrated, but would not be listed to; he then took the riot act, commenced reading, and was immediately seized upon by women; and the paper was attempted to be taken from him. He then gave the order to Mr Cumming to make way, when a heart-rending scene occurred. The men, who were armed with cudgels, and the women with stones, resisted considerably, until several on both sides were much hurt... It is reported this morning that one of the women is dead.'[27]

The *Inverness Courier* reported: 'The women, as they bore the brunt of the battle, were the principal sufferers. A large number of them – fifteen or sixteen, we believe, were seriously hurt, and of these, several are under medical treatment; one woman, we believe, still lies in a precarious condition. The policemen appear to have used their batons with great force, but they escaped themselves almost unhurt.' The article quoted two anonymous correspondents with opposing views: 'The judgement and energy with which Mr Taylor, the Sheriff Substitute at Tain, planned and conducted the present expedition, entitles him to the gratitude of every good member of society ... he has succeeded in upholding the authority of the law in a manner which, it is hoped, will prove a salutary lesson for the future.' The second considered 'Dr Gordon has been most assiduous in his attention to the wounded people... Among the worst of the cases are ten young women, and they happen to be all wounded in the back of the skull, and other parts of their person, which shows clearly that there was no resistance of any consequence... The wounds on these women show plainly the severe manner in which they were dealt with by the police when retreating, and when many of them fell forward on the ground. It was currently reported last night that one of them was dead.'[28]

Donald then wrote to the *Northern Ensign*:

I have read with considerable pain the accounts in the northern newspapers of the recent proceedings in connection with the serving of summonses on tenants on the Kindeace property... Even on the most favourable view of the recent procedure on the part of the Factor and Sheriff officers, and the constables, it cannot be described by any other name than that of *savage butchery*... The men who can hold up their heads, and brag that they maimed, and bruised, and levelled to the ground, with their sticks, so many females, in half-an-hour, are a disgrace to a civilized and christian country.[29]

On 10 April Donald wrote to the *NBDM* from Glasgow, based on information he had been sent:

1st, It is not true, as stated in the Courier, that there were four or five hundred people met to resist the sheriff-officers when on their way to serve the summonses of removal. There were only from 60 to 70 females assembled, and they had neither sticks nor stones in their hands, and they made no attack whatever upon the officers and constables.

2d, It is not true that the Sheriff read the Riot Act in presence of the people, and it is not true that he was struck by any of the females; on the contrary, it is averred, and it is quite correct, that none of the females offered any opposition to the Sheriff, or to the constables or officers, when the latter rushed upon them with their staves and batons, and beat, bruised, and assaulted them in a brutal and savage manner.

3d, It is not true that only four families were to be removed. There are in all 22 families under the ban of eviction, and these comprise no less than 120 souls...

Four females were handcuffed and were dragged to prison – a distance of twenty miles. Their clothes were clotted with blood, their heads cut, their hair dishevelled and red with blood; their backs were black and blue with the marks of the batons of the policemen, yet they were not allowed to have their heads bandaged, or their wounds tied up, but streaming in their blood were lodged in jail!

The constables, officers, and policemen, boast that notwithstanding of all this fearful bloodshed and onslaught on the females, they themselves escaped without a blow, or even a scratch.[30]

However, the statements lodged with Tain Court were consistent in that 200-300 people were present. Although only the four subtenants were served with a Summons, they probably further sub-let to families of cottars who would also have had to leave. Donald's next letter to the *Ensign* was written on 15 April at the Royal Hotel, Tain:

I have just returned from the scene of slaughter in Strathcarron, where I found matters much worse than was represented to me in letters and otherwise before I left Glasgow. Having spent two days in the district, collecting information and examining the wounded, I can form a pretty accurate opinion regarding this most melancholy tragedy, and the principal actors in it...

My information goes to show a shameful course of conduct on the part of the Sheriff. He did not warn the people of the intention on his part to let the police loose upon them. He read no Riot Act. He did not give them time to disperse; but, on the contrary, the moment he approached with his force, he, stick in hand, cried out, 'Clear the way,' and in the next breath said, '*Knock them down,*' and immediately a scene ensued which baffles description. The policemen laid their heavy batons on the heads of the unfortunate females, and levelled them to the ground, jumped and trumped upon them after they were down, and kicked them in every part of their bodies with savage brutality. The field was soon covered with blood. The cries of the women, and of the boys and girls, lying weltering in their blood, was rending the very heavens. Some of the females, pursued by the policemen, jumped into the deep and rapid rolling Carron, trusting in its mercies more than to that of the policemen or the Sheriff. There were females who had parcels of their hair torn out by the batons of the policemen, and one girl had a piece of the flesh, about 7 inches long by 1¼ broad, and more than a quarter of an inch thick, torn off her shoulder by a violent blow with a baton. A young girl, who was only a mere spectator, was run after by *three* policemen. They struck her on the forehead, cut open her skull, and *after she fell down* they kicked her. The doctor abstracted from the wound a portion of the cap sunk into it by the baton of the savage police. The marks of their hobnails *are still visible* in her back shoulders.

...There are still in Strathcarron thirteen females in a state of great distress, owing to the brutal beating they received at the hands of the police. Three of these are so ill that their medical attendant has no hopes whatever of their recovery... Among the number of seriously wounded is a woman advanced in pregnancy. She was not among the crowd who met the Sheriff, but at a considerable distance, just looking on; but she was violently struck and kicked by the policemen, and she is in a very dangerous condition.[31]

The *Ensign* added 'We think it right to state that we have considerably modified some of the statements in the foregoing letter, as they represent the conduct of the Sheriff and its results in such light as to be almost incredible, and require the strongest testimony before our readers could be induced to believe them.'

Donald wrote a long letter on 19 April to the Lord Advocate in Edinburgh:

The Sheriff arrived with his force of about 30 policemen, and on coming up to the women, he intimated who he was, and ordered them to retire, or clear the way for his force; and, this order not being instantly obeyed, he (the Sheriff) in the very next breath ordered the police to move on and knock them down. The police instantly obeyed, and with full force of their batons on the skulls of the women, knocked them to the ground, and a scene ensued which baffles description. The police struck with all their strength, not only when knocking down, but after the females were on the ground. They beat and kicked them while lying weltering in their blood. Such was the brutality with which this tragedy was carried through, that more than 20 females were carried off the field on blankets and litters; and the appearance they presented, with their heads cut and bruised, their limbs mangled, and their clothes clotted with blood, was such as would horrify any savage...

When the Sheriff and his party arrived at Greenyard the women had no weapons, no stones nor sticks, and they made no noise. They wanted to represent to the Sheriff, that Alexander Munro, the principal Tacksman, in whose name the summonses of removal were issued, positively denied all knowledge of them...

I may mention that on Thursday last I waited on Mr Munro, the Tacksman of Greenyard, and I found him still maintaining that he never authorised any one to apply for warrants of removing in his name against the tenants. This he solemnly declared in presence of witnesses, and he also stated, that he always told the tenants that he did not authorise the application for warrants against them...

...there was shown to me in Strathcarron two table-cloths filled with clothing which the unfortunate victims had on them at the time, and these were completely dyed red with their blood. There were caps with holes on them where the batons tore and carried the thin cotton with them into the skulls of the women; and there were pieces of the cotton of the caps afterwards abstracted by the doctor out of the heads of these unhappy sufferers. There were several strong ash batons left on the field, broken with the blows which the police gave with them. There are also pieces, or patches of the skin, which the police with their batons stript off the heads and shoulders of the women when they were beating them...

Four females were apprehended, or rather lifted off the ground, and were carried to jail. They were hand-cuffed, two and two, their heads and shoulders dreadfully cut, and their clothes completely wet with blood. Notwithstanding of this, the police went in to the Tacksman's house at Greenyard, and drank several bottles of whisky: the females all the while lying out on the grass, weltering in their blood. The spot where they laid still bears the mark of the blood where the poor females were lying on the ground...

Under these circumstances, it is respectfully submitted that your Lordship should cause immediate inquiry into the conduct of the police force and of the Sheriff, on the occasion referred to. It is absolutely necessary for the sake of order and good government that this should be done without delay: for independent of the rash and reckless conduct of the Sheriff, and the brutal and savage conduct of the police, the people are labouring under the impression that Her Majesty sanctions, nay encourages and authorises, these evictions, especially as the batons broken and left on the battle-field have the letters, 'V.R.,' painted in large characters on them. There are in all 22 families under the ban of eviction ... the feeling among them is, that the Government is conniving at these evictions – that the authorities under the Crown countenance and encourage them; and that the local authorities are in league with the proprietors for the expatriation of the people.[32]

Donald MacLeod later wrote 'I have seen myself in the possession of Mr. Ross, Glasgow, patches or scalps of the skin with the long hair adhering to them, which was found upon the field a few days after this inhuman affray.'[33]

The *Inverness Courier* printed a long article on 27 April, similar to the witness statements, though added 'One of the ringleaders has, however, since been apprehended, and another man has been taken into custody for attempting to take the life of the principal tenant by firing a shot into his house, on the assumption, we presume, of his being in league with the landlord.' However, a letter to Donald informed him that this was a 'false report.'[34] In the same newspaper an advert appeared for Donald's pamphlet, to be 'Published in a few days... Being a full account of the Battle of Greenyard, in Ross-shire, and of the whole proceedings of the Sheriff, Sheriff-Officers, Constables, and Policemen, when serving Summonses of Removal on the Tenants of Greenyard, on the 31st March last; together with a List of all the Females who were inhumanly assaulted and wounded by the Police on that occasion, on the bank of the river Carron.'[35]

Donald wrote another long letter to the *Ensign*, which criticised the paper for editing his previous letter.[36] The article provided the detailed background that formed the first few pages of the *Russians of Ross-shire*, which was advertised as 'Just published' on 12 May.[37] *Russians* repeated and expanded on what Donald had written previously and was similar in many respects to what was in the court documents, though had been given some embellishment. It is only worth outlining below differences from the above accounts. According to Donald, Robertson and Munro initially denied that summonses of removal had been drawn up. Rev. John Macdonald questioned Robertson who 'denied out and out that he had anything to do with the removals, – that Munro *alone* was the cause of them.' Munro gave the subtenants a copy of a letter he sent to Robertson on 6 March: 'I regret much that you told the Rev Mr M'Donald of Croick some days ago in Tain that you had no wish of removing any of the tenants, and that you said it was *my fault* to remove them. As you are perfectly aware I have no wish for removing the people, providing you wish to keep them in, as it is thoroughly in your power to keep them in or turn them out as you please. I consider myself aggrieved to put the whole burden on my shoulders.'

With regards to the initial deforcement 'the females ... made no attack whatever on Macpherson, but treated him very gently; and one or two of the men who came up after the summonses were burnt, went with him and with his assistant "Peter" to the Inn at Ardgay, and treated them to refreshments and some spirits.' Donald denied that Macpherson was stripped naked, and Macpherson didn't say he was stripped in his statement.

Regarding the incident with McCaig, apparently, on overhearing a discussion in a pub about the evictions, the three excise officers

> ...sallied forth, fully bent, as they said, on having "some fun with the women of Greenyard." Scarcely had they left the inn when they began to represent, and indeed announce themselves as sheriff-officers, on their way to warn out, *all* the tenants in Greenyard. This was enough. The news spread like wildfire – the swiftest boys ran up the banks of the Carron like roes, intimating at every house that three sheriff-officers were on their way... The women surrounded them and demanded a sight of their warrant, but no warrant could be shown; and at last the

imprudent fellows began to plead for mercy. One of them – a long ugly looking fellow with huge *moustaches* – confessed that they were only practising a small bit of imposition on the excited people; and begged to be let away as they were excisemen. But the women said they could scarcely believe men who came to them with a falsehood on their lips at the outset; and further, that they could not believe that excisemen could be guilty of such irregular conduct … one of them pulled out a loaded pistol, and presented it at the heads of some of the women. A young lad who had been near the scene came up; and seeing the gauger's pistol levelled it as his mother's head, took out an old rusty pistol he had for frightening away crows, and told the gauger that if he would dare meddle with his mother that he must stand the consequences. The gauger immediately put his pistol into his pocket and exhibited all the papers he had on him… After the females were satisfied that the parties were really excisemen, and not sheriff-officers, they allowed them to proceed on their way.[38]

However, Christy and Ann declared McCaig had pointed his pistol at their chests and McCaig stated he was made to return to Ardgay. Donald also wrote 'private meetings were held in Tain – the great heads of the evicting firms and the great sheep lords consulted together – and it was resolved upon to go to the district with a strong police force in order, as they said to "uphold the majesty of the law."' Although Robertson had complained about the deforcement, there is no evidence that any other proprietors were involved.

According to Donald, with regards to the 'Massacre' the policemen were instructed to assemble 'at the junction of the Tain and Ardross roads, at Midfearn.' Today, this is where the A836 running WNW from Tain meets the B9176 running north from Alness. 'The police force from Inverness and Dingwall arrived at the place appointed a little after midnight. The Tain brigade, headed by the Sheriff, Mr Stewart the law agent for Kindeace, and Mr Taylor the Fiscal, arrived an hour or two after. After several bottles of ale, porter, and whiskey had been drunk, and the roll called, the police stood in a row and the Sheriff administered an oath to them. Between Sheriff, Fiscal, Law Agent, Jehus [coach drivers] and policemen, there were more than 40 men.' However, none of the court documents mentioned that Stewart was present and both Sheriff-substitute Taylor and Superintendent Cumming stated that a total of 27 officers were present. Donald then let his imagination take over:

The morning … was dark and dismal … the hideous howl of the wild cats and badgers, and the unearthly screeches of owls and sea birds, disturbed from their night's repose by the sudden appearance among them of the Baton brigade – the solemn tread of the brigade with their heavy hob-nailed boots on the road, as they were drilled and sworn – their clothing and appearance as dark as the night they were out in, and as black as the job they were about to perpetrate, altogether rendered the scene, as well as the men, "truly horrible." ... The swearing over, and large quantities of liquor swallowed, the brigade tumbled into their carriages – the Jehus mounted their boxes, – crack went the whips, and round went the wheels; and with lashing and beating and furious driving, the brigade reached Gladfield, near Greenyard, by daylight in the morning. Here again they were "*refreshed,*" and thence marched on to the boundaries of Greenyard.[39]

There is no corroborating evidence that the policemen were plied with drink. After the event 'The fields were dotted with pools of blood – the dogs in the neighbourhood came and licked it up; and such was the awful nature of the scene, that Mr Munro's brother-in-law harrowed the ground under cloud of night, to hide the blood.'

Donald provided graphic descriptions of the injuries received by nineteen of the women, numbered 1 to 20 but without a No. 12, many of whom were listed in the 1851 census. Donald mentioned possessing medical reports and five of the cases described by Dr Gordon were expanded on by Donald: No. 1 Elizabeth Ross, 8 Margaret Macgregor or Ross, 11 Naomi Ross, 14 Ann Ross and 17 Grace Ross. Four other women – No. 2 Margaret Ross, 4 Margaret Ross, 9 Ann Ross and 10 Christina (Christy) Ross, were the ones taken to Tain Jail. Donald indicated that they would probably be tried at Inverness Circuit Court: 'I have already taken measures to secure an able Advocate to defend them.' Apparently, Christy had attempted to show Sheriff-substitute Taylor the copy of the letter that Munro had written to Robertson, but soon had 'three batons beating on her head.' Three of the women, No. 7 Helen Ross or Macgregor, Greenyards, 18 Margaret Ross, Cornhill, and 19 Ann Munro, Cornhill, reported hearing the Sheriff say 'knock them down.' In several accounts, after the women were down, they were repeatedly hit and kicked, and left for dead. For No. 1 Elizabeth Ross, the 'marks of the tacks of the policemen's boots were still visible on the breast and shoulders.' No. 14 Ann Ross was hit so hard on the shoulders that the policeman broke his solid ash baton. At least two of the victims have living descendants:

> 16th. Ann Ross, aged 43 years, wife of William Ross, *alias* Griasaich, tenant at Langwell, ran up on the bank of the river, and crossed at a wide ford, where the water was only about knee deep – as the channel was very wide. After landing on Greenyard, she heard the awful moaning and groaning of the bleeding and wounded females who were lying on the field: and she ran to assist them. She had only time to tear her apron into stripes for bandaging the broken and bleeding heads, when she saw two policemen making for her like blood-hounds. The poor woman got frightened, and ran for her life. At first she outran the police, by jumping over some ditches and drains, and was likely to get beyond their reach, and hide herself in a wood; but, just as she was near it, she

saw a policeman on his knees, watching her like a cat. She now turned to the right, and ran towards the river. The police however followed and came up to her, and beat her, several times on the head, and on the back, and shoulders, with their batons; still she kept her feet, although the blood, was gushing from every wound – forming a trail after her – still the police pursued – up one hill and down another – still she ran – still she was met, and chased out of one bush or thicket into another – still the batons beat on her head – still she hoped to escape, until at last, like the stag in the chase, her vision was failing – her blood-shot eyes, and streaming nostrils are telling that she is hotly pursued by the blood hounds. She is now frantic with despair – the police are close upon her – the river rapid and deep before her – there is not a moment to choose – a chance, a *slender* chance of escape is still left; and eyeing the gurgling pool with a confidence worthy of a heroine, she plunged in, and was carried along with the stream!

...Among those who ran, and watched on the north bank of the river, was William Ross, the husband of the pursued woman... He saw her plunge into the stream, and in the twinkling of an eye, he jumped in after her; and gliding down with the current, he caught hold of her; and after great exertions and no small risk of life, he managed to bring her to land. She sunk completely beneath the surface three times before her husband reached her; but the Almighty was kind towards her and saved her most wonderfully. After she was brought to land it was thought she was dead, but in a few minutes she rallied; and her husband and others carried her home.[40]

Six months later Ann and her family emigrated to Australia on the *Covenanter*, which left Liverpool on 28 September, after a cholera outbreak.[41] It arrived in Gelong, Victoria on 23 January 1855. They initially settled in Barunah Plains, Victoria and became sheep farmers. At the age of 80 Ann had 36 grandchildren and died four years later in 1895.[42]

17th. Grace Ross, aged 20 years, daughter of William Ross, Ca-dearg, a very respectable young girl, and noted in the district for her clean and tidy appearance, as well as for her good conduct and amiable disposition... She was looking on, a mere spectator, when a fierce looking policeman came up and struck her a savage blow with his baton on the forehead, which felled her, as if a cannon ball had gone through her heart. Such was the force with which the blow was given that it caused a cut 4 inches long; exposing the skull, shattering the frontal bone, and carrying into the fissures pieces of the cap that was on the poor girl's head. This blow caused concussion and compression of the brain, and for a few minutes she lay quite insensible. After she was able to crawl, she moved away in the direction of a wood; but the police on noticing her came back, and began to beat her. She was struck several times on the back

The Massacre of the Rosses

and shoulders; and being fearfully wounded by the blows she received, she ran into the river until the water reached her waist; and there she stood. The police remained at a distance watching her. Her clothing, such of it that appeared above the water, was completely red with blood; and her appearance was one of the most melancholy sights ever seen in a Christian country. At last the police moved away, and then the poor girl got out of the river; but she was so exhausted that she fell prostrate upon a sand bank, and appeared as if dead. Parties who had come now to the Langwell side of the river, and seeing Grace lying on a bank on the opposite side, joined hands and plunged into the stream, and made their way over. They lifted her up and brought her over, and thence they conveyed her to her father's house. She is still in a dangerous state.[43]

Grace married George Mackay from Spinningdale and had five children. The great-grandson of Grace still lives at Cawdearg today, who recalled that Grace 'had a deep dent in her skull for the rest of her life, she would demonstrate this by placing a coin into it.'[44]

Donald wrote that Donald Ross, aged about 68, a Waterloo veteran, declared 'that although he was at *nine* battles on the continent, he never saw such treatment of wounded soldiers or prisoners of war, as he saw of the helpless and inoffensive women of Greenyard.' George Ross, aged 80, one of subtenants in the summons, had served in the 85th Regiment for 29 years

Grace Ross of Ca-dearg, victim No. 17 in the *Massacre of the Rosses*. Grace received a severe head injury and ran into the river to escape. She was carried home and recovered though had a dent in her head for the rest of her life. Grace was twenty at the time, so this photo was taken much later.

and fought in ten battles. He had a wife and six children and had to vacate his house by 28 May but did not have anywhere to go. Donald sought character witness statements and Rev. Aird wrote 'For the last 13 years I have been acquainted with the people of the Strath... I can with freedom state, regarding the general body of the inhabitants of the whole district; that they are as quiet, inoffensive, and loyal a peasantry, as may be found in any part of the Highlands, or of Her Majesty's dominions.'[45]

Donald wrote to the *Ensign*, describing what happened on the day of the 'Massacre,' which was identical to what had just been published in his pamphlet. The next article would 'describe a few cases where the parties were seriously injured,' but there were no further articles in that newspaper.[46] A review in the *Northern Warder* considered Donald's pamphlet was an 'indignant and righteous protest' and 'Allowing for the colouring into which Mr Ross may even unconsciously have been led by the warmth of his feelings, enough remains to show that these poor people were outraged in a very brutal manner.'[47] The *NBDM* considered 'The contents of this publication are positively startling. No refutation of the statements made having been promulgated, we are bound to accept as facts the relation of the fiendish cruelties inflicted upon defenceless women... Why has the affair slumbered so long without investigation? Mr Donald Ross has done his work well – he is out-spoken, and his evidence, it would appear, is unimpeachable.'[48]

In *Russians*, Donald had mentioned that David Munro of Culrain was beaten by three policemen and, unbelievably, had seized one of the policemen 'and pitched him more than five yards.'[49] On 24 June Harry Taylor wrote to John C. Brodie, Crown Agent, Edinburgh, informing him that 'An attempt was made to apprehend some more of the men ... but the officer sent for the purpose found that they had left their houses and were in concealment.' Taylor established that 'David Munro residing at Culrain and Donald Ross alias Bain residing at Ardgay were present and formed part of the mob,' and requested a warrant for their arrest. On 14 July Munro, about 25, was arrested and declared 'I had a cane in my hand, but I did not make any use of it. I received two blows on my head but I cannot tell who struck them... I did not try to strike any of the officers before I got the blows on my head.' Cumming stated 'There was one man whom I saw taking a very active part in the mob, and I went up to him and attempted to speak to him, on which he raised his stick and tried to strike me with it, but I warded off the blow, and knocked him down with my baton. I have today seen David Munro in Prison and declare that I think he is the person whom I so Knocked down.' Peter Mackenzie identified 'David Munro as a person whom I saw struck down by Mr Cumming... Before he was struck he knocked off Mr. Cumming's hat with his stick.' Munro was released on bail the next day.[50]

On 20 July, Taylor wrote to Brodie:

> There is great difficulty in procuring evidence of the identity of the parties, because excepting the officers of the law, there were no witnesses

except persons engaged in the proceedings, or sympathizers with them, and the people were not previously known to any of the officers except Peter Mackenzie...

1st Case of M'Pherson. I have not been able to obtain any evidence in corroboration of Peter Mackenzie's with respect to the two women of the name of Margaret Ross. There is corroboration as regards Christy Ross, Ann Ross (also called Ann Ross Taylor) and Peter Ross.

2nd. Obstruction of Sheriff Substitute. The prisoners Christy Ross, Ann Ross, Margaret Ross and Margaret Ross, and a fifth woman released on the ground in consequence of having received a severe hurt, were the five persons referred to by the Sheriff Substitute as having been captured. The Precognition now contains all the evidence I have been able to procure of their having formed part of the mob. I have now included another prisoner, David Munro, in the charge, as being the only man against whom there seemed to be evidence of having taken an active part.

With reference to the statement of the witness Donald Ross [Mackinlay] ... that the Sheriff Substitute directed the police officers to knock down the persons composing the mob, I am personally able to contradict it, because I was at the Sheriff Subt's side during the whole affray.[51]

On 2 August it was decided 'Let Peter Ross (Bain) & Ann Ross (Taylor) be tried by the Sheriff & a jury... Only two persons are selected for trial – in order that, these cases being clear, a conviction may be secured ... the object being to vindicate the authority of the Law.' So, they were to be made scapegoats.

On 26 August it was declared that the Lord Advocate had raised an Indictment against Peter and Ann Ross 'accusing them of the crime of Mobbing and Rioting as also Breach of the Peace, as also Assault.' The wording for all three incidents was similar:

> ...you the said Peter Ross *alias* Bain and Ann Ross *alias* Taylor did, both and each, or one or other of you, form part of the said mob or great number of disorderly and evil-disposed persons, and were present, aiding and abetting, or exciting and actively engaged along with them, in the whole or part of the last above libelled unlawful acts of mobbing and rioting, and assaulting and obstructing the said sheriff-officer ... and others accompanying him as aforesaid, engaged in the execution of their duty.[52]

Two days later the Indictment was delivered to Peter and Ann by William Catharine Macpherson and witnessed by Peter Mackenzie, with an order to appear at Inverness Circuit Court on 14 September at 10am. All the witnesses who gave statements were also summoned. The *NBDM* reported 'The poor people to be tried have been lucky in securing the services of a very respectable and experienced Edinburgh agent, who, along with Mr Alexander Moncrieff, advocate, proceed to Inverness early next week, being engaged specially for the defence. The trial will excite great interest in the north.'[53]

At the trial 'The prisoners pled guilty to the charge of breach of the peace, and this modified charge was accepted by the Advocate-Depute.'[54] The Lord Justice Clerk ruled:

> Neither they nor their neighbours can be allowed to suppose that they can live in this kind of wicked and rebellious spirit against the law. They must be taught submission in the very first instance... Such opposition as was shown in this instance ... requires very severe chastisement indeed, and imposes upon the Court the necessity of making an example to repress the tendency to similar conduct in others... His lordship then sentenced the male prisoner to eighteen months' imprisonment, with hard labour, and the female prisoner to twelve months' imprisonment.[55]

There was some dissatisfaction with Peter and Ann pleading guilty, as given that 'the police were accused of having shown a wanton and cruel barbarity, a cold-blooded and savage violence, a spirit of ferocity and outrage, such as were scarcely credible... There is now but little probability that the dispute which has been so hotly waged regarding the circumstances of this painful affair will ever be settled by a discovery of the truth.' This article revealed that Donald was present at the trial.[56]

Before the trial, subtenants George, John and Ann Ross had been fighting against their eviction in a case brought before Tain Sheriff Court. They considered Alexander Munro had verbally agreed to a lease until Whitsunday 1855, that the removal was not authorised by Munro and they presented his letter of 6 March 1854 to Robertson as evidence. It differed slightly from Donald's quote in that the word 'blame' had been used instead of 'burden.' On 26 July Sheriff-substitute Taylor considered Munro had written the letter 'to ally the irritation of the people against the Pursuer at a time when he considered himself in danger from them' and decided against the subtenants. They appealed however on 23 August Sheriff Mackenzie dismissed the appeal and they were ordered to pay Munro £10 18s 6d expenses plus a 7s fee.[57]

The case then went before the Supreme Court in Edinburgh. On 4 September, Richard Arthur SSC submitted a Note of Suspension on behalf of the subtenants. It gave various reasons as to why the Sheriff's decisions regarding their removal were 'erroneous and contrary to law' and requested a suspension of their eviction. Alexander Munro stated that George Ross paid £12 12s 6d rent and John and Ann Ross paid £6 7s. A Sheriff Court Act was quoted in which 'it is incompetent to bring under review by "advocation, appeal, suspension, or reduction" a cause not exceeding the value of £25 sterling,' so on 27 September the Lord Ordinary refused the Note. The decision was appealed to the Inner House and the Law Lords agreed with the

Lord Ordinary. Expenses of £29 10s 9d after tax were due to be paid by the three Suspenders.[58] Subsequently George and John Ross were 'incarcerated in the Prison of Tain' for not paying the expenses. They could not afford to support themselves while in prison so on 6 February 1855 lodged petitions for aliment, drawn up by Thomas Munro, Writer, Tain.[59] George declared he was eighty-two and had served in the army for twenty-three years. He was a Chelsea pensioner receiving 1s 5½d per day, though had received his quarterly payment in January and could not afford to pay the debt as he had a family to support. On 8 February 1855 Sheriff-substitute Taylor found the petitioners entitled to aliment from Munro and Robertson at 1s each per day. George also declared.

> I do not consider I am due the debt for which I am incarcerated... I never gave my authority directly or indirectly to any of the agents employed in that matter; and in particular I gave no such authority to Thomas Munro, writer, Tain; nor to Mr Richard Arthur, S.S.C., Edinburgh; nor to Mr Donald Ross, Glasgow. Ross was twice in my house, but he never asked for authority from me, nor spoke of the matter. Depones – I did not recently, nor at any time receive any money from Donald Ross Glasgow, nor from any one employed by him, though I understand that a sum of about £200 was collected in Glasgow, besides subscriptions elsewhere, by Ross, for behoof of myself and other tenants at Greenyards, who were to be removed from their possessions. I did not get any money as a part of a subscription for said purpose by Misses Ross of Balnagown.

John declared 'I have not recently or at any time, got any money from Donald Ross, Glasgow, or from any other persons, out of subscriptions made in Glasgow or elsewhere, for behoof of the subtenants of Greenyards.' The article added 'The debtors have been liberated; one of them (the pensioner) having paid £12 in part of the costs.'[60] Donald responded that the article was 'injurious to his character,' however the *Inverness Courier* did not publish all of his letter because it was 'written in an intemperate style, and comments strongly on individuals.' Donald wrote 'The allegations in the garbled excerpts from the alleged depositions by George Ross and John Bain ... are palpable misrepresentations and untrue from beginning to end. I never collected nor received one shilling for behoof of George Ross or "the other sub-tenants of Greenyards." The money contributed by the Misses Ross of Balnagown, for the females who were wounded by the police at Greenyards, in March 1854, was sent by them to the Rev. Mr Aird.' The *Courier* considered that Donald threw 'doubt on the depositions made on oath by the Ross-shire men... Now the depositions are real, and the men, we believe, simple honest Highlanders.'[61] However, it pointed out that Thomas Munro had written to say he had been employed by George and acted as agent for both men 'in the proceedings adopted by them before the Sheriff.'

In February 1855 the *Ensign* reported that the remaining people of Greenyards had been evicted.[62] Both George and John Ross moved to Langwell on the north side of the river.[63] In September Rev. Aird wrote to Rev. A. Peterson in Perth. Peter Ross had been held at Perth Prison and his sentence had been shortened by six months. Aird included a pound note from his father, John Ross, Langwell, so that Peter could get home and mentioned he would be able to get work at the building of an embankment at Invercarron.[64]

Alexander Munro died on 13 March 1859 aged 80. The 1861 census only listed three households and ten people living in Easter Greenyard, including his widow Margaret and two children.

The Clearing of the Glens was a general account of the Highland Clearances, similar to what Donald and others had written before. Donald quoted two articles by the elder George Dempster and one by David Laurie from the *Farmers' Magazine*. He indicated that Dempster's were published in 1809 and Laurie's was written in 1810, but they were actually published in 1810, 1803 and 1808 respectively.[65] The second Dempster article included the line 'I would not give a little Highland child for ten of the highest Highland mountains in all Lochaber' which 'Charles Edward Gordon' had misquoted previously. Donald ended this section by publishing two long poems. 'The Clearing of the Glens' by 'an anonymous correspondent' began:

They'll speak of him for many a year, in Britain's sad decline,
In other lands, perchance than this, across the weltering brine–
They'll speak of him who drove them forth in alien fields to toil,–
Who forc'd them from their fathers hearths, the children of the soil.[66]

The second was by William D. Campbell, completed by his father, Donald Campbell, after William's untimely death. It was an attack at the Macdonells of Glengarry in the wake of the Knoydart evictions. Their crest featured a raven sitting on a rock. The first stanza, of eleven reads:

Glengarry he sat in his silent hall,–
   He gloomingly sat, and alone;–
Though the Yule-log's blaze illumined the wall,
   Of guests to the feast came none.
The chief, oblivious, exclaimed with a sneer
On his scornful lip, "'Tis somewhat queer
The clan pour not in to our Christmas cheer."
   "Alas, they are gone–and our lone glens mourn–
   Yes, gone–all gone–no more to return!"
Quoth the hoary old raven of CREAGAN-AN-FH'TCH.[67]

Prebble gave the most thorough later summary of the 'Massacre,' based predominantly on Donald's pamphlet, though incorrectly mentioned that

Alexander Munro lived at Braelangwell.[68] He also wrote that the *Northern Ensign* 'baulked' at printing all of Donald's letters, which others have repeated. However, it is likely that the publication of Donald's pamphlet meant that this was no longer news, particularly as forces were then being amassed to fight the Russians. Prebble mentioned that the 'women had drawn their red shawls over their heads' but there is no mention of red shawls in the contemporary accounts. He indicated that Donald had reported that two women, Elizabeth Ross and Margaret Macgregor Ross had died. However, Donald didn't say that any of the women had died. For Elizabeth Ross (No. 1), Donald had written 'She is now pining away – suffering from intense pain in the head, causing aberration of intellect and fever, together with a debility, which is sure to terminate her existence.'[69] Prebble reported that Elizabeth's great-nephew, Donald Ross of Letchworth had informed him that she had survived and lived to 'extreme old age.' Craig wrote that another relative of Elizabeth's, Willy MacDonald of Amatnatua, remembered her in old age and that the gable of her and her sister (No. 2 Margaret Ross)'s house was still standing as a memorial.[70] For Margaret Macgregor (No. 8) Donald wrote 'there was not the smallest hope of her recovery, and I much fear that, before what I now write can appear in print, Margaret M'Gregor has ceased to exist.'[71] It is not known what happened to her. Unfortunately, Kincardine Parish did not keep death records and they did not become mandatory until 1855. A trawl around the local graveyards did not reveal any positive matches for that year, so there is no known evidence that any of the victims died from their injuries.

Craig *On the Crofter's Trail* drove 'up Strath Carron in a kind of dread that flowed from its history.'[72] The valley certainly does have an eerie feel to it and you get the feeling that something dreadful happened in the past that has been hushed up, but maybe anyone who did not know about its history would not feel that way. There's not a single notice board about the 'Massacre' and perhaps this should be rectified.

21

The Crimean War

The outbreak of the Crimean War brought a distraction from reports of suffering Highlanders. On 27 March 1854, four days before the 'Massacre of the Rosses,' Britain and France declared war with Russia, and the area around Sevastopol, by the Black Sea, became the battleground. The war is well known for the suicidal 'Charge of the Light Brigade,' however one of the most heroic events took place in October at the Battle of Balaklava, where the 93rd Sutherland Highlanders repelled a 400-strong Russian cavalry charge, later referred to as 'The Thin Red Line.' The war was notorious for many deaths from cholera, scurvy, dysentery and a severe winter, however the care of the sick and wounded improved when Florence Nightingale arrived. Peace was declared on 30 March 1856 and nearly 100 men became the first recipients of the Victoria Cross.[1]

The 93rd Sutherland Highlanders were raised in 1799 and even by 1850 some recruits only spoke Gaelic and had to be taught English commands. They had the reputation of being well behaved and 'ready to go anywhere and do anything' as well as 'containing the strongest men of any regiment in the service.'[2] In the Crimean War they formed part of the Highland Brigade of the 1st Division, commanded by Sir Colin Campbell, who ordered the 93rd to form 'The Thin Red Line.' Campbell was born in Glasgow in 1792 and first saw action when only 15. He fought in numerous engagements and was wounded in action several times. He rose through the ranks and garnered much respect and loyalty from his men.[3]

In 1851, at a meeting held in Edinburgh to help destitute Highlanders, Rev. Macgregor stated that 'Skye had furnished since the Peninsular war no fewer than 21 Lieutenant-Generals and Major-Generals, 48 Lieutenant-Colonels, 600 Majors, Captains, and subalterns, 10,000 foot soldiers, 120 pipers, 4 Governors of British Colonies, one Governor-General, one Adjutant-General, one Chief Baron of England, and one Judge of the Court of Session.'[4] However, when the Russians became a threat, the army recruitment agents found it difficult to persuade any brave and loyal

Highlanders to enlist because of the Highland Clearances and broken promises to war veterans.[5] Donald, in *Russians*, reported that on Skye 'Captain Otter, after beating about all winter [1853-4], in the lochs and bays of that magnificent island, with all sorts of music, flags, and ribbons, and tempting offers, printed in English and in Gaelic, only succeeded in getting one Skyeman to enlist; and after getting him, he found the poor wretch was not worth keeping and dismissed him!' In Sutherland 'Capt. Craigie, R.N., the Duke's factor, a Free Church Minister and a Moderate Minister, had been piping for days, for volunteers and recruits in that county; and yet, after many threats on the part of the factor, and sweet music on the part of the parsons, the military spirit of the poor Sutherland serfs could not be raised to "fighting point." The truth is, as the men told the parsons, "we have no country to fight for: you robbed us of our country and gave it to sheep: therefore, since you have preferred sheep to men, let sheep defend you."'[6] According to MacLeod, the 2nd Duke then travelled to Sutherland and called a meeting at which 400 people attended. He offered £6 to anyone who would join the 93rd but no-one came forward. On asking why, an old man told him 'your predecessors and yourself expelled us in a most cruel and unjust manner from the land ... devoted now to rear dumb brute animals, which you and your parents consider of far more value than men. I do assure your Grace that it is the prevailing opinion in this country, that should the Czar of Russia take possession of Dunrobin Castle and of Stafford House next term, we could not expect worse treatment at his hands than we have experienced at the hands of your family for the last fifty years.'[7] A 'Committee of the young men of Sutherland' subsequently wrote to the *Northern Ensign*: 'We, the people of Sutherland, do not know what we are to come forward for. Where are our once happy homes, and where are our wives and children, and why are we forbidden to have them, and why are our straths and glens laid desolate, which might now, were the case otherwise, pour forth their thousands of men instead of sheep? ... For those wrongs and oppressions which we have endured so long, we are resolved that they shall have no volunteers from Sutherland.'[8]

The exact source of Donald's quote 'we have no country to fight for' is not known, however it was not the first such sentiment. In the 1780s when 550 people emigrated from Knoydart to Canada, Mrs Macdonald feared 'all the sheep that can be introduced and reared will form in their stead but a sorry defence against our enemies.'[9] George Dempster, in an 1810 *Essay on Sheep-Farming*, argued: 'That men are preferable to sheep, can hardly be doubted; since our kingdom is exposed to the invasion of foreign enemies; and since it is only by men, the sheep we prize so highly, and not only the sheep, but ourselves, our liberty, our constitution, our wives, children, friends, and all that is dear to us, are to be preserved from becoming the booty of plunderers, and the prey of our foes.'[10] MacLeod considered church ministers during the Sutherland Clearances 'literally prefer flocks of sheep to their human flocks, and lend their aid to every scheme for extirpating the latter to make room for the former.'[11]

In December 1854 Donald wrote a long letter to the newspapers, later reproduced in his pamphlet *Letters on the Depopulation of the Highlands*:

> I hope the Government and the proprietors of land in the Highlands of Scotland will now come to see the folly of their conduct in expelling our brave heroes from their ancient hills, and consigning them indiscriminately to foreign lands or to large cities, and supplying their place with sheep and deer... Is it not, then, a thousand pities that, in place of having only three Highland regiments in the Crimea, we have not a dozen Highland regiments there and another half-dozen Highland regiments to protect us at home? ... Alas! these robust sons have been driven across the Atlantic to feed the strength of other lands, sheep and game have been substituted for them, and only *a wreck* of a population is left behind.[12]

Donald then quoted a list of Scottish districts that in 1745 could gather a total of nearly 32,000 fighting men with only three days' notice. 'I know many districts which furnished 500, 700, and 800 soldiers in time of the wars, now without a single human being in them but one or two shepherds, and a brace of gamekeepers.' In his next article Donald quoted the Secretary of War about the gallant performance of the Highland Brigade in the Crimea and went on:

> Shame it is! Shame a hundred times told, that, while the brave Highlanders were on their way to the East, and while rendering their country such '*honourable and desperate*' service there, and making Britain's name a terror all over the world; many of the fathers, mothers, sisters, and brothers of these noble fellows, were deprived of their houses and lands in the Highlands of Scotland to make room for sheep. Shame it is, that the torch should be put to Christian homes in the Highlands, while these brave mountaineers were spilling their best blood on the heights of Alma, and in Balaklava's vales, for Britain, and for Britain's cause![13]

His next letter criticised the Government's new 'Foreign Enlistment Bill':

> That our nation, after a long period of peace, and before it was fully six months engaged in *active* hostilities against Russia, should be under the humiliating necessity of sweeping the continent for recruits to fight its battles, speaks trumpet-tongued against the monstrous policy which for years past tolerated the expatriation of the Highlanders of Scotland... The policy of expelling our own brave countrymen, and then establishing a system of kidnapping a set of foreigners, who may

be found passing through our country on their way to America, and inducing them to enlist into our army is, to say the least of it, as mad a piece of legislation as ever came under the notice of patriotic and sensible men...

For the last three of four years a society existed in London, designated the 'Highland and Island Emigration Society.' It is composed of two or three Highland dukes, half-a-dozen or so Highland lairds, a lot of money lenders; but among its most active members was the present *Secretary of War*, Mr Sidney Herbert!...

Mr Sydney Herbert is here found playing a double game. On the one hand he is active in removing the brave Scottish Highlanders out of their fatherland; on the other, he is found intercepting or rather kidnapping into the British army the miserable straggling Germans who are on their route through Britain to foreign lands.[14]

In January 1855 Rev. Coll Macdonald wrote 'there are five young men from the district of Knoydart fighting the battles of their Queen and country in the Crimea, while their parents have been shipped off to America, after having been driven out without a house to shelter them in the land of their forefathers.'[15] Later that month Donald wrote to the *NBDM*, subsequently reproduced in *Letters*:

> When Lord Madonald went through his properties in Skye, asking the young men who still remain in that mismanaged island to volunteer for military service, and that he would get some of the south country sheep farmers, and factors in the island, to drill them into military exercises at Portree, they indignantly spurned at his lordship's offer. They told him that they had been too long drilled and driven by such men, and that it was now adding insult to injury to ask them, the descendants of warriors and heroes, to submit to military direction at the hands of men who had not a spark of their ardour, and in whose souls their did not exist a particle of feeling congenial to that of the Highlanders.[16]

Donald paraphrased the young men of Sutherland and added the bold claim:

> Although I have no property in the Highlands, nor much influence with its people, I would have no difficulty in raising 2000 Highlanders, fit for home or foreign service, provided the Government should announce publicly that it will cause immediate inquiry, by Royal Commission, into the wrongs which affect the social position of the Highlanders, and afford all practicable redress. Let this be done, and I will undertake to convene at Fort William 2000 brave Highlanders, fit for home or foreign service, and that in less than 20 days.[16]

In November Donald wrote:

> Knowing well the very high respect which you entertain for Major-General Sir Colin Campbell, our brave countryman, now about to visit his native land, permit me, through your columns, to suggest to the Highlanders in Glasgow the propriety of giving this worthy and distinguished Highlander a real Highland welcome...
>
> Assemble, then, in hundreds in the City Hall in your native costume if possible, and give the distinguished Sir Colin such a shout of welcome and such a warm reception as he deserves, and as becomes you, as the descendants of a heroic and grateful people.[17]

It was subsequently reported:

> We learn that the Highlanders, acting upon the suggestion contained in Donald Ross's letter ... have fully resolved to present to Sir Colin Campbell a gold-mounted snuff horn, and a gold *cuach*, with suitable inscriptions upon each. This movement is not confined to one class of Highlanders, but to all – for Highlanders among the working classes are most enthusiastic in the cause, and are resolved that the brave Sir Colin will receive from them a real Highland welcome. A meeting of Highlanders was held on Wednesday night, when a large committee was formed, for the purpose of carrying out the above object.[18]

It doesn't say who was on the committee, but it can be imagined that Donald had a prominent position. On 30 November Donald sent an invitation to Sir Colin to attend a public dinner. However, he apologised for not being able to attend because he was only in England for a few days and had 'hoped to have been able to arrange presenting myself at Glasgow to have expressed personally the high sense I entertain of the gratifying and flattering intention of the Highlanders to convey to me their appreciation of my humble services.'[19]

After the war, a subscription was raised to present Sir Colin with an engraved sword and the Freedom of the City of Glasgow. The latter was presented by Archibald Alison at a dinner in the City Hall attended by 1,200 people.[20] Meanwhile, some of the soldiers who returned to Lairg in Sutherland found they had no homes to come back to, as while they were away their families had been evicted and their houses had been pulled down.[21]

22

Harriet Beecher Stowe

In *Real Scottish Grievances* Donald referred to Harriet Beecher Stowe's *Uncle Tom's Cabin*. This book, published in 1852, highlighted slavery in North America to a wider public and Harriet's campaign to end it made her famous.[1]

Harriet Beecher Stowe. Donald wrote to Harriet when she visited Scotland and was a guest of the 2nd Duke and Duchess of Sutherland.

The 2nd Duchess of Sutherland was sympathetic to the cause and in November 1852 held a meeting at which she read 'an "affectionate and Christian address of many thousands of the women of England to their sisters the women of the United States of America," setting forth the evils of slavery.'[2]

In 1853 Harriet embarked on a European tour and a book was published the following year entitled *Sunny Memories in Foreign Lands*. Harriet, along with the rest of her party, disembarked at Liverpool on 10 April and then travelled to Glasgow by train.[3] On the way they were startled by what appeared to be a castle on fire, though realised it was an iron-works, probably Dixon's, and as they 'drew near to Glasgow these illuminations increased, till the whole air was red with the glare of them.'[4] On 15 April about 2,000 people attended a soiree in Harriet's honour at Glasgow City Hall.[5] After visiting various places in Scotland she undertook a tour of England and in May arrived at Stafford House (today called Lancaster House), the London residence of the 2nd Duke and Duchess of Sutherland:

We were received at the door by two stately Highlanders in full costume; and what seemed to me an innumerable multitude of servants in livery, with powdered hair, repeated our names through the long corridors, from one to another...

When the duchess appeared... She was dressed in white muslin, with a drab velvet basque sashed with satin of the same colour. Her hair was confined by a gold and diamond net on the back part of her head...

We were presented to the Duke of Sutherland. He is a tall, slender man, with rather a thin face, light brown hair, and a mild blue eye, with an air of gentleness and dignity. The delicacy of his health prevents him from moving in general society, or entering into public life. He spends much of his time in reading, and devising and executing schemes of practical benevolence for the welfare of his numerous dependants...

When lunch was announced, the Duke of Sutherland gave me his arm, and led me through a suite of rooms into the dining-hall. Each room that we passed was rich in its pictures, statues, and artistic arrangements; a poetic eye and taste had evidently presided over all. The table was beautifully laid, ornamented by two magnificent *épergnes*, crystal vases supported by wrought-silver standards, filled with the most beautiful hothouse flowers; on the edges of the vases and nestling among the flowers were silver doves of the size of life. The walls of the room were hung with gorgeous pictures, and directly opposite to me was a portrait of the Duchess of Sutherland, by Sir Thomas Lawrence, which has figured largely in our souvenirs and books of beauty...

One of the dishes brought to me was a plover's nest, precisely as the plover made it, with five little blue speckled eggs in it. This mode of serving plover's eggs, as I understand it, is one of the fashions of the day... I had it not in my heart to profane the sanctity of the image by eating one of the eggs.[6]

Harriet wrote about the 'improvements' that had taken place on the Sutherland Estate and 'As to those ridiculous stories about the Duchess of Sutherland, which have found their way into many of the prints in America, one has only to be here, moving in society, to see how excessively absurd they are... Imagine, then, what people must think when they find in respectable American prints the absurd story of her turning her tenants out into the snow, and ordering the cottages to be set on fire over their heads because they would not go out.' However, she was confusing the 2nd Duchess with her mother-in-law. Harriet quoted James Loch's speech that he gave at the 2nd reading of the Poor Law Bill and referred to his 1820 *Account*. Loch supplied Harriet with a report that he gave to the Duke in May 1853 and informed her 'nothing could exceed the prosperity of the county during the past year; their stock, sheep, and other things sold at high prices; their crops of grain and turnips were never so good, and the potatoes were free from all disease: rents have been paid better than ever known.' Harriet concluded 'it is an almost sublime instance of the benevolent employment of superior wealth and power in shortening the struggles of advancing civilization, and elevating in a few years a whole community to a point of education and maternal prosperity, which unassisted, they might never have obtained.'[7] In response Donald MacLeod titled the 1857 3rd Edition of his pamphlet *Gloomy Memories* and was highly critical of her book.[8]

Harriet returned to Scotland in August 1856 and visited Inveraray Castle, Argyll. Donald wrote a letter to her on 2 September, though on not receiving a reply he sent a copy to the newspapers:

Will you kindly insert the following letter, which I deemed right to have sent to Mrs H. B. Stowe, to Inveraray Castle, the seat of his Grace the Duke of Argyle. I need scarcely tell you that the Duke of Argyle is married to the Duke of Sutherland's daughter, and that the clearances which Mrs Stowe so energetically defends in her "Sunny Memories" were carried out on the Duke of Sutherland's property... Of course, as Mrs Stowe is under the roof of "Young Argyle," and *viz-a-vis* at table with a branch of the Sutherland family, I need never expect so much as an acknowledgment of my humble communication...

Madam, – I have just read in a local print that you had proceeded from Glasgow to Inveraray, and to other districts in the West Highlands, 'to take notes on the clearances,' and to report in your future 'Memoirs of a Sojourn to the Highlands of Scotland.'

I am very glad of this announcement, and of your intention as indicated therein, for sure I am if you extend your visit to the northern counties, including Sutherlandshire, you will find scenes of desolation and oppression, which, if recorded faithfully, will form subject matter enough for you for a volume, well worthy of being bound up with your famous 'Uncle Tom.'

The most painful feature, however, in this case is that, when last in this country, you defended, in a lengthened and elaborate pleading, those clearances in Sutherlandshire which every man who was cognisant of the facts in connection with them universally condemned; and in this way, many hundreds in Scotland who read your 'Uncle Tom's Cabin' with admiration, turned aside from your 'Sunny Memories' with nothing less than disgust. There is not a shadow of doubt that those clearances in Sutherlandshire, which you laboured so much to defend, were notoriously wicked, oppressive, and cruel...

I much fear, then, madam, that you had your information on this matter from those parties whose hands are still stained with the guilt of the Sutherland clearances. With this, however, I send you a pamphlet, written by a gentleman who was an *eye-witness* to the scenes he so graphically describes...

I do not think that any apology is necessary for addressing to you this letter, nor yet for accompanying it with Mr Donald M'Leod's pamphlet. No one could have admired more your noble talents, humane and Christian disposition, as evinced in your 'Uncle Tom's Cabin,' than the individual who now addresses you; and certainly no one could have felt more disappointed, or more grieved, when those talents and disposition were made use of to prop up a system shocking to humanity, and a disgrace to a civilised nation.[9]

Harriet subsequently travelled to Dunrobin Castle and Donald wrote to her on 11 October, however she had already left by then.[10] Again he did not receive a reply, so sent his letter to the newspapers:

Mrs Stowe left Sutherlandshire last week. During her stay at Dunrobin, she was what may be said *"constantly watched,"* being seldom or ever out of the sight of some member of the Ducal family. She did *not* penetrate into the interior of the country to see the *"Desolations,"* and, for anything she may write of her *own* knowledge of the appearance or extent of the country under sheep, she might have been all the time in Kansas...

Madame,– ... At Dunrobin Castle you are in a manner tied to the Duchess of Sutherland's apron strings. You are shown all the glory and the grandeur of the Ducal residence – the fine old paintings, – the magnificently finished, and luxuriously and costly furnished apartments in that noble mansion. You are brought to see extensive gardens, aviarys, pleasure-grounds, waterfalls, and all that is beautiful and attractive in the vicinity of the castle; and you are occasionally treated to a drive along the coast road for some miles, through rich farms and beautiful corn-fields...

But you have not visited Strathnaver – you have not penetrated into Kildonan – you have not been up Strathbrora – you have not gone through Lairg, or Assynt, or Eddrachylis, or Durness, or Tongue, or Reay, or Farr – you have not seen the ruins of hundreds and hundreds of the houses of the burnt-out tenants – you have not seen those beautiful and fertile straths, once the happy and comfortable abodes of a loyal and virtuous peasantry, now a lying waste. If you had just penetrated through Rogart, and through the sheep-walks of the Halls of Shibercross, and on through Braegrudy to Crockan-a-chaillich, you could then begin to write the history of "The Desolation." Seating yourself, madam, on Crockan-a-chaillich you could see before you and around you one of the loveliest and most healthy portions of God's earth. Straths of beautiful and rich pasture, undulating valleys, table-lands, woods, rivers, lakes, and mountains, all forming a glorious landscape, and a truly suitable habitation for man. It is now the habitation of brutes. Sheep! sheep! sheep! occupy every corner of it. Upon the top of the hill just mentioned you can set a compass, with 25 miles of a *radius* upon it, and go round with it fully stretched; but, mark what I say, within this broad circumference you will not find a single human habitation, or one acre of land under cultivation, save that occupied by shepherds belonging to some sheep famers...

Madame, you will have your ears dunned with a vast amount of *sheepish* logic in Sutherlandshire. Factors and sheepfarmers will do all they can to run down the natives as indolent and ignorant, and the climate as cold and inhospitable. Do not believe the sheepocratic logicians. The natives indolent and ignorant! Fudge. Just mark the conduct of the 93rd Sutherland Highlanders. Is not this regiment the most active and the most intelligent in her Majesty's service. The act of this regiment, "the single red line" in Balaklava's vale resisting the charge and force of the Russian cavalry, stands unrivalled in the history of the world.[11]

Donald also sent the letters to *The Times*, but they weren't published, so he included them in *Letters on the Depopulation of the Highlands*.

23

Famine Relief

In 1854 the potato blight returned but this time it was a triple whammy as storms destroyed the corn crop and the fishing was abysmal. Donald ramped up his charity fundraising, even though the nation was more preoccupied with the Crimean War.

The first pamphlet Donald wrote with regards to the famine was *The Cry of the Hungry*. Unfortunately, the title page is missing from the only known copy, however it was mentioned in an appeal that Donald wrote on 30 December, so it was published before then. On 21 December Miss Gordon in Brighton, Sussex was gathering donations for 'The Cry of the Hungry – fearful famine in the western highlands and islands of Scotland,' which may have been in response.[1] The pamphlet begins:

> It may appear strange to some, that, after such a bountiful harvest in England and in the Lowlands of Scotland as we [h]ave this year been blessed with, a very large number of the inhabitants of the Western Islands should, at this moment, be in a state of actual starvation, arising from want of food. – It is nevertheless a fact, – alas! too true; for the cry of the poor sufferers is now piercing our ears. The causes of this destitution are sufficiently accounted for in the annexed letters from parties resident in the Islands. Last month, when visiting some of the districts referred to in these letters, – I saw sad proofs of the misery and the wretchedness of a large majority of the inhabitants. Much of this suffering, and misery, can be clearly traced to the conduct of the owners, and managers of property in those Islands. The cruel manner in which scores of families are, year after year, deprived of their lands and pastures, and driven to cold and barren moors, or to rocky eminences, in order to make room for deer, sheep, and game, is a cause of ruin, and consequent starvation to many hundreds of happy and industrious families...
>
> It must be borne in mind that provisions are at a famine price: whether this arises from the war or from other causes, it is not easy to

say. At any rate, meal is much dearer than it was at any period during the last ten years.

The pamphlet included thirteen letters, 'a mere tithe from a bundle of letters recently received,' mostly from ministers in the Hebrides pleading for help, some of whom had written to Donald before. The first, from Malcolm Morrison, Schoolmaster, Harris, dated 12 October:

> The blight has destroyed all their potatoes; indeed, by the end of August the fields were as black as they were when harrowed in Spring. The poor creatures who live almost *entirely* on this food are in a state of bewilderment. The change came on so sudden. In two or three nights there was not a green stem in the whole of this large parish. The corn crop is still ungathered. The weather is so stormy, with rain and wind every day, that there is no chance of it being gathered in with any safety, – the truth is, little as is of it, it is already half destroyed. The fishing was extremely bad. The herring appeared only once on the coast this year. They came up against a S.W. storm, and some of our fishermen went out, but caught none – as the sea was raging. Three men lost their lives in this attempt.

Many of the other letters gave similar accounts and a few thanked Donald for meal and clothes. Four of them were from Frank Mackenzie of Broadford, Skye who was caught up in the 'Weeping in the Isles' debacle. On 28 October Mackenzie wrote 'Dr. MacAllister was over at Strolamus and Dunan, yesterday and to-day, in consequence of a number of people having been seized with Diarrhoea around Scalpay Bay, of whom seven died within the last few days, some of them only survived a few hours illness. There are other four at this moment in the most precarious state. The disease can be distinctly attributed to the poverty of the sufferers, who have been entirely living on potatoes of the very worst description.' On 8 November he wrote:

> The meal, rice, arrowroot and clothing which you sent came safe, per steamer. Never was relief more timely, or more needed. I proceeded to Dunan and Strolamus early in the morning, accompanied by the minister, and brought a cart with the meal, and other articles. Having got weights and scales, we divided every ounce of the meal among the destitute families. May I never again see such a sight! It would melt a heart of stone to see the poor creatures, with their half-famished children, shivering in the cold, and with the marks of famine visible in their faces. I cannot describe the joy caused in these villages by your supply of meal, – neither can I describe their gratitude… Never in your life have you done a more charitable or Christian act than in the sending of this meal, – and oh! may God abundantly reward you. Cholera prevails in our immediate neighbourhood.[2]

Donald appealed for more donations and listed recipients in London, Manchester, Edinburgh and Glasgow. Appended letters encouraged Donald to continue his good work and not to give up. The *Glasgow Constitutional* later reported 'We find, from the docqueted accounts of Mr Ross intromissions with the "West Highland Relief Fund," that, from Feb., 1852, till Nov., 1854, he has expended and accounted for no less a sum than £1547 16s 6½d.'[3]

As mentioned above, on 30 December Donald submitted an appeal to the newspapers, 'Through the kindness of benevolent friends, whose contributions are noted below, we have been enabled to send several hundred bolls of meal within the last few weeks to the poor but patient sufferers.'[4] He quoted more recent letters; Morrison wrote:

> We received the meal, which was immediately distributed among the most necessitous. Such a cry for food as I heard the day of distribution was heartrending to listen to. Many declared, and the truth of their statements were proved by others, that they were fainting on the road – from pure want. I went over the most of the parish last week, and I found 267 cottar families in a most deplorable condition – their children wrapped in pieces of old blankets, or pieces of canvas, and without a particle of food in their houses. I am sure as I am of my own existence, that but for your meal we would have a black list of 'deaths by starvation' to send to the Government.

Then followed a list of eighty-two donations received during December, totalling £233 18s 6d, including £5 from Charles Darwin. The *Fife Herald* was critical of such charity as it considered 'the district or parish is liable, without fail, for the support of all the destitution within its bounds... The people who respond to these appeals – and they do so, we have no doubt, in the kindness of their hearts – are effecting no good, but evil rather. Every shilling they give is just a shilling saved to the Highland proprietor and rate-payer.'[5] Donald wrote another appeal on 31 January 1855, which included a long list of 130 donations received that month, totalling £262 19s, plus five donations of clothing.[6]

It wasn't long before Donald's next pamphlet *A Plea for the Famishing* appeared and was advertised in the newspapers towards the end of February.[7] It reproduced fourteen more letters received in December and January. Mackenzie on 13 January wrote 'I received your letter of the 10th this morning, intimating that you had shipped eighteen bolls of meal by the *Briton*, for the poor of Sleat and Strath, to be distributed by the Rev. Mr. M'Phail and myself... I cannot, in adequate terms, express to you the gratitude the poor people feel towards you.' Donald continued:

> From other districts the tale of want is equally distressing. From South Uist, in particular, the accounts are appalling. There is a little island,

Eriskay, within the bounds of this parish, and it is occupied by upwards of forty families – the victims of clearances in more favoured districts. They have been, as it were, *"transported"* to this island, and left to shift for themselves. Their potatoes have entirely failed, and the account received regarding them was that, unless relief reached them in some shape, every being on that island would perish in less than a month. A merchant at Lochboisdale, in South Uist was appointed by me to give them £10 worth of oatmeal, and last week I sent twenty bolls of meal to their rescue. To give an idea of their wretchedness – the deplorable misery to which the poor people have been reduced on this small island – their children are as naked as they came to the world. They have no bed-clothes, and, to preserve them alive, during cold weather, these children up to 12 years of age or so, *are kept under straw and bent, just like the litters of pigs*. The grown-up people and heads of families are not better off. A married woman gave birth to a child, and the tender infant had to be wrapped in a piece of an old hard, tarry sail; another made a frock for her infant, a week old, from one of the coarse sacks sent to the island at one time with meal![8]

Donald emphasised 'With regard to the distribution of meal, money, clothing, and other necessaries for the sufferers, that is most carefully done by trustworthy ministers… The distribution is of the most impartial character – Roman Catholics sharing equally with Protestants, and Dissenters equally with adherents of the State Church – the rule inviolably followed out being to give according to the *need* and not the creed of the sufferers.'

In February at a meeting in Wick, a local committee in charge of the Soup Kitchen Fund decided 'to transmit £15 to Mr Ross, wholly to be expended in oatmeal for the relief of the most necessitous districts in the West Highlands.'[9] However, this proposal caused an instant backlash. The *John o' Groat Journal* reported 'We are inundated with letters on this subject, all protesting against any foreign application of our local fund.' In one irate letter: 'Donald Ross cannot and will not touch six-pence of the Wick and Pulteneytown Soup Kitchen Fund.'[10] Donald subsequently wrote to the chairman of the committee and declined the offer.[11] The following month the *JOGJ* 'Notwithstanding our repeated warnings against such mal-direction of part of the Soup Kitchen Fund, and the dissatisfaction entertained by many here at the entrusting it to the administration of Mr Donald Ross' reproduced one of the *Reformers' Gazette*'s attacks on Donald and 'Had they asked advice as to whom they could apply to for information respecting the propriety of constituting Mr Donald Ross their almoner, we would have referred them to Mr Dempster of Skibo, than whom, on that particular point, there is no better authority in the north.'[12]

Over the next few months Donald submitted several more appeals to the newspapers and *The British Friend*, sometimes repeated in subsequent issues. Donald quoted more letters describing desperate conditions and thanking him for supplies. Money poured in from all over the country and Donald published long lists of donations. His network of donation hubs expanded to include Oxford, Cheltenham and Dublin and the appeals evolved from wanting money for meal to supplying seed and seed potatoes so that the people could plant crops.[13] Other articles reported Donald sending money, bundles of clothes and many sacks of meal, seed and potatoes to various places in the western Highlands and Islands.[14]

The British Friend reported that on 3 April at a Quarterly Meeting of the Society of Friends in Durham, £80-£100 was raised which was given to Isaac Sharp, the Secretary of the Society. Edwin O. Tregelles announced he wanted 'to visit the famine-stricken districts.' The Society raised more than £300 of which £100 was given to Tregelles, £100 was given to Donald and £100 was sent to the Island of Harris.[15] The *Glasgow Constitutional* reported on 28 April, 'Last week Mr Donald Ross shipped 344 sacks of potatoes, oats, and barley, and several hundred packages of turnip seed, and another larger quantity of the former was sent off on Thursday. Mr Ross has been enabled to make these purchases chiefly through the liberality of Mr Isac [sic] Sharp of the Society of Friends.'[16] It was stated that 'The introduction of turnip seed is a new feature in Highland agriculture;' however, the Highland Destitution Board had supplied large quantities of turnip seed in 1848.[17] Sharp, Tregelles and John R. Proctor travelled to Glasgow, then Tregelles and Proctor 'proceeded by rail to Greenock, and thence by steamer to Oban, being accompanied as far as Dunoon by Donald Ross.' Tregelles and Proctor went on to Arisaig, then Skye, and Proctor wrote back on 25 April that they had seen cases of 'severe suffering.'[18] The Society of Friends, still in existence today, are more commonly known as Quakers. The *NBDM* commented 'The Quakers have long distinguished themselves by deeds of Christian philanthropy.' However, because of their 'peace principles... A Quaker could not subscribe to the Patriotic Fund ... without countenancing the war.' The article pointed out that 'Completely absorbed by the war, and by the privations of our soldiers in the Crimea, the nation was not in any mood last winter to listen to the often repeated tale of Highland distress, and but for the interest opportunity aroused among the Quakers the result would probably have been many deaths by starvation... Hundreds of pounds have been sent within the last few weeks from England to the trust of Mr Donald Ross for the relief of the West Highlanders.'[19]

Donald's next pamphlet, *Destitution in the West Highlands*, dated 1 May, commenced:

> Through the active benevolence of those warm friends of the Highlanders, whose contributions for the past month are herewith published, nearly 1000 bags of oats, barley, and potatoes, for seed, have been sent to the West Highlands within the past few weeks; and still there is a great cry for more seed... It will not be too late for sowing corn or planting potatoes in the islands until near the middle of May; and now, owing

to the constant run of steamers to the Highlands, parties forwarding money contributions may rest satisfied that with such seed corn and potatoes will be purchased, and forwarded to the destitute crofters immediately after receipt.

Supplies of meal have been forwarded for the poor landless cottars; but it would be very desirable to furnish the most destitute cottar families with boats and nets, in order to put them in the way of earning their own living.

This was not a new idea; the Edinburgh Section of the Highland Destitution Board had supplied fishing boats to Skye.[20] Then followed a huge list of 305 donations received during April, totalling a whopping £868 10s 8d along with consignments of oats, potatoes, seeds and clothes. The donations included £200 from Sharp and another £2 from Darwin. Donald quoted letters from ministers received in the latter half of April, which all told a similar story: they were very grateful for the sacks of seeds and potatoes but needed more. Towards the end of the pamphlet was a detailed table listing quantities of potatoes, barley (bere) and oats, totalling 985 sacks, that Donald had shipped to twenty-four parishes in the Hebrides and west Highlands in April, along with thirty people, mostly ministers, entrusted to distribute the supplies.

Donald thanked all the donors, in particular the Society of Friends, and commented on the visit to the Hebrides by Sharp, Tregelles, and Proctor and the donation of turnip seeds. 'With these seeds we are sending some thousands of cabbage plants, and carrot seed, and with the blessing of heaven on these humble efforts, and a favourable season ensuing, we hope to see many scores of families, at present on the verge of starvation, emerging out of their difficulties.' Donald stated that bere could be sown up to 20 May, however for those donations received too late, the money would be spent on boats and fishing materials for the landless cottars. 'A boat costs from £14 to £16, 4 barrels of nets, about £10, other tackle, £4, in all, about £30; and this *one* boat will give constant employment to four families.'

Towards the end of the pamphlet Donald quoted the poem *The Clearing of the Glens*: 'Often have the following verses, from the pen of a Highlander, brought the tear into our aching eye, as we thought of the lovely vale, and the linn-watered glen in which we spent the first 28 years of our existence, but from which we were removed to make room for sheep.' Donald was actually thirty-two when he left. It is not stated who wrote the poem though it is clear why it meant something to Donald. Three of the stanzas read:

We sow'd the seed and reap'd the grain with thankful hearts and kind,
Our cattle grazed upon the hill that rose our homes behind,
Each Sabbath-day we worshipped God within the holy fane,
All circled by the blessed graves I ne'er shall see again,

And so it fell one weary day the bitter news was told,
That the fair land we loved so well was to a stranger sold.
The race that for a thousand years had dwelt within the glen,
Were rudely summoned from their homes to beg as broken men.

Death came, but came not quickly; pale and weak my mother grew,
With sharpened pain and wasting sobs her heavy breath she drew.
At last I laid her in her bed, when she could sit no more,
I kissed her poor and wasted cheek – I prayed, and all was o'er![21]

An article in the *Glasgow Constitutional* in May reported that £120 had 'been offered to provide boats on loan' and more than 1,300 bags of seed had been supplied to the Highlands.[22] The Skye correspondent of the *Inverness Courier* wrote on 30 May 'I was glad to see that the crofters, between one thing and another, have been enabled to lay down more crop this year than I thought in spring – thanks to Mr Donald Ross of Glasgow, and those who have helped him in his endeavours to assist the people here.'[23] In June the *Caledonian Mercury* reported:

> ...benevolent ladies in England ... have volunteered to provide funds sufficient to furnish at least a score of families with boats and nets for the herring fishing. These boats and nets are to be given to the cottars under strict guarantee of repayment by instalments... Three boats, named respectively the Friend, the Hope, and the Enterprise, with their full complement of nets and other tackle, were provided by Mr Donald Ross of Glasgow, for the poor cottars of Broadford, Skye; and we saw on Saturday, in the premises of Mr Ross, a large quantity of beautiful nets for the same purpose, purchased by him from the well-known firm of Messrs. J. & W. Stuart, *patent* net manufacturers, Musselburgh.[24]

It wasn't long before Donald wrote his next pamphlet, *Who will Help?*, dated 16 June. It ramped up the appeal for money for boats and nets, and included an ambitious boat scheme:

> It will take a large sum, about £2000, to accomplish this object ... A boat, with its full complement of nets, ropes, and other tackle fit for fishing in the lochs, bays, and sounds in the Hebrides, will cost £35 sterling. This boat we propose handing over to four cottars, under strict obligations and guarantee of repayment, by regular monthly or quarterly instalments. In order to encourage these fishermen, we shall open a store at the different fishing stations, where we shall receive any quantity of fish every morning from such fishermen, entering their full value to their credit in a book to be kept at the store. In this way such facilities will be afforded, and such encouragement given to industrious men, that even with an ordinary success in fishing, they may not only support their

families, but redeem their boats and nets in a year... The money to be realized from the sale of such fish we shall again apply in purchasing boats and nets, and so continue on until we shall have a fleet of 500 or 600 boats engaged in the herring-fishing in the West Highlands. Then, large-decked boats will be required for deep-sea fishing.

Donald failed to mention that herring fishing was fickle and had been dreadful the previous year. He then went on to report that the crops were doing well:

...the braid is strong, healthy, and far advanced, and, should a gracious Providence grant a favourable season for future growth and safe ingathering, there will be no fear of the crofters for the next year. To the different destitute districts we sent, in all, no less than 1436 bags of precious seed... In addition to the large quantities of corn and potatoes supplied for seed, we sent about 25,000 cabbage plants, considerable quantities of turnip, carrot, and other seeds, to the crofters for their gardens, besides packets of hemp and flax seeds, to be sown as "experiments" in some of their fields.

With regards to the donations of clothes:

...no less than 2500 young children were supplied with warm and suitable articles of clothing during the past season... There was clothing for the tender infant; little dresses for young children; frocks, polkas, and hoods for those attending school; pinafores, wrappers, and frocks for others; gowns, shawls, petticoats, and shifts for grown-up women; and coats, vests, trousers, and shirts for men and boys. Hundreds have been not only warmed and clad by such Christian bounty, but they have also, through these means, been enabled to attend public worship in their parish church... Large numbers of children are also regularly attending school.[25]

Some people still needed help and Donald quoted a letter from Rev. John Forbes of Sleat, the author of *Weeping in the Isles*: 'Destitution is at present pressing very heavily upon a number of the poor people here, and I have almost daily applications for relief, and very little to give at this time' An Appendix contained seven letters, mostly from Skye, received towards the end of May and early June. One from the Outer Hebrides was from a place he had not helped before: 'The people in Benbecula are in great want, more so than I can describe to you in a letter. I may now say that there is not a morsel of meal in this island, and the poor live *entirely* on fish and shell-fish.' Mackenzie wrote: 'Murdo M'Kenzie, the young lad whom you took by the hand some years ago, is now independent of all help. He has two boats and nets, and supports himself, his aged mother, and one or two sisters, in comfort. He is likely to make a good fishing this year, as he is fully ready to commence. Ever since you supplied him with nets, that family never asked nor received one ounce of meal, or one farthing of money from any charity.'[26]

Then it goes very quiet, so perhaps things were getting better. In *The British Friend* for November, Isaac Sharp reported that the Society of Friends had raised £475, of which five payments, totalling £310, had been given to Donald. Donald wrote 'the condition of the crofters in the islands was greatly improved, owing to the supplies of Seed Corn and Potatoes furnished to them; the cottars, however, owing to the *enormous* price of food, and the failure of the herring fishing, are even now very destitute.'[27] So Donald's ambitious scheme to make them self-sufficient from fishing had not taken off.

Donald's subsequent *Report on the Relief of Destitution in the West Highlands* was published in February or March 1856 and summarised the efforts of the previous year: 'The success which attended the appeals for aid for the destitute in the islands exceeded our most sanguine expectations, and the result was of the most gratifying character.' Donald reproduced ten letters 'out of a large bundle' which thanked him for the seed and potatoes though reported mixed results. Some of the crops had been good, others not so, and the blight had affected the potatoes to varying degrees. Most considered that the people did not have enough food to survive the winter and appealed for more help. One, from Rev. Coll Macdonald, reported fresh evictions on the west coast and 'The supplies of seed which you sent here in April last were of immense benefit to the poor in this extensive district... The produce, however, will be entirely consumed before the New-year, and then there will be distress, and want, and gloomy prospects. The herring fishing in this quarter was a complete failure.'[28] In an appendix Donald provided an informative account of the income received and expenditure for his West Highland Relief Fund. From 11 November 1854 to 31 January 1856, he had received £3,079 in donations plus £28 from fishing materials and £8 from the sale of empty sacks, and had spent £1,358 on meal, £1,003 on seed corn and potatoes, £153 on transport, £163 on printing pamphlets, adverts and stationary, £106 on clothing, £74 on postage etc and £190 on fishing materials. If the previously reported donations received from February 1852 up to November 1854 are added, then the total known income received over four years was a whopping £4,765, which equates to a relative income of £4,860,000 today![29] The accounts were signed off by sixteen men in Glasgow and included the statement 'In previous years Mr. D. Ross made no charge for commission, but in consideration of the assiduity, zeal, and great labour bestowed by him on this business during the past year, we approve of the charge now.' His 5% commission came to £152 10s 3d, equivalent to a salary of £116,900 today so he was really doing well out of this. Some may criticise this, but is it any different from the directors of charities receiving high salaries today? At the end Donald thanked the donors, appealed for more help and included a quote from Oliver Goldsmith's *The Deserted Village*.

Donald wrote a long advert on 5 March which appeared in five consecutive issues of the *Morning Chronicle*.[30] It included his accounts with a note:

'Should the fishing prove anyways favourable, the parties intrusted with nets, &c., will be able to repay, and in this way the balance due on commission will be paid up.' Donald was still due £102 so had only received £50 in commission. Another statement added 'The Gentlemen whose names appear to the above abstract have kindly agreed to act as a Committee to assist in raising the distributing funds for the Relief of Destitution in the West Highlands during 1856.'

Donald did not avoid criticism. A letter to the *Inverness Courier* considered that 'As many persons here (Mr Donald Ross's native county) have an idea that he makes "a good thing" out of his appeals to the English in behalf of the starving people in the Outer Hebrides and west coast, I have cut out the enclosed from an advertisement in a London paper. All that Donald receives or keeps to himself appears to be 5 per cent, charged for commission... The printing and stationary account, you will see, is somewhat extravagant.'[31] The *John o' Groat Journal* jumped at this and adjoined 'We have had occasion more than once to denounce the giving away of funds intended specially for the poor of this district, to be distributed in the Highlands through the agency of Mr Donald Ross, but we had not then any idea that Donald had such nice pickings off these charities.'[32] Abridged versions in other newspapers misprinted the printing expenses as £193.[33]

Donald went quiet again, though in May placed an advert for '26 Pieces (50 Yards Long each, and of best Hemp,) Herring Nets, quite New, and Four Large New Boxes, well suited for Conveying Lochfine Herring to market.'[34] So, it looks like Donald had given up on his grand scheme and was trying to recoup some expenses.

Donald's next pamphlet, *Cent per Cent*, appeared late in the year.

> In the spring of this year we sent upwards of three hundred bags of excellent seed corn to the poorest of the crofters in the islands; also, one hundred and eighty bags of potatoes, besides a quantity (ten bags) of potatoes received from Messrs. Sutton & Sons, the well-known seed merchants in Reading, Berkshire... The Messrs. Sutton, already mentioned, forwarded a large quantity of onion, carrot, turnip, and cabbage seed, for the use of the small crofters; the turnip and carrot seeds yielded rich crops, and the onions, on soil well cleaned and manured, produced a fair bulk; the cabbage seed did not yield so well, but the soil was not in good order for its reception. It is a new era in the history of the islanders to raise carrots and onions...
>
> In August last, having business to transact in one of the islands, we availed ourselves of an opportunity of making an extensive sojourn among the people. Having a quantity of nets, lines, ropes, salt, clothing, books, &c., for distribution, we placed the whole carefully on board a little vessel used by us in conveying meal, &c., to the islands, and then sailed for the Hebrides. We left parcels of clothing and books at Tobermory, for the poor of Iona and Coll, small islands near Mull.

> From Tobermory we sailed for Skye, and distributed clothing, nets, books, &c., in Sleat and in other places, until we arrived as Strolamus, a district in Skye, inhabited by a large population, having little or nothing to depend on but fishing. The misery in which the people who have got no land, and no boats nor nets, exist, can scarcely be credited; the children were in rags... With the clothing we gave away parcels of excellent tracts, periodicals, &c., furnished to us by Messrs. Oliver & Boyd, Edinburgh, and by Messrs. William & Robert Chambers of that city, both eminent publishers... It would gratify a heart of stone to see these little mountain Arabs grasp at the books and pamphlets; the fact is, ragged and suffering as they were, they preferred the books to the clothing. In two instances, a number of these little creatures, anxious to have some clothing and books, got into a little boat, and rowed out about half a mile to where our little vessel lay at anchor: when the poor little applicants approached within some yards of us, they appeared afraid, but on being spoken to they came close, and then fastened their little boat to our vessel; we soon supplied their wants, which the poor creatures acknowledged with grateful bows and smiles, and then rowed back to the shore. Some of them spoke English very correctly.

Donald went on to point out that the people were lacking medical services and provided a recipe for cough medicine. He then distributed the nets.

> Never was there a more pleasant, yet a more difficult task. We had before our eyes objects really and truly deserving, and would require more than £800 worth of nets among them, whereas we had scarcely more than £180 worth for distribution ... we distributed the nets, according to our judgment, among the poorest ... the people of Strolamus and of Arisaig are indebted for the nets they have received to the benevolence of Mr. Crossfield of London, Mr. Sinclair of Edinburgh, and to a kind-hearted and highly respected lady in London. This lady, with a liberality worthy of her Christian virtues, contributed a sum of £100 sterling for this purpose.[35]

Donald quoted eight letters, mostly requesting nets, received from June to September. Although the crofters had planted their crops, some had little to live off in the meantime. One letter was from a desperate man at Hallen, South Uist:

> You know my wife had three children at one birth, and we had not a stitch of clothes for two of them until you sent them. As we were poor, and could not pay a nurse, the mother had to give milk to the three. They are all daughters, and I wish you would get a friend to adopt one of them. They would get their choice. The one with black hair is the bonniest of the three. We are nine of a family, besides myself and

wife – eleven in all; and I have no lands, horse, cow, nor sheep, in order to help us, and therefore it is easily understood that we are exposed to several hardships; more so than the hearts of many could bear without feeling for them; much more a parent must feel, seeing his children starving before his eyes.

Before I was deprived of my lands and pasture, we lived comfortable; but now we have nothing to look to but the sea for support; and without fishing tackle what can we do? If you could send me two barrels of nets, it would save us alive; for we could fish all winter.

...If you would take one of the children, you can get the one with black hair and black eyes. She is the cleverest of the whole... We would part with two of the children, but this is from pure want of meat [meal?] for them.[36]

Another letter was from the schoolmaster in Benbecula who explained that sixty families were living off shellfish, so Donald sent sixty-one bolls of meal. One letter was from Rev. Forbes, so Donald supplied meal and clothing. Another mentioned that the people of Culnabruach, South Morar were about to be evicted and Donald also mentioned that twenty-four families on the Island of Eigg had received eviction notices. One man at Uig, Skye, with eight children, had been supplied with a boat and nets: 'His wife, who is a strong healthy woman, accompanied him to sea during thirty nights, took her place at the oar, and put down and drew up the nets like any ordinary fisher! Through the blessing of God in their labours, this couple have provided for themselves and their children until now, and are likely to do so during the winter.'[37] Donald finished the pamphlet with an appeal for contributions to supply more boats, nets and lines.

In May 1857 *The British Friend* published an article entitled 'The Skye Boat Scheme' describing a well-established system, initiated in 1851 by Rev. Alexander Adam, missionary in Portree and Rev. Dr. Fletcher in London who had supplied 42 boats. 'In addition to this, our friend Donald Ross has just now got built at Greenock, four large fishing boats for the poor cottars of South Uist, which, with their nets when complete, will be worth £400.'

In June Donald was again appealing for help for the poor in the western Highlands 'owing to a complete failure of their crops, and extraordinary inclement and tempestuous weather during the winter and spring.' He reported:

Many families were reduced to a state of starvation, and others, wishing to hold by their small lots of land, having committed the last grain of seed, and the last potato to the ground, are now in a state of extreme destitution, and requiring some aid to sustain them for a few months... A very large number of men, women, and children are in rags, being quite unable to get clothing, and are unfit for out-door work; and the children, consequently, cannot attend school, and hence grow up in ignorance, as well as in rags. Those entrusted with boats and nets last year will now support themselves without charity; but the number still in want, and the extent of applications for fishing materials, are so very great that one is at a great loss how to meet, or even reply to their applications.

We trust that the friends of these poor people will still hold out the hand of help by assisting them with boats and nets, so that they may be raised above their present deplorable destitution. The funds received for seed were judiciously applied, and many grateful acknowledgements have been received from, and on behalf of, the recipients. One of which, as a specimen, will be sufficient. John Fletcher, minister, Bracadale, Skye, says – "Your supplies of seed, for our poor crofters, was just in time to save many a nice plot of ground from being without a crop this year. The garden seeds are most valuable. Your great exertions, put forth year after year for the benefit and improvement of the islanders, are really beyond all praise and gratitude..."

It may be stated here that, in almost every instance, those families furnished with boats, nets, long-lines, hooks, &c., for fishing, have done [well]. In some instances parties have saved money, put on respectable clothing, and they can now regularly attend church. [I] have a list of upwards of fifty families, assisted into happy condition with little more than £600, or about £12 per family.[38]

Then followed a list of seventy-three donations totalling £277 5s 0d, plus six donations of potatoes and seeds, ten of clothes and two of books, received from March to the end of May. So, there was still a steady stream of money rolling in.

Clearly the effort that Donald had put in to help impoverished people during the 1850s potato famine was monumental. It must have been gratifying for him to know that he had saved many people from starvation and had enabled over fifty families to become self-sufficient.

24

The Glasgow Celtic Society

In May 1855 Donald wrote to the *Caledonian Mercury* proposing a new society called The Highland Association.[1] The aims of the association were to help destitute Highlanders who were victims of the clearances, to 'assist the aged and infirm poor in establishing their legal rights' with regards to the Poor Law, to instruct crofters in 'the best methods of cultivating their crofts,' to provide loans to landless cottars for the purchase of boats and nets, and to assist lowland managers in sourcing Highlanders for seasonal work. Members would pay five shillings per year. Clearly Donald had learned his lesson from his failed one-man Hebridean Benevolent and Industrial Society as this time the new association was to have a president, three vice-presidents, twenty directors, a treasurer and secretary. Donald indicated that when the committee positions were filled then there would be a public meeting. Further adverts added that members should contact Donald; J. F. Macfarlane, Edinburgh; Messrs Shirer, merchants, Cheltenham, and John Mackay, *Northern Ensign* Office, Wick.[2] It was subsequently reported:

> We are glad to learn that the friends of the Highlanders, clergymen and others, are enrolling their names in the lists of members of this laudable and patriotic Association, with an earnestness worthy of the cause. The other day no fewer than five gallant officers in the brave 93d Highland regiment, stationed at Dundee, forwarded their names as members, accompanied with a contribution of £2 15s in aid of the funds of the Association. Military gentlemen, majors and colonels, in other parts of the country, who know the noble qualities which distinguishes the sons of the mountain as soldiers, have also sent in their names, expressing at the same time their desire that every means should be used to retain the Highlanders in their native land, in order that those brave fellows, of strong arms and loyal hearts, be preserved to their country.[3]

Although the proposal was included in *Who will Help?*, there were no subsequent mentions of this association.[4]

The following year Donald was a judge at a 'competition of Highland pipers and Highland dancers' held in June 1856 at the City Hall, Glasgow.[5] He was also a judge at the first annual gathering of the Edinburgh Highland Society in September.[6] Other judges included William Campbell, Donald McLennan, and Dr David Mackay from Glasgow. McLennan and Mackay were signatories of Donald's accounts in his *Report*. Campbell was the former president of the defunct Glasgow Association in Aid of the Poor, so even though Donald had blotted his copybook regarding that association, they were probably still friends. In November Donald submitted an advert wanting, 'for a Highland Society now forming, a steady, intelligent, and active Young Lad as Piper. He must be a good Pibroch, March, and Reel Player, and also able to read and write accurately.'[7]

In October seventeen men met and 'agreed to form a society for "preserving the language, literature, music, poetry, antiquities, and athletic games of the Highlanders of Scotland, for encouraging the more general use of the national dress, and also for establishing a fund for affording temporary relief to destitute and deserving Highlanders, and to assist worthy persons coming from the Highlands in quest of employment."'[8] In January 1857 Donald submitted an advert announcing that the First Annual Meeting of The Glasgow Celtic Society, 'for the Election of a Chief, President, Vice-President, and other Office-Bearers, and for Approving of Rules for the guidance of the Society, will be held in the Merchants' Hall, Glasgow, on Thursday the 5th of February.'[9] The subsequently elected office bearers were Chief: the 6th Duke of Atholl (George Murray), President: William Campbell, Vice-President: James Watt MacGregor, Treasurer: Donald Campbell, Secretary: Donald Ross, plus 10 Directors, including McLennan and Mackay. It was reported that there were 518 paid-up members; many of whom had probably signed up to Donald's Highland Association beforehand.[10] The 6th Duke of Atholl had formed the Atholl Highlanders, which Queen Victoria made an official regiment and is still in existence today.

In June and July the newspapers advertised the First Grand National Gathering of the Glasgow Celtic Society, due to take place in August.[11] Sixteen patrons were listed including the Dukes of Atholl, Argyll and Montrose, Earls of Elgin, Perth and Seafield, Sir Archibald Alison, General Sir Colin Campbell and Cluny Macpherson. There were to be eighteen competitions:

1. For Pibrochs on the Great Highland Bagpipes
2. For Marches and Strathspeys
3. For Reel Playing
4. Dancing the Highland Fling
5. Reel of Tulloch Dancing
6. Sword Dance, or Gillie Callum
7. Reel Dancing
8. Best Dressed Highlander at his own Expense
9. Throwing the Heavy Stone

10. Throwing the Light Stone
11. Throwing the Heavy Hammer
12. Throwing the Light Hammer
13. Tossing the Caber
14. Foot Race (not exceeding 400 yards)
15. High Leap
16. Running Leap
17. Hurdle Race (300 yards)
18. For the best Gaelic Poem (not to exceed 100 lines) on the Military Services of the Highland Regiments during the late War

The competitors had to wear 'the Highland Garb' and 'Those wishing to compete for the Pipers' Prizes must lodge with the Secretary, at least ten days before the day of competition, a list of ten Highland Pipe Tunes... Those intending to compete for the Games must enrol their names, age, occupation, and address, with the Secretary, on or before Monday, the 3d of August.' It was subsequently advertised that the gathering would take place over two days, on 6 and 7 August. Rules, programmes and tickets (two for 1 shilling) were available from Donald and tickets for the evening dinner on the 2nd day were available from Donald, Donald Campbell and the directors.[12] Donald added a note requesting members to join the procession and wear Highland Dress.[13]

The most detailed report of the gathering was published over two issues of the *NBDM*. On the first day:

> The weather was delightful... At half-past ten o'clock morning the office-bearers and members of the society met in George Square, where they were joined by the Chief, his Grace the Duke of Athole, his son, the youthful Marquis of Tullibardine, his Grace's Highlanders, about forty rank and file, with their officers, the competitors and deputations from other societies, all – with three or four exceptions in Highland costume. Having formed into line, with pipers playing, and the standard flag of the Athole Highlanders floating overhead, the procession marched from George Square to St George's Church, down Buchanan Street, along Argyll Street and Trongate, up Candleriggs, through Albion Street, thence through College Street, and by the College gate into the Park... Immense crowds of people followed, rushing in hundreds from street to street to catch another glimpse, while the windows, housetops, and every available point of survey along the line of route, were occupied with spectators. On entering the College Park the procession marched round inside the ring formed to divide the spectators from the performers, the pipers playing the Gathering of the Clans, and then retired to the competitors' ground near the grand stand, a substantial wooden erection east of the ring, capable of accommodating about 1000 persons, having a specious roof to afford protection from the weather, and decorated with flags ... the numbers present were estimated at little less than 20,000... There

was a large number of competitors, all of them dressed in the Highland costume... The piping and dancing were excellent, as were all the other performances; the contest was keen, and close in many instances, and the spectators generally appeared much delighted with the proceedings.... In addition to the Duke of Athole, the occasion was likewise honoured with the presence of the Queen of the Netherlands... Her Majesty was present during the competition in putting, and the champion (Tait) had the honour of being afterwards introduced by Sir Archibald Alison to the Queen... The sports lasted till after four o'clock.[14]

The *Glasgow Herald* indicated it hadn't all gone smoothly: 'The ring was encroached upon during the day, and the crowd took up a position opposite the Grand Stand, thereby impeding the view from that quarter... The police arrangements were anything but satisfactory; but this is not to be wondered at, seeing that the great body of the force, as well as the chief officers, were stationed at the cattle show.'[15] The gathering had coincided with the Highland & Agricultural Society's Show. The *Glasgow Sentinel* added that the Duke of Atholl 'had gone to the cattle-show earlier in the day with his men as a body-guard for the Queen of the Netherlands.'[16] The 2nd day didn't go according to plan either and the *NBDM* took umbrage for not being supplied with the competition results by Donald:

> The sky looked somewhat threatening in the morning, but the day turned out favourable, and the concourse of spectators was considerably larger than on the previous day. The proceedings, as on Thursday, opened with a procession, which reached the grounds about half-past 10 o'clock... The champion of the athletic games was Mr John Tait, game-keeper to his Grace the Duke of Hamilton, who carried off some half-dozen prizes. The competition was very spirited, and excited great interest among the spectators, whose enjoyment of the scene, however, was much marred in consequence of the defective character of the arrangements for the preservation of order. Early in the afternoon the crowd outside the barrier surrounding the competition ground broke into the ring, and from that moment up to the close of the day, a great amount of confusion and discomfort prevailed, which neither the efforts of the police nor of the Highlanders present seemed capable of remedying... The Duke of Hamilton and party, including several ladies of distinction, might have been seen seated inside the enclosure, among other onlookers who had squatted themselves down upon the grass, familiarly conversing with those around them, delighting themselves with the exciting contest before them, and seeming altogether forgetful of rank and dignities. The work of competition lasted up till about seven o'clock, when the judges took their places on a reserved seat in front of the grand stand, the roll of the successful competitors was called over, and the prizes distributed by the President of the Society, Wm. Campbell, esq. of Tillichewan... The

The Glasgow Celtic Society

gentlemen in Highland costume, with the men of Athole, then formed into procession and marched back into the city, and the crowd gradually dispersed. The Secretary of the Society had engaged to furnish us with the official list of the prizes, but till the latest last night it had never reached our office, notwithstanding his promise to forward it in time for to-day's impression. The arrangements connected with the gathering, both as regards the accommodation for the press and the public, cannot be otherwise characterised than of the worst description.[17]

At the end of the day Donald was probably exhausted, and who knows how long the evening dinner went on for, which was attended by 160 people. The *Paisley Herald* also considered the arrangements were 'of a most reprehensible character... But with a singular lack of brains the managers placed the competition stage on the slope of one bank, and they erected their grand stand upon the other. Only those of the ordinary or shilling admission spectators (and these were thousands strong) who could force their way to the front had any chance of seeing what was going on.'[18] The article praised the Duke of Atholl for saving an elderly woman from being 'trampled to death' after she fell over during the returning procession. The Directors subsequently submitted a notice requesting 'that all parties having claims against the Society' should submit them to Donald Campbell or Donald within fourteen days.[19] The results of the competitions were published a few days later, except for the poem results, which were announced in November.[20]

The following year, the Glasgow Celtic Society's 2nd Grand Gathering featured in the *Illustrated News of the World*, but it is unlikely that Donald was present because he had resigned from the society eight months before.[21]

The 2nd grand gathering of The Glasgow Celtic Society, held in August 1858. Donald helped set up the society but resigned before this gathering, so was probably not present.

25

Miscellaneous Letters

There were several letters that Donald wrote about other subjects. In May 1856 a meeting was held in Stirling for 'adopting steps to have a national monument erected to the memory of Sir William Wallace, the Hero of Scotland.'[1] It was decided to hold a fundraising meeting in the King's Park on 24 June, the anniversary of the Battle of Bannockburn. 'The whole of the Scottish Peerage, the Lord Lieutenants and Deputy Lieutenants of Counties, the Provosts and Magistrates of Burghs, the Baronets of Scotland and Nova Scotia, and the Scottish Members of Parliament, have been specially invited to be present... A Procession will leave the Corn-Exchange.'[2] At a meeting in Glasgow, on behalf of the Lord Provost, it was decided that 'every exertion should be made to secure as large an attendance as possible.'[3]

The proceedings of the day were reported by the *Stirling Observer* which provided a long list of the bands, officials, societies and organisations that comprised the procession 'with their splendid banners, insignia, badges and dresses.'[4] 'At a quarter-past twelve the most Hon. the Earl of Elgin was met at the station of the Scottish Central Railway by twenty Highland gentlemen, accompanied by the Highland Chieftain, Cluny M'Pherson, and the Secretary. The Highlanders presented arms, and marched before his Lordship to the place of meeting.' The speakers and other eminent gentlemen took to the platform. 'Mr Paterson, the celebrated photographer here, was on the ground with his apparatus, and succeeded, after several attempts, in obtaining a splendid view of the platform, the Grand Stand and the multitude assembled.' The Earl of Elgin gave a long patriotic speech, followed by the Lord Provost of Edinburgh, who proposed the first resolution to 'erect a National Monument.' The second resolution by Sheriff-substitute Henry Glassford Bell proposed that the 'Monument be erected on the Abbey Craig, near Stirling.' The *NBDM* added that there were nearly 500 people in the procession and 8-12,000 present at the meeting.[5] 'Among those on the platform were 'several Highland gentlemen resident in Glasgow, dressed in their native costume.' The *Observer* later added:

Miscellaneous Letters

We have received numerous inquiries as to who the gentlemen Highlanders were ... they were all convened by Mr Donald Ross, of St Enoch Square, Glasgow, and it was solely on the suggestion of that gentleman that they appeared on the occasion. There were twenty-one of them in all, and their dresses and Highland appointments were of the most costly description, eliciting the admiration of all... Perhaps the highest compliment ... was paid to them by the noble chairman of the meeting, Lord Elgin, who, on returning into the town from the platform, expressed repeatedly his high admiration of them, and actually took his place in the middle of the Highlanders – a body guard, indeed, which even royalty itself would have graciously welcomed.

The gentlemen included William Campbell and Donald McLennan. In the same newspaper was a letter from Donald:

Now that a monument to the hero and patriot of Scotland, Sir William Wallace, is sure to be erected on the Abbey Craig, it will be desirable that all those having relics of the immortal hero should present them to the committee, in order to be placed in the monument. No doubt there are many relics of Wallace throughout the country. I find the following paragraph in Chambers' Biographical Dictionary, page 397, extracted from "Statistical Account of Scotland, xix., p. 561:–

'There is a respectable man in Longforgan, Perthshire, who has in his possession a stone called *Wallace's Stone*. It was what was formerly called in this country a *bear stone*, hollow like a large mortar, and was

James Bruce, 8th Earl of Elgin, who Donald escorted at a meeting held in Stirling in 1856, to raise funds for the Wallace Monument.

made use of to unhusk the bear or barley... Its situation was on one side of the door, and was covered with a flat stone for a seat when not otherwise used. Upon this stone Wallace sat, on his way from Dundee, when he fled after killing Selby, the Governor's son, and was fed with bread and milk by the good-wife of the house, from whom the man who now lives there, and is the proprietor of the stone, is lineally descended.'[6]

The stone was subsequently placed in the custody of the Laird of Castle Huntly; later donated to Dundee Museum and is on display in The McManus today.

Donald gave one guinea to the Wallace Monument Fund.[7] Its foundation stone was laid on 24 June 1861 by the Duke of Atholl and there was a spectacular 2-mile-long parade of up to 100,000 people, and 21 guns were fired from Stirling Castle. John Ross and his family may have attended and would have seen the 67m-high monument being built, which was completed in 1869.[8]

Donald's final letter in *Letters on the Depopulation of the Highlands* first appeared in the *NBDM* in November 1856.[9] It was in response to a letter written by John La Touche, who in turn was responding to one written by Prof. John Stuart Blackie of Edinburgh University.[10] Blackie had commented on depopulation in the Braemar district and that sheep walks were being converted to deer forests. However, La Touche of Ireland, who rented Highland deer forests, considered a link between depopulation and deer forests was 'totally imaginary,' that people 'never bred in the narrow glens, steep corries, and scowling heights that are now inhabited by deer' and that 'The proprietor of a deer forest ... employs more people, and of a better class; he circulates more money, he is more likely to forward education, civilization and all humanizing influences among his dependents.' Donald disagreed:

> Mr La Touche errs egregiously when he states that there are no lands fit for cultivation occupied as deer forests. In the parish of Glenorchy alone some 7000 acres of arable land were thrown out of cultivation to make room for deer, although the forest already exceeded 30,000 acres; and the population of the parish was reduced by 3010! ... generally, deer-stalkers care no more about the education of the people than they do about the shape of their noses. I could give proof of this, by showing how deer-stalking proprietors refused to grant sites for schools on their properties... If civilisation is to be promoted by savage butchery, such as deer-stalkers now resort to, all I can say is, may Heaven preserve my countrymen from such civilisation! ... I could illustrate this by several cases of gross inhumanity and savage cruelty perpetuated by gamekeepers, watchers, and gillies on poor natives, for simply trespassing on the ground set apart for deer. In the Inverness Courier of last week you will see the case of poor Isabella M'Gregor, who was

dragged from her house in the Lewis to Stornoway Jail, for taking a creelful of heather from a deer forest.

I fear Mr La Touche does not understand what "humanising influences" are, when he alleges that they are cherished by deer-stalking – seeing poor animals torn limb from limb by dogs, or having their throats cut, or brains knocked out by the well-directed balls of the deer-stalker.

Donald's last known pamphlet, *Letters in defence of the Highlands and Highlanders*, reproduced articles that he wrote in January 1857. The first, to the *NBDM*, was in response to letters published in *The Times* that suggested converting depopulated islands in the Hebrides into penal colonies for convicts.[11] This was not a new idea, in 1852 Sir James Matheson had offered the government the island of North Rona for this purpose.[12] Donald considered that if this happened 'Scotland, from being a nation glorious in historic reminiscences, and the Highlands, as being the birth-place of freedom, manliness, valour, and worth, will become a byeword and a nuisance.' He feared 'some of the loveliest spots in the Hebrides will erelong become the plague-spots of Britain – the abodes of murderers and thieves.' Donald pointed out that there were 20,000 people living in the Hebrides under proprietors Sir James Matheson, the Countess of Dunmore, the trustees of Lord Macdonald and Sir John Orde. If the scheme went ahead, the residents would have to 'go abroad, or settle down in the dirt, drink, dust, and smoke of Glasgow, and other large towns.' Donald suggested 'If England is overrun with convicts and ticket-of-leave men, let England provide for them. Send them to the Isle of Wight or to the Scilly Isles, or to Jersey or Guernsey, or to any other part of England.' The second letter was about the same subject: 'It is the intention of Government to convert many portions of the Highlands and Islands of the Hebrides into penal colonies ... and turn the beautiful and romantic land into a den of thieves and robbers.' It was written by 'Scotus' and first appeared in the *Glasgow Herald*.[13] In the pamphlet Donald said it was 'written by a Highland proprietor' but it is likely that it was written by him, otherwise why would he go to the trouble of re-publishing it? 'Scotus' trusted that 'there still remains sufficient patriotism and public spirit amongst the people of Scotland to defeat at once so gross an attempt.' Penal colonies in the Hebrides never materialised. The Government discussed the issue in February and decided to continue to deport convicts to Western Australia.[14]

Donald's next letter attacked Dr Frederic R. Lees and his essay on the 'prohibition of liquor traffic.'[15] Donald considered 'the old calumny about drinking and drunkenness in the Highlands is again revived and set forth, with no small amount of stupid cruelty.'[16] This wasn't the first letter Donald had written on the subject as he had sent a similar one to *The British Friend* in December.[17] Lees had used an old quote by Thomas Pennant about 6,000 bolls of barley being made into whisky in the Kintyre district, which led him to conclude, as Donald put it, that 'improvidence, dirt, dearth, and indolence have been engendered in the Highlands, and also been the cause of that "frequently recurring distress" in that part of the country.' However, although Lees certainly quoted Pennant, Lees actually wrote 'the improvidence, dirt, and indolence engendered by it, have as much to do with that frequently recurring "Distress in the Highlands," as any land-laws or absenteeism,' so Lees was not laying the blame solely on whisky production.[18] Donald commented that there were about 20 distilleries in Kintyre that converted 60,000 bolls of barley a year into whisky, 'which is no sooner done than it is shipped away in thousands of gallons to Greenock, Glasgow, Liverpool, Dublin, London, and to scores of other places in Britain, and also to the Continent. The inhabitants of Kintyre have little or nothing to do with these distilleries, and I question if there is any class of people in the West of Scotland more comfortable, and more peaceable and sober.' Certainly there was a lot of whisky being made in Scotland at that time; in 1857 13.3 million gallons was produced, of which half was for home consumption.[19] Lees stated that on the Isle of Mull in 1848 'the islanders spent on Whisky not less than £6,099' and that in Skye by the end of October 1850 'there had been expended on whisky, the sum of £10,855 – or more than double the sum distributed by the Relief Committee,' figures that he quoted from the *Quarterly Review*.[20] Donald attacked these figures as 'grossly untrue' and quoted a letter from the *Review* in which the Inland Revenue apologised to Macleod of Skye for making a mistake – in 1850 Skye had consumed 8,738 gallons, not 13,273.[21] Donald also wrote that fishermen from Ireland and elsewhere in Scotland bought 'large quantities of spirits, and often take home a supply' and that it was also purchased by tourists to take on their tours 'so that what is really drunk and carried away by strangers, is charged against the natives of Skye!' He continued 'Wherever much drinking prevails, there crime will assuredly prevail.' However, 'In 1853 (a famine year) the jail at Portree in Skye was four months empty!' and Donald went on to say 'In the Western Islands and in Ross-shire, Inverness, and Sutherland, smuggling, too, is at an end.' Donald ended his letter 'I can tell Dr. Lees that there is more guzzling and drinking, more brutal and savage conduct, more crime and more wickedness, perpetuated in one small county in England in a month, than in the whole Highlands of Scotland in half a dozen years.'[22] Maybe, but John Ross had certainly sold a lot of whisky in Dornoch Parish.

Lees replied 'Donald Ross, I perceive, is letting off his Highland steam in jets of "viperine" vituperation against my luckless self.'[23] He would correct the '£10,800 into the admitted sum of £6,300... No one will rejoice more than myself to learn than in Mull and Skye the people do not habitually drink whisky, and destroy the food to make it one year, for want of which they starve and demand charity the next.' Regarding Portree jail being empty in 1853: 'But surely a famine year is precisely the year when they cannot get the whisky.' He went on to say 'I have a revelation to make which will bring the Highland pony to a full stop.' The figures came from *Chambers' Edinburgh Journal*, who had quoted the *Quarterly Review*. Lees also provided quotes, reputedly from Donald, that were not in the previously published letters, so had Donald written to him privately? Lees ended his letter, 'I do not here say that Mr Ross is wrong in his facts, but that it is uncharitable and rude in inputing to me so many evil motives as my animating principle. I trust that Mr Ross's material charity, in reference to the Highlanders, so much indebted to him for his public appeals, will cover the want of "moral charity" towards an Englishman who is not one jot less sincere or unselfish than himself in his efforts to benefit mankind.'

Donald immediately replied that if Lees' 'expressions are not rude and uncharitable, certainly they are not very polite. They don't look very sober.'[24] He referred to Lees' corrected sum of £6,300 and wrote: 'In my letter no such admission appears,' and calculated that 8,738 gallons at 10s per gallon 'would amount to £4,369.' With regards to Portree jail being empty, 'there was no crime arising from drunkenness in Skye during the year the Doctor alleged the people had drunk £10,855 worth of whisky.' However, the erroneous figure was for 1850 whereas the jail was apparently empty in 1853. Donald ended his pamphlet: 'I am quite willing to discuss the matter calmly and candidly with Dr. Lees, but if he is not inclined to adopt this course, he will find that the Highland steam is not fully blown off yet, and that the "Highland pony" ... will not be brought to a "full stop" so easily.'

Lees wrote to *The British Friend* and included a letter from someone in the Highlands who wrote 'the people are not by any means *habitual* drinkers. It is only at weddings, on holidays, and on other special occasions, that they think of drinking,' and attributed the 'real cause of the *Highland distress*' to the clearances. But for 'the exertions of Donald Ross himself, in the way of soliciting and distributing relief in other years than 1848, many persons would have suffered death from absolute want. He has the entire confidence of the givers and recipients of relief... For *facts* you could not apply to a better informed, or better hearted man than to Donald Ross.'[25] Lees ended his letter 'as charity covereth a multitude of sins, I must excuse the little want of it displayed towards myself in Mr. Ross' imputations, while I assure him that I shall *effectually* correct the paragraph in the third edition of the essay, as amended. It will even strengthen my argument.' Lees deleted the incorrect figures from the 3rd edition of his book and added a footnote: 'In truth, however the poor Highlanders are now a temperate class; the class who *distil* and *drink*, are NOT now the class who *suffer* from famine.'[26] In another work Lees wrote: 'Donald Ross, in the Glasgow papers, fiercely assailed us for publishing an erroneous Excise Return – and, with the weakness of his countrymen, imputed it to *English* hostility!'[27]

26

Fraud

Towards the end of 1857 Donald wrote a letter to a lady in England; perhaps the same one who had donated £100 for nets. The lady sent his letter to the *Inverness Courier*:

> I am at present collecting money for the purpose of providing twenty-eight families at North Uist with boats and nets. They lost all their boats in April last during a fearful storm which suddenly overtook them, only a mile and a half from shore. They were driven before it and dashed against the rocks on the west coast of Uist. Four boats were broken to splinters, and three men were drowned. The fishing village comprised twenty-eight families entirely dependent on fishing. They expected help all summer, but obtained none. The fact is, they are in entire destitution. When I saw them early in October they were all in a deplorable condition. I ordered a dozen barrels of sea biscuit, and that and shell-fish has been their chief support since I saw them, only that I sent them half-a-dozen barrels of biscuit since my return.[1]

The accompanying editorial expressed surprise as 'The oats and potato crops in the Long Island have been good this season,' so the editor wrote to the local minister and Sheriff-substitute. The proprietor of North Uist, Sir John Orde, saw the article and wrote 'when I was in the Island in May last, I heard nothing of the kind, nor did I hear of it from my son, who was there all the early part of October.'[2] Rev. Finlay Macrae replied on the 30 November:

> There is no village in North Uist *entirely* dependent on *fishing*. There was no boat dashed against a rock on the west coast or on the east coast of North Uist, that I have heard of, for a long period of years, consequently, there was no man drowned on its coast from the cause assigned. There was no supply of biscuit sent to relieve the alleged distress of fishermen in this quarter. Donald Ross, Glasgow, has not, so far as I know, been

in North Uist either in April or October last. I have only known of his having been once in this part of the country, and that many years ago.

Sheriff-substitute C. Shaw replied on 2 December:

It is not possible, if such a calamity as the loss of so many men and boats had occurred in North Uist, but I would have heard of it at the time, and the Procurator-Fiscal and Inspector of Police would have officially reported the deaths of the three men, had they taken place. Just as improbable is it that the extent of destitution detailed by Mr Ross could have existed in North Uist without my being informed by it... There has not been an unusual amount of destitution in North Uist this year. On the contrary, I believe that during the autumn the people have been better off than for years back. All the crofters who chose to work got employment at kelp-making in summer, from Sir John P. Orde, the proprietor, and were by him liberally supplied with meal. About the 1st of August the potato crop became available. It has been the best crop raised in the island since 1845, and I think there is scarcely a family that has not had some in the ground... [The Registrar] writes me that there has not been a death by drowning registered in North Uist.

Donald saw the letter from Orde and wrote to the *Courier* on 8 December:

My informants from Uist, who were constantly among the people, are just as worthy of credit as Sir John Ord. One of them, Mr. John Clarke, missionary, writing on 5th May last, says – 'Dear Sir, – I have just arrived here, and having seen *the deplorable* state of the poor people, I at once write to you to see if you could do something for them, either by way of sending them seed for the small patches of ground they have – potatoes or barley – or clothing... If they can get no seed for the ground, another twelvemonth will have a mournful tale to tell.' Another correspondent, Mr. Donald Macdonald, Free Church teacher, Stonybridge, in Uist, in a letter dated 15th May last, says – 'I am sorry I have to state that most of the people here are suffering with want of daily sustenance. I understand that most of them cannot get what they tilled sown with want of seed, being compelled by starvation to eat the seeds usually laid aside for that purpose.' ... This shows the state of matters in May. In August and September, the Rev. Mr Macdougall, of Glasgow, visited the Uists, and found matters worse than represented above; and a letter from Mr. Clarke, missionary, dated Eriskay, and written last month, shows no improvement whatever in their condition, and urging providing the most destitute with fishing materials. Some families have been provided with nets, but a larger number still require a supply. It is in Eriskay the destitution is most severe; but who the proprietor of that island is as I am not aware.

The letters were published together and an accompanying editorial considered that Donald's explanation

> ...does not support the original statement given above. Part of it, indeed does not refer to North Uist at all, for Eriskay, as Mr. Ross must know, is a small island on the south side of South Uist... There is no mention of the lost boats or drowned men – no account of the twenty-eight families "entirely dependent on fishing," and "in entire destitution" – and no proof of Mr Ross's visit to North Uist in October last, or of his having sent eighteen barrels of biscuit – statements which appear to be expressly contradicted by the Sheriff and minister.[3]

The article was reprinted in the *Glasgow Herald*, so Donald responded on 15 December:

> At the request of the Rev. Mr. Macdougall, who was about to visit the outer islands, a number of barrels of biscuits – first 12, and then 6 – were forwarded, *per* Mr. John Campbell, master and owner of the Elizabeth, to Lochboisdale, for Eriskay; and, independent of this, Mr. Macdougall received from me two bales of articles of men and women's ready-made clothing for gratuitous distribution among the most destitute in *North Barra* and Eriskay.[4]

The editor of the *Herald* considered Donald's explanation to be unsatisfactory. 'At any rate, when we find a private individual attempting to collect money in a private manner for Highland destitution, real or alleged – and who for his intromissions is responsible to no one but himself – we are inclined to look upon the operation with disfavour, if not with suspicion.' Rev. Archibald Macdougall wrote to the *Herald* on 17 December:

> By appointment of the Free Church Highland Committee I visited South Uist, Eriskay, and Benbicula in the month of June last – not in August and September. Owing to reports that reached me before leaving Glasgow for these islands, relative to famine, starvation, &c., I did apply to Mr. Ross for such as he could spare... He gave me two bales of clothing, and it was arranged that he would immediately forward after me, and to my care, nine barrels of biscuits for general distribution among the people... But the nine barrels of biscuits never came, not even yet, whatever has become of them. It was not correct to say that I wished to send 12 or 18 barrels of biscuits to Eriskay and North Barra. Indeed there is no such place as *North Barra* at all – only that this might be a mere slip of the pen...
>
> Mr. Ross was not entitled to state that I "found matters worse than represented above," for I had no communication whatever with him about these islands since the month of June, and before I visited them ...

I was agreeably surprised to find matters not in a worse but in a better condition than was represented to me. I neither heard of nor saw anything like starvation or extreme suffering.[5]

The same issue reported that at a meeting of the Glasgow Celtic Society, 'a letter [dated 15 December] from Mr. Donald Ross, Secretary, was read resigning office, which, having been taken into consideration, was accepted.' Clearly Donald had realised he was not going to be able to dig himself out of this hole.

The Edinburgh-based *Scottish Press* praised Donald's charity work and gave him the benefit of the doubt: 'It is hoped that Mr Ross will do something to set himself right with the public, because in his capacity of self-constituted almoner for the West Highlanders he has long been entrusted with the collection and distribution of charity.'[6] Donald responded to Macdougall's letter, however, the *Herald* declined 'to insert correspondence which is entirely personal; but if Mr. Ross will give us something *authentic* as to his begging petition to the English lady, and as to the alleged terrible storm, and splintered boats, and drowned men at Uist, Barra, Eriskay, or wherever the real *locus* of the catastrophe is, he will be welcome to the use of our columns.'[7] Accusations in the press continued and Donald went quiet. A correspondent from North Uist wrote 'Donald Ross's statement of the destitution existing here is without the least foundation.' Another wrote 'Mr John Clarke, whose letter D. Ross quotes, resided in South Uist – I think the south end of it; that "Stonybridge," from which his other correspondent writes, is situated in the very centre of *South* Uist.'[8] Rev. Rod. Macdonald, Minister of South Uist, wrote: 'Mr Ross flies [from North Uist] to South Uist, and although they are different islands, different parishes, and under different proprietors, tries to map them into one.'[9] He confirmed that conditions were also good in South Uist: 'The good prices for cattle rendered it easy for the people to purchase such quantities of meal as they required. Great numbers were employed at kelp manufacture, who were liberally supplied with meal by the proprietor; there has been good fishing and an abundant harvest, so that instead of there being any unusual destitution during the last season, it would be difficult to point out any period in their past history in which the people of South Uist were more comfortable.' Macdonald mentioned a kelp-laden sloop that left South Uist on 29 September 'foundered at sea' and three men drowned, but 'Of course Mr. D. Ross could not have meant this, as they were people in good circumstances.'

In January 1858 the Glasgow Celtic Society held their Annual General Meeting. Although there was a detailed summary of the meeting, the only mention of Donald in the entire article and subsequent Annual Report was that he had resigned.[10] Clearly he had become an embarrassment to the society as there wasn't even a vote of thanks. Donald then became a subject of mockery. One article recounted a legendary tale about a boat crew from Barra who had discovered an enchanted isle: 'But stop my wayward fancy – your fond illusion is dispelled, Mr Donald Ross has discovered the island, and there is, alas! no golden age even in Ròca Barraidh; instead of peace, plenty, and happiness, they have ship-wrecks, deaths, and destitution – they have neither the nectar nor the ambrosia of the gods – but a miserable dole of eleemosynary biscuit and shell-fish from the shore to keep them from starvation.'[11]

Donald had really made a mess of this one and it appears that he had become a victim of his own success; the supply of seed, potatoes and seedlings enabled the Hebrideans to have a plentiful harvest in 1857. However, it appears Donald was still making a living from a cut of donations and thought he could get away with fabricating dire situations in private letters to generous donors. This does beg the question as to whether he had been making things up earlier, though in his published newspaper articles and pamphlets he probably made more of an effort to be factually correct, as he must have been acutely aware that his critics would pounce on anything untoward.

On 13 January Donald attended the 3rd annual Grand Highland Gathering and ball of the Fingalian Club at the Trades' Hall, Glasgow.[12] The club had been set up a couple of years before 'for the purpose of encouraging and promoting the moral and intellectual improvement of its members, who are required by the rules to be either Highlanders or of immediate Highland descent.'[13] He and Donald McLennan were among the gentlemen on the 'gaily decorated' platform, so Donald wasn't in complete disgrace and still had some friends. This may have been an opportunity for him to say goodbye as sometime after then he and his family emigrated to Canada.

27

A New Life in Nova Scotia

From 1773-1852, 30-40,000 Scots emigrated to Nova Scotia and Cape Breton in search of a better life.[1] Many had gone there because of the Highland Clearances, including some from Dornoch who had embarked at Cromarty.[2] Donald probably knew people who had left, so Canada would have been an obvious choice. By November 1859 Donald and his family were living in Halifax, Nova Scotia. An article in December revealed how he was getting on:

> Many readers of *The British Friend* will recollect that in the winters of 1853 and 1854, there was great distress in the Highlands of Scotland, and that the most active in rendering personal assistance and soliciting aid for others, was Donald Ross, late of Glasgow.
>
> It appears that such aid as he was so instrumental in procuring for others, he is now in much need of himself. The commercial crisis of 1857, which shattered the fortunes of so many did not spare him, and he emigrated to Canada, where, after a short time, he was seized with ague, entirely incapacitating him from work, and his medical advisers recommended that he should go to Halifax, Nova Scotia, where he now is, and though improved in health, yet still equal to but very little bodily exertion, and where he is in want of not only all the comforts he has been used to, but also of the necessaries of life.
>
> This adverse change in D. Ross's circumstances having become known to some Friends in this country, it has been determined to appeal to the liberality of those who have enough and to spare for the necessities of others, though he is not aware that such an appeal will be made.[3]

The financial crisis was caused by the collapse of the Western Bank due to mismanagement, which led to the loss of £3 million to shareholders.[4] This appears to have been a convenient excuse as to why Donald emigrated, though perhaps he lost money from it, too. In January 1860 *The British*

Friend listed 35 people who had donated a total of £55 12s to the Donald Ross Fund.[5] It subsequently reported:

> A letter has been received from our friend Donald Ross, from Halifax, Nova Scotia, on whose behalf a number of Friends have most kindly and liberally subscribed, in which he says: "The unexpected remittance was of the greatest service to me. It reached me on Saturday evening, the 31st ult. [December], when I had not one shilling in my possession, to take in any little necessaries for the following Sunday, and New Year." He speaks of the cold being intense, some nights at 14° below zero, and mentions how very severely they had been tried, and how very seasonable was the relief afforded. In the fullness of his gratitude he concludes with a wish, "that our Heavenly Father may guide and preserve, and bless with his countenance and presence in all their undertakings, all those generous Friends who have so handsomely contributed to meet his necessities, and to cheer up and comfort his drooping heart. May the Lord be their portion."
>
> We are truly glad to say that he reports his health as improved, and his limbs fast regaining strength, and it is also very gratifying to hear that he has temporary employment, which he hopes will become permanent, when the season opens; and in the meantime the money already collected we trust will suffice.[6]

An additional seven donations totalling £12 15s were listed. The money would have been a welcome windfall to Donald given his circumstances, and although it was not as much as his commission from donations, it was more than he was paid as Agent of the Poor.

Halifax is the capital of Nova Scotia, named after the Earl of Halifax and situated next to the second deepest natural harbour in the world.[7] It is not known where Donald and his family initially lived, though many of the scenes in Cornall's *Halifax* would have been familiar.[8] The city had access to piped water but no sewers, and had gas and oil lamps, but no electricity.[9] Halifax Harbour was renowned for being ice-free, though if the winter was particularly harsh then it could freeze over, whereby people walked or skated to and from Dartmouth on the other side.[10] The summers were pleasant and regattas were held in the harbour annually.[11]

In November 1859 Donald put his name to a list of people willing to become members of a volunteer rifle company.[12] This was set up in response to an Act passed in 1855, during the Crimean War, to form new volunteer companies.[13] Subsequently, Donald became the Acting Secretary of The Scottish Volunteer Rifle Company of Halifax which held its inaugural meeting in the Masonic Hall on 13 December 1859. Donald was elected Secretary on 13 January 1860, though resigned in March with 'a vote of thanks being tendered to the retiring official for his services.'[14] That year he became a member of the North British Society at a meeting held in the

Masonic Hall, and was still a member in 1868.[15] The society is still going strong today, known as The Scots.

On 5 January 1865 Donald, then as a merchant, wrote a letter to Prof. John Stuart Blackie at the University of Edinburgh:

> Accept the warm thanks of a Highlander from Scotland for your defence of Celtic Literature. I am a native of Sutherland, was 14 years of age before I could speak one word of English, and altho I was only three months at School, I can now speak the English pretty fair.–
>
> The Gaelic however is my favorite tongue. I do all my thinking in Gaelic. It answers better, and altho in somethings I cannot make myself sufficiently plain, it is not the fault of the fine old Gaelic, but, of the difficulty in coming down from it to low Saxon.–
>
> I noticed a review of a pamphlet, or printed lecture, or something of that kind, a production of yours in a recent [?] of the Inverness Courier. I was proud of it and doubly so because you a lowland Gentleman, appreciated so highly and had the credit of discovering beauty and merit in the dear old Gaelic.–
>
> If your pamphlet is for sale, will you let me have the name of the Publisher as I should like to have a few Copies.–
>
> It is my solemn Conviction that the Gaelic is the finest and the noblest language on earth:- Gods real Gift to man, when he permitted him to express his wishes, desires, and devotions in words. It is in truth the language of devotion; and I repeat here what I said a few years ago to an Oxford Professor who predicted that the Gaelic would be extinct throughout the world in 30 years, if so that, then, the world would not exist for more than 30 years; as the Great author of all Good who gave the language to our first parents would not keep roof over the human family one hour after the language was gone!
>
> This may be a rash thought, stile [sic] I believe it.–
>
> Many thanks then my dear Sir for your defence of the Gaelic, and, rest assured, that, hundreds on both sides the Atlantic who may never think of writing to you as I now do: express their thanks in their hearts and in Genuine Gaelic accent and sentiment may God long spare you, and bless you, are the wishes of your Celtic friend.[16]

It is surprising that Donald's use of English was not as good as in his previous writings, perhaps his illness had affected him. He would have had access to Scottish newspapers via the Cunard Royal Mail steamships.[17]

John Stuart Blackie is rarely heard about today, however in his lifetime he was referred to as the 'Apostle of the Celts' and 'the greatest living Scotsman.' After his death he was called 'the last great Scotsman,' previously applied to Sir Walter Scott.[18] He became the Professor of Greek at the University of Edinburgh in 1852 and was very popular with his students. Although he was born four years before Donald, Blackie didn't develop an interest in the

Highlands until relatively late. He wrote many books, including four about the Highlands and Highlanders and he was critical of the Highland Clearances.[19] Rev. Aird supplied Blackie with historical material for *Altavona*.[20] Although the Greek language was his main interest, Blackie became interested in Gaelic at a time when it was considered by many to be a dead language and he feared its extinction would be a major loss.[21] His 1864 pamphlet *The Gaelic Language* was the one that Donald wanted. The Education (Scotland) Act 1872 banned the teaching of Gaelic in schools, and Blackie considered teaching it was important.[22] To save Gaelic from extinction he tirelessly campaigned and raised money for a new Chair of Celtic Language, History, Literature and Antiquities, which became a reality in 1882. Donations came in from the poorest Highlander to the richest, including the Celtic Society of Glasgow, Queen Victoria and 3rd Duke of Sutherland.[23] Although this chair instigated the study of Gaelic at university level, it was not brought back as a mainstream language taught in Scottish schools until 1985. Blackie died in 1895 and the two-hour long procession from St Giles Cathedral to Dean Cemetery in Edinburgh, led by pipers of the Black Watch Regiment, was lined with thousands of grieving people from all backgrounds.[24]

In July 1868 the *Acadian Recorder* reported:

> Our esteemed Highland friend, Donald Ross, imported by last steamer for a Highland or Scottish Society, in Cape Breton, a beautiful set of No. 1 Military Bagpipes, from the celebrated pipe-maker, Mr. Glen of Edinburgh. Our respected fellow-citizen, Mr. Binney, always, when in full management of our Customs, admitted such pipes duty free. On this occasion Mr. Binney had not the full management. Tilley, Minister of Customs from Ottawa was here, and would not allow the Bagpipes out of his clutches until the sum of six dollars and 33 cents had been paid, as duty to the Dominion Government. Mr. Ross made a declaration that the pipes were not imported, as merchandise or for profit, but for a patriotic, and benevolent society, having for its objects, the preservation of the martial spirit, music, poetry, dress, and games of the Scottish Highlanders. Tilley, however, was inexorable, and insisted on the full amount of duty, which, of course, was paid by Mr. Ross.[25]

The *Halifax Citizen* added that Donald declared the pipes were 'for the Caledonia Club of Sydney, Cape Breton.'[26] By contrast the *Ottawa Daily Citizen* supported Tilley's decision and considered that 'If Donald Ross' "pipes" were allowed to enter free, the musical instruments of every Masonic, Temperance, National and other benevolent society, and of every individual who might chance to import an instrument for his own use, would be fairly entitled to claim the same thing.'[27] It is interesting that the bagpipes were destined for Sydney as this is nearly 200 miles from Halifax. Was Donald a member of the Club or did he use it as a ruse to try to avoid paying import duty? Today, the whereabouts of the bagpipes is unknown.[28]

A New Life in Nova Scotia

On 18 November 1869, Donald was elected President of the Highland Society of Nova Scotia and was listed as such in the *Halifax City Directory* for the years 1871-3.[29] His position was also mentioned in the *Annals of the North British Society*, but further details are elusive.[30]

In February 1870 it was widely reported in the newspapers that Donald had pre-ordered 400 copies of the new Gaelic edition of Queen Victoria's *Journal in the Highlands*; including the *Paisley Herald* where Donald's nephew, John Sutherland Ross had just commenced working as the Printer Compositor Foreman.[31] Queen Victoria's *Journal*, originally published in 1865 for private circulation, was an account of her early tours of Scotland and provided her subjects with the romantic view of Scotland. She and her entourage often travelled on the backs of ponies through the empty glens and over the hills, while Prince Albert and others were off stalking deer and other game. The book was extremely popular and several editions were published.[32]

The 1871 Canadian census indicated that Donald, 56, his wife 'Marjory', 61 and daughter 'Annie', 25, were living in Dartmouth and his occupation was given as 'Book Keeper.' His and Anna's ages were not too dissimilar from their real ages of 58 and 29, though May was actually 74, so they had probably narrowed the gap to appear more respectable. Dartmouth was predominantly residential, though did have its own industries making iron and brass castings, ice skates, nails, chocolate, ropes and ships, and harvesting ice from nearby lakes.[33] They probably watched the 'great four-oared boat-race for the championship of the world' row past on 1 September 1871.[34]

There were several churches that supported different denominations. Donald and his family were listed as Presbyterian in the census so probably attended St James Church. Initially it was situated 'near the eastern corner of King and North Streets' however in 1870 a new church was built at the

The great four-oared boat race going past Dartmouth in September 1871.

The Red Mill near Black Rock Point, Dartmouth; near where Donald lived.

junction of Portland Street with 'the Cole Harbour or Eastern Passage Road' and opened in January 1871. It is still there today at 181 Portland Street, but was badly damaged by fire in 1970 and was rebuilt.[35]

The Nova Scotia and Halifax directories provide more information (see Appendix 3). Donald was living in Dartmouth from at least 1865 and was variably listed from 1869 to 1878 as living at Craig Ross or Craig Rose cottage on Blackrock Road, Shore Road, Upper Water or Common. Black Rock Point is a promontory one mile W.N.W. of Dartmouth Harbour over which the Angus L. Macdonald Bridge heads across the water to Halifax today.[36] Near this point was the Red Mill, situated on Windmill Road. Two roads that run parallel to Windmill Road are Fairbanks Street and Shore Road today. The latter is referred to as Water Street on an 1878 map of Dartmouth.[37] It seems likely that Blackrock Road, Water Street and Shore Road are all the same road. There is a short road, Hare Lane, connecting Windmill and Shore roads and on the map, on the east side of this lane is a building marked 'D. Ross,' which must be Donald's house. The house was probably destroyed by the major explosion of 1917, when a ship carrying munitions blew up in Halifax Harbour and killed 2,000 people.[38]

From at least 1865 to 1871 Donald worked as a book-keeper for the merchant company Bauld, Gibson & Co. in Halifax, which was situated at the Steamboat Wharf.[39] In the Halifax directories the wharf is also referred to as the South or Steam Ferry Wharf, and the company address is also variably listed as Market Square, Market Slip or 1 Upper Water Street; these were all at the same place and their premises are clearly marked on a street atlas of 1878.[40] The company, of which the main proprietors were William Bauld and John Gibson, placed several adverts in the directories:

> BAULD, GIBSON & CO.
> Merchants, and Importers of
> BRITISH AND AMERICAN GOODS;
> Also of
> Sugars, Molasses, Rum, &c.
> From the West Indies;
> WINES, BRANDY, GIN, AND TEAS,
> From Spain, France, Holland, and London Markets;
> Together
> With a Large and Varied Supply of all kinds of Breadstuffs and General Groceries from American and European Markets, in Bond, or Duty Paid.
>
> ---
>
> STORES, AND BONDED WAREHOUSE,
> MARKET SQUARE, HALIFAX, N.S.[41]

There were three paddle steamer ferries operating between Dartmouth and Halifax, which Donald would have used to commute to work: the *Sir Charles Ogle*, *Micmac* and the *Boxer*, which was replaced by the *Chebucto* in 1869.[42] The ferry terminal at Steamboat Wharf, where Bauld Gibson & Co. were situated, would have been very convenient. The journey was described:

> The passage across the harbour is made in ten minutes. Dartmouth is seen to great advantage in the transit. The undulating hills in the distance, the luxuriant growth of native trees covering each elevation, the broad harbour stretching out to the Atlantic, the pretty villas dotted all over the land-scape from the Windmill to Fort Clarence, can all be seen and admired in one brief passage from shore to shore. The steamers with their varying passengers, are worlds in miniature, – grave men of business, light-hearted girls, noisy school-boys, merry darkies, solemn squaws, chattering French peasants, stolid labourers, men and women of leisure and of fashion, may all be seen on these boats as they pass to and fro, from six o'clock in the morning until midnight.[43]

By 1873 Donald had set up his own retail grocers in Halifax, also selling liquor, both wholesale and retail. The address was 9 or 11 Upper Water Street, between Steamboat Wharf and Stayner's Wharf, not far from Bauld & Gibson. Was he getting his stock from them, or had they fallen out? In April the *Stonehaven Journal* provided a rare description of Donald, quoting a letter from someone newly arrived in Halifax:

Last night we went into a place to have a "drink" – a Scotch house kept by a man named Donald Ross. He has been in Halifax for about 25 years, but hails originally from Durris. He is the rummest old gent, ever you saw; dresses in the tartan of the old country, and wears a big "Rob Rorrison" bonnet. When I told him we came from "Stanehive" you should have seen him jump. There were eight of us altogether but he treated us all to real Scotch bannock and cheese and every one had to accept an invitation to dinner at his house. "Mann" he said to me in the broadest of Scotch, "yer nae only a Scotchman but yer frae Stanehive, – fa wid hae thocht it! Gie's yer hand again." We stopped in his place for about three hours, and I am afraid we drank more Glenlivet than was good for us. We have a very small drop of Glenury left in the bottle, and he is coming down to the ship to taste it. Donald told me he came to Halifax poor and friendless, but he seems to be in a different position now. He has a splendid store with a bar-room at the back, and he has also a splendid villa across in Dartmouth, a rapidly rising place on the other side of the harbour.[44]

Given that Donald had left Scotland under a cloud then he was probably evasive when it came to telling strangers exactly where he was from. Perhaps he was familiar with Durris, Aberdeenshire, from when he was away, before he became the miller at Clashmore. Donald's retail venture appears to have

Sir John Douglas Sutherland Campbell, Marquis of Lorne and Princess Louise arriving in Halifax in 1878. Donald wrote a welcoming letter to the Marquis, the new Governor-General of Canada.

been short-lived as it is only listed in three volumes of the *Halifax City Directory*. The Dartmouth Council Minutes mentioned two letters written by him. No details are given for the first one, dated 16 September 1875, however the second one, dated 17 January 1876, is recorded as a 'letter from Donald Ross praying exemption from Taxes, owing to sickness and losses.'[45] The letters have not survived. Perhaps his 'losses' were due to him being too generous with his hospitality. The Dartmouth Property Assessment Rolls indicated the value of his property was $2000 from 1874-1876 but had dropped to $1200 in 1878.[46]

Donald's wife died on 10 July 1874, aged 77, and was buried in Dartmouth Common Cemetery.[47]

At a meeting of the Nova Scotian Institute of Natural Science in December 1876, it was reported that Donald had presented to the museum 'a Stone Axe found in Dartmouth.'[48] Donald wrote a series of articles on Highland history sent to the Halifax-based *Herald*, two of which, on the history of the Sutherland and Argyll families, were reprinted by *The Oban Times*.[49]

In 1878 the Marquis of Lorne, a son of the 8th Duke of Argyll and grandson of the 2nd Duke of Sutherland, became the new Governor General of Canada and arrived in Halifax with his wife, Princess Louise, one of Queen Victoria's daughters. 'There were the usual salutes from ships and forts, while flags, bunting, and arches decorated the streets. After the swearing-in ceremony church bells rang out and a seventeen-gun salute from the Citadel boomed the news to the entire area.'[50] In December Donald wrote a long welcoming letter; he was missing the Highlands:

> Please permit me, a Highlander from the county of Sutherland, but now resident in Nova Scotia, to address you, and to offer to your Excellency and to Her Royal Highness the Princess Louise, the assurance of my right hearty welcome, and the offer of my sincere congratulations on your safe arrival at the capital of the Dominion of Canada.
>
> Born, and long resident, in the romantic county of Sutherland, I could not fail to observe and to admire, the many noble qualities by which the illustrious family of Sutherland was ever and eminently distinguished; and I feel proud that a grandson of the "Good Duke" of Sutherland, in the person of your Excellency, has been chosen by Her Majesty to fill the important office of Governor-General of this extensive portion of Her Majesty's Dominions...
>
> Your Excellency's countrymen, the Scottish Highlanders, scattered throughout this great Dominion, one and all, hail with feelings of unmingled joy your Excellency's arrival among them, and in the true sincerity of warm Highland hearts greet your Excellency and your beloved Consort the Princess Louise, with many thousand Highland welcomes, and in event of their services being ever required, their fidelity and martial ardour is the same as of old; and right loyally they would

stand as a wall of fire around their Governor-General and his Royal partner...

I sincerely trust that your Excellency's stay in Canada will not be limited to any set term of years, but that it will be a very prolonged stay; and that when you do visit the "old country" it will be only for a visit; just to look once more on Scottish scenes, to admire again the magnificent scenery of Argyle and the Isles, to have a quiet look at the majestic Bencruachan and other heath-clad mountains, to wander by the beautiful and placid Loch Awe, to see the hills of Morven, Cowal, and Mull, made immortal by Ossian and the bards; and generally like Scotland's renowned bard, make leisurely pilgrimages through dear old Caledonia – gaze on her beautiful mountains, sit on the fields of her many battles, wander on the banks of her many lakes and meandering rivers, and muse by her old castles, stately towers, and venerable ruins; once the abode of her honoured statesmen, heroes, and bards.

May God bless your Excellency and your beloved Consort, the Princess Louise; may He make your stay in Canada a blessing to the people, a satisfaction to Her Majesty, and a source of very great pleasure to yourselves, is the sincere wish of your Excellency's devoted old Highland countryman, who has the honour to be your Excellency's very obedient humble servant, An là chi 's nach fhaic.[51]

Donald gave his address as 'Celtic Cottage, Dartmouth.' He received a reply from the Governor-General's secretary, Major F. De Winton, on behalf of the Governor-General, thanking him for his letter, 'the warm welcome and the many kind expressions.'

The 1881 Canadian census listed Donald as a widow, aged 66, living with Anna aged 35. He was a 'farmer,' so perhaps he had become self-sufficient. Donald died on 26 August 1882, aged 69, and was buried with his wife in Dartmouth Common Cemetery. Their red granite gravestone reads:

IN MEMORY OF
DONALD ROSS
A NATIVE OF
CLASHMORE SUTHERLANDSHIRE
SCOTLAND.
DIED AUG. 26TH 1882
AGED 66 YRS.
ALSO HIS WIFE
MARGORY BAIN
A NATIVE OF
WICK CAITHNESS-SHIRE
DIED JULY 10TH 1874
AGED 67 YRS.

A New Life in Nova Scotia

There are some errors, such as that his wife was born in Wick, where their daughter Anna was born, rather than near Perth, though it is close enough and was presumably erected by their daughter. There were two known obituaries. The first was in the *Halifax New Era* and reprinted in Scottish newspapers:

> Mr Donald Ross died at his residence, Dartmouth, on Saturday. The deceased was a native of Dornoch, Sutherlandshire, Scotland, and had been a resident of Nova Scotia for many years. He was very generally known, and was prominently identified with Scottish societies and all movements here in any way connected with his native land. His name was also a not unfamiliar one in the local press as a correspondent on matters of public interest.[52]

The second appeared in the *Celtic Magazine* in October, probably written by the editor, Alexander Mackenzie, who had visited Halifax in 1879.[53]

> We regret to learn from the Halifax (Nova Scotia) [electric] *Telegraph* that Mr Donald Ross, well known on both sides of the Atlantic for his warm interest in his Highland countrymen, and everything pertaining to their history, literature, and social position, died at his residence, Celtic Cottage, Dartmouth, N.S., on Saturday, the 26th of August last. Mr Ross, before he emigrated to Nova Scotia, took a very active and successful part in obtaining relief for the West Coast Highlanders, during and after the potato famine, from 1845 to 1851. He published several valuable pamphlets, now very rare, giving an account of the proceedings of that period in the West Highlands and Islands, including a graphic description of the Evictions in Knoydart, and in the Isle of Skye, and in other places. He was highly esteemed by Scotsmen, and indeed by all who knew him in his adopted country. When in better circumstances, his hospitality was unbounded, especially to the officers and men of the Highland regiments that were at times quartered in the City of Halifax. He was for many years a leading and respected member of the patriotic North British Benefit Society. The *Telegraph* informs us that "he will be long remembered as one of the principal organisers of the Scotch Volunteers (of Nova Scotia) some 23 years ago." When in the Dominion, a few years ago, we found him all that we have said of him, and much more; and his letters of introduction were excellent passports to the leading Scotsmen of Nova Scotia wherever we presented them.[54]

This was a fitting tribute and nicely rounds off the story of the life of Donald Ross. What happened to Anna after then is not known.

28

The Legacy of Donald Ross

To appreciate the importance of Donald's legacy with regards to the Highland Clearances it is necessary to summarise what others have written about him.

Rev. Richard Hibbs in his 1857 pamphlet *A Sermon for the Times* referred to the 2nd edition of *The Russians of Ross-shire* by 'Donald Ross – a gentleman whom all who feel sympathy for the down-trodden and oppressed must highly esteem.' Hibbs quoted Donald's letter to the Lord Advocate and wrote 'The publications of Mr. Ross are recommended to all who may desire further information on this subject.'[1]

Donald MacLeod, in *Gloomy Memories*, quoted Hibbs and praised Robert Somers and Donald 'to whom the Highlanders are much indebted for their disinterested advocacy in behalf of the poor, and their disclosure of the cruelty and ungodly conduct of proprietors.' MacLeod also mentioned that letters in newspapers by Donald and others had corroborated his own writings.[2]

In 1866 a Mr Murdock gave a lecture in Lerwick entitled 'The mischievous effects of the clearances elsewhere: a warning against the adoption of the system in Shetland.' When discussing the Sutherland Clearances 'hear this from the pen of one who knows the country well, – Mr Donald Ross' and quoted his second letter to Harriet Beecher Stowe.[3]

The Glengarry Evictions was mentioned in *A History of the Scottish Highlands* by Thomas MacLauchlan & John Wilson.[4] John Stuart Blackie in *The Scottish Highlanders* provided a long quote from *The Glengarry Evictions* and referred to Donald as an 'eye-witness.'[5]

Alexander Mackenzie, who probably wrote Donald's obituary in the *Celtic Magazine*, quoted *The Glengarry Evictions* in an 1880 article about that event. He referred to Donald, though not by name, as an 'eye-witness who described the proceedings at the time, in a now rare pamphlet, and whom I met last year in Nova Scotia.'[6] Donald was mentioned twice in the *Celtic Magazine* in an argument between Rev. Donald Mackinnon of Skye and Mackenzie about Lord Macdonald's role in the clearances. Mackenzie referred to Donald as 'an eye-witness' of the evictions at 'Boreraig and

Suisinish,' and quoted *Real Scottish Grievances*. Mackinnon responded: 'Mackenzie is theorising on matters of which he knows little or nothing, except what he has heard through Mr Donald Ross, who, like Mr Mackenzie himself, was known to be reckless in his statements, especially where his social superiors were concerned.'[7] Surprisingly, most of the mentions of Donald in Mackenzie's *History of the Highland Clearances*, were copied from MacLeod.[8] Extensive parts of *The Glengarry Evictions* and *Real Scottish Grievances* were reproduced, but Donald was not mentioned as the source. Three years later Mackenzie published the posthumous 3rd edition of *The Massacre of the Rosses* and confessed he had been 'unable to procure a copy' when he was writing his book. A review in the *Christian Leader*, reproduced in the *Celtic Magazine*, mentioned 'three decades after the faithful Highland citizen wrote it with his heart on fire, the story procures an audience.'[9]

Donald's disgrace was not forgotten, however. Rowland Hill Macdonald, in an 1885 pamphlet on *The Emigration of Highland Crofters*, considered that:

> The notorious Donald Ross ... who lived luxuriously for several years as a self-constituted philanthropist, writing to English newspapers, especially those of the religious type, harrowing tales of starvation, cruel evictions, and even the drowning of whole crews of fishermen, and other calamities that never happened, and receiving in response large sums of money, some of it anonymously, for the relief of these imaginary victims of oppression ... had the boldness to board in the Clyde a steamer full of emigrants from Skye and the Long Island, on their way to the Government depot at Birkenhead, there to embark for Australia ... to distribute amongst the emigrants tracts in the *Gaelic language*, denouncing emigration as only a milder type of penal servitude for life, concocted by rapacious landlords, with the approval of the Government and earnestly advising the poor people to return to their former homes.[10]

Presumably they were going to embark on the HMS *Hercules* and therefore the statement about Donald 'denouncing emigration' is nonsense.

Donald was largely forgotten until John Prebble's *The Highland Clearances* appeared in 1963. On the title page is the quote 'Since you have preferred sheep to men, let sheep defend you!' thus making it legendary. Donald was widely quoted and even though there were only six chapters, chapter five was titled 'The Massacre of the Rosses' and figure five comprised illustrations from *Real Scottish Grievances*. Prebble referred to six of Donald's works in the bibliography, including the first references to *The Scottish Highlanders* and *Letters on the Depopulation of the Highlands*, however *The Clearing of the Glens* was part of the 2nd edition of *The Russians of Ross-shire* so only five pamphlets were effectively cited. With regards to the 'Massacre': 'But for one man, little would have been heard of this obscene affray... This man was Donald Ross, a Glasgow lawyer who left little record of himself but his writings on the evictions and a list of his addresses in the Glasgow Directory... He was a Highlander by his name, and although it is a common enough one he may have been the Donald Ross of Dornoch who collected money for Mr. Spence's Glencalvie fund in 1845.'[11] Two of Donald's letters that Prebble quoted, one about 'Aunty Kate's Cabin,' and the other to Harriett Beecher Stowe, were later included in *A Scottish Postbag* by George Bruce and Paul Scott.[12]

The anonymous preface to the 1977 reprint of *The Russians of Ross-shire* included the first reference to *Pictures of Pauperism*. A short quote from *Pictures* was included by Anna Magnusson in her book *The Quarriers Story* on the history of the Quarrier's homes for orphan and destitute children.[13]

Donald, *The Russians of Ross-shire* and *Real Scottish Grievances* were mentioned or quoted by the late David Craig in *On the Crofters' Trail*.[14] They and *The Glengarry Evictions* were also cited by Craig and David Paterson in their lavishly illustrated book *The Glens of Silence*, where Donald was referred to as a 'campaigning lawyer.'[15]

Lucille Campey in *An Unstoppable Force* portrayed 'the redoubtable' Donald as anti-emigration. Unfortunately, she had accepted and quoted Rowland Macdonald's incorrect statement about Donald denouncing it. With regards to *The Glengarry Evictions*, she considered 'Ross's allegation that all of her [Josephine Macdonell's] tenants had been forced to emigrate is laughable... Donald Ross probably did not realize just how attractive Canada had become.'[16]

In Denis Rixson's *Knoydart*, Chapter 9, 'The 1853 Clearance,' commenced with 'All accounts of the Knoydart evictions begin and end with Donald Ross... Ross, a Glasgow advocate, was so incensed by the cruelty that he travelled to Knoydart, interviewed those who remained and wrote a passionate little book called *The Glengarry Evictions*... His arguments, although impassioned, are remarkably temperate. A deeply moral man and a strong Christian, his humanity was appalled at what he saw in Knoydart. His motives, as those of Coll Macdonald, the Catholic priest at Sandaig who tried to shelter those evicted, were wholly admirable.'[17]

A rare mention of Donald from his Dornoch days is in Michael Hook's *A History of the Royal Burgh of Dornoch* with regards to the Interdict to prevent the building of a road through the churchyard.[18] Equally rare mentions of Donald in Nova Scotia are in Stuart Wallace's biography of *John Stuart Backie*, referring to Donald's letter to Blackie, and John Gibson's *Traditional Gaelic Bagpiping*, which mentioned the import tax evasion incident.[19]

An article by Neil Bruce summarising the Barra exodus and Colonel Gordon's actions concluded 'Donald Ross made concerted efforts to ensure that the migrants' condition was kept in the public eye. He also used their presence to highlight the wider highland destitution he believed would soon reach the lowlands. However, following the debacle in Laurencekirk and reported unwillingness of the able-bodied migrants to work, Ross's efforts were neutralised.'[20]

Krisztina Fenyő in *Contempt, Sympathy and Romance* was the most fulsome in her praise of Donald and the other contemporary critics of the clearances. She referred to some of Donald's newspaper articles and four pamphlets (*Scottish Highlanders, Glengarry Evictions, Real Scottish Grievances* and *Russians of Ross-shire*). Fenyő described Donald, MacLeod and Mulock as '"true crusaders," the most radical of all journalists.' They were 'angry and passionate men ... hammering away at the landlords, at the government, and at other papers as no other critics had done before.' The two Donalds were 'perhaps the best-known defenders of the Gaels, even today... Donald Ross was from Ross-shire, probably from Dornoch, and became a lawyer in Glasgow. He became the only journalist to engage in practical campaigning for the Highlanders. Ross was best known for his accounts of the Knoydart eviction and the "Greenyards massacre."' Donald was from Sutherland, not Ross-shire. Fenyő wrote that after Mulock had given up the fight in 1851 and MacLeod had emigrated to Canada:

> Another Highland native, however, remained firmly on the scene and through the untiring *Northern Ensign* sustained the battle throughout the first half of the 1850s. This last remaining crusader was Donald Ross.
>
> Donald Ross was the most energetic and idealistic journalist of the 1850s. Although very little is known about him, not even his date of birth, there was something youthful both in his character and his writings. He was tireless in his campaign against the Clearances, even when he had to overcome his own disillusionment. He had enough energy and faith to flood newspapers with his long articles, to go on investigative trips, to organise practical aid for the destitute, to set up charity schemes, and to publish pamphlets and books based on his newspaper articles.
>
> Ross was the only journalist at the time who not only wrote about the Clearances in indignation but actually went out to find tents and blankets for evicted people: a practical '*engagé*' journalist.
>
> He also differed markedly from other journalists in his style of writing. His investigative journalism produced an early documentarist genre, which was unique at the time. He tirelessly recorded cases of abuses and evictions, with long and detailed descriptions. This factual documentarist style, however, was mixed with frequent romanticising passages both about the bygone 'golden age', and about the Highland people themselves.[21]

The three main authorities on the Highland Clearances – Prof. Sir Thomas Devine, Prof. James Hunter and the late Prof. Eric Richards – were less flattering. Devine mentioned Donald several times in *The Great Highland Famine*, including as a 'pamphleteer,' and three of Donald's pamphlets were referred to (*Scottish Highlanders, Glengarry Evictions, Real Scottish Grievances*).[22] One of the eviction scenes from *Real Scottish Grievances* was reproduced in Devine's *Clanship to Crofters' War* and in *The Scottish Clearances* Donald was mentioned briefly along with his contemporaries.[23]

Donald Ross and the Highland Clearances

Hunter, in *The Making of the Crofting Community*, briefly mentioned Donald as 'the Glasgow advocate and pamphleteer.'[24] In *Insurrection* Hunter quoted the plight of one of the families from *The Glengarry Evictions* and referred to Donald as 'a man who would be described today as an investigative journalist.'[25]

Richards was the most critical of Donald and his works. In *The Leviathan of Wealth*, after discussing Macleod, 'Equally trenchant denunciation came from the pen of Donald Ross, whose writings helped to consolidate the popular impression of the resolute wickedness of the Sutherland policies... Nevertheless, the influence of Macleod and Ross on the public mind was irresistible; it was part of the growing literature of popular protest which prepared the way for the Napier Commission Reports of 1884.'[26] In *The Highland Clearances* Richards referred to four of Donald's pamphlets (*Scottish Highlanders, Glengarry Evictions, Real Scottish Grievances, Russians of Ross-shire*) and discussed aspects of them at length. With regards to the Barra exodus, Richards wrote that Donald '(another prominent anti-eviction writer) added this cause to his campaign against Highland landlords' and Mulock 'turned on fellow critic Donald Ross and denounced him as a showman who was gaining cheap personal publicity from the sufferings of the Barra folk in Edinburgh.' However, the latter statement is unconfirmed as the source is vague. With regards to the 'Massacre,' Richards wrote 'Ross was eyewitness to some of the episodes; his transparent purpose was to rouse public opinion against the landlords of the Highlands. Ross's anger led him into hyperbole which naturally places his credibility at risk.' The newspaper reports 'were greatly refuelled by the passionate and detailed accounts in Donald Ross's letters to the press, although his florid style caused many contemporaries to be sceptical.'[27] In *Debating the Highland Clearances* Richards wrote 'Donald Ross was the best-known journalist/recorder who wrote inflammatory accounts of evictions in Ross-shire in the 1850s.' He reproduced Donald's letter to the Lord Advocate about the 'Massacre' and wrote 'This has become the document most often quoted against landlords as a class. It demonstrates the growing power of journalism by mid-century. Ross's version was treated with incredulity but, in retrospect, conforms well with many other fracas during the Highland Clearances. The vehemence of Ross's language probably distracted attention from the wealth of corroboration of the main facts of the evictions.'[28]

I consider most of the comments about Donald are just, however perhaps Fenyő's are a bit over the top and some of Richards' and Campey's are unfair, though they did drive me to look for other accounts and corroborating evidence. Donald wasn't against Highland landlords *per se*, more against unscrupulous landlords and the system that allowed them and their factors to evict their tenants with impunity. Also, he wasn't against emigration for those who wanted to leave, but was against the emigration of those who had to leave against their will.

Donald's writings and exploits have captured the imagination of fiction writers. *A Bowdon Romance* by Alice Frank summarised the *Weeping in the*

The Legacy of Donald Ross

Isles episode and mentioned Donald.[29] Donald is also mentioned in three other novels based on the 'Massacre': *A Pistol in Greenyards* by Mollie Hunter, *Greenyards* by Joan Lingard and *The Greenyards Legacy* by Jane King.[30]

The 1970s play *The Cheviot, the Stag, and the Black Black Oil* by John McGrath was televised and told the story of the Highlands from after Culloden through to the exploitation of oil reserves in the North Sea. It quoted three of Donald's pamphlets, including the injuries of seven of the victims of the 'Massacre,' the evictions of John Mackinnon and his family from Knoydart and Flora Matheson and her grandchildren from Suishnish. The 'let sheep defend you!' line was also mentioned.

Donald and/or his writings have been mentioned in three documentaries. The 'Massacre' featured in an episode about the Highland Clearances in a series entitled *Highlands*, presented by John Michie for the History Channel. Although not mentioned by name, Donald was referred to as an 'eye-witness' and his letter to the Lord Advocate was quoted. With regards to the *Weeping in the Isles*, Donald was unfairly referred to as a 'people trafficker' in an episode of the BBC series *Who Do You Think You Are?* about comedian David Mitchell, who is a direct descendent of Rev. John Forbes. In the WB Australian *Who Do You Think You Are?* TV presenter Grant Denyer was found to be descended from Ann Ross, who was victim No. 16 in *The Russians of Ross-shire*. The title page of Donald's pamphlet was shown and Ann's injuries were quoted.

What do I think of Donald Ross? He was certainly quite a character. His writings demonstrate anger stemming from the injustice he and his family suffered and he clearly wanted to publicise atrocious clearance events and help fellow sufferers. He was not averse to exaggerating and even lying, which casts doubt on the validity of his writings, however there is enough corroborating evidence to support most of what he wrote. Donald had to resort to sensationalism to get the public's attention, particularly when the Crimean War was filling the newspapers and the public were growing weary of stories of impoverished Highlanders. He demonstrated a mastery of the English language, though given his first language was Gaelic, he probably had help, perhaps from friends and his lowland-born wife. He was supremely confident in fighting and winning court cases without any formal legal training, but at times became complacent and made mistakes which came back to bite him hard. However, every time his world collapsed around him, he reinvented himself and bounced back – a true survivor. It is quite astonishing how incredibly productive Donald was during the twelve years from when he became Agent of the Poor up until he emigrated, and the huge amount of money he raised for famine relief. In spite of his flaws, I am immensely proud of him as his publicising of the 'Massacre of the Rosses' probably prevented any such atrocity from happening again on Scottish soil. Also, he probably saved hundreds, if not thousands of people from starving to death during the later Potato Famine. I hope that the information I have uncovered about Donald and his life will enable researchers of the clearances to see him in a new light and I also hope that anyone who has read this book will agree that he was a true hero of the poor.

Notes

Birth, marriage and death records were obtained from the relevant parish or statutory records at the NRS unless otherwise stated. Scotland census records were obtained from the NRS unless otherwise stated.

Chapter 1

1. Ann Gordon or Ross v George Dempster & others, NRS CS237/R/14/30; Donald Ross v Duke of Sutherland & others, NRS CS275/7/314.
2. NRS CS237/R/14/30.
3. Pigot, *National Commercial Directory*, p. 785.
4. Statute Labour Lists, Dornoch, HCA/CS/2/2/4.
5. Gauldie, *Scottish Country Miller*.
6. Loch, *Account of the Improvements*, Appendix II, p. 9.
7. NRS CS237/R/14/30.
8. Report by Bauchope, NRS CS237/R/14/30.
9. Will of Donald Ross, NRS SC9/36/3.
10. NRS CS237/R/14/30.
11. Letter from George [Soper] Dempster to Donald Cameron, 22 December 1853, DNHHL 2001_415.
12. Valuation by Graham, NRS CS237/R/14/30.
13. Goudie, *Horizontal Water Mills*, pp. 282-283.
14. Henderson, *Agriculture of Sutherland*, pp. 64-77.
15. Connor & Simpson, *Weights and Measures*, p. 297.
16. *Farmers' Magazine*, 1800, v. 1, p. 444.
17. Henderson, pp. 64-77.
18. Dempster, *Estates of Skibo and Pulrossie*, p. 378.
19. Tucker, *Millstone making in Scotland*, p. 539.
20. Gauldie, *Scottish Country Miller*.
21. 1841 census; Petition of Ann Gordon, NRS SC9/7/122/1844; death record.
22. Robert Gordon v Roderick & George Gordon, NRS SC9/7/119/1841G.
23. Cowper & Ross, *Tombstone Inscriptions in Sutherland*, p. 109, no. 86.
24. Bethune, OSA, Dornoch; Sage, *Memorabilia Domestica*, p. 68.
25. Mackay, *Old Dornoch*, p. 113.
26. Bentinck, *Dornoch Cathedral*, pp. 311, 353.
27. Daniell, *Voyage*, v. 5.
28. NLS Adv.MS.30.5.23.
29. Henderson, p. 115; Sage, pp. 164-5.

Notes

30. Hook, *History of Dornoch*, p. 66.
31. Hook, p. 69; Bentinck, pp. 299, 351.
32. Sage, p. 162; Bentinck, p. 365; Mackay, p. 119.
33. Report by Bauchope, NRS CS237/R/14/30.
34. Loch, *Account*, p. 33.
35. Dalrymple et al., *Reports*, Dornoch, p. 27.
36. Bentinck, pp. 368-369.
37. Calder, *Estate and Castle of Skibo*.
38. Wall, *Skibo*, p. 22.
39. Evans, *Gentleman Usher*, p. 181.
40. Fergusson, *Letters of George Dempster*, p. 157.
41. Dempster, *Estates of Skibo and Pulrossie*, pp. 375-376.
42. *Inverness Courier*, 30 August 1826.
43. Fergusson, p. 235.
44. *Inverness Courier*, 16 December 1835.
45. Fergusson, p. 219.
46. NRS CS237/R/14/30.
47. *Anno Sexto & Septimo Gulielmi IV. Regis*, Cap. 27, pp. 591, 594, 1836; Fergusson, p. 326.
48. Wall, p. 29.
49. *Perthshire Courier*, 17 May 1821; Dempster, *George Dempster*, p. 9.
50. Dempster, *George Dempster*, p. 4; *Inverness Courier*, 13 September 1826.
51. *Perthshire Courier*, 17 May 1827.
52. Calder, p. 33.
53. *Inverness Courier*, 3 April 1844.
54. *Inverness Courier*, 30 October 1851.
55. Dempster, *George Dempster*, p. 10.
56. *Perthshire Courier*, 14 November 1823; Dempster, *George Dempster*, p. 4.
57. *Inverness Courier*, 17 July 1823; e.g. *Inverness Courier*, 3 October 1827; *Glasgow Herald*, 14 January 1848.
58. *Inverness Courier*, 11 February 1835; Dempster, *Report relative to Plantations*.
59. Anon, *Elizabeth*, p. 5.
60. Fraser, *Sutherland Book*, pp. 461-463; Bell, *Prospect of Sutherland*, p. 38.
61. Prebble, *Highland Clearances*, p. 60.
62. Lee, *Dictionary of National Biography*, v. 33, Leveson-Gower, p. 147.
63. Kennedy, *Days of the Fathers*, p. 16.
64. Devine, *Scottish Clearances*.
65. Loch, *Account*, p. 51.
66. Henderson, pp. 103-6.
67. Anon, *Balnagown*, pp. 68-69.
68. Loch, *Account*, p. 97; Richards, *Highland Clearances*, pp. 4, 107, 226.
69. *Farmers' Magazine*, 1804, v. 5, p. 49.
70. Hunter, *Making of the Crofting Community*.
71. *Farmers' Magazine*, 1807, v. 8, p. 172.
72. MacLeod, *Destitution in Sutherlandshire*, p. 4.
73. *Farmers' Magazine*, 1801, v. 2, p. 394.
74. Grimble, *Trial of Patrick Sellar*; Richards, *Highland Clearances*, chapter 9; Edgar, *Sutherland Clearances*.
75. Richards, *Leviathan of Wealth*, pp. 207-8.
76. MacLeod, *Destitution*, p. 21.
77. MacLeod, *Gloomy Memories*, p.92.
78. Sage, p. 294.
79. Johnston, *Strathnaver Trail*; Gibson, *Highland Clearances Trail*, pp. 36-37.
80. Park, *Highland Clearances in Southeast Sutherland*, pp. 10-11.
81. Hunter, *Set Adrift*, pp. 290-300.
82. Hunter, *Set Adrift*, p. 365.
83. *JOGJ*, 15 August 1845.
84. *Inverness Courier*, 14 March 1827.
85. *Inverness Courier*, 9 July 1828.
86. Fiars prices, NRS SC9/67/3.
87. *Inverness Courier*, 16 January 1833, 14 August 1833, 30 November 1836.

88. *Anno Sexto & Septimo Gulielmi IV. Regis*, Cap. 27, pp. 589-603.
89. *Standard*, 14 January 1840.
90. *Caledonian Mercury*, 23 April 1840.
91. *Caledonian Mercury*, 15 July 1841.
92. *Inverness Courier*, 11 September 1844.
93. Loch, *Memoir of George Granville*, pp. 35-6.
94. Uncles, *Memories of East Sutherland*, p. 62.
95. Simpson, *Dornoch Cathedral*; p. 227; Hook, p. 76.
96. Sage (1899), p. 169; MacLeod, *Gloomy Memories*, p. 69; Craig, *Crofters' Trail*, p. 135.
97. Bentinck, p. 373.
98. Connor & Simpson, pp. 446-8.
99. *Inverness Courier*, 18 June 1857; *Paisley Herald*, 20 June 1857.
100. Evans, *Gentleman Usher*, p. 325; *Stonehaven Journal*, 4 April 1861; *Inverness Courier*, 27 October 1864.
101. *JOGJ*, 17 May 1866; e.g. *Inverness Courier*, 3 May 1866.
102. Evans, p. 325.
103. *Edinburgh Evening News*, 27 July 1885.
104. McLean, *Borthwick Parish Church*.
105. Inventory and Will of George Dempster, 1889, NRS.
106. Bentinck, p. 355.
107. Nicholson, *Golspie*, p, 75.
108. Kennedy, NSA, Dornoch, p. 6.
109. Calder, p. 75.
110. Sage, p. 150.
111. Adam, *Sutherland Estate Management*, v. 1, p. 184.
112. Sage, pp. 407-8; Kennedy, NSA, Dornoch, pp. 14-15.
113. Sage, pp. 158-9.
114. Nicholson, *Golspie*.
115. HCA/CS/2/2/4.
116. NRS CS275/5/7/314.
117. HCA/CS/2/2/4.
118. George Dempster v John Gordon & others, NRS SC9/7/119/1841C.
119. Donald Ross v Alexander Graham & Roderick Forsyth, NRS SC9/7/122/1844.
120. Dornoch Parochial Board Minute Book, HCA/6/4/1.
121. NRS CS237/R/14/30.
122. HCA/6/4/1.
123. HCA/6/4/2.

Chapter 2

1. Statute Labour Lists, Dornoch, HCA/CS/2/2/4.
2. MacPherson, NSA, Golspie, p. 41; Grant, *Golspie's Story*.
3. Loch, *Account of the Improvements*, Appendix 2, p. 21; Adam, *Sutherland Estate Management*, v. 1, p. 38.
4. HCA/CS/2/2/4.
5. Pigot, *National Commercial Directory*, p. 785.
6. George Dempster v John Ross & others, NRS SC9/7/124/1846.
7. Donald Sutherland v John Ross, NRS SC9/7/123/1844.
8. Sillett, *Illicit Scotch*.
9. Brander, *Original Scotch*.
10. John Gordon v John Ross, NRS SC9/7/123/1844.
11. *Poor Law Inquiry (Scotland)*, 1844, Appendix 4, p. 399b.
12. Small Debt Court Book, NRS SC9/58/1.
13. John Ross v Hugh Ross, NRS SC9/7/117/1839G.
14. *Inverness Courier*, 22 & 29 July 1840.
15. Donald Sutherland v John Ross, NRS SC9/7/123/1844.
16. measuringworth.com
17. Donald Sutherland v John Ross, NRS SC9/7/123/1844.
18. John Gordon v John Ross, NRS SC9/7/123/1844.
19. John Gordon v John Ross, NRS SC9/7/123/1844 (different bundle to above).
20. Beith *et al.*, NSA, Stirling, p. 414.

Notes

21. Forrest, *Sanitory Condition, Stirling*, pp. 263-5.
22. Ronald, *Landmarks of Old Stirling*, pp. 1-95.
23. Beith et al., NSA, Stirling, pp. 440-442; *Poor Law Inquiry (Scotland)*, 1844, Appendix 3, p. 208.
24. Post Office Directory, Stirling, 1870-1, p. 24.
25. Stirling Council Minutes, SCA SBC/11/15; Lockhart Whiteford, *Stirling Burgess List*, p. 37; Drysdale, *Old Faces*, p. 296.
26. Drysdale, *Old Faces*, Preface, p. 160.
27. SCA SBC/11/15; *Greenock Advertiser*, 17 August 1849.
28. SCA SBC/11/15.
29. Mitchell & Mitchell, *East Stirlingshire monumental inscriptions*, pp. 243-4, no. 359; Anon, *Stirling's Talking Stones*, p. 29, plot. 431.

Chapter 3

1. *Witness* 29 March 1854; Letter to John Stuart Blackie, 5 January 1865, NLS MS.2626 ff.132-5.
2. Statute Labour Lists, Dornoch, HA CS/2/2/4.
3. Hunter, *Insurrection*, p. 50.
4. Bill, 1840, DNHHL 2004_325.
5. Miss Jess Davidson v Donald Ross, NRS SC9/7/122/1844.
6. HA CS/2/2/4; Dornoch Sheriff Court Jury Rolls, NRS SC9/76/3.
7. Ann Gordon or Ross v George Dempster & others, NRS CS237/R/14/30.
8. Donald Ross v Duke of Sutherland & others, NRS CS275/7/314.
9. Dornoch Town Council Minutes, HCA/BD/1/1/4.
10. NRS CS275/7/314.
11. HCA/BD/1/1/4.
12. Uelsh, *Shearmoinéan*, p. 13.
13. Burke, *Portrait Gallery*, pp. 1-2; Lee, *Dictionary of National Biography*, v. 33, pp. 147, 152; Bell, *Prospect of Sutherland*, p. 46.
14. Alison, *Life and Writings*, v. 1, p. 508.
15. MacLeod, *Gloomy Memories*, p. 171.
16. Adam, *Sutherland Estate Management*, v. 1.
17. MacLeod, *Gloomy*, p. 42.
18. *JOGJ*, 22 January 1841.
19. Tindley, *Sutherland Estate*.
20. Alison, *Life*, v. 1, p. 509.
21. Edinburgh Post-Office directories and Almanacs.
22. Clark et al., NSA, Edinburgh, p. 655; Grant, *Old and New Edinburgh*, v. 2, pp. 126-9.
23. MacLeod, *Gloomy*, p. ix.
24. *Scotsman*, 1 March 1843.
25. *Witness*, 21 August 1844.
26. MacLeod, *Gloomy*, p. ix.
27. *Scottish Herald*, in *Stirling Observer*, 13 March 1845.
28. *Times*, 3 April 1845.
29. *Inverness Courier*, 14 May 1845.
30. *Times*, 13 June 1845.
31. *Times*, 30 July 1845.
32. *Scotsman*, 21 May 1845.
33. *Caledonian Mercury*, 2 June 1845.
34. *Witness* 28 June 1845.
35. Fenyő, *Contempt, Sympathy and Romance*; Lee, *Dictionary of National Biography*, v. 53, pp. 229-230.
36. *Scotsman*, 7 June 1845.
37. *Witness*, 13 August 1845.
38. *Scotsman*, 25 April 1846.
39. *Caledonian Mercury*, 4 June 1846.
40. *Edinburgh Almanac*, 1850, p. 456.
41. *Witness*, 24 July 1850; *Elgin Courier*, 16 August 1850.
42. MacLeod, *Gloomy*, pp. 119-122.

Chapter 4

1. Ann Gordon or Ross v George Dempster & others, NRS CS237/R/14/30.

2. George Dempster v John Gordon & others, NRS SC9/7/119/1841C.
3. Mackay, *Old Dornoch*, pp. 2-3.
4. George Dempster v Ann Gordon or Ross & others, NRS SC9/7/121/1843E.
5. Robert Gordon v Roderick & George Gordon, NRS SC9/7/119/1841G.
6. NRS SC9/7/119/1841C; NRS SC9/7/121/1843E.
7. NRS SC9/7/121/1843E; George Dempster v John Gordon & others, SC9/7/121/1842A.
8. NRS CS237/R/14/30.
9. Petition for George Dempster, NRS SC9/7/122/1843.
10. NRS CS237/R/14/30; measuringworth.com.
11. Petition of Ann Gordon or Ross, NRS SC9/7/122/1844.
12. Dornoch Parochial Board Minute Book, HCA/6/4/1.
13. Summons of Removing for Mrs May or Mary Bayne or Ross, NRS SC9/7/123/1845.
14. NRS CS237/R/14/30.
15. Grant, *Old and New Edinburgh*, v. 1, pp. 157-166; Cullen, *Parliament House*.
16. Clark *et al.*, NSA, Edinburgh, pp 712-715; Cullen, p. 41.
17. NRS CS237/R/14/30.
18. extrapolated from 1851 census.
19. NRS CS237/R/14/30.
20. George Dempster v John Ross & others, NRS SC9/7/124/1846.
21. NRS CS237/R/14/30.
22. *Scottish Jurist*, 1848, v. 20, pp. 471-473; *Journal of Agriculture*, July 1847 – March 1849, New Series, pp. 607-608.
23. NRS CS237/R/14/30.

Chapter 5

1. Robert Gordon v Roderick & George Gordon, NRS SC9/7/119/1841G.
2. George Dempster v John Gordon & others NRS SC9/7/121/1842A.
3. Execution of Ejectment, John Gordon & others, NRS SC9/48/4.
4. W.S. Fraser, Procurator Fiscal against John Gordon & others, NRS SC9/48/4.
5. Bentinck, *Dornoch Cathedral*, pp. 346-347.
6. Hook, *History of Dornoch*, p. 70.
7. Miscellaneous papers, NRS SC9/84/34.
8. Anon, *Town Jail Craft Centre*.
9. NRS SC9/48/4.
10. *Inverness Courier*, 4 January 1843.
11. *JOGJ*, 6 January 1843.
12. John Gordon v John Ross, NRS SC9/7/123/1844.
13. Dornoch Small Debt Court Book, NRS SC9/58/1.

Chapter 6

1. Dornoch Small Debt Court Book, NRS SC9/58/1.
2. Precognition, Procurator Fiscal against Donald Ross, NRS AD14/44/475; Register of Instruments of Protest, Book III, NRS SC9/30/3.
3. Dornoch Jury trial book, NRS SC9/47/1; NRS AD14/44/475.
4. Declaration of Donald Ross, NRS JC26/1844/10.
5. Inventory of Productions, NRS AD14/44/475.
6. Letter to Sangster, 16 February 1843, NRS JC26/1844/10.
7. NRS AD14/44/475; NRS SC9/30/3
8. Letter to Munro, 19 September 1843, NRS JC26/1844/10.
9. NRS AD14/44/475; NRS SC9/30/3
10. NRS AD14/44/475.
11. Second Declaration of Donald Ross, NRS JC26/1844/10.
12. Donald Ross v Alexander Graham & Roderick Forsyth, NRS SC9/7/122/1844.
13. NRS SC9/58/1.
14. NRS SC9/7/122/1844.

Notes

15. Lord Advocate v Donald Ross, NRS JC26/1844/10.
16. Register of Warrants to Imprison, NRS SC9/14/2.
17. NRS JC26/1844/10.
18. Groome, *Ordnance Gazetteer*, p. 306; Pollitt, *Historic Inverness*, pp. 55, 60-61; Meldrum, *Inverness in Pictures*, No. 8.
19. *JOGJ*, 3 May 1844.
20. Donald Ross v Graham & Forsyth, NRS SC9/7/122/1844.
21. NRS SC9/7/122/1844.
22. Miss Jess Davidson v Donald Ross, NRS SC9/7/122/1844.
23. Donald Ross v Graham & Forsyth, NRS SC9/7/122/1844.
24. NRS SC9/58/1.
25. Davidson v Donald Ross, NRS SC9/7/122/1844.
26. Donald Ross v Graham & Forsyth, NRS SC9/7/122/1844.
27. NRS SC9/58/1.
28. Donald Ross v Graham & Forsyth, NRS SC9/7/122/1844.

Chapter 7

1. *Stirling Observer*, 9 March 1843.
2. *Stirling Observer*, 30 March 1843.
3. *Stirling Observer*, 27 April 1843.
4. *Stirling Observer*, 6 July 1843.
5. Brown, *Annals of the Disruption*, pp. 28-9.
6. Brown, *Annals*, pp. 43-44, 49-51.
7. Brown, *Annals*, pp. 88-92.
8. Fowler, *Hill's Big Picture*.
9. Brown, *Annals*, p. 242.
10. Bentinck, *Dornoch Cathedral*, p. 355.
11. Sage, *Memorabilia Domestica*, p. 287.
12. Miller, *Sutherland*, p. 13.
13. *Inverness Courier*, 18 January 1843.
14. Kennedy, *Apostle of the North*, pp. 301, 304.
15. Brown, *Annals*, p. 64.
16. MacRae, *Life of Gustavus Aird*, pp. 103-104.
17. Baillie, *Proceedings of the General Assembly*, p. 8.
18. *Standard*, 24 May 1843; Baillie, p. 49.
19. *Inverness Courier*, 14 June 1843.
20. Dornoch Presbytery Minutes, 12 June 1843, HCA/CH2/1290/6.
21. *Inverness Courier*, 21 June 1843.
22. *Inverness Courier*, 28 June 1843.
23. Mackay, *Old Dornoch*, p. 144.
24. *Inverness Courier*, 21 June 1843; *Stirling Observer*, 6 July 1843.
25. *JOGJ*, 11 August 1843.
26. *Inverness Courier*, 30 August 1843; 11 June 1845.
27. Hook, *History of Dornoch*, p. 90.
28. *JOGJ*, 6 October 1843; *Standard*, 28 November 1843.
29. *Inverness Courier*, 29 November 1843.
30. Hook, p. 90.
31. Dornoch Presbytery Minutes, 14 September 1843, HCA/CH2/1290/6.
32. Dornoch Presbytery Minutes, 4 & 11 October 1843, HCA CH2/1290/6.
33. *Inverness Courier*, 15 November 1843; Dornoch Presbytery Minutes, 22 November 1843, HCA/CH2/1290/6.
34. Sage, pp. 17, 287.
35. Scott, *Fasti Ecclesiae Scoticanae*, p. 85; MacRae, *Life of Gustavus Aird*, pp. 106-9.
36. *Stirling Observer*, 26 October 1843.
37. *JOGJ*, 29 December 1843.
38. *Inverness Courier*, 3 January 1844.
39. *Stirling Journal*, 12 January 1844.
40. *Stirling Journal*, 26 January 1844.
41. *Northern Warder*, 23 October 1845; *JOGJ*, 24 October 1845.
42. *Inverness Courier*, 11 October 1855.
43. Napier et al., *Crofters' Commission*, pp. 2584, 2599-2600.

44. Brand *et al.*, *Royal Commission*, p. 611.
45. Park, *Highland Clearances in Southeast Sutherland*.

Chapter 8

1. Prebble, *Highland Clearances*, pp. 221-239; Richards, *Highland Clearances*, pp. 19-28; Fenyő, *Contempt, Sympathy and Romance*, pp. 47-52.
2. MacRae, *Life of Gustavus Aird*, pp. 16, 19.
3. *Standard*, 11 November 1840; *Inverness Courier*, 30 December 1840.
4. MacRae, pp. 40, 178-9; Campey, *After the Hector*, pp. 156-157.
5. Allan, NSA, Kincardine, p. 421.
6. *Inverness Courier*, 9 February 1842.
7. 'National', in *Witness*, 4 September 1844; Prebble, p. 226.
8. *JOGJ*, 1 April 1842.
9. *Inverness Courier*, 6 April 1842.
10. Baillie, *Proceedings of the General Assembly*, p. 72.
11. MacRae, *Life of Gustavus Aird*.
12. *Times*, 25 May 1888; MacRae, pp. 205-10.
13. *Scotsman*, 21 December 1898; MacRae, pp. 227-230; Cowper & Ross, *Tombstone Inscriptions in Sutherland*, p. 239.
14. *Scotsman*, 26 December 1898.
15. *Poor Law Inquiry (Scotland)*, 1844, Appendix 2, p. 46.
16. *Greenock Advertiser*, 23 May 1845, 3 June 1845.
17. Prebble, pp. 232-3.
18. *Times*, 20 May 1845.
19. *Times*, 21 May 1845.
20. *Times*, 13 June 1845.
21. *Times*, 27 June 1845.
22. *Scottish Guardian*, in *Aberdeen Journal*, 18 June 1845.
23. *JOGJ*, 28 November 1845
24. Brand *et al.*, *Royal Commission*, pp. 781-783.
25. Prebble, p. 236; MacLeod, *Gloomy Memories*, p. 199.
26. Macrae, p. 180.
27. *Inverness Courier*, 4 February 1846.
28. *Times*, 22 October 1846.
29. *NBDM*, 11 May 1847.

Chapter 9

1. Cunnison & Gilfillan, *Third Statistical Account, Glasgow*, p. 317; Thomas & Patterson, *Regional History of the Railways, Vol. IV*.
2. Cunnison & Gilfillan, p. 309; Gibb, *Glasgow*, pp. 43-44.
3. Cunnison & Gilfillan, chapter 3; Devine, *Scotland's Slavery Past*.
4. Oakley, *Second City*, pp. v, 39.
5. MacFarlan *et al.*, NSA, Glasgow, p. 201.
6. McQueen, *Clyde Paddle-wheels*, pp. 180-1.
7. Cunnison & Gilfillan, p. 27.
8. Pagan, *Glasgow, Past and Present*, p. 110.
9. Pagan, in Fairbairn, *Relics of Ancient Architecture*, Avenue in the Green.
10. MacDonald, *Rambles Round Glasgow*, p. 16.
11. Cunnison & Gilfillan, pp. 461, 557.
12. *Witness*, 24 August 1850.
13. MacFarlan *et al.*, p. 148; Black & Black, *Economical Guide through Glasgow*, p. 6; *Witness*, 24 August 1850.
14. MacFarlan *et al.*, p. 163; Thomson, *Chemical Manufactures*, pp. 58-64; Oakley, pp. 44, 218.
15. Brown, *Midnight Scenes*, p. 81.
16. Cunnison & Gilfillan, pp. 43, 419-421, 788, 799.
17. Gibb, p. 127; Cunnison, & Gilfillan, p. 810.
18. Gibb, pp. 105-6; Devine, *Clearance and Improvement*, p. 177.

Notes

19. *1st Annual Report of the Board of Supervision*, 1847, Appendix D, p. 53; MacDonald, *Glasgow's Gaelic Churches*, p. 4.
20. *Scottish Highlanders*, p. 24.
21. Baird, *Sanitary Condition*, pp. 162-6.
22. Chalmers, *Public Health Administration in Glasgow*, p. 189.
23. Chalmers, *Public Health Administration*; Cunnison & Gilfillan, pp. 561-2.
24. Chalmers, p. 3.
25. Cunnison & Gilfillan, p. 480; Gibb, p. 109.
26. Cowan, in Baird, *Sanitary Condition*, p. 185.
27. Baird, *Sanitary Condition*, p. 176.
28. *Poor Law Inquiry (Scotland)*, 1844, Appendix 1, p. 436.
29. Baird, *Legal Provisions*, pp. 72-3.
30. Brown, *Midnight Scenes*, pp. 42-3.
31. Logan, *Moral Statistics of Glasgow*, p. 46.
32. Baird, *Sanitary Condition*, p. 192; Logan, p. 43.
33. Osborne, *Immortal Sewerage*, p. 9.
34. *Poor Law Inquiry*, Appendix 1, pp. 326, 465, 470.
35. Alison, *Principles of Population*, v. 2, p. 317; Baird, *Sanitary Condition*, p. 189.
36. Pagan, *Glasgow, Past and Present*, p. 135.
37. Brown, *Midnight Scenes*, pp. 47-8.
38. Pagan, p. 4.
39. Stuart, *Views and Notices of Glasgow*, p. 88.
40. Chalmers, p. 12.
41. Pagan, pp. 5, 90.
42. Cunnison & Gilfillan, pp. 304-5.
43. Baird, *Sanitary Condition*, p. 181.
44. Baird, *Sanitary Condition*, pp. 190-1; Alison, *Principles*, v. 1, p. 191.
45. Logan, pp. 65-6.
46. *Poor Law Inquiry*, Appendix 1, pp. 357, 470-1.
47. Brown, *Midnight Scenes*, pp. 43, 63.
48. Brown, *Midnight Scenes*, pp. 88-9; *Poor Law Inquiry*, Appendix 1, p. 323.
49. Alison, *Principles*, v. 2, pp. 120, 535-6; measuringworth.com.
50. Logan, pp. 34, 40; *Poor Law Inquiry*, Appendix 1, p. 323.
51. Logan, pp. 35-38.
52. Logan, pp. 49, 52.
53. *Poor Law Inquiry*, Appendix 1, p. 649.
54. Logan, pp. 18, 30.
55. Anon, *Scottish Temperance League Register*, pp. 46-7.
56. Lees, *Legislative Prohibition of the Liquor Traffic*, p. 66.
57. Brown, pp. 22-7, 48-50, 53; Alison, *Life and Writings*, v. 2, pp. 306-7.
58. MacDonald, *Rambles Round Glasgow*, p. 13.
59. Baird, *Sanitary Condition*, p. 183.
60. MacFarlan et al., NSA, Glasgow, pp. 218-219.
61. *ILN*, 11 June 1853
62. Pagan, pp. 144-156; Simpson, *Glasgow in the "Forties"*, XVII-III.
63. *ILN*, 19 April 1851; *Glasgow Herald*, 6 January 1854.
64. McQueen, *Clyde Paddle-wheels*, frontispiece.
65. Pagan, p. 99.
66. McKean et al., *Central Glasgow*, p. 92.
67. Pagan, pp. 129, 187.
68. Oakley, pp. 156-7.
69. Chalmers, p. 3.
70. Smart, *Villages of Glasgow*, p. 56; Cunnison & Gilfillan, p. 907.
71. Oakey, p. 137.
72. MacDonald, *Glasgow's Gaelic Churches*.
73. 1828 map in Moore, *Maps of Glasgow*, Plate 4.
74. Oakley, pp. 123-4, facing p. 134; Alison, *Life*, v.1, pp. 609-610; *Greenock Advertiser*, 17 August 1849.
75. Black & Black, *Economical Guide*, p. 18.

76. Brown, *Midnight Scenes*, pp. 82-84.
77. Simpson, *Glasgow*, VII; Brown, pp. 59-60.
78. Smart, p. 75.
79. MacDonald, *Rambles Round Glasgow*, pp. 266-7.
80. Brotchie, *History of Govan*, pp. 126, 153, 271-273.
81. Brotchie, pp 158, 293-297; Dalglish & Driscoll, *Historic Govan*, p. 73.
82. Cunnison, & Gilfillan, pp. 179-180.
83. Smart, p. 85.
84. Brotchie, pp. 131, 181.
85. *Glasgow Herald*, 4 July 1855; Lyall, *Vanishing Glasgow*, p. 80.
86. Brotchie, pp. 105, 121; Cunnison, & Gilfillan, p. 324.
87. MacDonald, *Rambles*, pp. 109-110.
88. Simpson, *Glasgow*, XXVII; Smart, p. 35-37.
89. Smart, p. 30; MacDonald, *Rambles*, p. 112.

Chapter 10

1. *Witness*, 25 & 28 June 1845.
2. *Glasgow Saturday Post*, in *Glasgow Chronicle*, 8 May 1850.
3. *NBDM*, 27 January 1851.
4. Campbell *et al.*, *Second Annual Report*, p. 11.
5. *NBDM*, 2 October 1847.
6. Campbell *et al.*, *Second Annual Report*, pp. 12, 15.
7. *London Daily News*, 23 October 1846.
8. *Inverness Courier*, 16 December 1846.
9. *Glasgow Citizen*, in *Inverness Courier*, 9 December 1846.
10. Campbell *et al.*, *Second Annual Report*, p. 13.
11. Anon, *One Hundred Glasgow Men*, p. 76; Oakley, *Second City*, p. 223; Gibb, *Glasgow*, p. 93.
12. *Poor Law Inquiry (Scotland)*, Appendix 1, p. 643; *1st Annual Report of the Board of Supervision*, 1847, Appendix D, pp. 53-4.
13. *2nd Annual Report of the Board of Supervision*, 1848, p. xii, Appendix C, p. 97; *3rd Annual Report*, 1849, Appendix A, p. 21.
14. *Greenock Advertiser* 28 August 1846.
15. *Glasgow Argus*, in *Scotsman*, 19 December 1846.
16. *Dublin Weekly Nation*, 19 December 1846.
17. *Glasgow Constitutional*, in *Banner of Ulster*, 29 December 1846.
18. *Glasgow Argus*, in *Scotsman*, 20 January 1847.
19. *Glasgow Chronicle*, 5 May 1847.
20. *Pictures of Pauperism*, p. 3.
21. *Pictures of Pauperism*, p. 7.
22. *London Daily News*, 22 September 1847.
23. *Pictures of Pauperism*, pp. 4, 10.
24. Smith, *et al.*, *Dictionary of National Biography*, pp. 288-290.
25. Hall, in Devine, *Scotland's Slavery Past*, pp. 206-224.
26. 'Gazette', in *Witness*, 16 June 1852; Anon, *National Portrait Gallery*.
27. Alison, *Life and Writings*, v. 1, Preface.
28. Smith, *et al.*, *Dictionary of National Biography*, pp. 290-2; Alison, *Management of the Poor*; *Generation of Fever*, pp. 13-33; *Epidemic Fever*; *Poor Law Inquiry (Scotland)*, Appendix 1, pp. 73-84; Appendix 3, pp. 901-3.
29. Alison, *Principles of Population*, v. 1, pp. x-xi, 76-77; v. 2, p. 218; *Life and Writings*, v. 1, pp. 457-8.
30. *Pictures of Pauperism*, p. 8; *Greenock Advertiser*, 22 December 1846.
31. *Pictures of Pauperism*, pp. 11-2.
32. Guthrie, *Plea for Ragged Schools*, p. 24; Defoe, *Giving Alms no Charity*, p. 12.
33. *Pictures of Pauperism*, p. 17.

34. *Poor Law Inquiry (Scotland)*, Appendix 1, pp. 342-345, 667-669.
35. *Pictures of Pauperism*, p. 36.
36. Campbell *et al.*, *Second Annual Report*, pp. 13-16.
37. Campbell *et al.*, *Second Annual Report*, p. 8.
38. Campbell *et al.*, *Second Annual Report*, p. 4.
39. Ellice, *Poor Law (Scotland)*.
40. Campbell *et al.*, *Second Annual Report*, pp. 7-8.
41. *Glasgow Chronicle*, 21 July 1847.
42. Campbell *et al.*, *Second Annual Report*, p. 9.
43. *NBDM*, 25 March 1848.
44. *3rd Annual Report of the Board of Supervision*, 1849, p. i, Appendix A, p. 8.
45. *Glasgow Saturday Post*, in *Glasgow Chronicle*, 8 May 1850.
46. *1st Annual Report of the Board of Supervision*, 1847, p. xiii.
47. *1st Annual Report of the Board of Supervision*, 1847, Appendix E, pp. 152, 168-9, 176-7; *2nd Annual Report*, 1848, Appendix D, pp. 136, 158-161, 196; *3rd Annual Report*, 1849, Appendix B, pp. 65, 86-7, 115-6; *4th Annual Report*, 1850, Appendix B, pp. 46, 66-7, 95-6.
48. Logan, *Moral Statistics of Glasgow*, pp. 25-6.

Chapter 11

1. *Pictures of Pauperism*, p. 7.
2. Campbell *et al.*, *Second Annual Report*, p. 11.
3. e.g. *Greenock Advertiser*, 28 August 1846.
4. *Edinburgh Evening Post*, 30 September 1846; *Dumfries & Galloway Standard*, 24 February 1847; *Glasgow Argus*, in *Dundee, Perth & Cupar Advertiser*, 26 March 1847; *NBDM*, 23 April 1847; *NBDM*, 23 July 1847; *NBDM*, 13 August 1847; *Glasgow Courier*, 28 August 1847; *Dundee, Perth & Cupar Advertiser*, 22 October 1847; *Glasgow Courier*, 25 March 1848; *Glasgow Courier*, 6 July 1848; *Glasgow Chronicle*, 27 December 1848.
5. McNeel-Caird, *Poor-Law Manual*, pp. 302-304, 318-325.
6. *NBDM*, 26 June 1847, 8 July 1847.
7. *NBDM*, 8 February 1848.
8. *NBDM*, 9 February 1848.
9. e.g. *NBDM*, 12 June 1848; McNeel-Caird, pp. 412-419.
10. Christina Rice v William Thomson, NRS CS230/T/7/9.
11. *Scottish Jurist*, 1848, v. 20, pp. 462-465.
12. *Perthshire Advertiser*, 15 June 1848.
13. NRS CS230/T/7/9.
14. *Glasgow Courier*, 20 January 1848.
15. Circular, NRS GD1/955/5.
16. William Thomson v William Lindsay, NRS CS236/T/17/12.
17. *NBDM*, 14-15 June 1848.
18. NRS CS236/T/17/12.
19. *Glasgow Chronicle*, 14 June 1848.
20. *NBDM*, 14, 17, 20 July 1848.
21. *NBDM*, 17 August 1848.
22. *NBDM*, 14 October 1848.
23. *NBDM*, 9 November 1848.
24. *Caledonian Mercury*, 7 & 11 December 1848; *NBDM*, 8 December 1848.
25. *Glasgow Herald*, 26 February 1849; *Scotsman*, 28 February 1849.
26. *Glasgow Herald*, 6 November 1848.
27. e.g. *Glasgow Citizen*, in *Stonehaven Journal*, 7 November 1848.
28. *NBDM*, 6 November 1848.
29. *Glasgow Herald*, 6 November 1848.

30. [Glasgow?] 'Constitutional', in Glasgow Herald, 27 November 1848.
31. Glasgow Courier, 14 December 1848.
32. NBDM, 4 December 1848.
33. NBDM, 6 December 1848.
34. NBDM, 7 December 1848.
35. Glasgow Herald, 23 February 1849.
36. Glasgow Saturday Post, in Glasgow Chronicle, 8 May 1850.
37. Greenock Advertiser, 12 October 1849; McNeel-Caird, pp. 386-9.
38. Glasgow Sheriff Court Extract Decree Books, NRS SC36/14/18.
39. Glasgow Sheriff Court Extract Decree Books, NRS SC36/14/19.
40. NBDM, 16 April 1850.
41. NBDM, 18 April 1850.
42. NBDM, 22 April 1850.
43. [Glasgow?] Saturday Post, in Dumfries & Galloway Standard, 26 March 1851.
44. NBDM, 12 July 1851.
45. [Glasgow?] Saturday Post, in Dumfries & Galloway Standard, 16 July 1851.
46. e.g. Elgin & Morayshire Courier, 11 July 1851.
47. Morning Advertiser, 15 July 1851.
48. Scotsman, 19 July 1851.
49. Glasgow Sentinel, 26 July 1851.
50. Scottish Highlanders, pp. 4-5.
51. Scotsman, 27 March 1852; Scottish Jurist, 1852, v. 24, pp. 391-400.
52. Glasgow Sheriff Court Extract Decree Books, NRS SC36/14/24.

Chapter 12

1. Pictures of Pauperism, p. 28.
2. Fenyő, Contempt, Sympathy and Romance.
3. Inverness Advertiser, 22 January 1850.
4. Hutchinson, Martyrs, p. 17.
5. McNeill, Report to the Board of Supervision, p. xxxix.
6. Mackinnon, NSA, Strath, pp. 307-8.
7. Devine, Scottish Clearances, p. 306.
8. Inverness Courier, 26 August 1846.
9. Hunter, Insurrection.
10. Devine, Great Highland Famine, p. 57.
11. Glasgow Herald, 15 January 1847.
12. Devine, Great Highland Famine, p. 44.
13. Nicolson, History of Skye, p. 272; Devine, Great Highland Famine, p. 137.
14. Devine, Great Highland Famine, p. 127.
15. MacLeod, Gloomy Memories, pp. 100-101.
16. Somers, Letters from the Highlands, pp. 93, 97, 100, 109.
17. Nicolson, Skye, pp. 251-252.
18. Devine, Great Highland Famine, pp. 39, 86-7, 185-6.
19. Witness, 17 July 1850.
20. Devine, Great Highland Famine, p. 189.
21. JOGJ, 2 August 1850.
22. Mulock, Western Highlands, p. 230.
23. Inverness Advertiser, 2 July 1850.
24. Letters from the Mountains, Introduction.
25. Douglas, Modern Athenians, pp. 66-7; Cairns & MacQueen, Learning and the Law.
26. Scotsman, 1 March 1843; NBDM, 15 June 1848.
27. Letters from the Mountains, p. 2.
28. Uncles, Last Ferry to Skye, pp. 74-77, 82.
29. Mackinnon, NSA, Strath, p. 311.
30. Uncles, Last Ferry, p. 65.
31. OS 25 inch maps XLI.13, XLVII.1 and XLVI.4, 1881, surveyed 1876.
32. Letters from the Mountains, pp. 1-3.
33. Letters from the Mountains, pp. 3-4.
34. Letters from the Mountains, p. 8; Mackinnon, p. 312; Uncles, Last Ferry, p. 64.
35. Uncles, Last Ferry, p. 62.

36. *Letters from the Mountains*, p. 10.
37. Personal observation: tree stumps with 51 rings, probably planted when one year old.
38. *Letters from the Mountains*, pp. 11-12.
39. *Letters from the Mountains*, pp. 19-22.
40. *Letters from the Mountains*, pp. 24-25.
41. *Letters from the Mountains*, pp. 28-29.
42. *Letters from the Mountains*, pp. 38, 41-42.
43. *Inverness Advertiser*, 29 October 1850.
44. *Scotsman*, 21 December 1850.
45. McNeill, *Report*, p. xxxix.; 1851 census.
46. *Scottish Highlanders*, pp. 12-13.
47. Portree Small Debt Court Book, NRS SC32/12/2.
48. HIES passenger lists, NRS HD4/5.
49. Napier *et al.*, *Crofters' Commission*, p. 223.
50. Brand *et al.*, *Royal Commission*, p. 154.

Chapter 13

1. Brand *et al.*, *Royal Commission*, p. 931; Devine, *Great Highland Famine*, p. 94; Hunter, *Insurrection*, p. 90.
2. Nicolson, NSA, 'Barray,' p. 212; Charnley, *Western Isles*, pp. 28-30.
3. Nicolson, NSA, 'Barray,' p. 208; Devine, *Great Highland Famine*, p. 75.
4. Craig, *Crofters' Trail*, p. 90.
5. *Poor Law Inquiry*, 1844, Appendix. 2, pp. 362-364.
6. *2nd Annual Report of the Board of Supervision*, 1848, Appendix. B, pp. 64-68, 84-85.
7. *Inverness Advertiser*, 28 August 1849.
8. *Witness*, 9 November 1850.
9. *JOGJ*, 14 February 1851.
10. Devine, *Great Highland Famine*, pp. 75, 180.
11. *NBDM*, 6 December 1850.
12. *Glasgow Herald*, 9 December 1850.
13. *Reformers' Gazette*, 14 December 1850.
14. *Scottish Press*, 25 December 1850.
15. *Caledonian Mercury*, 23 December 1850; *NBDM*, 27 December 1850.
16. *Caledonian Mercury*, 19 December 1850.
17. *Inverness Advertiser*, 24 December 1850.
18. *Witness*, 21 December 1850.
19. *Scotsman*, 18 December 1850.
20. '*Courant*', in *Glasgow Herald*, 20 December 1850; *Inverness Advertiser*, 31 December 1850.
21. *NBDM*, 17 December 1850.
22. *Caledonian Mercury*, 19 December 1850.
23. *Glasgow Herald*, 20 December 1850; '*Courant*', in *Glasgow Herald*, 23 December 1850.
24. *NBDM*, 23 December 1850.
25. *Inverness Courier*, 30 January 1851.
26. *Daily Mail*, in *Northern Star*, 28 December 1850.
27. *NBDM*, 26 December 1850.
28. *NBDM*, 27 December 1850.
29. *Edinburgh Evening Post*, in *Standard*, 1 January 1851.
30. *Perthshire Advertiser*, 2 January 1851.
31. *Caledonian Mercury*, 30 December 1850.
32. *NBDM*, 15 March 1851.
33. *Witness*, 1 January 1851.
34. *Montrose, Arbroath & Brechin Review*, 10 January 1851.
35. *Edinburgh Evening Courant*, 11 January 1851.
36. *Scotsman*, 11 January 1851.
37. *Montrose, Arbroath & Brechin Review*, 24 January 1851.
38. *Scotsman*, 22 January 1851; *Caledonian Mercury*, 13 January 1851.

39. *Witness*, 12 March 1851; *Edinburgh Evening Courant*, 15 March 1851.
40. *Scotsman*, 15 January 1851.
41. *Inverness Courier*, 13 February 1851.
42. *Caledonian Mercury*, 13 February 1851.
43. *JOGJ*, 14 February 1851.
44. *Inverness Courier*, 6 March 1851; *JOGJ*, 7 & 14 March 1851.
45. *Inverness Courier*, 20 March 1851.
46. *6th Annual Report of the Board of Supervision*, 1851, pp. v, Appendix A, 11-13; *Edinburgh Evening Courant*, 26 July 1851.
47. MacLeod, *Gloomy Memories*, p. 136.
48. McNeill, *Report to the Board of Supervision*, pp. xxiv-xxv.
49. *Inverness Courier*, 3 July 1851.
50. *Inverness Courier*, 10 July 1851.
51. *Inverness Courier*, 5 February 1852.
52. *Glasgow Herald*, 4 August 1851.
53. MacLeod, *Gloomy*, p. 138.
54. Prebble, *Highland Clearances*, p. 285.
55. Devine, *Great Highland Famine*, pp. 325-326.
56. *NBDM*, 8 November 1851.
57. *Inverness Courier*, 29 January 1852.
58. *Inverness Advertiser*, 20 July 1852.
59. *Inverness Courier*, 15 January 1852.
60. *Inverness Courier*, 5 February 1852.
61. *Inverness Advertiser*, 3 February 1852.

Chapter 14

1. *Scottish Press*, 25 December 1850.
2. *Caledonian Mercury*, 23 January 1851.
3. *NBDM*, 10 February 1851.
4. *Inverness Advertiser*, 4 February 1851.
5. *Edinburgh Evening Courant*, 20 February 1851, 20 March 1851.
6. McNeill, *Report to the Board of Supervision*, pp. 50-51.
7. McNeill, pp. 33-4.
8. McNeill, pp. 48-9.
9. McNeill, p. 55.
10. McNeill, pp. vi-vii, xiii, xxxvi.
11. Devine, *Great Highland Famine*, p. 202.
12. *NBDM*, 28 April 1851.
13. 'Mail', in *Scotsman*, 4 June 1851.
14. *Scotsman*, 18 June 1851.
15. *NBDM*, 19 June 1851.
16. *NBDM*, 29 May 1851.
17. *NBDM*, 7 June 1851.
18. *Reformers' Gazette*, 5 July 1851.
19. *Witness*, 28 June 1851; *Inverness Courier*, 10 July 1851.
20. *Glasgow Herald*, 14 July 1851.
21. *NBDM*, 17 July 1851.
22. Letter to Breadalbane, 21 July 1851, NRS GD112/11/10/13/27-8.
23. *Perthshire Advertiser*, 23 June 1853.
24. MacLeod, *Gloomy Memories*, p. 159.
25. e.g. *Edinburgh Evening Courant*, 26 July 1851.
26. *NBDM*, 1 August 1851.
27. *Patriot*, 14 August 1851.
28. *NBDM*, 16 August 1851.
29. *NBDM*, 9 August 1851.
30. *Inverness Advertiser*, 12 August 1851.
31. *Oxford Journal*, 23 August 1851; *Oxford Chronicle*, 23 August 1851.
32. *Oxford Journal*, 6 September 1851.
33. *Berrow's Worcester Journal*, 4 September 1851.
34. *West of England Conservative*, 24 September 1851.
35. e.g. *Oxford Journal*, 1 November 1851.
36. *NBDM*, 6 November 1851.

Notes

37. e.g. *Oxford Journal*, 6 December 1851.
38. Checkland, *Philanthropy in Victorian Scotland*, p. 5.
39. e.g. *Morning Advertiser*, 25 December 1851.
40. *Quarterly Review*, 1851, v. 90, pp. 163-205.
41. *Reformers' Gazette*, 31 January 1852.
42. *Morning Advertiser*, 31 January 1852.

Chapter 15

1. *NBDM*, 5 November 1851.
2. *NBDM*, 10 January 1852.
3. *Scottish Guardian*, in *Stirling Observer*, 29 January 1852.
4. Devine, *Great Highland Famine*, pp. 138-9.
5. Alison, *Management of the Poor*, pp. 180-181; Somers, *Letters from the Highlands*, pp. 173-4.
6. *Scottish Highlanders*, p. 7.
7. *Scottish Highlanders*, pp. 9-12.
8. *Scottish Highlanders*, p. 14.
9. McCulloch, *Statistical Account*, p. 310; *Scottish Highlanders*, p. 19.
10. *Scottish Highlanders*, p. 21.
11. *Caledonian Mercury*, 26 February 1852.
12. *Scotsman*, 31 July 1852.
13. *Manchester Times*, 17 March 1852.
14. *NBDM*, 26 March 1852.
15. *Times*, 22 March 1852.
16. *Times*, 26 March 1852.
17. *Times*, 7 April 1852.
18. *Reformers' Gazette*, 27 March 1852.
19. *Caledonian Mercury*, 22 April 1852; *Manchester Times*, 22 May 1852.
20. *Glasgow Saturday Post*, in *Glasgow Chronicle*, 08 May 1850.
21. *Inverness Advertiser*, 22 June 1852.
22. *NBDM*, 12 June 1852.
23. *British Friend*, 1852, v.10(8), p. 214.
24. *British Friend*, 1852, v.10(9), p. 229; 1853, v.11(1), p. 18.
25. *NBDM*, 12 November 1852.
26. *Worcester Journal*, 17 February 1853.
27. *Reformers' Gazette*, 9 April 1853, in Forbes, *Weeping in the Isles*, pp. 49-50.
28. *Witness*, 27 April 1853.
29. *Glasgow Constitutional*, 1 June 1853.

Chapter 16

1. Campey, *After the Hector; Unstoppable Force*.
2. *Glasgow Herald*, 10 October 1853; Beechey, *Loss of the "Annie Jane"*.
3. *Inverness Courier*, 28 August 1851.
4. *Witness*, 11 February 1852.
5. *Witness*, 25 February 1852.
6. *Witness*, 16 June 1852.
7. Devine, *Great Highland Famine*, p. 204.
8. *British Friend*, 1852, v.10(8), p. 214.
9. Devine, *Great Highland Famine*, pp. 245-268.
10. *Morning Herald*, 8 September 1852; *Standard*, 13 November 1852.
11. *British Friend*, 1853, v.11(1), pp. 16-17.
12. *Witness*, 19 March 1853.
13. *Campbeltown Journal*, in *Inverness Courier*, 30 December 1852.
14. *Campbeltown Journal*, in *British Friend*, 1853, v.11(1), p. 17.
15. Devine, *Great Highland Famine*, p. 256.
16. HIES passenger lists, NRS HD4/5.
17. *Glasgow Constitutional*, 1 January 1853.
18. *NBDM*, 4 January 1853.
19. *NBDM*, 8 January 1853.
20. *Campbeltown Journal*, in *British Friend*, 1853, v.11(2), p. 43.

21. *NBDM*, in *British Friend*, 1853, v.11(2), pp. 43-44.
22. *British Friend*, 1853, v.11(2), p. 44.
23. *Witness*, 5 February 1853.
24. *Witness*, 9 February 1853.
25. *Inverness Courier*, 10 February 1853.
26. *NBDM*, 24 January 1853.
27. *Cork Constitution*, 25 January 1853.
28. *Cork Constitution*, 29 January 1853; *NBDM* 1 February 1853.
29. *Sun*, 15 February 1853.
30. *Perthshire Courier*, in *Glasgow Herald*, 28 February 1853.
31. *Cork Examiner*, 11 March 1853.
32. *Witness*, 19 March 1853.
33. *Plymouth Mail*, in *NBDM*, 28 March 1853.
34. *Cork Examiner*, 8 April 1853.
35. *Witness*, 3 August 1853.
36. *NBDM*, 3 August 1853.
37. *Inverness Advertiser*, 20 September 1853.
38. *Glasgow Herald*, 11 November 1853.

Chapter 17

1. *Reformers' Gazette*, 29 May 1852.
2. Hearle, *Hollins Mill*.
3. Forbes, *Weeping in the Isles*, pp. 39-41.
4. Forbes, *Weeping*, pp. 43-44.
5. Forbes, *Weeping*, pp. 1-3.
6. *Reformers' Gazette*, 20 November 1852.
7. Forbes, *Weeping*, pp. 50-51, 58-60.
8. *Reformers' Gazette* 11 December 1852.
9. Forbes, *Weeping*, pp. 46-47.
10. Forbes, *Weeping*, pp. 60-61.
11. *Reformers' Gazette*, 25 December 1852.
12. *NBDM*, 18 December 1852.
13. *Glasgow Sentinel*, 8 January 1853.
14. *Reformers' Gazette*, 8 January 1853, in Forbes, *Weeping*, pp. 66-7.
15. Forbes, *Weeping*, p. 60.
16. HIES passenger lists, NRS HD4/5, p. 83; *NBDM*, 3 August 1853.
17. Forbes, *Weeping*, pp. 72-73.
18. Forbes, *Weeping*, pp. 12-13, 16, 74.
19. Forbes, *Weeping*, pp. 78-79.
20. Forbes, *Weeping*, p. 83.
21. *Fifeshire Journal*, 11 August 1853.
22. *Church of Scotland Magazine and Review*, July 1853, p. 278; *Elgin Courant*, 19 August 1853; *Montrose Standard*, 19 August 1853.
23. *JOGJ*, 26 August 1853.
24. *Inverness Courier*, 8 September 1853.
25. Hazlitt, *Faiths and Folklore*, p. 563.
26. *Am Ministear*, p. 9.
27. Forbes, *Double Grammar*.
28. *Glasgow Constitutional*, 27 August 1853.
29. *Inverness Advertiser*, 27 September 1853.
30. *Inverness Advertiser*, 25 October 1853; *JOGJ*, 18 November 1853.
31. *Times*, 30 March 1852.
32. *Glasgow Free Press*, 23 April 1853.
33. *Real Scottish Grievances*, p. 24.
34. *Fife Herald*, 29 September 1853.
35. *Glasgow Sentinel*, 1 October 1853.
36. *Northern Ensign*, in *Scottish Guardian*, 4 October 1853.
37. *Witness*, 8 October 1853.
38. *Northern Ensign*, in *Witness*, 2 November 1853.
39. *Inverness Courier*, 5 January 1854.

Chapter 18

1. Woolf, *Knoydart*, p. 3.
2. Lees, *County of Inverness*, p. 249.
3. Beith, NSA, Glenelg, pp. 135-136.
4. Hunter, *Dance Called America*; Campey, *Unstoppable Force*; *Freeholder*, in *Inverness Courier*, 31 March 1853.

Notes

5. Rixon, *Knoydart*, p. 120.
6. *Inverness Courier*, 17 February 1847.
7. Devine, *Great Highland Famine*, pp. 263-4.
8. *Inverness Courier*, 18 August 1853.
9. *Scotsman*, 22 October 1853; Richards, *Highland Clearances*, p. 335.
10. *Inverness Courier*, 8 September 1853.
11. *Inverness Advertiser*, 6 September 1853.
12. *Inverness Advertiser*, 13 September 1853.
13. *Inverness Courier*, 15 September 1853.
14. *Times*, 20 September 1853.
15. Uncles, *Last ferry to Skye*, p. 84.
16. *Inverness Advertiser*, 27 September 1853.
17. *Inverness Courier*, 29 September 1853.
18. *Inverness Courier*, 13 October 1853.
19. *Inverness Advertiser*, 18 October 1853.
20. *Northern Ensign*, 20 October 1853, in *Witness*, 5 November 1853; *Inverness Advertiser*, 25 October 1853.
21. *British Friend*, 1853, v. 11(11), p. 292.
22. Stewart, *Sketches*, p. 127.
23. *Inverness Courier*, 10 March 1847.
24. *Glengarry Evictions*, p. 5.
25. *Glengarry Evictions*, pp. 7-8.
26. *Glengarry Evictions*, pp. 17-19, 21, 23.
27. Ellice, *Place-names in Glengarry*, pp. 118-121.
28. *Glengarry Evictions*, pp. 27-28.
29. *Glengarry Evictions*, p. 30.
30. *Belfast Chronicle*, 19 November 1853.
31. *Scotsman*, 22 October 1853.
32. Rixon, pp. 141-142.
33. Craig & Paterson, *Glens of Silence*, p. 72.
34. *Scotsman*, 26 October 1853.
35. *Glasgow Constitutional*, 16 November 1853.
36. *Inverness Courier*, 24 November 1853.
37. *Morning Advertiser*, 25 November 1853.
38. *Inverness Advertiser*, 13 December 1853.
39. *Northern Ensign*, in *Scottish Press*, 16 December 1853.
40. *British Friend*, 1854, v. 12(1), pp. 3-4.
41. *Highland Clearances*, p. 10.
42. Ellice, *Place-names in Glengarry*, p. 7.
43. *Poor Law Inquiry*, 1844, Appendix. 2, pp. 472-478.
44. *Real Scottish Grievances*, pp. 27-28; *Scotsman*, 3 May 1854; *Glasgow Herald*, 18 July 1855.
45. *Northern Ensign*, 26 January 1854.
46. Letter from McNeill to Palmerston, 3 February 1854, NRS GD371/288.
47. *Inverness Courier*, 16 February 1854.
48. *Inverness Courier*, 23 February 1854.
49. *British Friend*, 1854, v. 12(3), p. 76.
50. *Northern Ensign*, 2 March 1854.
51. *Northern Ensign*, 16 March 1854.
52. Campbell, *Raid of Albyn*, publisher's note at end.
53. *Real Scottish Grievances*, pp. 20-21.
54. *Northern Ensign*, 16 March 1854.
55. *Real Scottish Grievances*, pp. 25-27.
56. *Inverness Courier*, 30 March 1854.
57. *Northern Ensign*, 20 April 1854.
58. *Scotsman*, 9 December 1854.
59. *Inverness Courier*, 21 September 1854; *Scotsman*, 9 December 1854; Ellice, *State of the Highlands*, pp. 43-44.
60. *Scotsman*, 3 May 1854.
61. *Inverness Advertiser*, 23 May 1854.

62. *Scotsman*, 27 May 1854.
63. *Inverness Courier*, 1 June 1854.
64. *Scotsman*, 9 December 1854.
65. *Scotsman*, in *Inverness Courier*, 1 June 1854.
66. *Inverness Courier*, 15 June 1854.
67. *Inverness Courier* 22 & 29 June, 6, 13, 27 July 1854.
68. *Scotsman*, 9 December 1854.
69. *Witness*, 26 August 1854.
70. *Scotsman*, 12 August 1854
71. *NBDM*, 29 August 1854.
72. *Inverness Advertiser*, 3 October 1854.
73. *Cry of the Hungry*, pp. 6-7.
74. *Scotsman*, 9 December 1854; *Poor in Knoydart*.
75. *Plea for the Famishing*, pp. 4-7.
76. *Fife Herald*, 1 February 1855, *Scottish Guardian*, 20 February 1855.
77. McNeill, *Poor Law in the Parish of Glenelg*; *Glasgow Herald*, 4, 18, 25 July, 1 & 22 August 1855.
78. *Scotsman*, 21 February 1855; *Inverness Courier*, 1 March 1855.
79. *Scotsman*, 7 April 1855.
80. *Leeds Mercury*, 2 May 1857.
81. Brand et al., *Royal Commission*, pp. 1043-1046.

Chapter 19

1. *Inverness Advertiser*, 25 October 1853.
2. *Inverness Courier*, 27 October 1853.
3. *Real Scottish Grievances*, p. 14.
4. *Real Scottish Grievances*, pp. 5-6.
5. HIES passenger lists, NRS HD4/5.
6. *Inverness Courier*, 3 November 1853.
7. Geikie, *Scottish Reminiscences*, p. 226.
8. *Morning Advertiser*, 25 November 1853.
9. *Inverness Advertiser*, 29 November 1853.
10. *Morning Advertiser*, 25 November 1853.
11. *Real Scottish Grievances*, p. 12.
12. *Inverness Courier*, 3 November 1853.
13. *Real Scottish Grievances*, p. 13.
14. *Highland Clearances*, p. 5.
15. *Inverness Advertiser*, 10 January 1854.
16. *Northern Ensign*, 2 February 1854.
17. Geikie, p. 234.
18. *Inverness Advertiser*, 17 January 1854.
19. *Real Scottish Grievances*, pp. 19-20.
20. *Northern Ensign*, 26 January 1854.
21. *Northern Ensign*, 2 March 1854.
22. *Northern Ensign*, 16 March 1854.
23. *Scotsman*, 24 June 1854.
24. Hansard HC Deb 3 May 1855 v. 138, ee34-55.
25. Hutchinson, *Martyrs*.
26. Napier et al., *Crofters' Commission*, pp. 236, 242-244, 293-295.
27. Devine, *Great Highland Famine*, pp. 264-5, 331; Hunter, *Making of the Crofting Community*, p.83.
28. *Real Scottish Grievances*, p. 17; Brand et al., *Royal Commission*, pp. 162-164.
29. Hunter & Maclean, *Skye*, pp. 14-15; Craig, *Crofters' Trail*, pp. 8, 17, 28, 30, 33-35; Craig & Paterson, *Glens of Silence*, pp. 137-8.

Chapter 20

1. *NBDM*, 7 July 1854.
2. Richards, *Highland Clearances*, pp. 343-352.
3. Allan, NSA, Kincardine, pp. 420, 423.
4. Roy, Military Survey of Scotland, 1747-55, NLS, area ref: C.9.b 35/5a, 2.
5. Precognition against Peter Ross, NRS AD14/54/192.
6. Richards, *Highland Clearances*, p. 324.

Notes

7. Letter to Munro, NRS JC26/1854/76.
8. NRS AD14/54/192.
9. Summons of Removing, NRS JC26/1854/76.
10. NRS AD14/54/192.
11. Letters to Lord Advocate, NRS AD56/309/3.
12. NRS AD14/54/192.
13. *Inverness Advertiser*, 28 March 1854.
14. *Inverness Courier*, 30 March 1854.
15. Petitions, NRS AD14/54/192.
16. NRS AD56/309/3.
17. Precognition, NRS AD14/54/192.
18. *Russians of Ross-shire*, pp. 9, 29.
19. Alastair McIntyre, pers. comm.
20. Report by William Gordon, NRS AD14/54/192.
21. Report by N. B. Ross, NRS AD14/54/192.
22. Declarations, NRS AD14/54/192, JC26/1854/76.
23. Petitions for Bail and Bonds of Caution, NRS SC34/14/3.
24. Declaration and Defences for Peter Ross, NRS JC26/1854/76.
25. NRS AD56/309/3.
26. *Inverness Advertiser*, 4 April 1854.
27. *Northern Ensign*, 6 April 1854.
28. *Inverness Courier*, 6 April 1854.
29. *Northern Ensign*, 13 April 1854.
30. *NBDM*, 18 April 1854.
31. *Northern Ensign*, 20 April 1854.
32. *Northern Ensign*, 4 May 1854.
33. MacLeod, *Gloomy Memories*, p, 199.
34. *Russians of Ross-shire*, p. 34.
35. *Inverness Courier*, 27 April 1854.
36. *Northern Ensign*, 11 May 1854.
37. *NBDM*, 12 May 1854.
38. *Russians of Ross-shire*, pp. 5-6.
39. *Russians of Ross-shire*, p. 8.
40. *Russians of Ross-shire*, pp. 16-17.
41. *Liverpool Mercury*, 19 September 1854; HIES passenger lists, NRS HD4/5.
42. Pam Keown pers. comm.; *Who Do You Think You Are?* Australia.
43. *Russians of Ross-shire*, pp. 17-18.
44. Alastair McIntyre, pers. comm.
45. *Russians of Ross-shire*, pp. 19-20, 22-23, 28-29.
46. *Northern Ensign*, 25 May 1854.
47. *Northern Warder*, 13 July 1854.
48. *NBDM*, 9 August 1854.
49. *Russians of Ross-shire*, p. 20.
50. NRS AD/14/54/192; Petition for David Munro SC34/14/3.
51. Letters, Taylor to Brodie, NRS AD14/54/192.
52. Indictment, NRS JC26/1854/76.
53. *NBDM*, 8 September 1854.
54. *Inverness Courier*, 14 September 1854.
55. *JOGJ*, 22 September 1854.
56. *Inverness Advertiser* 19 September 1854.
57. Tain Court minute book, NRS SC34/1/12; Register of decrees, NRS SC34/3/4.
58. George Ross & Others v Alexander Munro, NRS CS275/16/12.
59. Petitions for Aliment, NRS SC4/4/102.
60. *Reformers' Gazette*, in *Inverness Courier*, 15 March 1855.
61. *Inverness Courier*, 29 March 1855.
62. *Northern Ensign*, 15 February 1855, in Richards, *Highland Clearances*, p. 352.
63. Summons of Forthcoming, NRS SC4/4/102.
64. Letter, Aird to Peterson, 4 September 1855, TANDM 2795.
65. *Farmers' Magazine*, v. 11, pp. 3-5; v. 4, pp. 126-127; v. 9, pp. 23-42.
66. *Russians of Ross-shire*, p. 42.
67. *Russians of Ross-shire*, p. 45.
68. Prebble, *Highland Clearances*, pp. 240-253.
69. *Russians of Ross-shire*, pp. 9-10.
70. Craig, *Crofters' Trail*, pp. 312-3.
71. *Russians of Ross-shire*, p. 13.
72. Craig, p. 309.

Chapter 21

1. Selby, *Thin Red Line*.
2. Selby, pp. 19-20; *Inverness Courier*, 23 June 1853.

3. Greenwood, *Victoria's Scottish Lion.*
4. *Witness*, 16 April 1851.
5. Prebble, *Highland Clearances*, pp. 316-323.
6. *Russians of Ross-shire*, pp. 27-28.
7. MacLeod, *Gloomy Memories*, pp. 165-6.
8. *Northern Ensign*, in *Aberdeen Free Press*, 26 January 1855.
9. Fraser-Mackintosh, *Letters of Two Centuries*, pp. 311-312.
10. Dempster, *Essay on Sheep-Farming*, p. 3.
11. MacLeod, *Destitution in Sutherlandshire*, p. 74.
12. e.g. *Witness*, 13 December 1854.
13. *Northern Ensign*, 21 December 1854.
14. *Northern Ensign*, 28 December 1854.
15. *Glasgow Free Press*, in *Plea for the Famishing*, p. 7.
16. *NBDM*, 27 January 1855.
17. *NBDM*, 26 November 1855.
18. *NBDM*, 1 December 1855.
19. *NBDM*, 12 December 1855.
20. Alison, *Life and Writings*, v. 2, p. 167-170.
21. Prebble, p. 323.

Chapter 22

1. Grimble, *Trial of Patrick Sellar*, p. 99.
2. *Witness*, 1 December 1852.
3. *Elgin Courier*, 29 April 1853.
4. Stowe, *Sunny Memories*, pp. 36-7.
5. *Witness*, 20 April 1853.
6. Stowe, pp. 210-213.
7. Stowe, pp. 219-228.
8. MacLeod, *Gloomy Memories*, pp. 71-84, 141-2.
9. *Northern Ensign*, in *Glasgow Sentinel*, 13 September 1856.
10. *Northern Ensign*, in *The Globe*, 7 September 1856.
11. *Glasgow Sentinel*, 18 October 1856.

Chapter 23

1. *Brighton Gazette*, 21 December 1854.
2. *Cry of the Hungry*, p. 9.
3. *Glasgow Constitutional*, 3 March 1855.
4. e.g. *Morning Chronicle*, 18 January 1855.
5. *Fife Herald*, 25 January 1855, 12 April 1855.
6. *Witness*, 7 February 1855.
7. e.g. *Morning Advertiser*, 23 February 1855.
8. *Plea for the Famishing*, p. 10.
9. *Inverness Courier*, 22 February 1855.
10. *JOGJ*, 23 February 1855.
11. *JOGJ*, 2 March 1855.
12. *JOGJ*, 23 March 1855.
13. e.g. *Caledonian Mercury*, 1 March 1855, 2 April 1855; *Witness*, 24 March 1855; *Glasgow Constitutional*, 11 April 1855; *British Friend*, 1855, v. 13(4), pp. 6-7, v. 13(5), pp. 8-10, v. 13(6), pp. 4-5.
14. *NBDM*, 15 March 1855, 26 April 1855; *Glasgow Constitutional*, 17 March 1855; *Caledonian Mercury*, 12 & 19 April 1855.
15. *British Friend*, 1855, v. 13(5), p. 114
16. *Glasgow Constitutional*, 28 April 1855.
17. *Times*, 13 April 1848.
18. *British Friend*, 1855, v. 13(5), pp. 114-5.
19. *NBDM*, 11 May 1855.
20. *Witness*, 17 July 1850.
21. *Destitution in the West Highlands*, pp. 17-18.
22. *Glasgow Constitutional*, 16 May 1855.
23. *Inverness Courier*, 7 June 1855.
24. *Caledonian Mercury*, 11 June 1855.
25. *Who will Help?*, pp. 8-9.
26. *Who will Help?*, pp. 9, 23-24.
27. *British Friend* 1855, v. 13(11), p. 6, v. 13(12), p. 5.

28. *Report on the Relief of Destitution*, p. 8.
29. measuringworth.com.
30. e.g. *Morning Chronicle*, 8 March 1856.
31. *Inverness Courier*, 13 March 1856.
32. *JOGJ*, 21 March 1856.
33. *Greenock Advertiser*, 28 March 1856; *Scottish Guardian*, 1 April 1856.
34. *Greenock Advertiser*, 23 May 1856.
35. *Cent per Cent*, pp. 9-10.
36. *Cent per Cent*, p. 13.
37. *Cent per Cent*, pp. 17-18.
38. *British Friend*, 1857, v. 15(6), p. 5.

Chapter 24

1. *Caledonian Mercury*, 14 May 1855.
2. e.g. *Greenock Advertiser*, 15 May 1855.
3. 'Glasgow Paper,' in *Witness*, 9 June 1855.
4. *Who will Help?*, pp. 15-17.
5. *NBDM*, 28 June 1856.
6. *Caledonian Mercury*, 6 September 1856.
7. *NBDM*, 28 November 1856.
8. *NBDM*, 7 February 1857.
9. *Glasgow Herald*, 30 January 1857.
10. *NBDM*, 7 February 1857.
11. e.g. *NBDM*, 18 June 1857.
12. *Glasgow Herald*, 31 July 1857.
13. *Glasgow Herald*, 5 August 1857.
14. *NBDM*, 7 August 1857.
15. *Glasgow Herald*, 7 August 1857.
16. *Glasgow Sentinel*, 8 August 1857.
17. *NBDM*, 8 August 1857.
18. *Paisley Herald*, 15 August 1857.
19. *NBDM*, 14 August 1857.
20. *Glasgow Herald*, 10 August 1857, 30 November 1857.
21. *Illustrated News of the World*, 28 August 1858.

Chapter 25

1. *Stirling Observer*, 15 May 1856.
2. *NBDM*, 11 June 1856.
3. *Glasgow Herald*, 13 June 1856.
4. *Stirling Observer*, 26 June 1856.
5. *NBDM*, 25 June 1856.
6. *Stirling Observer*, 3 July 1856.
7. *Dundee Advertiser, Supplement*, 12 December 1856.
8. Drysdale, *Old Faces*, pp. 212-214; MacInnes (2004).
9. *NBDM*, 12 November 1856.
10. *Times*, 27 October 1856, 8 November 1856.
11. *NBDM*, 21 January 1857; e.g. *Times* 5 January 1857.
12. *Scotsman*, 7 April 1852.
13. *Glasgow Herald*, 21 January 1857.
14. *Morning Chronicle*, 10 February 1857.
15. Lees, *Legislative Prohibition of the Liquor Traffic*.
16. *NBDM*, 6 January 1857.
17. *British Friend*, 1857, v.15(1), pp. 23-24.
18. Pennant, *Tour in Scotland*, p. 221; Lees, *Legislative*, p. 126.
19. Sillett, *Illicit Scotch*, pp. 70, 102.
20. *Quarterly Review*, v.90, p. 171.
21. *Quarterly Review*, v.90, p. 594.
22. *NBDM*, 6 January 1857.
23. *NBDM*, 12 January 1857.
24. *NBDM*, 13 January 1857.
25. *British Friend*, 1857, v.15(2), pp. 52-53.
26. Lees, *Traffic in Strong Drink*, p. 140.
27. Lees, *One Hundred Objections*, p. 106.

Chapter 26

1. *Inverness Courier*, 26 November 1857.
2. *Inverness Courier*, 3 December 1857.
3. *Inverness Courier*, 10 December 1857
4. *Glasgow Herald*, 14 December 1857, 16 December 1857.

5. *Glasgow Herald*,
   18 December 1857.
6. *Scottish Press*, 18 December 1857.
7. *Glasgow Herald*
   21 December 1857.
8. *Inverness Courier*,
   24 December 1857.
9. *Inverness Courier*, 14 January 1858.
10. *Glasgow Herald*, 22 January 1858;
    Campbell *et. al.*, *First Annual Report*.
11. *Inverness Courier*,
    4 February 1858.
12. *Glasgow Sentinel*,
    16 January 1858.
13. *Glasgow Herald*, 18 January 1856.

Chapter 27

1. Campey, *After the Hector*, p. 181.
2. Hunter, *Set Adrift*, pp. 319-324;
   Campey, *Hector*, pp. 98, 131,
   Appendix 2.
3. *British Friend*, 1859, v.17(12),
   p. 315.
4. Cunnison & Gilfillan, *Third Statistical Account, Glasgow*,
   p. 393.
5. *British Friend*, 1860, v.18(1), p. 14.
6. *British Friend*, 1860, v.18(2),
   p. 40.
7. Payzant, *Halifax*, pp. 16, 75.
8. Cornall, *Halifax*.
9. Payzant, pp. 47-54.
10. Chapman, *Wake of the Alderney*,
    p. 135.
11. Payzant, p. 98.
12. Egan, *Halifax Volunteer Battalion*,
    pp. 67, 86.
13. Edwards, *Militia of Nova Scotia*,
    p. 93.
14. Egan, pp. 67-70, 88.
15. Macdonald, *North British Society*,
    pp. 319, 402, 683.
16. Letter to Blackie, 5 January 1865,
    NLS MS.2626 ff.132-5.
17. Payzant, p. 72.
18. Stoddart, *John Stuart Blackie*,
    pp. 113, 176; Wallace, *John Stuart Blackie*, pp. 7-8.
19. Blackie, *Lays of the Highlands,
    Language and Literature,
    Altavona, Scottish Highlanders*.
20. Blackie, *Altavona*, p. xi; MacRae,
    Life of Gustavus Aird, pp. 99-100.
21. Blackie, *Gaelic Language*,
    Stoddart, pp. 5, 93, Wallace,
    pp. 198, 266-267.
22. *Inverness Courier*,
    15 October 1874.
23. Wallace, pp. 272-6; Stoddart,
    pp. 114-5, 212.
24. *Scotsman*, 7 March 1895;
    Stoddart, pp. 346-49; Wallace,
    p. 315.
25. *Acadian Recorder*, 20 July 1868.
26. *Halifax Citizen*, 23 July 1868.
27. *Ottawa Daily Citizen*,
    31 July 1868.
28. Gibson, *Traditional Gaelic Bagpiping*, p. 213.
29. *London Scotsman*,
    18 December 1869; *McAlpine's Halifax City Directory*, 1871-2,
    p. 480, 1872-3, p. 543.
30. Macdonald, *North British Society*,
    p. 430.
31. e.g. *Inverness Courier*,
    17 February 1870; *London Scotsman*, 19 February 1870;
    Paisley Herald, 26 February 1870.
32. Huxley, *House of Smith Elder*,
    p. 149.
33. Lawson, *Townships of Dartmouth*,
    pp. 114-122; Chapman,
    pp. 99-118.
34. *ILN*, 30 September 1871.
35. Lawson, pp. 82-85; Chapman,
    pp. 82, 434-435.
36. Chapman, p. 352.
37. Hopkins, *Map of the Town of Dartmouth*, 1878, Nova Scotia Archives V7 239.
38. Payzant, pp. 136-8; Chapman,
    pp. 194-8.
39. Akins, *History of Halifax City*,
    p. 83.
40. Hopkins, *City Atlas of Halifax*,
    Plate A, Nova Scotia Archives O/S G 1129 H3 H67.
41. *McAlpine's Maritime Provinces Directory*, 1870-1, p. 215.

Notes

42. Lawson, pp. 53-4; Parker, *Historic Dartmouth*, pp. 39, 79.
43. Lawson, pp. 58-59.
44. *Stonehaven Journal*, 24 April 1873.
45. Town of Dartmouth Council Minutes, 1873-1882, pp. 148, 159, Halifax Municipal Archives, 101-1A.
46. Dartmouth Property Assessment Rolls, Halifax Municipal Archives.
47. Donald's gravestone.
48. *Proceedings and Transactions of the Nova Scotian Institute of Natural Science*, 1877, v.4(3), p. 234
49. *Oban Times*, 7 December 1878.
50. Payzant, pp. 151-2.
51. *Celtic Magazine*, 1880, v. 5, pp. 39-40.
52. *Halifax New Era*, reprinted *Aberdeen Journal*, 28 October 1882; *JOGJ*, 2 November 1882.
53. *Celtic Magazine*, 1879-1880, v. 5, pp. 23-24, 109-112.
54. *Celtic Magazine*, 1882, v. 7, p. 561.

Chapter 28

1. Hibbs, *Sermon for the Times*, pp. 7-8.
2. MacLeod, *Gloomy Memories*, pp. 161, 182, 196-8.
3. *Northern Ensign*, 4 January 1866.
4. Maclauchlan & Wilson, *History of the Scottish Highlands*, p. 57.
5. Blackie, *Scottish Highlanders*, pp. 67-70.
6. *Aberdeen Free Press*, 17 December 1880.
7. *Celtic Magazine*, 1882, v. 7, pp. 370, 411.
8. Mackenzie, *History of the Highland Clearances*, pp. 156, 219-230, 236-248, 265-284.
9. *Christian Leader*, in *Celtic Magazine*, 1886, v. 11, p. 313.
10. Macdonald, *Emigration of Highland Crofters*, pp. 14-15.
11. Prebble, *Highland Clearances*, p. 240
12. Bruce & Scott, *Scottish Postbag*, pp. 166-7.
13. Magnusson, *Quarriers Story*, p. 21.
14. Craig, *Crofters' Trail*, p. 28, 309-13.
15. Craig & Paterson, *Glens of Silence*, pp. 71-3, 137.
16. Campey, *Unstoppable Force*, pp. 126, 153, 156-8.
17. Rixson, *Knoydart*, p. 133.
18. Hook, *History of Dornoch*, p. 67.
19. Wallace, *John Stuart Blackie*, pp. 267, 292; Gibson, *Traditional Gaelic Bagpiping*, p. 213.
20. Bruce, 'What I propose doing with the people? I say – nothing.'
21. Fenyő, *Contempt, Sympathy and Romance*, pp. 4, 145-6, 150, 180.
22. Devine, *Great Highland Famine*, pp. 130, 249, 257, 260-1, 263.
23. Devine, *Clanship to Crofters' War*, pp. 57, 169; Devine, *Scottish Clearances*, pp. 6, 359.
24. Hunter, *Making of the Crofting Community*, p. 79.
25. Hunter, *Insurrection*, pp. 219-220.
26. Richards, *Leviathan of Wealth*, p. 276.
27. Richards, *Highland Clearances*, pp. 277-8, 344-5.
28. Richards, *Debating the Highland Clearances*, pp. 17, 186, 194-7.
29. Frank, *Bowdon Romance*, p. 62.
30. Hunter, *Pistol in Greenyards*, pp. 93-5, 103, 128-130, 179; Lingard, *Greenyards*, pp. 128-9, 166; King, *Greenyards Legacy*, p. 356.

Illustration sources and credits

Photographs are by the author unless otherwise stated.

Frontispiece. Depping, *L'Angleterre*.
p. 16. Sewell, *George Dempster*.
p. 17. From *The Estate of Skibo* sale prospectus DNHHL 2011_037_02. Reproduced with the permission of Historylinks, Dornoch.
p. 18. Loch, *Account*.
p. 23. DNHHL 2003_038_019. Reproduced with the permission of Historylinks, Dornoch.
p. 24, left. Cadell & Davies, *British Gallery*; based on a painting by William Owen.
p. 24, right. 1807 mezzotint by Charles Turner; enhanced from a painting by Thomas Phillips.
p. 41. Part of OS Town Plan of Glasgow, sheet no. VI.11.7. Reproduced with the permission of the National Library of Scotland.
p. 43. DNHHL 2004_325. Reproduced with the permission of Historylinks, Dornoch.
p. 48. NRS SC9/7/121/1843E. Reproduced with the permission of the National Records of Scotland.
p. 50. Billings, *Baronial and Ecclesiastical Antiquities*.
p. 54. NRS SC9/48/4. Reproduced with the permission of the National Records of Scotland.
p. 58. Beattie, *Scotland Illustrated*.
p. 66. *ILN*, 3 June 1843.
p. 75. *National Gazetteer*, Virtue and Co., 1868.
p. 76. MacRae, *Life of Gustavus Aird*.
p. 81. Blackie, *Imperial Gazetteer*.
p. 86. Pagan & Stoddart, *Relics of Ancient Architecture*.
p. 89. Knight, *Land we Live in*.
p. 90. Anon, *Views of Glasgow*.
p. 91, top. Simpson, *Glasgow in the "Forties"*.
p. 91, bottom. By John Rapkin, in Montgomery, *Illustrated Atlas*. Reproduced with permission from the Carson Clark Gallery, Edinburgh.
p. 93, top. Simpson, *Glasgow in the "Forties"*.
p. 93, bottom. *ILN*, 18 August 1849.
p. 94. Pagan & Stoddart, *Relics of Ancient Architecture*.
p. 95. *ILN*, 14 July 1855.
p. 96. Simpson, *Glasgow in the "Forties"*.

Illustration sources and credits

p. 98. Anon, *One Hundred Glasgow Men*.
p. 109, left. Anon, *One Hundred Glasgow Men*.
p. 109, right. Anon, *The Drawing-room Portrait Gallery*.
p. 110. NRS CS230/T/7/9. Reproduced with the permission of the National Records of Scotland.
p. 122. Douglas, *Modern Athenians*.
p. 125. *ILN*, 15 January 1853.
p. 159. *ILN*, 15 January 1853.
p. 189, top. By William Johnson; published by John Thomson, Edinburgh, 1830.
p. 200. NLS Special Collections 3.2643(5). Reproduced with the permission of the National Library of Scotland.
p. 207. Part of OS 6-inch map LI. Reproduced with the permission of the National Library of Scotland.
p. 208. Part of OS 6-inch map LI. Reproduced with the permission of the National Library of Scotland.
p. 214. NLS Special Collections 3.2643(5). Reproduced with the permission of the National Library of Scotland.
p. 227. Part of OS 6-inch map XXVI. Reproduced with the permission of the National Library of Scotland.
p. 239. Alastair McIntyre, reproduced with permission.
p. 251. *The Ladies' Repository*, 1858, v. 18.
p. 273. *Illustrated News of the World*, 28 August 1858.
p. 275. *ILN*, 3 December 1859.
p. 289. *ILN*, 30 September 1871.
p. 290. *Gleason's Pictorial Drawing-Room Companion*, 1853.
p. 292. *ILN*, 14 December 1878.

Plates
pl. 1, top. Loch, *Account*.
pl. 1, bottom. Part of OS 25-inch map CXII.8. Reproduced with the permission of the National Library of Scotland.
pl. 2, top. Daniell, *Voyage*. NLS Special Collections MS.6140(v). Reproduced with the permission of the National Library of Scotland.
pl. 2, bottom. Beattie, *Scotland Illustrated*.
pl. 3, top. Sandra Ross.
pl. 4, bottom. NRS SC9/7/123/1844. Reproduced with the permission of the National Records of Scotland.
pl. 5, bottom right. Drysdale, *Old Faces*.
pl. 6, bottom. By Henry G. Duguid, published by J. Menzies, Edinburgh, 1854.
pl. 7, top left. Douglas, *Modern Athenians*.
pl. 7, bottom. NRS SC9/7/122/1844. Reproduced with the permission of the National Records of Scotland.
pl. 8, top. Brown, *Annals of the Disruption*.
pl. 10, top. Published by John Bartholomew & Co., Edinburgh, 1915.
pl. 14, bottom left. Pam Keown, reproduced with permission.
pl. 14, bottom right. Nolan, *History of the War against Russia*.
pl. 15, top. Cram's atlas, 1887.
pl. 15, bottom. Anon, *National Portrait Gallery*.
pl. 16, top. *The Pictorial World*, 14 December 1878.
pl. 16, bottom. Joyce Wylie, reproduced with permission.

Appendix 1
The addresses of Donald Ross from the Glasgow Post Office directories

Plus dates from newspaper articles and the 1851 census.
FD= First known date
LD= Last known date
OD= Only known date

1847-8

Agent for the Glasgow Association in aid of the Poor, and agent for the National Friendly Society, 16 Buchanan Street; house 51 Adelphi Street.
FD 16 Buchanan Street, *Greenock Advertiser*, 28 August 1846.

1848-9

Agent for the Glasgow Association in aid of the Poor, and agent for the National Friendly Society, 16 Buchanan Street; house 51 Adelphi Street.
LD 16 Buchanan Street, *Glasgow Courier*, 23 March 1848.
Late entry:
Writer and agent for the National Friendly Society, 29 Brunswick Place.
FD 29 Brunswick Place, 14 June 1848 in *NBDM*, 15 June.

1849-50

Writer, 29 Brunswick Place.
LD 29 Brunswick Place, 11 January 1850 in *Inverness Advertiser*, 22 January.

1850-1

Writer, 31 North Frederick Street, house, Cathcart.
OD 31 North Frederick Street, 28 June 1850 in *Inverness Advertiser*, 2 July.

1851-2

Writer, 143 London Street.
FD 143 London Street, 31 March 1851 census
LD 143 London Street, 30 May 1851 in *The Scotsman*, 4 June.
Late entry:

The addresses of Donald Ross

Writer, 20 St Enoch Square.
FD 20 St Enoch Square, 15 July 1851 in *NBDM*, 17 July.

1852-3

Writer, and agent for Hebridean Benevolent and Industrial Society, 20 St Enoch Square.

1853-4

Writer, 20 St Enoch Square, house, Naples Place, Govan.
Writer, Napier's Place, Govan.

1854-5

Writer, 20 St Enoch Square; house, Cathcart.
Writer, Napier's Place, Govan.

1855-6

Writer, 20 St Enoch Square; house, Cathcart.
LD 20 St Enoch Square, 5 March 1856 in *Morning Chronicle*, 8 March.

1856-7

Writer, 28 St Enoch Square; house, Cathcart.
OD 28 St Enoch Square, *Greenock Advertiser*, 23 May 1856.

1857-8

Writer, secretary to the Glasgow Celtic Society, 1, Oswald Street; house, Cathcart.
FD 1 Oswald Street, 25 June 1856 in *Stirling Observer*, 3 July.
LD 1 Oswald Street, 12 August 1857 in *NBDM*, 14 August.

1858-9

Writer, secretary to the Glasgow Celtic Society, 1, Oswald Street; house, Cathcart.

1859-60

Writer, secretary to the Glasgow Celtic Society, 1, Oswald Street; house, Cathcart.

1860-1

Writer, secretary to the Glasgow Celtic Society, 1, Oswald Street; house, Cathcart.

Appendix 2
The published pamphlets of Donald Ross

See abbreviation list for repositories.
1. *Pictures of Pauperism. The Condition of the Poor described by themselves, in fifty genuine letters, addressed by paupers to the agent of the Glasgow Association in Aid of the Poor; with some preliminary observations on the present working of the Scottish Poor Law* (Glasgow: George Gallie, 1847) [BL, MLG]
2. *Letters from the Mountains: or, the present condition and future prospects of the people in the Highlands of Scotland* (Glasgow: George Troup, 1850) [EUL]
3. *Famine in the Hebrides, or the present condition of the Highlanders in the Western Islands of Scotland* (Glasgow: 1851)
[not found; referred to in *The West of England Conservative*, 24 December 1851]
4. *A Voice from the Hebrides* (Glasgow: 1851)
[not found; referred to in the *Oxford Journal*, 6 December 1851; *The Oxford University, City, and County Herald*, 6 December and *Morning Advertiser*, 25 December]
5. *The Scottish Highlanders: their Present Sufferings and Future Prospects: together with observations on the state of the poor – the capabilities of the soil, and the general natural resources of the Highlands* (Glasgow: Hebridean Benevolent and Industrial Society, 1852)
[NLS]
6. *The Skye Girls in England; or the True History of their Case: with Letters regarding their Treatment at Marple. Being a Complete Refutation of certain Calumnious Statements made in a Glasgow Newspaper* (Glasgow: Archibald Sinclair, 1852)
[not found; referred to in *The Glasgow Sentinel*, 8 January 1853 and Forbes, *Weeping in the Isles*]
7. Scotus, *The Poor Man's Guide to Parochial Relief: Containing instructions to poor persons how to apply for and enforce Parochial Relief* (Glasgow: Archibald Sinclair, 1853)
[not found; referred to in the *Glasgow Free Press*, 23 April 1853 and *Real Scottish Grievances*]
8. *Am Ministear air "An lair mhaide." Focal no dha do mhuinntir an eilein sgiathanaich, mu dhfighinn an leabhair bhreugaich agus chfalgaich sin a chuireadh a mach le Iain Forbeis, Minister Sgire Shleit, fo ainm "Gal 's na h-eileinean;" maille ri comhadh eadar triuir ghaidheal, mu'n Mhinistear agus m'a ghramar dubailt* (Glasgow: Archibald Sinclair, 1853)

328

The published pamphlets of Donald Ross

[NLS]
9. *Humanity Defended, and Calumny Refuted* (Glasgow: Archibald Sinclair, 1853)
[not found; English version of the above, referred to in the preface of *Am Ministear*; *Fife Herald*, 29 September 1853; *Scottish Guardian*, 4 October; *The Witness*, 8 October and *Inverness Courier*, 5 January 1854]
10. *The Glengarry Evictions; or, Scenes at Knoydart, in Inverness-shire* (Glasgow: W.G. Blackie & Co., 1853)
[AUL, BL, CUL, EUL, FWL, IRL, NAK, NLS, OUL]
11. *Highland Clearances. Sufferings of the Outcasts in Knoydart and in Skye: with a list of contributions received for their relief* (Glasgow: 1853)
[AUL, NAK]
12. *Real Scottish Grievances: or, Injustice to the Scottish Highlanders Exposed: being Another Chapter on Highland Evictions; together with an account of Aunty Kate's Cabin* (Glasgow: George Gallie, 1854)
[IRL, MLG, NLS]
13. *The Russians of Ross-shire, or Massacre of the Rosses in Strathcarron, Ross-shire; by policemen, when serving the tenants in Strathcarron with summonses of removal in March last. Also a warning against the Clearing of the Glens* 2nd Edition (Glasgow: George Gallie, 1854)
[1st Edition not found; 2nd Edition GUL, MLG, NLS, SAUL, V&AL; 3rd Edition (1886) AUL, EUL, GUL, NLS, SMO]
14. *The cry of the hungry* (Glasgow: 1854)
[AUL, title page missing]
15. *A Plea for the Famishing: being a record of sufferings in the West Highlands of Scotland. With a list of contributions for relief of the sufferers* (Glasgow: W. G. Blackie & Co., 1855)
[AUL]
16. *Destitution in the West Highlands. With list of contributions received during the month of April, 1855; and note of seed, corn, and potatoes, supplied to the crofters* (Glasgow: W. G. Blackie & Co., 1855)
[AUL]
17. *Who will help? Being an appeal for Boats and Nets, to enable poor cottars in the West Highlands to help themselves by fishing. With a prospectus of the Highland Association* (Glasgow: W. G. Blackie & Co., 1855)
[AUL]
18. *The West Highlands. Report on the Relief of Destitution in the West Highlands, in 1855. With letters illustrative of the great good done by providing the poor crofters, last year, with seed corn and potatoes. Also, abstract of receipts and disbursements* (Glasgow: W. G. Blackie & Co., 1856)
[AUL]
19. *Cent per cent: or, Plain Reasons for the Judicious Exercise of Christian Charity towards deserving and needy objects* (Glasgow: William MacKenzie, 1856)
[AUL]
20. *Letters on the Depopulation of the Highlands* (1856)
[MLG]
21. *Letters in defence of the Highlands and Highlanders, or, the last kick at Scotland; and, Dr. Lees' charges against the Highlanders refuted* (Glasgow: William Mackenzie, 1857)
[MLG]

Appendix 3

The addresses of Donald Ross from the Nova Scotia directories

HNS = Hutchinson's Nova Scotia Directory
MHC = McAlpine's Halifax City Directory
MMP = McAlpine's Maritime Provinces Directory
MNS = McAlpine's Nova Scotia Directory

HNS 1864-5

Halifax: Ross Donald, bookkeeper, Bauld, Gibson & Co., h Dartmouth.

HNS 1866-7

Halifax: Ross Donald, bookkeeper, Water, h Dartmouth.

MNS 1868-9

Halifax: Ross Donald, bookkeeper, h Craig Ross cottage, Dartmouth.
Dartmouth: Ross Donald, bookkeeper, h Blackrock road.

MHC 1869-70

Dartmouth: Ross Donald, bookkeeper, h Craig Rose Cottage, Black Rock.

MMP 1870-1

Halifax: Ross Donald, bookkeeper, h Dartmouth
Dartmouth: Ross D. bookkeeper, h Craig Rose cottage, Black rock

MHC 1871-2

Halifax: Ross Donald, bookkeeper Bauld, Gibson & Co, h Dartmouth.
Dartmouth: Ross Donald, bookkeeper, h Craig Rose Cottage, Shore rd.
Highland Society of Nova Scotia: Office-bearers for the year 1871; President, Ronald [sic] Ross, Ross Cottage, Dartmouth.

The addresses of Donald Ross from the Nova Scotia directories

MHC 1872-3

Halifax: Ross Donald, grocers retail, liquors wholesale and retail, 11 Upper Water, h Dartmouth.
Dartmouth: Ross Donald, grocer, Upper Water, Hx, h Black Rock road.
Highland Society of Nova Scotia: Office-bearers for the year 1871; President, Donald Ross, Dartmouth.

MHC 1873-4

Halifax: Ross Donald, grocers retail, liquors wholesale and retail, 9 Upper Water, h Dartmouth.

MHC 1874-5

Halifax: Ross Donald, grocers retail, liquors wholesale and retail, 9 Upper Water, h Dartmouth.
Dartmouth: Ross Donald, grocer and liquor, (city), h Black Rock road.

MHC 1875-6

Dartmouth: Ross Donald, h Upper Water.

MHC 1876-7

Dartmouth: Ross Donald, h Craig Ross Cottage, Water.

MHC 1877-8

Dartmouth: Ross Donald, Craig-Ross cottage, h Common.

MHC 1878-9

Dartmouth: Ross Don. Craig Ross cottage, h Com'n.

MHC 1879-80

Dartmouth: Ross Donald, h Water.

MHC 1880-1

Dartmouth: Ross Donald, h Water.

MHC 1882-3

Dartmouth: Ross Donald, book agent, h Water.

Bibliography

Adam, R. J., *Papers on Sutherland Estate Management 1802-1816* Vol. 1. Scottish History Society, Ser. 4, Vol. 8 (Edinburgh: T. & A. Constable Limited, Edinburgh, 1972)

Akins, Thomas B., History of Halifax City. *Collections of the Nova Scotia Historical Society*, 1895, Vol. 8, 1-272.

Alison, Archibald, *The Principles of Population, and their connection with Human Happiness* 2 Vols (Edinburgh: William Blackwood and Sons, 1840)

Alison, Archibald, *Some Account of my Life and Writings, an Autobiography* 2 Vols (Edinburgh: William Blackwood and Sons, 1883)

Alison, William Pulteney, *Observations on the Management of the Poor in Scotland, and its effects on the health of the great towns* (Edinburgh: William Blackwood & Sons, 1840)

Alison, William Pulteney, Observations on the Generation of Fever. In: *Reports on the Sanitary Condition of the Labouring Population of Scotland, in consequence of an inquiry directed to be made by the Poor Law Commissioners* (London: Clowes & Sons, 1842)

Alison, William Pulteney, *Observations on the Epidemic Fever of MCCCCXLIII in Scotland, and its connection with the destitute condition of the poor* (Edinburgh: William Blackwood & Sons, 1844)

Allan, Hector, Parish of Kincardine, 1840. In: *The Statistical Account of Inverness-shire. By the ministers of the respective parishes, under the superintendence of a committee of the society for the benefit of the sons and daughters of the clergy* (Edinburgh: William Blackwood and Sons, 1842)

Anon, Illustrative memoir of the most noble, Elizabeth, Marchioness of Stafford, Countess of Sutherland, and Baroness of Strathnaver. *La Belle Assemblée or Court and Fashionable Magazine*, 1831, Vol. 14 (No. 74).

Anon, *The Scottish Temperance League Register and Abstainer's Almanac for 1851* (Glasgow: League Office, 1851)

Anon, *The Drawing-room Portrait Gallery of Eminent Personages* Second Series (London Joint Stock Newspaper Company Limited, 1859)

Anon, *Views of Glasgow, Clyde and Vicinity* (Edinburgh: Banks & Co., c.1870)

Anon, *The National Portrait Gallery*, 4th Series (London: Cassell, Petter & Galpin, c.1878)

Anon, *Memoirs and Portraits of One Hundred Glasgow Men who have died during the last thirty years, and in their lives did much to make the city what it now is* Vol. 1 (Glasgow: James Maclehose & Sons, 1886)

Bibliography

Anon, *Town Jail Craft Centre, A Brief History, Cathedral Square, Dornoch, Sutherland, Scotland* (Torquay: Bendles, c.1980)

Anon, *Balnagown, ancestral home of the Clan Ross, a Scottish Castle through five centuries* (London: Brompton Press, 1997)

Anon, *Stirling's Talking Stones* (Stirling Council Libraries, 2002)

Baillie, John (ed.), *Proceedings of the General Assembly of the Free Church of Scotland; with a sketch of the Proceedings of the Residuary Assembly* (Edinburgh: John Johnstone, 1843)

Baird, Charles R., Report on the Legal Provisions available in Glasgow for the Removal of Nuisances. In: *Reports on the Sanitary Condition of the Labouring Population of Scotland, in consequence of an inquiry directed to be made by the Poor Law Commissioners* (London: Clowes & Sons, 1842)

Baird, Charles R., On the general and Sanitary Condition of the Working Classes and the poor in the City of Glasgow. In: *Reports on the Sanitary Condition of the Labouring Population of Scotland, in consequence of an inquiry directed to be made by the Poor Law Commissioners* (London: Clowes & Sons, 1842)

Beattie, W., *Scotland Illustrated in a series of views taken expressly for this work by Messrs. T. Allom, W. H. Bartlett and H. M'Culloch* Vol. 2 (London: George Virtue, 1838)

Beechey, F.W., *Report of an Investigation into the Loss of the "Annie Jane," made by direction of the board of trade* (London: Her Majesty's Stationery Office, 1854)

Beith, Alexander, Parish of Glenelg, 1836. In: *The Statistical Account of Inverness-shire. By the ministers of the respective parishes, under the superintendence of a committee of the society for the benefit of the sons and daughters of the clergy* (Edinburgh: William Blackwood & Sons, 1842)

Beith, Alexander, Cupples, G. & Leitch, A., Parish of Stirling, 1841. In: *The new Statistical Account of Scotland. By the ministers of the respective parishes, under the superintendence of a committee of the society for the benefit of the sons and daughters of the clergy*, Vol. 8, Dunbarton – Stirling – Clackmannan (Edinburgh & London: William Blackwood & Sons, 1845).

Bell, Gilbert T., *A Prospect of Sutherland* (Edinburgh: Birlinn Ltd, 1995)

Bentinck, Charles D., *Dornoch Cathedral and Parish* (Inverness: Northern Counties Publishing Company, 1926)

Bethune, John, Parish of Dornoch. In: Sinclair, John (ed.) *The [old] Statistical Account of Scotland. Drawn up from the communications of the ministers of the different parishes*, Vol. 8 (William Creech, 1793)

Billings, Robert William, *The Baronial and Ecclesiastical Antiquities of Scotland* Vol. 2 (Edinburgh: William Blackwood & Sons, 1852)

Black, Adam & Black, Charles, *Black's Economical Guide through Glasgow; arranged in three walks* 2nd Edition (Edinburgh: Adam & Charles Black, 1843)

Blackie, John Stuart, *The Gaelic Language, its Classical Affinities and Distinctive Character, A Lecture Delivered in the University of Edinburgh* (Edinburgh: Edmonston & Douglas, 1864)

Blackie, John Stuart, *Lays of the Highlands and Islands* (London: Strahan & Co., 1872)

Blackie, John Stuart, *The Language and Literature of the Scottish Highlands* (Edinburgh: Edmonston & Douglas, 1876)

Blackie, John Stuart, *Altavona, Fact and Fiction from my Life in the Highlands* (Edinburgh: David Douglas, 1882)

Blackie, John Stuart, *The Scottish Highlanders and the Land Laws, an historico-economical enquiry* (London: Chapman & Hall, 1885)

Blackie, W. G., *The Imperial Gazetteer; a general Dictionary of Geography, Physical, Political, Statistical, and Descriptive* Vol. 2 (Glasgow: Blackie & Son, 1856)

Brand, David, Shaw-Stewart, M. H., Sutherland, A., Forsyth, J. N. M., Gordon, G., M'Callum, J. M., Macleod, J. & Munro, H., *Report of the Royal Commission (Highlands and Islands, 1892)* (Edinburgh: Her Majesty's Stationary Office, 1895)

Brander, Michael, *The Original Scotch, a History of Scotch Whisky from the earliest days* (London: Hutchison & Co Ltd, 1974)

Brotchie, T. C. F., *The History of Govan* 2nd Edition (The Old Govan Club, 1938)

Brown, Alexander, *Midnight Scenes and Social Photographs: Sketches of life in the streets, wynds, and dens of the City* (Glasgow: Thomas Murray & Son, 1858)

Brown, Thomas, *Annals of the Disruption; with extracts from the narratives of ministers who left the Scottish Establishment in 1843* New Edition (Edinburgh: MacNiven & Wallace, 1892)

Bruce, George & Scott, Paul H., *A Scottish Postbag, Eight centuries of Scottish letters* (Edinburgh: W & R Chambers Ltd, 1986)

Bruce, Neil M., 'What I propose doing with the people? I say – nothing'; In the news: The 'richest commoner' and his Barra tenants. *History Scotland*, 2018, 18(5), 16-21.

Burke, J., *The Portrait Gallery of distinguished females, including Beauties of the Courts of George IV. and William IV.* Vol. 1 (London: Edward Bull, 1833)

Cadell, T. & Davies, T., *The British Gallery of Contemporary Portraits, being a series of engravings of the most eminent persons now living or lately deceased, in Great Britain and Ireland: from drawings accurately made from life or from the most approved original pictures. Accompanied by short biographical notices* Vol. 1 (London: T. Cadell, London, 1822)

Cairns, John W. & MacQueen, Hector L., *Learning and the Law, a short History of Edinburgh Law School* (University of Edinburgh, 2013)

Calder, William, *The Estate and Castle of Skibo* (Edinburgh: Albyn Press, 1949)

Campbell, William, et al., *Second Annual Report by the Directors of the Glasgow Association in Aid of the Poor, now the Association for the Protection of the Poor* (Glasgow: James Hedderwick & Son, 1847)

Campbell, William, et al., *First Annual Report of the Glasgow Celtic Society, submitted to the members at the Annual General Meeting held on the 20th January, 1858* (Glasgow: Buckie & Co., 1858)

Campbell, William D., *The Raid of Albyn, A Historic Poem* (Glasgow, Edinburgh & London: William Mackenzie, 1854)

Campey, Lucille H., *After the Hector, the Scottish Pioneers of Nova Scotia and Cape Breton 1773-1852* 2nd Edition (Toronto: Natural Heritage Books, 2007)

Campey, Lucille, H., *An Unstoppable Force, The Scottish Exodus to Canada* (Edinburgh: Birlinn Limited, 2008)

Chalmers, A.K. (ed.), *Public Health Administration in Glasgow. A memorial volume of the writings of James Burn Russell* (Glasgow: James Maclehose and Sons, 1905)

Chapman, Harry, *In the Wake of the Alderney* (Dartmouth Historical Association, 2000)

Charnley, Bob, *The Western Isles, A Postcard Tour, 1. Barra to North Uist* (Isle of Skye: Maclean Press, 1992)

Checkland, Olive, *Philanthropy in Victorian Scotland: Social Welfare and the Voluntary Principle* (Edinburgh: John Donald Publishers Ltd, 1980)

Clark, Thomas, Crawford, T. J., Gilchrist, J., Bonar, A., Paul, J., Veitch, A. M., Stevenson, R. H., Glover, W., Robertson, W., Lee, R., Arnot, D., M'Letchie, J., Frazer, R. W., Bennie, A., Grant, J., Clark, J., Muir, W., Smith, G., Steve, W., Brunton, A., Hunter, J., Nisbet, R., City of Edinburgh. *The new Statistical Account*

Bibliography

of Scotland. By the ministers of the respective parishes, under the superintendence of a committee of the society for the benefit of the sons and daughters of the clergy, Vol. 1 (Edinburgh & London, William Blackwood & Sons, 1845).

Connor, R. D. & Simpson, A. D. C. In: Morrison-Low, A. D. (ed.), *Weights and Measures in Scotland: a European perspective* (Edinburgh: National Museums of Scotland, 2004)

Cornall, James, *Halifax, South End* (Charleston: Arcadia Publishing, 1998)

Cowper, A. S. & Ross, I., *Pre-1855 Tombstone Inscriptions in Sutherland Burial Grounds* (Scottish Genealogy Society, 1999 reprint)

Craig, David, *On the Crofters' Trail, In search of the Clearance Highlanders* (London: Jonathan Cape, 1990)

Craig, David & Paterson, David, *The Glens of Silence, Landscapes of the Highland Clearances* (Edinburgh: Birlinn Ltd, 2004)

Cullen, W. Douglas, *Parliament House, a short history and guide*. (Scottish Courts Administration, 1992)

Cunnison, J. & Gilfillan, J.B.S. (eds), *The City of Glasgow. The Third Statistical Account of Scotland* (Glasgow: William Collins Sons & Co. Ltd., 1958)

Dalglish, Chris & Driscoll, Stephen. T., *Historic Govan, Archaeology and Development* (York & Edinburgh: Council for British Archaeology and Historic Scotland, 2009)

Dalrymple, J.H., Murray, W. & Pringle, J.W., *Reports upon the boundaries of the several cities, burghs, and towns, in Scotland, in respect to the election of members to serve in Parliament* 1832.

Daniell, William, *A Voyage Round Great Britain, undertaken in the summer of the year 1813, and commencing from the Land's-End, Cornwall. With a series of views, Illustrative of the Character and Prominent Features of the Coast* Vol. 5 (London: Longman, Hurst, Rees, Orme and Brown, 1821)

Defoe, Daniel, *Giving Alms no Charity, And Employing the Poor. A Grievance to the Nation, Being an Essay Upon this Great Question* (London, 1704)

Dempster, George, Plan for improving the Estates of Skibo and Pulrossie. In: Rainy, George, Parish of Criech. In: Sinclair, John (ed.) *The* [old] *Statistical Account of Scotland. Drawn up from the communications of the ministers of the different parishes*, Vol. 8 (Edinburgh: William Creech, 1793)

Dempster, George, Essay on the Sheep-Farming of the Highlands of Scotland. *Farmers' Magazine*, 1810, Vol. 11, pp. 3-6.

Dempster, George Soper, Report relative to Plantations made on the Estates of Skibo, in the County of Sutherland. *Prize-essays and Transactions of the Highland and Agricultural Society of Scotland*, 1837, Ser. 2, Vol. 5.

Dempster, Joanna Hamilton, *George Dempster (of Skibo) In Memoriam* (Privately printed, 1889)

Depping, G.-B., *L'Angleterre, ou Description Historique et Topographique du Royaume Uni de la Grande-Bretagne* Vol. 2, *L'Écosse* (Paris: Étienne Ledoux, 1824)

Devine, Thomas Martin, *Clanship to Crofter's War; the social transformation of the Scottish Highlands* (Manchester University Press, 1994)

Devine, Thomas Martin, *The Great Highland Famine; hunger, emigration and the Scottish Highlands in the Nineteenth Century* (Edinburgh: John Donald Publishers Ltd, 1996 reprint)

Devine, Thomas Martin, *Clearance and Improvement; land, power and people in Scotland 1700-1900*. (Edinburgh: John Donald, 2006)

Devine, Thomas Martin (ed.), *Recovering Scotland's Slavery Past, the Caribbean Connection* (Edinburgh University Press Ltd, 2015)

Devine, Thomas Martin, *The Scottish Clearances, A History of the Dispossessed 1600 – 1900* (Penguin Books, 2019 reprint)

Douglas, W.S., *Modern Athenians, a series of original portraits of memorable Citizens of Edinburgh drawn and etched by Benjamin W. Crombie, miniature painter 1837 to 1847* (Edinburgh: Adam & Charles Black, 1882)

Drysdale, William, *Old Faces, Old Places, and Old Stories of Stirling* (Stirling: Eneas Mackay, 1898)

Edgar, Alwyn, *The Sutherland Clearances* (Theory and Practice, 2022)

Edwards, Joseph Plimsoll, The Militia of Nova Scotia, 1749-1867. *Collections of the Nova Scotia Historical Society*, 1913, Vol. 17, 63-110.

Egan, Thomas J., *History of the Halifax Volunteer Battalion and Volunteer Companies, 1859-1887* (Halifax: A. & W. Mackinlay, Publishers, 1888)

Ellice, Edward, *Poor Law (Scotland). Return, in reference to the Record of Applications to the Board of Supervision for Relief of the Poor in Scotland* (London: House of Commons, 1849)

Ellice, Edward, *The state of the Highlands in 1854* (Inverness: Courier Office, 1855)

Ellice, Edward C., *Place-names in Glengarry and Glenquoich and their origin* (London: Swan Sonnenschein & Co. Ltd, 1898)

Evans, John, *The gentleman usher, the life and times of George Dempster (1732-1818), member of Parliament and Laird of Dunnichen and Skibo* (Barnsley: Pen & Sword Military, 2005)

Fairbairn, Thomas, *Relics of Ancient Architecture and other Picturesque Scenes in Glasgow* (Glasgow: Miller & Buchanan, 1851)

Fenyő, Krisztina, *Contempt, Sympathy and Romance, lowland perceptions of the Highlands and the clearances during the famine years, 1845-1855* (East Linton: Tuckwell Press, 2000)

Fergusson, J., *Letters of George Dempster to Sir Adam Fergusson 1756-1813 with some accounts of his life* (London: MacMillan and Co., Limited, 1934)

Forbes, John, *A Double Grammar, of English and Gaelic, in which the principles of both languages are clearly explained; containing the grammatical terms, definitions, and rules, with copious exercises for parsing and correction* (Edinburgh: W. Whyte & Co., 1843)

Forbes, John, *Weeping in the Isles, or the death of three of the girls who were taken from the Isle of Skye to England in May, 1852; and a consoling address to the bereaved parents, with a statement of remarkable facts respecting the adventure of the Skye girls to England, and their return home; to which are annexed remarks on the industrial character of the highland people* (Edinburgh: Alexander C. Moodie, 1853)

Forrest, W. H., Report on the Sanitary Condition of the Labouring Classes of the town of Stirling. In: *Reports on the Sanitary Condition of the Labouring Population of Scotland, in consequence of an inquiry directed to be made by the Poor Law Commissioners* (London: Clowes & Sons, 1842)

Fowler, John, *Mr Hill's Big Picture, the Day that Changed Scotland Forever: Captured on Canvas* (Edinburgh: Saint Andrew Press, 2006)

Frank, Alice, *A Bowdon Romance* (Cirencester: Memoirs Publishing, 2012)

Fraser, William, *The Sutherland Book* Vol. 1 (Edinburgh: William Fraser, 1892)

Fraser-Macintosh, Charles, *Letters of Two Centuries chiefly connected with Inverness and the Highlands, from 1616 to 1815* (Inverness: A. & W. Mackenzie, 1890)

Gauldie, Enid, *The Scottish Country Miller, 1700-1900, a History of Water-powered Meal Milling in Scotland* (Edinburgh: John Donald Publishers Ltd, 1999 reprint)

Geikie, A., *Scottish Reminiscences* (Glasgow: James Maclehose & Sons, 1904)

Gibb, Andrew, *Glasgow, the Making of a City* (London: Croom Helm Ltd, 1983)

Bibliography

Gibson, John G., *Traditional Gaelic Bagpiping, 1745-1945* (Edinburgh: NMS Publishing Limited, 1998)

Gibson, Rob, *The Highland Clearances Trail* (Edinburgh: Luath Press Limited, 2010 reprint)

Goudie, Gilbert, On the Horizontal Water Mills of Shetland. *Proceedings of the Society of Antiquaries of Scotland*, 1886, Vol. 20.

Grant, James, *Cassell's Old and New Edinburgh: Its History, its People, and its Places* Vol. 1 (London: Cassell, Peter, Galpin & Co., c.1881)

Grant, James, *Cassell's Old and New Edinburgh: Its History, its People, and its Places* Vol. 2 (London: Cassell, Peter, Galpin & Co., 1882)

Grant, Margaret Wilson, 1991. *Golspie's Story* (Golspie: Northern Times Limited, 1991 reprint)

Greenwood, Adrian, *Victoria's Scottish Lion, the life of Colin Campbell, Lord Clyde.* (Stroud: Spellmount, 2015)

Grimble, Ian, *The Trial of Patrick Sellar, The Tragedy of the Highland Evictions* (London: Routledge and Kegan Paul, 1962)

Groome, Francis H. (ed.), *Ordnance Gazetteer of Scotland: a survey of Scottish Topography, Statistical, Biographical, and Historical* Vol. 4 Hartree – Libberton (Edinburgh: Thomas C. Jack, 1885)

Guthrie, Thomas, *A Plea for Ragged Schools; or, Prevention Better than Cure* (Edinburgh: John Elder, 1847)

Hazlitt, W. Carew, *Faiths and Folklore, A Dictionary of national beliefs, superstitions and popular customs, past and current, with their classical and foreign analogues, described and illustrated* Vol. 2 (London: Reeves & Turner, 1905)

Hearle, Ann, *Hollins Mill, The heart of Marple for over one hundred years* 2nd Edition (Marple Local History Society, 2015)

Henderson, John, *General view of the Agriculture of the County of Sutherland; with observations on the means of its improvement* (London: Sherwood, Neely & Jones, 1815)

Hibbs, Richard, *A Sermon for the Times, Preached in the United Church of England and Ireland Chapel, St. Vincent Street, Edinburgh, on Ash-Wednesday, and re-delivered (by Request) on Sunday Evening, March 15, 1857* (London: Seeley, Jackson, & Halliday, 1857)

Hook, Michael, *A History of the Royal Burgh of Dornoch* (Dornoch: Historylinks Museum, 2005)

Hopkins, Henry W., *City Atlas of Halifax, Nova Scotia* (G.B. Vanderwoort, 1878)

Hunter, James, *The Making of the Crofting Community* (Edinburgh: John Donald Publishers Ltd, 1997 reprint)

Hunter, James, *A Dance Called America* (Edinburgh: Mainstream Publishing, 1998 reprint)

Hunter, James, *Set Adrift Upon the World; the Sutherland Clearances* (Edinburgh: Birlinn, 2015)

Hunter, James, *Insurrection, Scotland's Famine Winter* (Edinburgh: Birlinn, 2019)

Hunter, James & Maclean, Cailean, *Skye: The island* (Edinburgh: Mainstream Publishing, 1986)

Hunter, Mollie, *A Pistol in Greenyards* (London: Evans Brothers Limited, 1965)

Hutchinson, Roger, *Martyrs, Glendale and the revolution in Skye* (Edinburgh: Birlinn Limited, 2015)

Huxley, Leonard, *The House of Smith Elder* (London: Printed privately, 1923)

Johnston, Jim, A., *Strathnaver Trail, The Story of a North Highland Landscape* (Inverness: The Highland Council, 2003)

Kennedy, Angus, Parish of Dornoch, 1834. In: *The Statistical Account of Sutherlandshire. By the ministers of the respective parishes, under the superintendence of a* committee of the society for the benefit of the sons and daughters of the clergy (Edinburgh: William Blackwood and Sons, 1841)

Kennedy, John, *The Days of the Fathers in Ross-shire* 2nd Edition (Edinburgh: John MacLaren, 1861)

Kennedy, John, *The "Apostle of the North." The life and labours of the Rev. Dr. M'Donald* (London: T. Nelson and Sons, 1866)

King, Jane, *The Greenyards Legacy* (Marston Gate: Amazon.co.uk Ltd, 2014)

Knight, C., *The Land we Live in. A Pictorial and Literary Sketch-book of the British Empire* Vol. 2 (London: Charles Knight, 1848)

Lawson, Mary Jane, *History of the Townships of Dartmouth, Preston and Lawrencetown, Halifax County, N. S.* (Halifax: Morton & Co., 1893)

Lee, Sidney (ed.), *Dictionary of National Biography* Vol. 33, Leighton – Lluelyn (New York: MacMillan & Co., 1893)

Lee, Sidney (ed.), *Dictionary of National Biography* Vol. 53, Smith – Stanger (London: Smith, Elder & Co., 1898)

Lees, Frederic Richard, *An Argument Legal and Historical for the Legislative Prohibition of the Liquor Traffic* (London: William Tweedie, 1856)

Lees, Frederic Richard, *An Argument Legal and Historical concerning the Traffic in Strong Drink* 3rd Edition (London: William Tweedie, 1857)

Lees, Frederic Richard, *One Hundred Objections to a Maine Law; being a Sequel to the 'Argument' of the United Kingdom Alliance for the Legislative Prohibition of the Liquor Traffic* (London: W. Smith & Son, 1857)

Lees, J. Cameron, *A History of the County of Inverness (Mainland)* (Edinburgh: William Blackwood & Sons, 1897)

Lingard, Joan, *Greenyards* (London: Hamish Hamilton Ltd, 1981)

Loch, James, *An Account of the Improvements on the Estates of the Marquess of Stafford, in the counties of Stafford and Salop, and on the estate of Sutherland* (London: Longman, Hurst, Rees, Orme & Brown, 1820)

Loch, James, *Memoir of George Granville, late Duke of Sutherland, K.G.* (London: not published, 1834)

Lockhart Whiteford, J., Stirling Burgess List 1800 – 1902. *Central Scotland Family History Society, Occasional Monograph Series,* No. 3 (1992)

Logan, William, *The Moral Statistics of Glasgow* (Glasgow: Office of the Scottish Temperance League, 1849)

Lyall, Heather, F. C., *Vanishing Glasgow* (Aberdeen: AUL Publishing, 1991)

McCulloch, J. R., *A Descriptive and Statistical Account of the British Empire* 3rd Edition Vol. 1 (London: Longman, Brown, Green, and Longmans, 1847)

MacDonald, Hugh, *Rambles Round Glasgow, Descriptive, Historical, and Traditional* 2nd Edition (Glasgow: Thomas Murray & Son, 1856)

MacDonald, Ian R., *Glasgow's Gaelic Churches, Highland religion in an urban setting 1690-1995* (Edinburgh: Knox Press, 1995)

Macdonald, James, S., *Annals of the North British Society, Halifax, Nova Scotia, with Portraits and Biographical Notes, 1768-1903* 3rd Edition (McAlpine Publishing Company, Limited, 1905)

Macdonald, Rowland Hill, *The Emigration of Highland Crofters under the auspices of the Imperial Government, shown to be inevitable and obligatory in a letter to the Lord Advocate* (Edinburgh: William Blackwood & Sons, 1885)

MacFarlan, Duncan, Forbes, J., Lockhart, J., Buchanan, R., Lorimer, J.G., Smyth, J., Paterson, N., Henderson, J., Brown, T., Muir, J., Burns, J., Black, W. & Turner, A., City of Glasgow, and suburban parishes of Barony and Gorbals. *New Statistical Account of Scotland*, Vol. VI, Lanarkshire (1835)

Bibliography

McIan, Robert Ronald, *The Clans of the Scottish Highlands, illustrated by appropriate figures, displaying their dress, tartans, arms, armorial insignia, and social occupations* Vol. 1 (London: Ackermann & Co., 1845)

MacInnes, Ranald, *The National Wallace Monument* (Edinburgh: Someone Publishing Ltd, 2004)

Mackay, H. M., *Old Dornoch: Its Traditions and Legends* (Dingwall: North Star Office, 1920)

McKean, Charles, Walker, D. & Walker, F. A., *Central Glasgow, an Illustrated Architectural Guide* (Edinburgh: Mainstream Publications (Scotland) Ltd, 1989)

Mackenzie, Alexander, *The History of the Highland Clearances; containing a reprint of Donald MacLeod's "Gloomy Memories of the Highlands"; Isle of Skye in 1882; and a verbatim report of the trial of the Braes Crofters* (Inverness: A. & W. MacKenzie, 1883)

Mackinnon, John, Parish of Strath, 1840. In: *The Statistical Account of Inverness-shire. By the ministers of the respective parishes, under the superintendence of a committee of the society for the benefit of the sons and daughters of the clergy* (Edinburgh: William Blackwood & Sons, 1842)

Maclauchlan, Thomas & Wilson, John, *A History of the Scottish Highlands, Highland and Highland Regiments, with an account of the Gaelic Language, Literature, and Music, and an essay on Highland Scenery* Vol. 2 (Edinburgh & London: A. Fullarton & Co., 1875)

McLean, Margaret, *Borthwick Parish Church* (Gorebridge: J.E.T.S. Training Workshop, 2001)

MacLeod, Donald, *History of the Destitution in Sutherlandshire. Being a series of letters published in the Edinburgh Weekly Chronicle, in the years 1840 & 1841; with an Appendix, containing some additional information* (Edinburgh: Chronicle Office, 1841)

MacLeod, Donald, *Gloomy Memories in the Highlands of Scotland: versus Mrs. Harriet Beecher Stowe's Sunny Memories In (England) a Foreign Land: or a faithful picture of the Extirpation of the Celtic Race from the Highlands of Scotland* (Toronto: Thompson & Co., 1857)

McNeel-Caird, Alexander, *The Poor-Law Manual for Scotland: carefully revised, greatly enlarged, and brought down to the present time* 6th Edition (Edinburgh: Adam & Charles Black, 1851)

McNeill, John, *Report to the Board of Supervision by Sir John M'Neill, G.C.B., on the Western Highlands and Islands* (Edinburgh: Murray & Gibb, 1851)

McNeill, John, Report by Sir John M'Neill, G.C.B., Chairman of the Board of Supervision on the Administration of the Poor Law in the Parish of Glenelg. In: *Ninth Annual Report of the Board of Supervision*, Appendix A (Edinburgh: Murray & Gibb, 1854)

MacPherson, Alexander, Parish of Golspie, 1834. In: *The Statistical Account of Sutherlandshire. By the ministers of the respective parishes, under the superintendence of a committee of the society for the benefit of the sons and daughters of the clergy* (Edinburgh: William Blackwood, 1842)

McQueen, Andrew, *Echoes of old Clyde Paddle-wheels* (Glasgow: Gowans & Gray Ltd, 1924)

MacRae, Alexander, *The Life of Gustavus Aird, A.M., D.D., Creich* (Stirling: Eneas MacKay, 1908)

Magnusson, Anna, *The Quarriers Story, A History of Quarriers* 2nd Edition (Edinburgh: Birlinn Limited, 2006)

Meldrum, Edward, *Old Inverness in Pictures* (Edinburgh: Paul Harris Publishing, 1978)

Miller, Hugh, *Sutherland as it was and is; or, how a Country may be Ruined* (Edinburgh: John Johnstone, 1843)

Mitchell, J. F. & Mitchell, S., *East Stirlingshire monumental inscriptions pre-1855* (Edinburgh: Scottish Genealogy Society, 1972)

Montgomery, M.R., *The Illustrated Atlas, and Modern History of the World: geographical, political, commercial, and statistical* Part 43 (London: John Tallis & Company, 1851)

Moore, John N., *The Maps of Glasgow* (Glasgow University Library, 1996)

Mulock, Thomas, *The Western Highlands and Island of Scotland, socially considered, with reference to Proprietors and People: being a series of contributions to the periodical press* (Edinburgh: John Menzies, 1850)

Napier, Francis, B., Mackenzie, K. S., Cameron, D., Fraser-Mackintosh, C., Nicolson, A. & MacKinnon, D., *Report of Her Majesty's Commissioners of Inquiry into the condition of the Crofters and Cottars in the Highlands and Islands of Scotland* (Neill & Company, Edinburgh, 1884)

Nicholson, Edward, W.B. (ed.), *Golspie, Contributions to its Folklore* (London: David Nutt, 1897)

Nicolson, Alexander, Parish of Barray, 1840. In: *The Statistical Account of Inverness-shire. By the ministers of the respective parishes, under the superintendence of a committee of the society for the benefit of the sons and daughters of the clergy* (Edinburgh, William Blackwood & Sons, 1842)

Nicolson, Alexander, *History of Skye* 3rd edn (Kershader: The Islands Book Trust, 2012)

Nolan, E. H., *The Illustrated History of the War against Russia* Vol. 2 (London: James S. Virtue, 1857)

Oakley, C. A., *The Second City* (London and Glasgow: Blackie & Son Limited, 1948 reprint)

Osborne, Sidney Godolphin, Immortal Sewerage. In: Ingestre, Viscount (ed.) *Meliora: or, Better Times to Come. Being the contributions of many men touching the Present State and Prospects of Society* 2nd Series (London: John W. Parker & Son, 1853)

Pagan, James, *Glasgow, Past and Present: illustrated in Dean of Guild Court Reports, and in the Reminiscences and Communications of Senex, Aliquis, J. B., &c.* Vol. 1 (Glasgow: James Macnab, 1851)

Pagan, James & Stoddart, J. H., *Relics of Ancient Architecture and other picturesque scenes in Glasgow, thirty drawings by Thomas Fairbairn* (Glasgow: David Bryce & Son, Glasgow, 1885)

Park, Graham, *The Highland Clearances in Southeast Sutherland* (Dornoch: Historylinks Museum, 2010)

Parker, Mike, *Historic Dartmouth, Reflections of Early Life* (Halifax: Nimbus Publishing Ltd, 1998)

Payzant, Joan M., *Halifax, Cornerstone of Canada* (Windsor Publications (Canada) Ltd., 1985)

Pennant, Thomas, *A Tour in Scotland, and Voyage to the Hebrides; MDCCLXXII* (London: Benjamin White, 1790)

Pigot, J., *Pigot and Co.'s National Commercial Directory of the whole of Scotland, and of the Isle of Man* (London: J. Pigot & Co., 1837)

Pollitt, A. Gerald, *Historic Inverness* (Perth: Melven Press, 1981)

Prebble, John, *The Highland Clearances* (London: Secker & Warburg, 1965 reprint)

Richards, Eric, *The Leviathan of Wealth* (London: Routledge & Kegan Paul Limited, 1973)

Richards, Eric, *Debating the Highland Clearances* (Edinburgh University Press, 2007)

Richards, Eric, *The Highland Clearances, people, landlords and rural turmoil*. 2nd Edition (Edinburgh: Birlinn Ltd, 2008)

Bibliography

Rixon, Denis, *Knoydart, A History* 2nd Edition (Edinburgh: Birlinn Ltd, 2011)
Ronald, James, *Landmarks of Old Stirling* (Stirling: Eneas Mackay, 1899)
Ross, Donald, [See Appendix 2]
Sage, Donald, *Memorabilia Domestica; or, parish life in the north of Scotland* (Wick: W. Rae, Wick, 1889)
Scott, Hew, *Fasti Ecclesiae Scoticanae; The Succession of Ministers in the Church of Scotland from the Reformation* New Edition Vol. VII, Synods of Ross, Sutherland and Caithness; Glenelg, Orkney and of Shetland (Edinburgh: Oliver & Boyd, 1928)
Selby, John, *The Thin Red Line* (London: History Book Club, 1970)
Sewell, J., George Dempster, Esq. *The European Magazine and London Review*, 1793, Vol. 24.
Simpson, William, *Glasgow in the "Forties"* (Glasgow: Morison Brothers, 1899)
Simpson, W. Douglas, Dornoch Cathedral: the High Church of Caithness. *Proceedings of the Society of Antiquaries of Scotland*, 1924, Vol. 58.
Sillett, Steve W., *Illicit Scotch* 2nd Edition (Aberdeen: Impulse Books, 1970)
Smart, Aileen, *Villages of Glasgow, Volume 2* (Edinburgh: John Donald Publishers Ltd, 1998 reprint)
Smith, George, Stephen, L. & Lee, S., *The Dictionary of National Biography*, Volume 1, Abbadie – Beadon (Oxford University Press, 1922)
Somers, Robert, *Letters from the Highlands on the Famine of 1846* (Perth: Melven Press, 1985 reprint)
Stewart, David, *Sketches of the character, manners, and present state of the Highlanders of Scotland; with details of the military service of the Highland Regiments* 3rd Edition, Vol. 1 (Edinburgh: Archibald Constable & Co., 1825)
Stoddart, Anna M., *John Stuart Blackie, a Biography* Vol. 2 (Edinburgh: William Blackwood & Sons, 1895)
Stowe, Harriet Beecher, *Sunny Memories of Foreign Lands* (London: Sampson Low, Son & Co., 1854)
Stuart, Robert, *Views and Notices of Glasgow in Former Times* (Glasgow: Robert Stuart & Co., 1848)
Thomas, John & Paterson, Alan J. S., *A Regional History of the Railways of Great Britain. Volume VI Scotland: The Lowlands and the Borders* 2nd Edition (Nairn: David St John Thomas, 1984)
Thomson, Thomas, On the most important Chemical Manufactures carried on in Glasgow and the Neighbourhood. *Report on the Tenth Meeting of the British Association for the Advancement of Science; held at Glasgow in August 1840.* Notices and Abstracts of Miscellaneous Communications to the Sections (1841)
Tindley, Annie, *The Sutherland Estate, 1850-1920, Aristocratic Decline, Estate Management and Land Reform* (Edinburgh University Press, 2010)
Tucker, D. Gordon, Millstone making in Scotland. *Proceedings of the Society of Antiquaries of Scotland*, 1984, Vol. 114.
Uelsh, Eoin [Welsh, Jonathan], *Da fhichead 'sa h ochid do Shearmoinéan taghta, a Shermoinicheadh* (Inverness, 1845)
Uncles, Christopher J., *Memories of East Sutherland* (Catrine: Stenlake Publishing Ltd, 2007)
Uncles, Christopher J., *Last Ferry to Skye* (Catrine: Stenlake Publishing Ltd, 2009)
Wall, Joseph Frazier, *Skibo* (Oxford University Press, 1984)
Wallace, Stuart, *John Stuart Blackie, Scottish Scholar and Patriot* (Edinburgh University Press, 2006)
Woolf, Joanne, *Knoydart: Landscape, History, People* (Madwolf Design, 2013)

Index

Abbey Craig, Stirling 274-5
Aberdeen, Aberdeenshire 135-6, 150
Aberdeen Town & County Banking Company, Golspie 58-61
Achnahannait, Skye 141
Adam, Alexander, Rev., Portree 267
Adam of Melrose, Bishop, Caithness 182
Adams, Alexander Maxwell, Inspector, Glasgow 113, 115, 117-8
Adamson, Ebenezer, Inspector, Glasgow 194
Adamson, Robert, Photographer, Edinburgh 67
Adelaide, Australia 165
Admiral, ship 139
Adolphus, Gustavus, King of Sweden 74
Advocates' Library, Edinburgh 44
Ailsa Craig, island 159
Aird, Gustavus, Rev., Croick and Migdale 69, 73-80, 76, 240, 243-4, 288
Airor, Knoydart 188, *189*, 193, 204, 206
Albert, Prince 46, 92, *93*, 157, 289
Alison, Archibald, Rev. 102
Alison, Archibald, Sir, Sheriff of Lanarkshire 44, 85, 87-8, 92, *93*, 102, 106, 108-9, *109*, 111-3, 116-7, 155, 158, 212, 250, 270, 272
Alison, William Pulteney, Prof., Edinburgh 102, 113, 135, 141, 144, 150
Allan, Hector, Rev., Kincardine 74, 78-9
Allan, Robert, Insurer, Edinburgh 153-4
Alltan Doirein (Alt Dorain), burn, Greenyards boundary 226, 227
Alma, Crimea 248
Alness, Ross & Cromarty 34, 236
Amat, Strathcarron 75, 227-8
Amatnatua, Strathcarron 79, 228, 245
Anderson, George, Inspector, Inverness 193
Anderston, Glasgow 82, 103
Annie Jane, ship 157
Ardgay, Ross & Cromarty 78, 222, 224, 235-6, 240
Ardrishaig, Argyll & Bute 134
Ardross, Ross & Cromarty 229, 236
Argyll, 8th Duke of 253, 270, 293
Arinacraig, Skye 122, 124, 130
Arincreaga, Skye 124

Arisaig, Lochaber 260, 266
Armadale Castle, Skye 215
Arran, Isle of 160
Arthur, Richard, SSC, Edinburgh 242-3
Ashaig, Skye 123
Assynt, Sutherland 255
Atholl, 6th Duke of 90, 270-3, 276
Atholl Highlanders 270-1
Baillie, W. R., Lawyer, Glengarry 192-3, 197
Baird, Charles R., Lawyer, Glasgow 83, 108, 112, 120, 135
Baird, Robert, Lawyer, Glasgow 108, 112
Balaklava, Crimea 246, 248, 255
Ballingal, Factor to Lord Macdonald 212
Balnagown, Ross & Cromarty 25, 243
Bannockburn, Battle of, Stirling 274
Barony, Glasgow 82, 103-5, 107, 109, 135
Barra, Outer Hebrides 131-9, 147-148, 153, 157, 194, 282-3, 298, 300
Barunah Plains, Australia 238
Bauchope, Alexander Lockhart, Surveyor 51
Bauld, William, Merchant, Halifax 291
Bayne (or Ross), May (or Marjory), Donald's wife 42, 50, 59, 63, 289, 293-5
Baynton, Benjamin, Captain of the *Hercules* 158, 160, 165
Begg, James, Rev. 46, 134
Beith, Alexander, Rev., Lochaber 184
Bell, Henry, Engineer, Glasgow 82
Bell, Henry Glassford, Sheriff-substitute, Lanarkshire 108, *109*, 109-113, 117, 274
Ben Bhraggie, Sutherland 28
Benbecula, Outer Hebrides 131, 145, 148, 263, 267, 282
Bethune, Divie, Skye 147, 149
Bethune, John, Rev., Dornoch 20, 30, 42
Birichen Muir, Sutherland 26
Birkenhead, England 161, 297
Black Isle, Ross & Cromarty 44
Black Sea 246
Blackie, John Stuart, Prof., Edinburgh 276, 287, 296
Blackie, W. G., Printer, Glasgow 118
Board of Supervision 45-6, 97, 99-100, 104-7, 116, 128, 131, 141, 196, 202, 204-5, 211, 218-9

Index

Bonar Bridge, Sutherland 57, 59, 69, 77, 222, 228
Bond Charles, Secretary of the Royal Patriotic Society of Scotland 46, 135, 154
Boreraig, Skye 207-214, *208*, 216, 218-9, 296
Borthwick Church, Midlothian 23, 28, *29*
Boxer, Halifax-Dartmouth ferry 291
Boyle, David, Lord Justice General, Edinburgh 52, 112-3
Bracadale, Skye 140, 155, 268
Braelangwell, Strathcarron 245
Braemar, Highlands 276
Braes, Skye 219
Breadalbane, 2nd Marquis of 145-6
Breakish, Skye 123, 141, 219
Brebner, William, Governor, Glasgow Prison 85
Bridge of Earn, Perthshire 143
Brighton, England 162, 256
British Linen Company Bank, Golspie 57
Briton, ship 258
Broadford, Skye 119, 122-4, *123*, 126, 128-9, 140-1, 147, 153, 167-8, 177, 179, 181, 216, 218, 257, 262
Brodie, John, C., Crown Agent, Edinburgh 240
Broomielaw, Glasgow 82, 90, 95, 123, 132
Brown, Alexander ('Shadow'), Glasgow 84-5, 87-8, 94
Brown, James, Accountant, Golspie 60
Brown, Robert, Commissioner to the Duke of Hamilton 148
Bruce, George, Author 298
Bruce, James, 8th Earl of Elgin 275
Bruce, James, Author 144
Bruce, Neil, Author 298
Buie, Loch, Sutherland 66
Bute, Marchioness of 161
Caledonian Banking Company, Dornoch 35, 57-60, 62-3
Calton, Glasgow 82
Calvie Burn, Glencalvie 74
Cambridge, England 22, 173
Cameron, Alexander, Knoydart 204
Cameron, John, local manager, Knoydart 192, 197, 200, *200*, 205
Cameron, Mary, Reidh an Daraich 202-3
Camismary, Skye 122
Campbell, Colin, Sir, Major-General 246, 250, 270
Campbell, Donald, Glasgow 270-1, 273
Campbell, Donald, Poet 244
Campbell, Ewen, Inspector, Glenelg 195, 198, 201-4, 206

Campbell, John, 2nd Marquis of Breadalbane 145-6
Campbell, John Douglas Sutherland, Marquis of Lorne 292
Campbell, John, Pensioner, Clashmore 55
Campbell, John, ship owner 282
Campbell, Rory, Roag 141-2, 146-7, 149
Campbell, William, Amatnatua 79
Campbell, William D., Poet 199, 244
Campbell, William, Tullichewan 97-8, *98*, 117, 120, 270, 272, 275
Campbeltown, Argyll & Bute 158, *159*, 162, 174
Campey, Lucille H., Author 298
Canonmills, Edinburgh 67
Cape Breton, Canada 131, 285, 288
Cape Clear, Ireland 162
Cape of Good Hope, South Africa 165
Cape Town, South Africa 164
Carey, Lawrence, Surgeon on *Hercules* 159-160, 163-4
Carlisle, Earl of 117
Carnegie, Andrew, Philanthropist 30
Carron, River, Strathcarron 74-5, 220, 232, 235
Cart, River, Renfrewshire 96
Cassels (or Cassells), John, Inspector, Govan Parish 106, 109-110
Cathcart Castle 96
Cathcart, Renfrewshire 92, *96*, 96
Cawdearg (Ca-derg), Strathcarron 227, 239
Celt, steamer 158
Ceres, Fife 45, 97, 122
Chambers, Robert, Publisher, Edinburgh 266
Chambers, William, Publisher, Edinburgh 266
Chant, James, Birkenhead Emigration Depot 161, 164
Chatham Dockyard, London 158
Chebucto, Halifax-Dartmouth ferry 291
Cheltenham, England 260, 269
Cheviot sheep 25-7
Cholera 21, 83, 92, 198, 238, 246, 257
Christie, George, Sydney 51
Christie, William, Accountant, Golspie 33-5, 39, 51
Cill Criosd (Kilchrist) Church, Skye 124, *127*
Clark, John, Missionary, South Uist 281, 283
Clashmore Mill, Sutherland 17-9, 33, 42-3, 47, 49, 51, 69, 71
Clashmore, Sutherland 17-9, *18*, 21, 26, 30, 33-4, 39, 42-3, 47, 48-51, 56, 58-60, 62-4, 69, 70-3, 78, 80, 292, 294
Clashmugach, Sutherland 17, 22, 33, 48, 52-53, 56-7

Cluny, Aberdeenshire 133-6
Cluny Castle 136
Clyde, River, Glasgow *81*, 82, *89*, 89-90, 92, 94, 297
Cobh, Ireland 162, 164
Coigach, Wester Ross 220
Coll, island, Inner Hebrides 265
Colquhoun, Sheriff-substitute 204, 212
Comet, first steamboat on the Clyde 82
Comet, HMS 141
Conordan, Skye 141
Convocation of the Church 67
Cornhill, Strathcarron 237
Coruisk, Loch, Skye 129
Covenanter, ship 238
Craig, David, Author 219, 245, 298
Craigie, Captain 247
Crawford, S., MP 45
Creich, Sutherland 21, 69, 77
Crimea 246, 248-9, 255, 260
Crimean War 220, 246, 256, 260, 286, 301
Croick Church 74, 76, 226
Croick, Ross & Cromarty 74-7, 226, 235
Cromarty, Easter Ross 285
Cuillin Mountains, Skye 208
Culloden, Battle 301
Culrain, Strathcarron 240
Cumming, George, Police Superintendent, Inverness 226, 229-231, 236, 240
Cunard Shipping Line 95, 287
Cuninghame, John, Lord Ordinary, Edinburgh 51-2, 112
Cuthbert, William, Dornoch 59, 61-3
Cyderhall, Sutherland 26
Dalmore Distillery, Alness 34-5, 37-9
Daniell, William, Artist 20
Dartmouth, Nova Scotia 286, *289-290*, 289-295
Darwin, Charles, Naturalist 258, 261
Davidson, James, Golspie 34
Davidson, Jess, Dornoch 42, 49, 61-3
Davie, William, Clerk, Glasgow 87
Davies, John, Rector 148, 156
Dean Cemetery, Edinburgh 102, 288
Deed of Demission 67-8, 77
Defoe, Daniel, Author 103
Dempster, Eleanor Soper 28
Dempster, George, MP, Skibo *16*, 16-7, 19, 21-2, 24, 26, 47, 65, 244, 247
Dempster, George Soper, Skibo 22-3, *23*, 27-8, 29, 30, 33, 42, 45, 47-54, 65-6, 68-73, 77, 259
Dempster, Harriet, Skibo 18, 20, 51-2
Dempster, John Hamilton, Captain, Skibo 22

Dempster, William John Soper, Skibo 22, 51
Denyer, Grant, TV Presenter 301
Devine, Thomas (Tom), Sir, Prof., Edinburgh 299
Devine, William, Glasgow 103
Dickson, J. B., Rev. 170
Dingwall, Ross & Cromarty 24, 225, 236
Disruption of the Church 66, 66-8, 77, 215
Dixon's Ironworks, Glasgow 82, 252
Docherty, John, Excise Officer, Inverness 223-4
Donn, Rob, Gaelic Poet 176
Dornoch Castle 55
Dornoch Cathedral 20, 28, 30, 32-3, 42, 68-9
Dornoch Free Church 52, 69-70
Dornoch Jail 23, *55*, 59-60, 70
Dornoch Sheriff Court 34, 38, 42, 47, *48*, 51, 53, 55, 221
Dornoch, Sutherland 16-7, 20-1, 23, 28, 30, 32-6, 38, 42-4, 47, 49, 51-3, 55-61, 63-4, 68-72, 221, 278, 285, 295, 298-9
Dougal, John, Assistant Inspector, Gorbals 114-5
Doune, Knoydart 184, 187, 192-3, *194*, 198, 200, 202-4, 206
Dounie (Downie), Strathcarron 222, 226, 230
Drumfearn, Skye 168, 219
Dublin, Ireland 260, 278
Duirinish, Skye 140-2
Duke of Cornwall, steamer 158
Dunan, Skye 257
Duncan, Elspeth, Ceres 45
Dundas (or Dempster), Joanna Hamilton, Skibo 23, 28, 29, 30
Dundas, Robert, Lord Chief Baron, Arniston 23, *50*
Dundas, William Pitt, Registrar General 23, 29
Dundee, Tayside 269, 276
Dunmore, Countess of 277
Dunn, William, Contractor, East Calder 136
Dunnichen, Angus 50
Dunoon, Argyll & Bute 132, 260
Dunrobin Castle, Golspie 19, 23, 247, 254
Duntroon Castle, paddle steamer 123, 153
Durham, England 260
Durness, Sutherland 255
Durris, Aberdeenshire 292
East Calder, West Lothian 136
Eddrachillis, Sutherland 255
Edinburgh, Midlothian 22, 25, 27-8, 44-6, 48, 50-1, 59, 67, 81, 97, 102, 112-3, 120, 122, 126, 129, 133-7, 141, 143, 153-4, 157,

Index

198, 206, 233, 240, 242-3, 246, 258, 261, 266, 269-270, 274, 276, 283, 287-8, 300
Eigg, Island of, Inner Hebrides 267
Eishort, Loch, Skye 208
Elgin, 8th Earl of 270, 274-5, *275*
Elgol, Skye 121-2, 124, 126, 129-130
Elizabeth, ship 282
Ellice, Edward, MP 45, 105, 117, 196, 201-6, 218-9
Eriskay, Outer Hebrides 259, 281-3
Evelix, Sutherland 62, 73
Fairy, Queen Victoria's yacht 92
Farr, Sutherland 255
Fenyő, Krisztina, Author 298
Feolin, Skye 122
Ferguson, Peter, Inspector, Glasgow 83
Fergusson, Adam, Sir 22
Fingalian Club, Glasgow 284
Finlay, John, Glasgow 153
Fitzroy, Henry, MP 202
Fleming, John, Factor, Barra 131-2, 139
Fletcher, John, Rev., Bracadale 155, 268
Fletcher, Rev., London 267
Forbes, George, Factor, Skibo 47-8, 65, 72
Forbes, John, Rev., Sleat 167, 167-183, 263, 267, 301
Forbes Mackenzie Act 88
Forbes, Robert, Glasgow 153
Forbes, William, Lawyer 60
Forsyth (or Gordon), Ann 'Nanny,' Clashmore 20, 47
Forsyth, Roderick ('Rory'), Carpenter, Clashmugach 57, 59, 61-4
Fort William, Lochaber 137, 152, 184, 198-9, 249
Frank, Alice, Author 300
Fraser, Andrew, Sheriff-substitute, Fort William 184, 198-9, 202-4, 206, 218
Fraser, Thomas, Sheriff-substitute, Skye 121, 126, 157, 162
Fraser, William Sutherland, Lawyer, Dornoch 55, 57, 60, 69
Fullerton, John, Lord, Edinburgh 52, 112-3
Gaelic 20, 34, 43, 68-9, 79, 83, 92, 100, 128, 141, 158, 166-7, 176-7, 179-180, 212, 228, 246-7, 271, 287-9, 297, 301
Gairloch, Wester Ross 46, 152
Geikie, Archibald, Geologist 210, 219
Gelong, Australia 238
Gibson, John, Author 298
Gibson, John, Merchant, Halifax 291
Gillanders, James F., Factor, Glencalvie 74-5
Gilpin, Charles, Emigrants' Lending Library Association 158

Glasgow (Jamaica) Bridge, Glasgow *81*, 89-90, 92, *93*
Glasgow, Lanarkshire 32, 41, *41*, 52, 78, *81*, 81-90, *86*, *89-91*, 92, *93*, 94, 97-109, 111-120, 123, 132-7, 139, 143, 145-7, 149, 152-6, 158, 161, 166, 170, 174-6, 180, 192, 194, 197, 206, 231-2, 234, 243, 246, 250, 252-3, 258, 260, 262, 264, 270-5, 277-285, 288, 297-300
Glasgow Sheriff Court 89, 105, 108, 113, 117-8
Glasnakelt, Skye 122
Gledfield, Strathcarron 237
Glencalvie, Ross & Cromarty 74-6, 78-80, 220-1, 226, 298
Glencoe, Lochaber 129
Glendale, Skye 219
Glenelg, Lochaber 120, 184, 194, 202-3, 205-6
Glengarry, 16th Chief of 184-5, 196-7
Glengarry County, Nova Scotia 184
Glengarry, Lochaber 184-6, 192, 194, 196-8, 200, 204, 214, 244
Glenorchy, Argyll & Bute 276
Glenquoich, Glengarry 196, 203
Goldsmith, Oliver 264
Golspie Burn, Sutherland 33
Golspie Mill, Sutherland 33
Golspie, Sutherland 21, 23, 27-8, 30, 33-4, 39, 47, 57-60, 68, 72
Gorbals, Glasgow 82, 89, *91*, 92, 104, 107, 109, 112-6, 122
Gordon, Alexander, Sheriff-substitute, Sutherland 34, 38-40, 47-50, 52-3, 55-7, 60
Gordon (or Ross), Ann, Clashmore, Donald's mother, 20, 32, 42, 47-52, 69
Gordon, Charles Edward 65, 68-73, 78
Gordon, Elizabeth, Countess of Sutherland 23-8, *24*
Gordon, George, Shoemaker, Clashmore, Donald's uncle 47-8, 53-5
Gordon, Isabella, wife of Robert 53, 55
Gordon, John, Colonel, Cluny 131-6, 138-9, 298
Gordon, John, Lawyer, Clashmore, Donald's uncle 38-40, 47-8, 51, 53-6, *54*, 62
Gordon, Robert, Labourer, Clashmore, Donald's uncle 47-8, 53-6, 221
Gordon, Roderick, Farmer, Clashmore, Donald's uncle 47-8, 53-6
Gordon, William, Clashmugach, Donald's grandfather 20, 47, 53

Gordon, William, Surgeon, Tain 226, 231, 237
Govan, Lanarkshire 94, 94-6, 104, 106, 109
Gower, Earl 27, 44
Graham, Alexander, Mason, Allardie/Ardalie, Sutherland 49-50, 59, 61-4
Graham, Duncan, Kilbrandon 145-6
Grant, Alexander, Factor, Glengarry 185-6, 190, 192
Gray, Bell, Clashmore 62
Gray, William, Skibo 21
Greenock, Renfrewshire 260, 267, 278
Greenyards (Gruinards), Strathcarron 74, 220-8, 233-5, 237, 239, 243-4, 299, 301
Grey, George, Home Secretary 206
Guernsey, island 277
Guthrie, Thomas, Rev. 103
Halifax, Earl of 286
Halifax, Nova Scotia 285-6, 288, 290-3, 295
Hall, Robert, Evelix 62
Hallen, South Uist 266
Halyburton, James, Meikle Ferry 62
Hamilton, Duke of 148, 272
Hamilton, Ontario 139
Hardy (or Hardigan or Harigan), Thomas, Gorbals 116
Harrapool, Skye 123, 141, 151
Harris, Outer Hebrides 148, 151, 153, 158, 257, 260
Haulbowline, island, Ireland 163
Hawkins, Catherine, Skibo 50-2
Hawkins, Charlotte, Skibo 50-2
Hawkins, George Dempster, Dunnichen 50-1
Hawkins, Gertrude, Skibo 50-2
Hawkins, Helen, Skibo 50-2
Heast, Strath 211
Helmsdale, Sutherland 21, 34, 61
Herbert, Sidney, Secretary of War 249
Hercules, HMS 158-162, *159*, 164-5, 174, 178, 209-210, 219, 297
Hibbert, James, Marple 170-2
Hibbs, Richard, Rev. 296
Hill, David Octavius, Painter, Edinburgh 67
Hogg, William, Aberdeen 150
Hollins Mill, Marple 167, 172-3
Holy Rood Church, Stirling 40, 40-41
Hook, Michael, Author 298
Hourn, Loch, Lochaber 184, 188, *189*
House of Commons, London 45, 117, 230
House of Lords, London 24, 28, 45, 51, 117-8, 148
Houston, Lewis, Bank Agent, Golspie 57
Howard, Harriet Elizabeth Georgiana, 2nd Duchess of Sutherland 44

Howatt, William, Inspector, Gorbals Parish 109
Hunter (or Scobie), Ann, Barony 109
Hunter, James, Prof. 219, 299-300
Hunter, Mollie, Author 301
Huntingtower, Perthshire 42
Hutcheson Bridge, Glasgow 89, 89-90
Inglis, Sarah, Glasgow 108
Iona, island, Inner Hebrides 265
Inveraray, Argyll & Bute 253
Inveraray Castle 253
Invergordon, Easter Ross 225
Inverguseran, Knoydart 193
Inverie, Knoydart 184, 186, 188, 192, 200, 200, 204, 206
Inverness Castle 58, 60
Inverness, Inverness-shire 58, 60, 69-70, 77, 83, 120, 137-9, 153, 193, 197, 203-4, 211, 223, 236-7, 241-2
Isle of Man 159
Isle of Wight, England 277
Isleornsay, Sleat 185-186, 219
Jeffrey, Francis, Lord, Einburgh 52, 112-3
Jersey, island 277
John o' Groats, Caithness 148
Johnston, James F. W., Prof. 26-7
Johnstone, William, Barony 109
Kelly, Farquhar, Skye 219
Kelly, Neil, Boreraig 219
Kennedy, Angus, Rev., Dornoch 30, 34, 42, 68-70
Kennedy (or Macdonald), Christy, Doune 187
Kennedy, George Rainy, Rev., Dornoch 68-70, 77
Kennedy, John, Rev., Dingwall 24
Kennedy, Rev., Stepney Green 147
Keppoch (Capach), Skye 121-2, 124, 130
Kilbrandon, Argyll & Bute 145-6
Kilbride, Strath 210, 216
Kilchoan, Knoydart 202
Killean, Argyll & Bute 159
Kilmore, Skye 122, *167*
Kilmuir, Skye 141
Kilninver, Argyll & Bute 145
Kincardine, Ross & Cromarty 74, 221-3, 245
Kindeace, Easter Ross 75, 221, 224, 231, 236
King, Jane, Author 301
Kingston, William H. G., Australasian emigration officer 157
Kintyre, Argyll & Bute 277-8
Kirkfield Church, Gorbals *91*, 92
Kirkibost, Skye 122
Kirkwall, Orkney Isles 44

Index

Knoydart, Lochaber 184-206, *189*, 208, 216, 218, 244, 247, 249, 295, 298-9, 301
Kyleakin, Skye 122-3, 151
Kylerhea, Skye 120, 123
Kyles, Knoydart 202
La Touche, John, Ireland 276-7
Lairg, Sutherland 250, 255
Lamont, Rev., Waternish 182-3
Langwell, Stratharron 27, 222, 227-8, 237-9, 244
Laurencekirk, Aberdeenshire 136-7, 298
Laurie, David 244
Lawrence, Thomas, Sir, Painter 252
Lees, Frederick R., Dr 277-9
Leslie, Alexander, Clerk, Dornoch 58, 60
Letchworth, England 245
Leveson-Gower, George Granville, Earl Gower 44
Leveson-Gower, George Granville, Marquis of Stafford 23-8, *24*
Leveson-Gower, Lord Francis, MP 27
Lewis, Outer Hebrides 277
Lindsay, William, Cotton-spinner, Gorbals 112-3, 117-8, 122
Lingard, Joan, Author 301
Liverpool, England 130, 238, 252, 278
Livingstone, William, Glasgow 166
Loch, James, Commissioner 25-7, 45, 69, 253
Lochaber, Highlands 73, 184, 244
Lochboisdale, South Uist 138-9, 259, 282
Lochmaddy, Outer Hebrides 147
Logan, William, Scottish Temperance League 84
London, England 51, 82, 118, 145, 147, 149, 153-4, 157, 165, 199, 229, 249, 252, 258, 265-7, 278, 291
Long Island, Outer Hebrides 131, 145, 147-8, 280, 297
Longforgan, Perthshire 275
Lorne, Marquis of 292, 293-4
Louise, Princess 292, 293-4
Luib, Skye 141
Lumsden, Hugh, Sheriff of Sutherland 49, 54
Lusk, John, Glasgow 78
Lusk, Robert Baillie, Glasgow 106, 111
Lützen, Battle 74
McAfferty, John, Labourer, Glasgow 115
McAffray, John, Glasgow 115
Macalister, Alexander, Torrisdale 124, 128, 130
Macalister, Norman M., Doctor, Strath 148, 151, 257
McCaig, Dugald, Excise Officer, Inverness 223-4, 228-9, 235-6

Macdonald, Alexander, Doune 187
Macdonald, Ann, Samadalan 192
Macdonald, Archibald, Inspector, Barra 131
Macdonald, Coll, Rev., Knoydart 187-8, 192, 194-6, 200-1, 204-5, 249, 264, 298
Macdonald, Donald, Rev., Barra 131
Macdonald, Donald, Samadalan 191-2, 199, 202
Macdonald, Donald, Scullamus 168
Macdonald, Donald, Teacher, Stonybridge 281
Macdonald, Godfrey, Lord of the Isles 121, 128-9, 142, 207, 209, 211, 213, 215, 217-8, 249, 277, 296
Macdonald, Hugh, Author, Glasgow 82, 94, 96
Macdonald, Hugh, Schoolmaster, Barra 131
Macdonald, Isabella ('Bella'), Scullamus 166, 168, 179, 181
Macdonald, J., Commissioner, Glasgow 111
Macdonald, James, Sawyer, Clashmore 58-60
MacDonald, John, Rev., 'Apostle of the North' 68
Macdonald, John, Rev., Croick 235
Macdonald, John, Sawyer, Clashmore 58-60
Macdonald, Mary, Doune 202-3
Macdonald, Mary, Niag-àrd 202-3
Macdonald, Ranald, Ground officer of Lord Macdonald 211-2, 216-7
Macdonald, Rod., Rev., South Uist 283
Macdonald, Rowland Hill, Glasgow 297-8
Macdonald, W., Glasgow 153
MacDonald, Willy, Amatnatua 245
Macdonell, Josephine, Torquay 184-8, 190, 193-4, 197, 200, 298
Macdougall, Archibald, Rev., Glasgow 281-3
MacFarlan, Patrick, Rev. 69
Macfarlane, J. F., Edinburgh 269
McGillivray, C. R., Dr, Glasgow 154-5
McGrath, John, Playwrite 301
MacGregor, Isabella, Lewis 276
MacGregor, James Watt, Glasgow 270
Macgregor (or Ross), Margaret, Greenyards 227-8, 237, 245
Macinnes, Alexander, Suishnish 211-2, 216
Macinnes, Donald, Suishnish 216-7, 219
Macinnes, Neil, Suishnish 216
MacIntosh, James, Merchant, Clashmore 59, 62
McIntyre (or Neilson), Mary, Glasgow 117
McIsaac, Archibald, Doune 190-2, 195, 205-6
McIsaac, Gillies, Inverie 206
MacIvor, Alexander, Rev., Sleat and Dornoch 49-50, 69

Mackay, Alexander, Shoemaker's Apprentice, Clashmore 55
Mackay, C., murderer, Glasgow 88
Mackay, David, Dr, Glasgow 270
Mackay, George, Spinningdale 239
Mackay, Hugh, Burgh Officer, Tain 228
Mackay, James, Rev., Inverness 139
Mackay, John, Wick 269
Mackay, Neil, Shoemaker's Apprentice, Clashmore 55
Mackay, Philip, Messenger at Arms, Dornoch 57-60
McKean, Alexander, Cotton-spinner, Gorbals 114-5
Mackenzie, Alexander, Editor 220, 295-7
Mackenzie, Donald, Greenyards 224
Mackenzie, Francis Humberston ('Frank'), Broadford or Harrapool 147, 149, 151, 167-171, 173, 175-7, 218, 257-8, 263
Mackenzie, J. H., Lord, Edinburgh 52, 112-3
Mackenzie, Kenneth, Sir., Gairloch 46, 152
McKenzie (or Gordon), Marian, Clashmore, Donald's grandmother 20
Mackenzie, Murdo, Skye 263
Mackenzie, Peter, Police Officer, Ross & Cromarty 222-3, 226, 228, 235, 240-1
Mackenzie, Roderick, Baker, Tain 32, 57-60
Mackenzie, Thomas, Sheriff, Ross & Cromarty 223-4, 229, 242
Mackinnon, Angus, Doune 202-3
Mackinnon, Ann, Knoydart 187
Mackinnon, Anne (or Ann), Tarskavaig 166, 168, 173, 175
Mackinnon, Catharine, Broadford 128
Mackinnon, Catharine ('Kate'), Inverie 191-2, 196, *200*, 200-3, 205
Mackinnon, Donald, Elgol 130
MacKinnon, Donald, Rev., Skye 296-7
Mackinnon, Flora, Tarskavaig 168
Mackinnon, Hector, Schoolmaster, Torrin 218
Mackinnon, John, Knoydart 187, 301
Mackinnon, John, Rev., Kilbride 119-120, 216
Mackinnon, Margaret ('Peggy'), Inverie 191-2, 201, 203, 205
Mackinnon, Mary, Tarskavaig 166, 168-9, 173-4
Mackinnon, Miles, Tarskavaig 168-9, 174
MacKinnon, Peggy, Teacher, Skye 219
Maclaren, John, Treasurer, Barony Parochial Board 103
MacLauchlan, Thomas, Author 296
MacLean, Alexander, Missionary, Glasgow 153
MacLean, Donald, Barra 132, 137-8

MacLean, Joseph, Master spinner, Glasgow 114
Maclean, Niel, Factor, Glenquioch 203
Macleay, William, Clashmore 73
McLennan, Donald, Glasgow 153, 270, 275, 284
Macleod, Alexander, Doctor, Portree 147-8
Macleod, Alexander, Doctor, Sleat 201
Macleod, Alexander, Excise Officer, Inverness 223-4
MacLeod, Donald, Stonemason, Sutherland 26, 28, 44-6, 69, 79, 97, 120, 157, 234, 247, 253-4, 296, 299-300
McLeod, Ewen, Skye 147, 149
MacLeod, George, Glasgow 155
MacLeod, Norman, 25th Chief 121, 278
Macleod, Norman, Rev. 120
Maclure, David, Glasgow 107
McNeill, Colonel, Barra 132
McNeill, Duncan, Lord Advocate 45
McNeill, John, Sir, Chair of the Board of Supervision 45, 137-8, 141-4, 146-7, 149, 152, 157-8, 161-2, 165, 184, 187, 197-8, 204-6, 218-9
McNicol, Ann, Sleat 166
McPhaill, Ann, Scottas 203
McPhaill, George, R., Strath 218
McPhaill, Rev., Sleat 218, 258
MacPhee, Catharine ('Kate'), Inverie 191-2, 201, 205
MacPhee, Ewen, Glengarry 192
Macpherson, A., Rev., Golspie 68
Macpherson, Alexander, Ground officer, Portree 141
Macpherson, Cluny 270, 274
Macpherson, John, Schoolmaster, Roag 142
Macpherson, William Catharine, Sheriff Officer, Tain 222, 224, 228-9, 235, 241
McQueen, Rev., Harrapool 147, 151, 171
Macrae, Duncan, Suishnish 211-2, *214*
Macrae, Finlay, Rev., North Uist 280
Macrae, Flora, Suishnish *214*
Macrae, John, Broadford 182
Macrae, John, Sheriff Officer, Skye 212
Macrae, John, Suishnish 211-2
Macrae, Marion, Strath 166
Macrae, Sarah, Broadford 168, 174-5, 179, 181-182
Macrimmon, John, Skye 144
McTavish, John, Rev., Killean 159, 163-4
McTear, John, Inspector, Gorbals 114, 118
McWilliams, William, Boilermaker, Glasgow 113, 117-8
Magnusson, Anna, Author 298

Index

Mallaig, Lochaber 184
Manchester, England 77, 153, 166-7, 170, 174, 183, 258
Marlborough, Duchess of 44
Marple, Stockport 167-182
Martin, Angus, Rev., Snizort 144-5
Masonic Hall, Halifax 286-7
Matheson, Alexander ('Sandy'), Suishnish 210-1, 215, 217, 219
Matheson, James, Sir, MP 46, 277
Matheson, Lachlan, Doctor, Portree 148
Matheson, Neil, Greenyards 224
Matheson, Peter, Greenyards 224
Matheson, Thomas, Skibo 72
Meek, John, Inspector, Barony Parish 105, 109
Meikle Ferry, Tain-Dornoch 21, 26-7, 30, 35-6, 44, 62
Melbourne, Australia 165
Michie, John, Actor 301
Micmac, Halifax-Dartmouth ferry 291
Midfearn, Ross & Cromarty 236
Migdale Church, Bonar Bridge 69, 77
Miller, Henry, Captain, Police Superintendent, Glasgow 84-5, 88
Miller, Hugh, Editor 46, 68, 134, 182
Mitchell, David, Comedian 301
Mitchell, David, Sheriff Officer, Tain 224, 226, 229
Moidart, Lochaber 153, 204
Moncreiff, James, Lord Advocate 219, 229-230
Moncrieff, Alexander, Advocate 242
Montreal, Canada 193
Montrose, Angus 202, 270
More, John Shank, Prof., Edinburgh 112-3, 122, *122*, 134
Morrison, Malcolm, Schoolmaster, Harris 151, 257-8
Mull, Isle of, Inner Hebrides 119, 148-9, 152-3, 156, 265, 278, 294
Mulock, Thomas, Editor 119, 122, 299-300
Munro, Alexander, Principal Tenant, Greenyards 80, 221-3, 226, 233-5, 237, 242-5
Munro, Alexander, Rev., Manchester 170-2, 177, 183
Munro, Ann, Cornhill 237
Munro, Catrina (or Catherine), Strath 166, 168
Munro, David, Culrain 240-1
Munro, George Gunn, Sir, Poyntzfield 69
Munro, George, Rector, Stirling 69, 71-2
Munro, Hector, Captain, Hamilton, Ontario 139
Munro, John, Acre-Dhu, Greenyards 221
Munro, Margaret, Greenyards 221, 244
Munro, Thomas, Lawyer, Tain 243
Munro, William, Accountant, Dornoch 57-8, 60-1
Murdoch, John, Dornoch 23
Murray, Angus, Clashmore 62
Murray, Donald, Gamekeeper, Skibo 62
Murray, George, 6th Duke of Atholl 270
Murray, George, Rosemount 77
Murray, John, Cuthill 62
Musselburgh, East Lothian 262
Nairn, Nairnshire 137-8
Napier, Robert, Shipbuilder, Govan 95
Ness, River, Inverness *58*, 60
Netherlands, Queen of 272
Nevis, Loch, Lochaber 184, 204
Niag-àrd, Knoydart 184, 193, 198-9, 202-3
Nicholson, Alexander, Schoolmaster on *Hercules* 159-160, 164
Nicolson, Angus, Drumfearn 168
Nicolson, Christina, Drumfearn 166, 168, 175
Nicolson, Donald, Torrin 130
Nicolson, Mary, Drumfearn 166, 168, 175
Nicolson, Neil, Sleat 181
Nightingale, Florence, Nurse 246
North Rona, island 277
North Uist, Outer Hebrides 144, 280-3
Nova Scotia, Canada 26, 74, 131, 184, 274, 285-6, 288-296, 298
Oban, Argyll & Bute 260
Ogg, Daniel, Furniture Dealer, Glasgow 117
Ontario, Canada 139
Ontario, ship 130
Ord, Caithness 30
Orde, John P., Sir 277, 280-1
Ormiston Hall, East Lothian 28
Ornsay, Isle, Sleat 185, 190, 199
Osborne, Sidney Godolphin, Rev., Glasgow 85
Otter, Captain 247
Oxenham, Prebendery, Rev. 148
Oxford, England 147-149, 153, 260, 280, 287
Pagan, James, Editor, Glasgow 85
Paisley, Renfrewshire 289
Palmerston, Lord, 3rd Viscount 196, 198, 202, 204-5
Parliament House, Edinburgh *50*, 51, 134
Paterson, David, Photographer 298
Pattison, George, Lawyer, Glasgow 108, 112-3
Pearson, Alexander, Inspector, Glasgow 115
Pennant, Thomas, Author 277-8
Persia, RMS *95*, 95
Perth, Perthshire 41-2, 81, 92, 244, 270, 295
Peterkin, William, A., Board of Supervision 131, 142, 146-7, 149
Peterson, A., Rev., Perth 244

Phytophthora infestans, potato blight 120
Pictou, Nova Scotia 74
Plaiden Ell, St Barr's Churchyard 28, 43
Polson, William, Miller, Skibo 62
Portland Street Suspension Bridge, Glasgow 89-90
Portree, Skye 121, 126, 130, 141-2, 145, 147-8, 153, 157, 211, 214-5, 249, 267, 278-9
Possil House, Glasgow 102
Poyntzfield, Ross & Cromarty 69
Prebble, John, Author 244-5, 297
Prince Edward Island, Canada 131
Proctor, John R., Society of Friends 260-1
Pulteneytown, Caithness 259
Quakers (Society of Friends) 260
Quebec, Canada 139
Queenstown, Ireland 162-4
Ranaldson, Aeneas, 16th Chief of Glengarry 184
Reading, England 265
Reay, Sutherland 255
Reidh an Daraich, Knoydart 193, 202-3, 206
Rice, Jean (or Janet), Glasgow 111
Rice, Patrick, Glasgow 111
Rice, Peter, Glasgow 111
Richards, Eric, Prof. 299-300
Rixson, Denis, Author 298
Roag, Skye 141-2
Robertson, Alexander ('R. Alister'), Dundonachie 146
Robertson, Alexander ('Sandie'), Tarskavaig 168, 170, 173
Robertson, Ann, Broadford 129
Robertson, Catherine, Tarskavaig 166, 168-9, 173-5
Robertson, Charles, Major, Kindeace 74, 80, 221, 224, 229, 235-7, 242
Robertson, Ewen, Tarskavaig 168, 175
Robertson (or Matheson), Flora, Suishnish 217, 301
Robertson, John, Constable, Skye 212
Robertson, Marian, Tarskavaig 166, 168-9, 174
Robertson, Mary, Strath 166
Robertson, Patrick, Lord Ordinary, Edinburgh 112-3
Rosebank, Clashmore 33, 42, 48-50, 63, 69, 70-3, 80
Ross, Alexander, Clashmore, Donald's brother 32, 43
Ross, Alexander, Sheriff Officer, Dornoch 61
Ross, Andrew, Clerk, Tain 228

Ross (or Mackenzie), Ann, Clashmore, Donald's sister 30, 32, 52
Ross (or Mackinlay), Ann, Greenyards 223-4
Ross, Ann, Langwell, Victim No. 14 in the 'Massacre' 227, 237
Ross, Ann, Langwell, Victim No. 16 in the 'Massacre' 237, 301
Ross (or Taylor), Ann, Rhein-Rhiach, Greenyards 221, 223-4, 228-9, 236-7, 241-2
Ross, Anna, Donald's daughter 42, 289, 295
Ross, Betty, Greenyards 223
Ross (or Bain), Charles, Greenyards 223-4
Ross, Christina ('Christy'), Greenyards 227-9, 236-7, 241
Ross, Christy, Clashmore, Donald's sister 32, 49, 51-2
Ross, David, Greenyards 224
Ross, David, Rev., Tobermory 149, 156
Ross (or Bain), Donald, Ardgay 240
Ross, Donald, Greenyards 239
Ross (or Bain), Donald, Greenyards 223-4
Ross (or Mackinlay), Donald, Langwell 222, 226, 241
Ross, Donald, Letchworth 245
Ross, Donald, Miller of Skibo, Clashmore, Donald's father 16-22, 24, 28, 30, *31*, 43, 47, 51-2
Ross, Elizabeth, Amat 227-8, 237, 245
Ross, George, Lawyer 112-3, 118
Ross, George, Pensioner, Balmeanach, Greenyards 221, 223, 239, 242-4
Ross, George, Sheriff Officer, Dornoch 54
Ross, Grace, Ca-derg (Cawdearg) 227, 237-9, 239
Ross (or Macgregor), Helen, Greenyards 237
Ross, Hugh, Greenyards 224
Ross, Hugh, Tacksman, Dornoch 34
Ross, James, Clashmore 32
Ross, Jean, Clashmore, Donald's sister 30
Ross, Joan, Innkeeper, Spinningdale 36
Ross, John, Innkeeper, Bonar Bridge 57
Ross, John Lockhart Ross, Sir, Balnagown 25
Ross, John, Millwright, Donald's brother 19, 32-42, 48-56, 63, 69, 72-3, 221, 278
Ross (or Bain), John, Rhein-Rhiach, Greenyards 221, 223, 227-8, 242-4
Ross, John Sutherland, Printer, Paisley 289
Ross, Margaret, Amat 228, 237, 241
Ross, Margaret, Amatnatua 228, 237, 241, 245
Ross, Margaret, Clashmore, Donald's sister 32, 51-2
Ross, Margaret, Cornhill 237

Index

Ross, Marrion, Clashmore, Donald's sister 32, 52
Ross, Marrion, Langwell 228
Ross, N. B., Doctor, Tain 228-9
Ross, Naomi, Langwell 228, 237
Ross (or Bain), Peter, Greenyards 223-4, 229, 241-2, 244
Ross, Robert, Lawyer, Dornoch 56, 63-4
Ross, Simon, Greenyards 224
Ross, Thomas, Amatnatua 228
Ross, William, Ca-derg (Cawdearg) 238
Ross, William, Clashmore, Donald's brother 32, 52
Ross, William, Greenyards 227
Ross, William, Kincardine 222
Ross (or Griasaich), William, Langwell 237-8
Ross, William, Merchant, Bonar Bridge 59
Ross, William, Shepherd, Ross & Cromarty 229
Rothesay, Isle of Bute 160-3
Roy, William, Surveyor 220
Royal Commission 45, 73, 79, 130, 206, 219, 249
Royal Infirmary, Glasgow 88
Russell, John, Secretary, Glasgow 99
Ryre Farm, Clashmore 17, 48, 50-1
Sage, Donald, Rev. 20-1, 26, 28, 30, 68
Samadalan, Knoydart 184, 192-3, 198, 206
Sandaig, Knoydart 195, *196*, 206, 298
Sangster, Robert Barclay, Bank Agent, Golspie 58, 60
Scilly Isles, England 277
Sconser, Skye 141-2
Scott, George, Rev., Chaplain, Glasgow 88
Scott Monument, Edinburgh 44
Scott, Paul, Author 298
Scott, Walter, Sir 287
Scottas, Knoydart 186, 193, 203
Scullamus, Skye 168, 212, 219
Sellar, Patrick, Sutherland 26-7
Sevastopol, Crimea 246
Sharp, Isaac, Secretary, Society of Friends 260-1, 264
Shaw, C., Sheriff-substitute, Outer Hebrides 131, 281
Sidera, Sutherland 26
Sillery, ship 184, 190
Sinclair, Archibald, Publisher, Glasgow 180-1
Sinclair, George, Sir, Caithness 148
Sinclair, John, Sir, Caithness 25
Sir Charles Ogle, Halifax-Dartmouth ferry 291
Skibo, Sutherland 16-7, *17*, 19-22, 27-8, 30, 42-3, 48, 50-1, 62, 65-6, 70-3, 259
Skibo, cow breed 22

Skye, Isle of, Inner Hebrides 69, 119-124, *125*, 126, *127*, 128-130, 140-5, 147-153, 155-8, 163, 166-174, 176-185, 193, 196, 198-9, 201, 207-219, 246-7, 249, 260-3, 266-8, 278-9, 295-7, 301
Slapin, Loch, Skye 124, *127*, 208
Sleat, Skye 69, 129, 163, 166-170, 172, 176-7, 179-180, 193, 201, 212, 218-9, 258, 263, 266
Smallpox 83, 137, 163
Smeal, Robert, merchant, Glasgow 155
Smeal, William, merchant, Glasgow 155
Smith, Archibald, Sheriff-substitute, Glasgow 118
Smith, Donald Macleod, Sheriff Clerk, Sutherland 60
Smythe, William, Secretary, Board of Supervision 99
Snizort, Skye 144
Somers, Robert, Editor 46, 97, 119-121, 150, 296
Soper, William John, Skibo 22
South Morar, Lochaber 267
South Uist, Outer Hebrides 83, 131-2, 138-9, 145, 153, 258-9, 266-7, 282-3
Spar Cave, Skye 129
Spence, Charles, SSC, Edinburgh 43-6, 49-52, 72, 78, 97, 108, 111-2, 122, 134, 140-1, 298
Spinningdale, Sutherland 36, 239
Spruel (or Spruell or Rice), Christina, Glasgow 110-2
St Andrew Square, Edinburgh 133-4, 153
St Andrew's Church, Edinburgh 66, 67
St Andrew's Church, Golspie 33
St Andrews, Fife 22-3
St Andrew's Suspension Bridge, Glasgow 90
St Anthony's Chapel, Sandaig 195, *196*
St Barr's Churchyard, Dornoch 20-1, 43
St Enoch Square, Glasgow 92, 94, 153-4, 156, 275
St George's Church, Glasgow *90*, 271
St Giles Cathedral, Edinburgh 51, 288
St James Church, Dartmouth 289
St Magnus Cathedral, Kirkwall 44
St Rollox, Glasgow 82
Stafford (Lancaster) House, London 247, 252
Stafford, Marchioness of 24-7
Stafford, Marquis of 18, 21, 24-7, *24*, 146
Steel, James, Grain Merchant, Glasgow 143
Stepney Green, London 147
Stewart, Donald, Lawyer, Tain 56, 221, 229, 236
Stewart, P. M., MP 45

Stirling Castle 276
Stirling, Stirlingshire 40-1, 52, 69, 71-3, 274-5
Stockport, England 167
Stockwell Bridge, Glasgow 89-90, 92
Stonehaven, Aberdeenshire 292
Stonybridge, South Uist 281, 283
Stornoway, Outer Hebrides 277
Stowe, Harriet Beecher, Author *251*, 251-4, 296, 298
Stratford-upon-Avon, England 95
Strath, Skye 119-121, 124, 128-9, 141, 147-8, 166-9, 207, 218, 258
Strath Suardal, Skye 124, *127*
Strathaird Peninsula, Skye 119-120, 122, 124, 129, 151
Strathbrora, Sutherland 255
Strathcarron, Ross & Cromarty 75, 202, 220, 232-234, 245
Strathnaver, Sutherland 26, 255
Strollamus, Skye 257, 266
Suishnish, Skye *207*, 207-214, 216-9, 297, 301
Supreme Court, Edinburgh 44-5, 51, 59, 112-4, 117, 242
Sutherland, 1st Duke of 18, 24, 28, 47, 253
Sutherland, 2nd Duchess of 44, 252-3
Sutherland, 2nd Duke of 26-7, 43-4, 46, 55, 69, 120, 220, 247, 252-3, 293
Sutherland, 3rd Duke of 221, 288
Sutherland, 93rd Highlanders 246-7, 255
Sutherland (or Ross), Catharine, John Ross's wife 33, 38-9
Sutherland, Countess and 1st Duchess of *24*, 24-8
Sutherland, Donald, Distiller, Alness 34-9
Sutherland, John, Merchant, Clashmore 59
Sydney, Australia 51, 130
Sydney, Cape Breton 288
Tain, Ross & Cromarty 21, 56-7, 60, 75, 79, 221-2, 224-5, 228-232, 235-7, 242-3
Tain Sheriff Court 222, 229, 232, 242
Tait, John, Gamekeeper to Duke of Hamilton 272
Tanfield, Canonmills 67
Tarskavaig, Skye 168, 219
Tay, Loch, Perthshire 146
Taylor, George Sutherland, Lawyer, Golspie 43, 47, 53
Taylor, Harry Munro, Procurator Fiscal, Ross & Cromarty 224, 226, 228, 236, 240
Taylor, Joseph, Lawyer, Glasgow 117
Taylor, Robert Sutherland, Sheriff-substitute, Ross & Cromarty 59, 223-4, 226, 228-234, 236-7, 241-3

Temple, Henry John, 3rd Viscount Palmerston 196
Tennant, Charles, Businessman, Glasgow 82
Thomson, William, Inspector, Glasgow 87, 110-3
Thurso, Caithness 21, 148
Tibbermore Church, Perthshire 42
Tobermory, Mull 134-5, 149, 156, 265-6
Tongue, Sutherland 255
Toronto, Canada 149
Torquay, England 85, 184
Torrin, Skye 124, 130, 207, 212
Torrisdale Castle, Argyll & Bute 124
Tregelles, Edwin O., Society of Friends 260-1
Trevelyan, Charles, Sir, Treasury, London 157-8
Trinity College, Cambridge 22
Tullibardine, Marquis of 271
Tullichewan Castle, West Dunbartonshire 98
Typhus 83, 92, 103, 148-9, 163-4
Uig, Skye 267
Valentine, James, Photographer *40*
Vatersay Bay, Barra 157
Victoria, Australia 238
Victoria Bridge, Glasgow 90
Victoria Cross 246
Victoria, Queen 41, 44, 46, 74, 92, *93*, 102, 157, 270, 280, 288-9, 293
Wallace Monument, Stirling 274-6
Wallace, Stuart, Biographer 298
Wallace, William, Sir 274-6
Walmsley, Betty, Marple 167, 174-5, 182
Walmsley, Charles, Marple 167-176, 179, 182-3
Walmsley, William, Marple 167-176, 179, 182-3
Waterloo, Battle of 151, 239
Waternish, Skye 182
Waterston, Charles, Bank Manager 58-9
Watson, Thomas, Doctor, Glasgow 106
Watt, James, Engineer 82
Welsh, David, Dr 67
Whisky 20, 33-8, 87-8, 107, 132, 178, 205, 234, 236, 277-9, 292
Wick, Caithness 42, 259, 269, 294-5
Williamson, Robert, Rev., Croick and Pictou 74
Willis, Rev., Toronto 149
Willock (or Willox), Richmond, Assistant Inspector, Glasgow 111-2, 115, 136
Wilson, John, Author 296
Winton, F. De, Major 294
Wortley, Stuart, Lawyer 118
Young, William, Sutherland 26-7